Frederick Stoutland
What Philosophers Should Know About Truth

Berlin Studies
in Knowledge Research

―

Edited by
Günter Abel and James Conant

Volume 15

Frederick Stoutland

What Philosophers Should Know About Truth

Edited by Jeff Malpas

DE GRUYTER

Series Editors
Prof. Dr. Günter Abel
Technische Universität Berlin
Institut für Philosophie
Straße des 17. Juni 135
10623 Berlin
Germany
e-mail: abel@tu-berlin.de

Prof. Dr. James Conant
The University of Chicago
Dept. of Philosophy
1115 E. 58th Street
Chicago IL 60637
USA
e-mail: jconant@uchicago.edu

ISBN 978-3-11-061875-4
e-ISBN (PDF) 978-3-11-062078-8
e-ISBN (EPUB) 978-3-11-061830-3
ISSN 2365-1601

Library of Congress Control Number: 2019933617

Bibliographic information published by the Deutsche Nationalbibliothek
The Deutsche Nationalbibliothek lists this publication in the Deutsche Nationalbibliografie;
detailed bibliographic data are available on the Internet at http://dnb.dnb.de.

© 2021 Walter de Gruyter GmbH, Berlin/Boston
This volume is text- and page-identical with the hardback published in 2019.
Printing and binding: CPI books GmbH, Leck

www.degruyter.com

Acknowledgments

This volume would not have been possible without the support and advice of Lilli Alanen, as well as of Harry Alanen and Andrea Stoutland. I am very grateful to Tim Crane for writing the Foreword, and to James Conant for his assistance in placing the volume with de Gruyter. Thanks are also due to Christoph Schirmer, and the editorial staff at de Gruyter, for bringing the volume to press. However, I owe a very special debt to Celina Luzi Stoutland for the enormous amount of work she undertook, with Andrea's assistance, to get from the original scanned versions of the essays to a form that was suitable to be submitted for final formatting and printing. It is Celina who has done most of the real work that was required to make this volume of her grandfather's work a reality.

Jeff Malpas
Hobart, August 2018

Contents

Foreword —— IX

Editorial Introduction —— XI

Original Publication Details —— XV

1   What Philosophers Should Know about Truth and the Slingshot —— 1
1.1   Some Background Principles and Distinctions —— 3
1.2   Davidson and the Slingshot —— 11
1.3   Gödel and the Slingshot —— 20
1.4   Consequences for Correspondence —— 29

2   Wittgenstein on Certainty and Truth —— 35
2.1   Wittgenstein on Certainty —— 36
2.2   How Certainty Involves Truth —— 39
2.2.1   Wittgenstein on Truth and Propositions —— 40
2.2.2   One Example of Certainty —— 48

3   Putnam on Truth —— 52
3.1   Metaphysical Realism —— 53
3.2   Internal Realism —— 64
3.3   The Turn to Wittgenstein —— 73

4   Do We Need Correspondence Truth? —— 88

5   Making True —— 100

6   A Mistaken View of Davidson's Legacy: Reading Lepore and Ludwig —— 112
6.1   Postscript – Radical Misinterpretation Indeed: Lepore and Ludwig Revisited —— 129

7   Davidson and Dewey: A Critical Comparison —— 140
7.1   The Natural World —— 141
7.2   Dewey on Experience —— 143
7.3   Davidson on Experience —— 149
7.4   Some Critical Comparisons —— 154

8 Common Sense Psychology and Physical Science —— 158
- 8.1 CSP and Teleological Explanation —— 159
- 8.2 Causal Explanation and Physical Science —— 163
- 8.3 CSP and Causal Explanation —— 169
- 8.4 CSP and Physical Science —— 173

9 Philosophy of Mind with and against Wittgenstein —— 186
- 9.1 Wittgenstein and the Philosophy of Mind —— 187
- 9.2 Physicalism and the Philosophy of Mind —— 195
- 9.3 Davidson and the Philosophy of Mind —— 201

10 The Ontology of Social Agency —— 210
- 10.1 Social Agents —— 211
- 10.2 Social Actions —— 213
- 10.3 Social Attitudes —— 216
- 10.4 Ascribing Attitudes to Social Agents —— 220
- 10.5 Social Agents' Knowledge of What They Are Doing —— 223
- 10.6 Bodily Movements and Action —— 226
- 10.7 Individuating Agents —— 228

11 Searle's Consciousness —— 230

12 Self and Society in the Claims of Individualism —— 241
- 12.1 Philosophical Individualism —— 243
- 12.2 The Dignity of the Individual —— 249
- 12.3 The Ideal of Individuality —— 252
- 12.4 Moral Individualism —— 256
- 12.5 Liberalism as a Political Conception —— 270

13 Interpreting Davidson's Philosophy of Action —— 277

14 The Problem of Congruence —— 301

15 Analytic Philosophy and Metaphysics —— 323

Bibliography —— 347

Index of Names —— 355

Index of Subjects —— 358

Foreword

Fred Stoutland was a very fine philosopher who made important contributions to a number of central philosophical debates. His writings on truth, on the mind and action, on Ludwig Wittgenstein, Donald Davidson and other philosophers display a deep understanding of the complexity and obscurity of philosophical problems, and a sure grip on the good sense required to resolve or settle them.

Stoutland once cited Wittgenstein and Davidson as the 20th-century philosophers he most admired, and knowing his work a little makes it clear why: he shares with both a suspicion of the metaphysical machinery philosophers invent to solve problems, many of which are their own making (the idea of truth as involving some metaphysically weighty relation of "correspondence with reality" is one of Stoutland's prime examples). He is also drawn to their very different treatments of the mind-body problem, and to their linguistic sensitivity.

Stoutland's writings might give the impression that he was something of a miniaturist in philosophy – he dealt with arguments in meticulous detail, avoiding big statements of doctrines or theses. In this way too he resembles Wittgenstein, who recommended that philosophy should refrain from advancing theses but untangle our "knotted understanding". But it would be wrong to think of him, for this reason, as a purely critical or negative philosopher, taking potshots at the silliness of metaphysical fancies and elaborate conceptual constructions. Rather, he was concerned, like Wittgenstein, to keep the phenomena firmly in view, to get a correct vision of the lived world and our ordinary conception of it. In this way, he could be called a phenomenologist – not in Husserl's doctrinal sense, but just in the sense of aiming to give a lucid overview of the phenomena (what Wittgenstein called a "perspicuous representation").

An example is his treatment of action and its explanation. Some philosophers have rejected the idea that explanations of action are causal explanations on the grounds that this would lead to an unacceptable kind of reductionism about the human mind, which makes genuine agency invisible. Stoutland argues by contrast that explanations of action in commonsense intentional psychology are often causal (though not always) but no unacceptable reductionist consequences follow from this, once we take care in distinguishing causal explanations of actions from explanations that are instances of laws, and in giving a proper place to what is 'fundamental' in philosophy and science.

Stoutland once described Davidson as "a splendid example of how to do philosophy of mind in a manner inspired by Wittgenstein without being a Wittgensteinian" – a description that would fit Stoutland himself. While he is without question one of the clearest expositors of Wittgenstein around, Stoutland is not one of those slavish followers who repeats the sayings of the *Philosophical Investigations* as a substitute for philosophical argument. In his discussion of the revival of metaphysics in the late 20th century, he says that he often learns "more from working through the works of philosophers who do not try to avoid the metaphysical way than from those who do". This is partly because those who try and avoid metaphysics often try to avoid argument – and without argument we are lost as philosophers. But it is also because some of "those who think of themselves as followers of Wittgenstein too often fail to avoid the ways of metaphysics because they put external 'Wittgensteinian' constraints on philosophical activity, which are more restrictive than any put on it by those committed to metaphysics". In these essays Stoutland shows clearly how one may learn from a powerful philosopher like Wittgenstein without becoming a dogmatic follower.

Contemporary philosophy of mind and metaphysics needs more voices like Fred Stoutland's. To obtain a proper conception of ourselves, our minds and our place in the rest of the world requires the kind of clarity, caution, phenomenological and historical sensitivity that his work exhibits. It is a very good thing for philosophy to have this collection of his writings made available.

Tim Crane
Budapest, August 2018

Editorial Introduction

Frederick Stoutland is best known to most readers of recent and contemporary analytic philosophy through his work in the philosophy of action. His very first published paper, in the *Journal of Philosophy*, was "Basic Actions and Causality" (Stoutland 1969), and that paper was the first in a long series of publications that explored questions of action, reason, causality, intention, and explanation. Having completed a PhD thesis on "The Nature of Historical Knowledge", Stoutland was very much a product of an American post-war philosophical milieu that was strongly oriented around questions of knowledge and explanation, and within which the question of *historical* knowledge and explanation, and with it of the explanation of human action and decision, was of particular importance – especially among those concerned to defend the possibility of a distinct mode of understanding that might apply to human thought and action. It is this same background that gave rise to Donald Davidson's seminal paper "Actions, Reasons, and Causes" (Davidson 1963) – a paper that looms large in the background of Stoutland's thinking on these matters. Yet Stoutland's work was not restricted to the philosophy of action alone, and was intimately connected, much as was Davidson's also, to his thinking in the philosophy of mind and language, with that latter focus coming more to the fore in Stoutland's later writings.

While not entirely neglecting his work on action, the essays collected in this volume aim to draw together Stoutland's main essays on questions of truth, language, mind, and metaphysics, thereby providing an indication of the larger context in which Stoutland's work on action must be placed. In addition, the choice of essays reflects Stoutland's own estimation of his best and most significant essays. Stoutland had already drawn up a list of papers as the basis for a volume (or possibly two) of collected papers from which most of the papers included here are taken. That original list also included many papers on the philosophy of action that do not appear here. A separate volume, *Acting for Reasons*, that focuses on Stoutland's thoughts on action (and so includes many of the essays absent from the present volume), is currently in preparation by James Conant, Dawa Ometto, and Harry Alanen.

Stoutland's life and career was divided largely between North America (notably Northfield, Minnesota) and Scandinavia (Finland and Sweden). Born of Norwegian immigrant parents in Illinois, in 1933, Stoutland graduated from Saint Olaf College in 1954, and received his PhD in philosophy from Yale University in 1959. He taught at Trinity College in Hartford, Connecticut from 1958 to 1962, and at Saint Olaf College from 1962 to 1996. Among other awards, Stoutland was the recipient of three grants from the US National Endowment for the Humanities and one from the American Council of Learned Societies (for study at Oxford). In 1995, Stoutland was named Docent at the University of Helsinki, and in 1998 he was welcomed as Permanent Visiting Professor at Uppsala. He died in Helsinki in 2011. Stoutland was not only an accomplished philosopher, but also a skilled carpenter, spending time in his workshop as well as in his study, and working on a range of building projects from boat houses to homes. A much-loved and respected figure both at St Olaf and Uppsala, Stoutland combined philosophical insight and acuity with a gentle humor and great generosity of spirit. Always ready to admit when he was wrong, he was nevertheless a committed thinker who cared deeply about the topics with which he was engaged.

Stoutland's readiness to admit mistakes is especially evident in his work on Davidson, and it is thus a trait that is of particular relevance to the essays collected here. Stoutland's thinking was heavily influenced by the work of the later Wittgenstein, and Stoutland developed a close relationship with Georg Henrik von Wright, who had been Wittgenstein's successor at the University of Cambridge, and who was also a major contributor to 20th-century thinking on questions of action and explanation (see e.g. von Wright 1971). Like von Wright, Stoutland was an early critic of the causal theory of action, including its exemplification in Davidson's work – Davidson being routinely taken as arguing against the position of the later Wittgenstein. Yet as Stoutland himself acknowledges, Davidson's thinking was itself heavily influenced by Wittgensteinian ideas (especially as mediated through the work of Elizabeth Anscombe), and Stoutland himself came to adopt a much more nuanced approach to the reading of Davidson than is common among many of Davidson's critics or supporters. As the horizons of Stoutland's work expanded, he also engaged more directly with other aspects of Davidson's thinking, publishing a long two-part discussion in 1982, "On Realism and Anti-Realism in Davidson's Philosophy of Language" (Stoutland 1982a, 1982b), that was essentially Stoutland's first published foray outside of the philosophy of action. If that essay is not included here, the reason is simply that Stoutland regarded it as an almost complete misreading of Davidson's position, and a reading that he later aimed to correct. It is notable that in his writing on Davidson thereafter, especially in his work from the 1990s onwards, Stoutland develops an approach to Davidson that, if not entirely in agreement, certainly shows considerable sympathy for, and is in some respects convergent with, many aspects of the Davidsonian account, even on some topics in the philosophy of action (though on this topic important differences still remain).

These essays, which engage with Davidson no less than Wittgenstein or von Wright, are testimony to Stoutland's more developed and later thinking, and to the broadening of scope that was characteristic of the last twenty years or so of Stoutland's philosophical work. Significantly, just as in Davidson's work, the question of truth became increasingly important, something similar also occurs in Stoutland. The rejection of the correspondence theory of truth, on which Stoutland largely follows Davidson, becomes a significant part of Stoutland's own criticism of the metaphysical pretensions of contemporary analytic thought (in contrast to the anti-metaphysical tenor of much previous analytic philosophy). In many ways, this can be seen as a return to as well as a reiteration of key themes in the later Wittgenstein.

Most of the essays included here come from this latter stage of Stoutland's career – the earliest, "Self and Society in the Claims of Individualism", was first published in 1990, and the majority of the essays appeared after the turn of the millennium (only five of the sixteen appeared prior to 2000). The essays fall into five broad groupings. Essays 1–5 deal with the issue of truth, and especially with the criticism of the standard approaches to truth that are extant in the existing philosophical literature. Here Stoutland discusses both Wittgenstein and Davidson on truth, and gives considerable attention to the so-called 'slingshot' argument (so-called because it uses what appears to be a relatively small point to demolish a very large claim) as that is deployed, by Davidson especially, against traditional correspondence accounts. Essays 6–8 deal specifically with the reading of Davidson – with what Stoutland viewed as the highly tendentious, but nevertheless influential reading of Davidson advanced by Ernest Lepore and Kirk Ludwig in the years immediately following Davidson's death, and with the pragmatist Deweyan reading of Davidson advanced by Richard Rorty. Essays 9–12 take up various topics within and around the philosophy of mind, broadly conceived, especially as these relate to issues concerning the social character of human mindedness, and including specific discussion of Wittgenstein as well as the work of John Searle. Essays 13–14 are the only essays included here that directly represent Stoutland's work in the philosophy of action, and they focus specifically on Davidson, in essay 13, and von Wright, in essay 14. The final essay, essay 15, comes back to a set of broader meta-philosophical considerations regarding the problematic character of that type of metaphysical philosophical that is nowadays so widespread, and that Stoutland claims "ought to be resisted" since "it is at best an unproductive diversion, and at worst dialectical illusion".

Jeff Malpas
Hobart, August 2018

Original Publication Details

Chapter 1 first appeared as "What Philosophers Should Know About Truth and the Slingshot", in M. Sintonen, P. Ylikoski and K. Miller, eds., *Realism in Action* (Doredrecht: Springer, 2003), pp. 3–32. Chapter 2 first appeared as "Wittgenstein: On Certainty and Truth", *Philosophical Investigations* 21 (1998), pp. 203–221. Chapter 3 first appeared as "Putnam on Truth", in M. Gustafsson and L. Hertzberg, eds., *The Practice of Language* (Dordrecht: Kluwer, 2002), pp. 147–176. Chapter 4 first appeared as "Do We Need Correspondence Truth?", in J. Peregrin, ed., *Truth and Its Nature (if Any)* (Dordrecht: Kluwer, 1999), pp. 81–90. Chapter 5 first appeared as "Making True", in R. Sliwinski, ed., *Philosophical Crumbs: Essays Dedicated to Ann-Mari Henschen-Dahlquist on the Occasion of Her Seventy-fifth Birthday* (Uppsala: University of Uppsala, Department of Philosophy, 1999), pp. 235–247. Chapter 6 first appeared as "A Mistaken View of Davidson's Legacy", *International Journal of Philosophical Studies* 14 (2006), pp. 579–596, with the Postscript to the chapter appearing as "Radical Misinterpretation Indeed: Response to Lepore and Ludwig", *International Journal of Philosophical Studies* 15 (2007), pp. 587–597. Chapter 8 first appeared as "Common Sense Psychology and Scientific Explanation", as part of T. Rønnow-Rasmussen, B. Petersson, J. Josefsson and D. Egonsson, eds., *Hommage à Wlodek: 60 Philosophical Papers Dedicated to Wlodek Rabinowicz* (Lund: University of Lund, 2007), online at http://www.fil.lu.se/hommageawlodek. Chapter 9 first appeared as "Philosophy of Mind with and Against Wittgenstein", in S. Heinämaa and M. Reuter, eds., *Psychology and Philosophy: Inquiries into the Soul from Late Scholasticism to Contemporary Thought* (Dordrecht: Springer, 2009), pp. 285–305. Chapter 10 first appeared as "The Ontology of Social Agency", *Analyse & Kritik* 30 (2008), pp. 533–551. Chapter 11 first appeared as "Searle's Consciousness: A Review of John Searle's *The Rediscovery of the Mind*", *Philosophical Books* 35 (1994), pp. 245–254. Chapter 12 first appeared as "Self and Society in the Claims of Individualism", *Studies in Philosophy and Education* 10 (1990), pp. 105–137. Chapter 13 first appeared as "Interpreting Davidson on Intentional Action", in J. Malpas, ed., *Dialogues with Davidson: Acting, Interpreting, Understanding* (Cambridge, MA: MIT Press, 2006), pp. 297–324. Chapter 14 first appeared as "The Problem of Congruence", in I. Niiniluoto and R. Vilkko, eds., *Philosophical Essays in Memoriam: Georg Henrik von Wright*, Acta Philosophical Fennica 77 (2005), pp. 127–150. Chapter 15 first appeared as "Analytic Philosophy and Metaphysics", in S. Philström, ed., *Wittgenstein and the Method of Philosophy*, Acta Philosophica Fennica 80 (2006), pp. 67–95.

List of Abbreviations

The following abbreviations have been used within this volume:

CSP	common sense psychology
EP	Equivalence Principle
LHS	left hand side
RHS	right hand side
SUB-LE	substitution – logical equivalence
ιCONV	iota-conversion
ι-SUB	iota substitution

1 What Philosophers Should Know about Truth and the Slingshot

> A champion came out from the Philistine camp, a man named Goliath; he was over nine feet in height ... When the Philistine began moving towards him, David ran quickly to engage him. He put his hand into his bag, took out a stone, slung it, and struck the Philistine on the forehead. The stone sank into his forehead; and he fell flat on his face on the ground. So David proved the victor with his sling and stone; he struck Goliath down and gave him a mortal wound, though he had no sword. (First Samuel, chapter 17)

The slingshot argument is so called[1] because, like the sling David used to slay Goliath, it uses so little to accomplish so much – or so its defenders claim. It has been used to reject the claim that sentences designate propositions or states of affairs, to undermine concepts like "necessarily" or "because", to show the futility of talk about mental or linguistic representations of reality, and much else besides. I am not going to discuss these uses of the argument, however, but only its use to show that the correspondence theory of truth – the theory that a sentence is true just in case it corresponds to a particular fact – should be rejected on the ground that, given a couple of unobjectionable premises, it can be proved that if a true sentence corresponds to any fact, it corresponds to every fact. That means that every true sentence corresponds to the same thing – which is to say there really is only one fact – which would be a mortal wound for the correspondence theory.

The inspiration for the slingshot is Frege and hence it is often called "the Frege argument". Frege held that all three kinds of non-logical, truth-relevant expressions – singular terms, predicates, and sentences – have both *Sinn* and *Bedeutung*: each has a sense and each signifies[2] (designates, means) something. In the case of a sentence (with a truth value) its sense is the thought one grasps in understanding it, while what it signifies depends only on whether it is true or false: if it is true, it signifies The True, and if it is false, it signifies The False. While non-synonymous sentences differ in their sense, all true ones signify the same thing, and this parallels precisely the conclusion of the slingshot that all true sen-

---

[1] The argument evidently acquired this marvelous name from Barwise and Perry (1983).
[2] I follow Gödel, who suggested in Gödel 1944 that Frege's 'bedeuten' be translated as "signifies". It's a fairly ordinary term and it relates Frege to medieval discussions of similar notions which are typically translated as "signify" ("signification").

tences correspond to the same fact. Needless to say, Frege did not hold a correspondence theory of truth, a major reason being that he put forward considerations analogous to those used in the slingshot. The argument itself, however, is not found in his work, but he nevertheless deserves credit for inspiring it and for creating the logical resources which made its formulation and evaluation possible.

The slingshot is a deductive argument, expressible in first order predicate logic with identity, which can be so formulated as to leave no question that, given the principles of inference used, its conclusion follows from its premises. This suffices to convince some philosophers that it establishes straightaway that the correspondence theory of truth must be rejected. But it also suffices to convince others that the argument can be ignored because it must involve formal tricks with no bearing on philosophical questions like how to understand the concept of truth. Both attitudes are wrong: although the slingshot can be made rigorously valid, its conclusion can be evaded by challenging one or more of its assumptions, not all of which are by any means self-evident. At the same time, reflection on these assumptions sheds a great deal of light on philosophical questions, and anyone who thinks about issues like truth ought to know what is at stake in accepting or rejecting the argument and the assumptions it requires.

My aim in this paper is to state the argument as clearly as I can, focusing on two versions of it (which I shall call the "Davidson version" and the "Gödel version"), and to explain its significance for the correspondence theory of truth. The technical parts are derivative on the work of others,[3] my intention not being to develop that work, but to make it more accessible and to draw out the philosophical significance of alternative ways of stating the argument and evading its conclusion. This does not mean that I have no view of my own. I take my discussion to show that, while there are good reasons not to accept all the assumptions required by the slingshot (either the Davidson or the Gödel version), the correspondence theory of truth by no means escapes its effects. Some versions accept the assumptions the slingshot requires, and they are mortally wounded by it, while others reject them at the price of a correspondence theory so devoid of explanatory force as to be indistinguishable from a deflationist conception of truth.

---

[3] Particularly Needham 2006; Neale 1995; and Neale and Dever 1997. Neale 1995 has an excellent and comprehensive bibliography of discussions of the slingshot.

1.1 Some Background Principles and Distinctions

Before considering the argument, I want to discuss the principles on which its evaluation must turn. These principles are philosophically elementary, but it is easy to lose sight of them when considering the slingshot as a formal argument. The decisive thing is to get clear about the philosophical significance of various substitution principles used in different versions of the argument.

The slingshot is directed against any correspondence theory of truth which claims that a true sentence must correspond to some particular fact, where a fact is an entity whose existence makes true a sentence which corresponds to it. While accounts of facts differ in many ways, two things are essential, which Russell put as follows. First, facts must be "what they are whatever we may choose to think about them" (Russell 1956, p. 182), which implies that we can refer to them in different ways and that how we refer to them makes no difference to what they are. Second, a fact must be "the sort of thing expressed by a whole sentence, not by a single name" (Russell 1956, pp. 182–183), where this latter point might be put by saying that a fact must be a sentence-like entity. For example, the sentence 'The author of Waverley lived in Scotland' is true not because it corresponds to the author of Waverly or to Scotland but because it corresponds to the fact that the author of Waverley lived in Scotland, where 'the fact that' must be followed by a (true) sentence.

The correspondence theory holds that a true sentence must correspond to some *particular* fact because simply corresponding to the facts is far too general. A false sentence may very well correspond to *some* fact, but it is false because it does not correspond to the right fact – the fact which would make it true – and it is this notion of each true sentence corresponding to a particular fact which the slingshot purports to undermine. It argues that, given that 'the author of Waverly lived in Scotland' corresponds to the fact that the author of Waverley lived in Scotland, then it also corresponds to the fact that Truman lived longer than Roosevelt, that sugar maples turn red in the fall, that Strindberg was born in Stockholm, etc., where one can put any true sentence after 'the fact that'. This could be taken as the claim that any true sentence corresponds to *every* fact, but it can also be taken as the claim that every true sentence corresponds to the *same* fact, since if a true sentence corresponds to the fact that p, where 'p' is any true sentence, then any other true sentence also corresponds to the fact that p. But if every true sentence corresponds to the same fact, then there is only one fact, which rules out any notion of a true sentence corresponding to a particular fact.

If correspondence is a relation between a true sentence and a particular fact, then we must be able to refer both to sentences and to facts. A sentence is what is true (or false), and we refer to a sentence, say 'Strindberg was born in Stockholm', in various ways: by quoting it (as I just did), by describing it ('the last sentence in the previous paragraph'), by nominalizing it ('that Strindberg was born in Stockholm'), and so on. How we refer to sentences is not crucial to our discussion, nor is it crucial that we speak of sentences, rather than statements, utterances, or propositions, as what are true (or false), and I will speak of sentences because that is customary among logicians when constructing formal arguments.[4]

How we refer to facts, however, is crucial. Because facts are sentence-like, sentences must figure in referring to them, and because facts are entities, we must be able to refer to them by using singular terms. This has often led defenders of the correspondence theory to conclude that sentences are themselves singular terms, but a more plausible version is as follows. Take a paradigm correspondence claim:

> A. The true sentence that Stockholm is a large city corresponds to the fact that Stockholm is a large city.

It is natural to construe this as involving the relational predicate 'corresponds to' flanked by two singular terms, *'the true sentence that Stockholm is a large city'*, which refers to a sentence, and *'the fact that Stockholm is a large city'*, which refers to a particular fact. While there is nothing wrong with this way of construing the claim, it does not clarify the crucial role of sentences since it construes the claim as consisting only of a predicate and two singular terms. But it is not difficult to reconstrue the claim so that it consists of sentences and a sentence connective:

> B. The true sentence that [*Stockholm is a large city*] corresponds to the fact that [*Stockholm is a large city*].

If we suppress the two sentences in brackets and replace them with variables, the result is a two-placed sentence connective – the 'correspondence connective':

> C. The true sentence that p corresponds to the fact that q.

---

[4] Though not crucial to evaluating the slingshot, the issue of what are taken to be true or false lies just beneath the surface of my central points, and the issue is surely very important for wider questions about an adequate conception of truth.

This enables us to reformulate the slingshot as purporting to show that, given obvious assumptions, whatever *true* sentences the correspondence connective connects (whatever true sentences we substitute for 'p' or 'q' in C), the result will be true. In other words, the correspondence connective, appearances to the contrary notwithstanding, is, defenders of the slingshot maintain, fully extensional in that any true sentence in its scope may be substituted *salva veritate* by any true sentence. It is indeed, they maintain, a truth-functional connective: the truth value of sentences containing it depends only on the truth value of the sentences it connects.

Defenders of the correspondence theory must obviously deny that we get a true sentence no matter what true sentence we substitute for 'p' or 'q' in C. It is equally obvious that they cannot deny that we get a true sentence whenever we substitute the *same* (or a synonymous) true sentence for both 'p' and 'q' in C: the true sentence that p always corresponds to the fact that p. That sets up the crucial question: are there principles which permit the substitution *salva veritate* of *some* but not all true sentences for 'p' and for 'q' in C? For instance, given that the true sentence 'Stockholm is a large city' corresponds to the fact that Stockholm is a large city, are there principles that permit the substitution *salva veritate* of *some* true sentences in 'the fact that Stockholm is a large city' which do not also permit the substitution of *all* true sentences? Is there something *between* permitting the substitution of only synonymous sentences – in which case the correspondence connective is fully *intensional*[5] – and permitting the unlimited substitution of true sentence – in which case the connective is fully *extensional*?

To consider that question, however, we must consider the substitution not only of sentences but also of the singular terms and predicates which are their constituents. A singular term is a term which, in a given context, signifies (or purports to signify) a particular individual. Examples are proper names like 'John' or 'Stockholm', pronouns like 'he', 'she' or 'it', demonstratives like 'this' or 'that', and definite descriptions like 'the capital of Sweden' or 'the fact that Stockholm is a large city'. The standard substitution principle for singular terms 'a' and 'b' is that 'a' may be substituted for 'b' *salva veritate* in a sentence just in case 'a' and 'b' refer to the same individual (so that a = b). For example, since Stockholm is (identical to) the Capital of Sweden, we may substitute one for the other *salva veritate*: if it is true that Stockholm is a large city, then it is true that the capital of Sweden is a large city. Or to use a classical example, since 'Cicero' and 'Tully' both refer to

---

5 In this respect it is just like a (*de dicta*) belief context: John's belief that Stockholm is a large city can be characterized only as the belief that Stockholm is a large city – not even as the belief that the capital of Sweden is a large city (for John may not believe that Stockholm is the capital of Sweden).

the same Roman statesman (Cicero = Tully), we may substitute 'Tully' for 'Cicero' in sentences like 'Cicero often gave speeches in Rome'.

The standard principle of substitution for singular terms is based on the sound idea that if a term is used to refer to a particular individual, then any other term which refers to that same individual will do as well. If it is true that Cicero often gave speeches in Rome, then the sentence 'Rome's greatest orator often gave speeches in Rome' will also be true, whether or not Cicero really was Rome's greatest orator, *provided* the point of using the definite description, 'Rome's greatest orator', was simply to refer to Cicero. We may, therefore, substitute co-referring singular terms *salva veritate* in any sentence in any context in which the terms simply refer to the same individual. That also includes the context of the correspondence connective, in which case, from:

> D. The true sentence that Cicero often gave speeches in Rome corresponds to the fact that Cicero often gave speeches in Rome

we may infer:

> E. The true sentence that Cicero often gave speeches in Rome corresponds to the fact that Tully often gave speeches in Rome.

A predicate contrasts with a singular term in not referring to a particular individual but in being *true of* an individual or set of individuals. The individuals of which a predicate is true comprise the *extension* of the predicate. 'Is a large city', for example is true of Stockholm, New York, London, and all other large cities, which comprise its extension. A predicate can be thought of as what remains of a sentence if we remove singular terms. Thus, if we remove 'Stockholm' from 'Stockholm is a large city', the result is the predicate 'x is a large city', which logicians call an 'open sentence' since replacing the variable with a singular term produces an ordinary ('closed') sentence. If we remove both singular terms from 'Stockholm is larger than Helsinki', we get the open sentence, 'x is larger than y', which is a relational predicate requiring (in this case) two singular terms to become a (closed) sentence. A quantified sentence like 'Some cities are dangerous' has predicates but no singular terms; it is taken to express that there is at least one individual which is in the joint extension of the predicates 'x is a city' and 'x is dangerous'. 'All cities are dangerous' is taken to express that if any individual is in the extension of 'x is a city', it is also in the extension of 'x is dangerous'.

According to this account, predicates do not *refer* but are rather *true of* various individuals, and hence it would be incoherent to formulate a substitution principle in terms of *co-referring* predicates. The substitution principle Frege proposed (which is valid in extensional contexts) is that predicates may be substituted in sentences *salva veritate* if they are *co-extensive* – that is, true of the very same individuals. We cannot substitute 'is a city' for 'is large' since their extensions are not the same: not every city is large nor is every large individual a city. We can, of course, substitute *synonymous* predicates ('is a pair of glasses' for 'is a pair of spectacles') *salva veritate* since they necessarily have the same extension. But the principle also permits the substitution of predicates which are co-extensive as a matter of contingent fact – predicates which as a matter of fact are true of the same individuals. Quine's nice example is 'is a creature with a heart' and 'is a creature with a kidney', which are co-extensive because there are no organisms which have a heart but do not have a kidney. Another example is 'lives in California' and 'lives in the most populous state in the USA'; still another is 'broke her arm in Nelspruit on January 6, 2000' and 'is a grandchild of mine born in 1996'.

It is clear that co-extensive predicates may not be substituted *salva veritate* in the context of the correspondence connective, as can be seen by considering examples. For example, from:

> The true sentence that Celina broke her arm in Nelspruit on January 6, 2000 corresponds to the fact that Celina broke her arm in Nelspruit on January 6, 2000

we cannot infer:

> The true sentence that Celina broke her arm in Nelspruit on January 6, 2000 corresponds to the fact that Celina is a grandchild of mine born in 1996

even though those predicates are co-extensive in that both are true only of my granddaughter, Celina. This is particularly clear if we consider the converse of 'correspond', namely 'make true', for we surely cannot claim that what makes it true that Celina broke her arm in Nelspruit on January 6, 2000 is the fact that she is a grandchild of mine born in 1996. Nor could we claim that what makes it true that the governor of California lives in California is the fact that the governor of California lives in the most populous state.

A more general way of making this point is to note that, although co-extensive predicates, like 'has a heart' and 'has a kidney', are true of the same individuals, to predicate 'has a heart' of an individual is to predicate something quite different from predicating 'has a kidney', and even though any (living) creature which has the one will have the other, any surgeon better know the difference. Similarly, to say of Celina that she broke her arm in Nelspruit on January 6, 2000 is to say something quite different than to say of her that she is my grandchild born in 1996.

The latter example is of special relevance for our topic. It concerns predicates which are co-extensive just because they are true of exactly one individual. They are significant because there are contexts in which, if such predicates can be substituted *salva veritate*, then any sentences with the same truth value may also be substituted *salva veritate*. The intuitive point is that if you can substitute predicates just because they are true of exactly one individual, then, *in a context where all that counts is that one individual*, you can also substitute any sentences with the same truth value. Such contexts (which have to be *devised*) are such that to permit the substitution of co-extensive predicates is *thereby* to permit the substitution of co-extensive sentences (that is, sentences with the same truth value). To put it in other terms: since predicates are open sentences, (closed) sentences are a special case of predicates, and hence there are contexts in which permitting the substitution of co-extensive predicates is *thereby* to permit the substitution of co-extensive sentences. This, as we shall see, is central to constructing the slingshot argument.

Let me sum up this discussion so far. Defenders of the correspondence theory cannot hold that the correspondence connective sets up a fully *extensional* context, for that would mean that *any* true sentences may be substituted *salva veritate* for 'p' or 'q' in this schema:

F. The true sentence that p corresponds to the fact that q.

But they do not have to accept the notion that the correspondence connective sets up a fully *intensional* context – which would require that the same (or a synonymous) true sentence must always be substituted for *both* 'p' and 'q' – the reason being that a context in which co-referring terms are substitutable *salva veritate* need not be a context in which true sentences are substitutable *salva veritate*. Given that 'Stockholm' and 'the capital of Sweden' refer to the same city, it does not follow from:

G. The true sentence that Stockholm is a large city corresponds to the fact that the capital of Sweden is a large city

that *any* true sentence may be substituted *salva veritate* for 'the capital of Sweden is a large city'. The principle of the substitution of co-extensive *predicates*, however, works quite differently: co-extensive predicates may not be substituted *salva veritate* in the context of the correspondence connective.

If this were all there is to say about principles of substitution, however, the slingshot would be utterly unpersuasive. What I take to be its crucial assumption is expressed by Davidson as the assumption that we should permit the "substitution of singular terms for others with the same extension" (Davidson 2001a,

p. 152), and Davidson's use of the slingshot amounts to the claim that if we accept that principle of substitution in the context of the correspondence connective, we have thereby accepted the substitution *salva veritate* of sentences with the same truth value. But if the "substitution of singular terms for others with the same extension" (Davidson 2001a, p. 152) is the same as the principle of the substitution of co-referring singular terms, then Davidson is claiming that any context which permits the substitution of co-referring singular terms *salva veritate* must be a fully extensional context and there is, as we just saw, no reason to accept that. We have been given no reason to think, for example that we cannot substitute *salva veritate* 'Tully' for 'Cicero', or 'the capital of Sweden' for 'Stockholm', in the context of the correspondence connective.

What this shows is that the notion of singular terms with the same *extension* cannot be the same as the notion of singular terms with the same *reference*, which suggests a complication in the notion of singular terms our discussion so far has ignored. I used 'singular term' to refer to names, pronouns, demonstratives and definite descriptions, but that blurs a distinction which is crucial to evaluating the slingshot. Names, pronouns, and demonstratives are (almost always) used as *referring* terms, that is, used simply to refer to a particular individual[6] their use is, as it were, exhausted by their successful reference. Definite descriptions, on the other hand, have two distinct uses, which Keith Donellan called 'attributive' and 'referential':

> A speaker who uses a definite description attributively in an assertion states something about whoever or whatever is the so-and-so. A speaker who uses a definite description referentially in an assertion, on the other hand, uses the description to enable his audience to pick out whom or what he is talking about and state something about that person or thing. In the first case the definite description might be said to occur essentially, for the speaker wishes to assert something about whatever or whoever fits that description; but in the referential use the definite description is merely one tool for doing a certain job – calling attention to a person or thing – and in general any other device for doing the same job, another description or a name, would do as well. (Donellan 1966, p. 285)

Donellan illustrates this distinction with the sentence 'Smith's murderer is insane'. If we utter it in the presence of the murdered Smith but do not know who Smith's murderer is, then we are saying that whoever murdered Smith is insane.[7] That is an *attributive* use of the description, 'Smith's murderer'. On the other hand, if we utter it in the presence of the person we believe to be Smith's

---

[6] Or occasionally, particular individuals considered as a unit, as with the demonstrative 'those'.
[7] It is not necessary for the attributive use that we not know who Smith's murderer is, but the idea is more easily grasped when that assumption is made.

murderer, simply in order to say of that particular person that she is insane, then what we are saying is true as long as that particular person is insane, whether or not she was Smith's murderer. That is a *referential* use of the description, 'Smith's murderer'.

If definite descriptions are used referentially, then they (like names, pronouns, and demonstratives) conform to the principle of substitution for co-referring singular terms. I illustrated this above when I argued that we could substitute 'Rome's greatest orator' for 'Cicero', whether or not Cicero was Rome's greatest orator *provided* we used the terms simply to refer to the particular man Cicero. However, if definite descriptions are used *attributively*, the principle of substitution of co-referring singular terms is not acceptable because there will be contexts (including that of the correspondence connective) in which definite descriptions cannot be substituted *salva veritate*. The reason is that when used attributively, definite descriptions are used not only (and not primarily) to *refer* but to *describe*. As Donellan put it in the quotation above, "A speaker who uses a definite description attributively in an assertion states something about whoever or whatever is the so-and-so." (Donellan 1966, p. 285) An utterance of 'Smith's murderer is insane' which involves an *attributive* use of the definite description 'Smith's murderer', is true, therefore, only if whoever is Smith's murderer is insane.

This means that substitution of definite descriptions which function attributively is tantamount to the substitution of *predicates*. But we have seen that the principle for the substitution of co-extensive predicates works very differently from the principle for the substitution of co-referring singular terms. Whereas co-referring singular terms may be substituted *salva veritate* in the context of the correspondence connective, co-extensive predicates may not be. We must, therefore, distinguish between a principle for the substitution of definite descriptions as used attributively – which involves *predicate* substitution – and a principle for the substitution of definite descriptions as used referentially – which involves no predicate substitution. Insofar as names, pronouns, and demonstratives are (as they generally are) used referentially, the latter principle will, of course, also apply to them.

This distinction is obscured by Davidson's reference to the "substitution of singular terms for others with the *same extension*" (Davidson 2001a, p. 152).[8] Predicates have extension though (as Davidson and I agree) not reference, and singular terms can also be spoken as having extension, whether used referential-

---

[8] Just as it is obscured by speaking of the substitution of singular terms for others which 'stand for', or 'designate' the same things. The common use of the term "represent" in this context is even more obscuring since it can indicate not only both *extension* and *reference* but also *sense*, as when it is said that a false sentence may represent what is not the case.

ly (the extension is the particular individual actually referred to) or attributively (the extension is whichever individual the description happens to fit). But to leave it at that blurs the distinction between referential and attributive uses of definite descriptions, which obscures the point that, although the principle of substitution for *co-referring* singular terms is acceptable in any context, it does not follow that the principle applies to definite descriptions in their *attributive* use. As we shall see, definite descriptions in their attributive use are substitutable *salva veritate* only in extensional contexts, which is the decisive point for evaluating the slingshot.

The distinctions just made are, from the point of view of formal logic, *pragmatic* points and hence cannot be incorporated directly into formal arguments like the slingshot. But they must be reflected in the formal arguments if they are to be relevant to philosophical issues like truth, and to help with this, I will make some terminological stipulations. From now on, I will use 'singular term' as the generic term for names, pronouns, demonstratives, and definite descriptions. There will be two species of the genus: names and definite descriptions. I will use 'names' to cover referring terms in the strict sense, hence not only names proper, but pronouns, demonstratives, and definite descriptions understood *referentially*. This means that the principle I called the substitution principle for co-referring singular terms is renamed the substitution principle for co-referring names. I will use 'definite descriptions' to cover singular terms as used *attributively* rather than referentially, and the principle of substitution for co-referring names will not apply to them for reasons just given.

The canonical expression for a definite description in this restricted sense will be the iota sign: 'ιx'. 'The capital of Sweden' will be symbolized as Russell did: '$(\iota x)Fx$', to be read as 'the unique individual x such that x is the capital of Sweden'. The principle of substitution for definite descriptions, abbreviated 'ι-SUB' ('iota substitution'; it will be formulated later) will specify the conditions under which, given that $(\iota x)Fx == (\iota x)Gx$, it is acceptable to substitute '$(\iota x)Fx$' for '$(\iota x)Gx$' in a sentential context. The principle will, of course, function differently from the principle of substitution for co-referring names since the latter (unlike the former) never involves the substitution of co-extensive predicates.

1.2 Davidson and the Slingshot

The most discussed version of the slingshot (which I will call 'Davidson's version') was first published in Church's review of Carnap's *Introduction to Semantics* in the 1943 *Philosophical Review* (Church 1943). Carnap had proposed replacing Frege's notion that sentences signify truth values with the notion that they signify propositions, his aim being to reject the unsettling notion that what a sentence signifies depends only on its truth value. Church argued that, on Carnap's own assumptions, if a sentence signifies any proposition, then every true sentence signifies the same proposition, which means that Carnap's connective, 'the sentence S signifies proposition p', is in fact truth-functional and hence no advance over the Fregean idea that sentences signify truth values.

This form of argument has since been used to make analogous criticisms of other proposed connectives, notably by Quine in his criticism of quantified modal logic and by Davidson in his critique of the correspondence theory of truth, which is our subject. Davidson first used the argument in his "Truth and Meaning" (Davidson 2001b)[9] to undermine the proposal that we might think of the meaning of a sentence as something the sentence signifies, and then think of the meaning of singular terms and predicates as the contribution they make to sentence meaning thus construed. That proposal is a non-starter, he claimed, because, given "two reasonable assumptions" (Davidson 2001b, p. 19), every true sentence signifies the same thing, and so does every false sentence, so that the proposal would amount to the absurd claim that "all sentences alike in truth value must be synonymous" (Davidson 2001b, p. 19). The two 'reasonable assumptions' referred to are "that logically equivalent singular terms [sic] have the same reference, and that a singular term does not change its reference if a contained singular term is replaced by another with the same reference" (Davidson 2001b, p. 19).

Davidson next used the argument in his paper on "Causal Relations", also published in 1967 (Davidson 2001a) to argue that the notion of a *causal* connective is incoherent because we can show that it too must be truth-functional in that any true sentences can be substituted *salva veritate* for 'p' and 'q' in the schema, 'The fact that p was the cause of the fact that q'. To show that, we need the same two reasonable assumptions, though now reformulated. The assumption that logically equivalent singular terms have the same reference is reformulated as the principle that logically equivalent sentences may be substituted *salva veritate*. The assumption that "a singular term does not change its reference if a contained singular term is replaced by another with the same reference" (Davidson 2001b, p. 19) is reformulated as the principle (discussed in the previous section) that "substitution of singular terms for others with the same extension" (Davidson 2001a, p. 152) is always permissible.

---

[9] Davidson wrote there that "the argument derives from Frege" (Davidson 2001b, p. 36), citing Church's *Mathematical Logic*.

Davidson appealed to these two assumptions again in "True to the Facts" (Davidson 2001b), where he first used the slingshot in discussing truth, and where he used it twice. Its first use was to undermine a deflationary conception of truth which attempts to show, by using the principle, '(∀p) (the sentence that p is true ↔ p)', that the truth predicate is redundant. Davidson argued that the principle would enable us to eliminate 'is true' only if its variable ranges over entities "that sentences may be construed as naming", but, he went on, "There are very strong reasons, as Frege pointed out, for supposing that if sentences, when standing alone or in truth functional contexts, name anything, then all true sentences name the same thing" (Davidson 2001b, p. 39), which shows that a redundancy theory based on (objectual) quantification can't work.

Davidson's other use of the argument in "True to the Facts" dealt explicitly with the role of facts in this schema:

> The sentence that p corresponds to the fact that q

which leads to a correspondence theory of truth, he noted, if we add that "a statement is true if there is a fact to which it corresponds" (Davidson 2001b, p. 41). The problem with the schema is to determine what we could substitute for 'p' and 'q', the difficulty being that if we substitute anything other than the same sentence for each, then any true sentence will do, so that "if a statement corresponds to one fact, it corresponds to all" (Davidson 2001b, p. 43). Then he states the argument itself, using the same two assumptions:

> ... If a statement corresponds to the fact described by an expression of the form 'the fact that p', then it corresponds to the fact described by 'the fact that q' provided either (1) the sentences that replace 'p' and 'q' are logically equivalent, or (2) 'p' differs from 'q' only in that a singular term has been replaced by a coextensive singular term. The confirming argument is this. Let 's' abbreviate some true sentence. Then surely the statement that s corresponds to the fact that s. But we may substitute for the second 's' the logically equivalent '(the x such that x is identical with Diogenes and s) is identical with (the x such that x is identical with Diogenes)'. Applying the principle that we may substitute coextensive singular terms, we can substitute 't' for 's' in the last quoted sentence, provided 't' is true. Finally, reversing the first step we conclude that the statement that s corresponds to the fact that t, where 's' and 't' are any true sentences. (Davidson 2001b, p. 43)

As Searle notes, the argument is given with "breathtaking speed" (Searle 1995, p. 221) but before spelling it out, let me say a few more words about Davidson's attitude to the correspondence theory of truth.

In "True to the Facts", Davidson defended a correspondence theory in spite of endorsing the slingshot. What he took the slingshot to show was that appeal to *facts* has no place in an account of truth because, given the two reasonable assumptions, "Descriptions like 'the fact that there are stupas in Nepal', if they describe at all, describe the same thing: The Great Fact. No point remains in distinguishing among various names of The Great Fact when written after 'corresponds to'" (Davidson 2001b, p. 42), which amounts to "ontological collapse" as far as the notion of facts is concerned (Davidson 2001b, p. 43). To respond to this by rejecting the two assumptions is to "leave the frying-pan of extensionality for the fires of intension" (Davidson 2001b, p. 43), which means there would be precisely as many facts as there are distinct true sentences, so that the correspondence theory could claim no more than what makes it true that p is the fact that p. While there is every reason to accept that claim, there is no reason to think it could explain anything – either what it is for a sentence to be true or why a sentence is true – and hence no reason to think it supports a correspondence theory of truth.

What Davidson defended in "True to the Facts", therefore, was a correspondence theory which makes no use of facts. He took this to be possible on the basis of Tarski's truth theory, which explains truth in terms of satisfaction and explains satisfaction as a relation between expressions and sequences of objects. The fact that in Tarski's theory, true sentences are satisfied by *all* sequences is thus a reflection of what the slingshot shows, but the fact that non-sentential expressions can be satisfied by some but not all sequences permits an explanatorily relevant specification of the relation of language and world.

> The semantic concept of truth as developed by Tarski deserves to be called a correspondence theory because of the part played by the concept of satisfaction; for clearly what has been done is that the property of being true had been explained, and nontrivially, in terms of a relation between language and something else ... All true sentences end up in the same place [as satisfied by all sequences], but there are different stories about how they got there; a semantic theory of truth tells the story for a particular sentence by running through the steps of the recursive account of satisfaction appropriate to the sentence. (Davidson 2001b, p. 48)[10]

Davidson soon ceased to defend the correspondence theory of truth in any form, the break becoming explicit in "A Coherence Theory of Truth and Knowledge"

---

10 It is worth noting that although Davidson defended this notion of a correspondence theory without facts by reference to Tarski's semantics for quantificational logic, it is in fact closer to older correspondence theories than to the fact-based ones which became current only after the latter part of the 19th century (central figures being Meinong and Russell). Earlier philosophers did not think of a sentence as signifying a fact, state of affairs, or other sentence-like entity. They thought of a sentence as signifying the object (or objects) which its subject term signified and predicating something of that object (or objects). This is not Tarski, but closer to the Tarskian point of view Davidson used than to the fact-based correspondence he rejected.

(1983, reprinted: Davidson 1986). In a sense, this was only a terminological change, because the main reason he gave for rejecting the correspondence theory was that it thinks of sentences as representations, which makes sense only if there are facts to be represented, which the slingshot shows to be untenable. Since this is the view he held in "True to the Facts", where he defended the theory ("[it] deserves, not elimination, but elaboration" (Davidson 2001b, p. 54)), it looks as if he has only changed the label on the ground that it is misleading to call a conception of truth which makes no use of facts a correspondence theory. But the change also reflected greater appreciation of the significance of the fact that Tarski's theory defines truth only in the context of a particular language and hence yields a different definition of the truth predicate for each language and, moreover, has nothing to say about what each of those differently defined predicates has in common. What conception of truth Davidson presently holds, given his firm rejection not only of the correspondence theory but of epistemic theories of truth is another question, which I will not pursue here.

Let me now give a precise formulation[11] of Davidson's version of the slingshot, which presents it as a formally valid argument proving that if we accept *any* instance of the scheme, 'the sentence that p corresponds to the fact that q' we must, given a couple of 'reasonable assumptions', accept *every* instance of the scheme which results from substituting any true sentence for 'p' and any true sentence for 'q'. We can accomplish the same end more smoothly if we take 'p' to stand for a particular true sentence (for example, 'Stockholm is a large city' – abbreviated as 'S'), and hence use 'S' instead of the variable 'p' after 'the sentence that', thus construing the scheme as expressing a *one-place* sentence connective. Hence I define 'C' (the 'correspondence connective') as follows:[12]

'Cq' =$_{df.}$ 'The true sentence S corresponds to the fact that q'

---

11 My formulation is indebted to Neale 1995 and to Needham 2006.
12 Note that Davidson formulates the correspondence connective as "The *statement* that p corresponds to the fact that q", not as "The *true sentence* that p corresponds to the fact that q." I use 'sentence' rather than 'statement' as explained above, and I use "*true* sentence" to simplify the exposition but it does not affect the proof. My version requires that true sentences go in for both 'S' and 'q' on the ground that fact-based correspondence theories generally deny that false sentences correspond to anything. Davidson's version of the slingshot requires that what goes in for 'q' have *the same truth value* as 'S', which yields the claim that a false sentence corresponds to the fact that q, provided 'q' is a false sentence: that would make the fact that q a *false* fact, which is something correspondence theories want to avoid. The proof goes through either way.

The task then is to show that, given the reasonable assumptions, we may, in the context of C, substitute *salva veritate* any true sentence for 'q', which amounts to saying that, whatever anyone may have thought, the connective is fully extensional and hence useless in a substantive account of truth. I will follow Davidson's statement of the argument, abbreviating 'the x such that x is identical with Diogenes' as 'the x such that Fx' (so that 'Fx' stands for 'x is identical with Diogones') and using the iota sign '(ιx)' for 'the x such that'.[13]

The inference rules for this version of the slingshot are the standard rules of predicate logic with the addition of two substitution principles, which correspond to Davidson's two assumptions. The first permits the substitution, in the context of C, of logically equivalent sentences – sentences which have the same truth value in every model (or possible situation) – a principle I abbreviate as SUB-LE, whose formal statement is as follows:

> SUB-LE: given that 'p ↔ q' holds just in case 'p' and 'q' have the same truth value in every model, then from 'p↔q' and 'Σ(p)' you may infer 'Σ(q)', where 'Σ(q)' is the result of replacing at least one occurrence of 'p' in 'Σ(p)' by 'q'.

The second substitution principle corresponds to Davidson's assumption that we may substitute "co-extensive singular terms" in the context of C, which clearly functions as a principle for the substitution of singular terms in the *generic* sense, which includes definite descriptions. I will (following Neale) call the principle 'iota-substitution' and abbreviate it as ι-SUB. It permits the substitution of a definite description for a definite description, of a definite description for a name and of a name for a definite description, and hence its formal statement requires three rules:

ι-SUB:	(ιx)p = (ιx)q	(ιx)p = a	(ιx)p = a
	Σ[(ιx)p]	Σ[(ιx)p]	Σ[a].
	Σ[(ιx)q]	Σ[a]	Σ[(ιx)p]

where 'Σ(ψ)' is the result of replacing at least one occurrence of 'φ' in 'Σ(φ)' by 'ψ':

---

[13] Standard statements of the argument (like Davidson's) use sentences of the form '(ιx)(x = a)' because in standard predicate logic, singular terms ('names' in my terminology) like 'a', which can flank the identity sign, are taken to have a reference, so that '(ιx)(x = a)' is understood to refer to one and only individual. I use '(ιx)Fx' to simplify the formulation of the argument, but for the argument to go through, 'Fx' must be understood to have the form 'x = a'.

Here is the Davidson slingshot set out formally (Table 1.1).

Table 1.1

(1)	p ↔ q	premise
(2)	Cp	premise
(3)	p ⇔ ((ιx)(Fx) = (ιx)(Fx . p))	(Logical equivalence)
(4)	C[(ιx)(Fx) = (ιx)(Fx . p)]	2, 3 SUB-LE
(5)	(ιx)(Fx . p) = (ιx)(Fx . q)	1
(6)	C[(ιx)(Fx) = (ιx)(Fx . q)]	4, 5 ι-SUB
(7)	q ↔ ((ιx)(Fx) = (ιx)(Fx . q))	(Logical equivalence)
(8)	Cq	6,7 SUB-LE

Let me explain the proof informally. Line 1 uses '↔' for the biconditional and can be read as "'p' and 'q' are materially equivalent", that is, have the same truth value. Line 2 abbreviates 'The sentence S corresponds to the fact that p'. The aim of the proof is to show that it is permissible to substitute 'q' for 'p' in 'The sentence S corresponds to the fact that p' ('Cp') even if the only thing 'q' and 'p' share is that both are true.

The inference from line 1 to line 5 occurs outside the scope of C and depends only on the definition of 'ιx' together with standard rules of predicate logic with identity. Reading '(ιx)Fx' as "the unique object x such that x is F" means that '(ιx)(Fx . p)' is to be read as 'the unique object x such that x is F and p'. If 'p' is true, this will be true of the unique object x such that x is F; but if 'p' is false, there will be no such thing as the unique object x such that x is F and p of which the formula can be true.[14] This means that the role of 'p' in the reference of '(ιx)(Fx . p)' depends *only* on whether 'p' is true or false, and hence substituting 'q' for 'p' will not change the reference of '(ιx)(Fx . p)', provided 'q' and 'p' have the same truth value. According to line 1, 'q' does have the same truth value as 'p', and hence '(ιx)(Fx . p)' and '(ιx)(Fx . q)' have the same reference, which is to say that '(ιx)(Fx . p) = (ιx)(Fx . q)', which is just line 5.

Lines 3 and 7 express the logical equivalences which are used to get lines 4 and 8 respectively. Since lines 3 and 7 are both outside the scope of C, reference to SUB-LE or ι-SUB is not required for their justification, which depends only on predicate logic with identity and parallels that given for line 5 in the previous

---

14 If we take 'Fx' to signify 'is President of the U.S.' and 'p' to signify 'Today is Friday', then '(ιx)(Fx & p)' can be read as 'the unique individual such that he is President of the U.S. and today is Friday'. If today *is* Friday, that description (at this writing) signifies Bill Clinton; if today is not Friday, it doesn't signify anybody, since in order for the description to signify something it has to be Friday today.

paragraph. Line 3 says that 'p' and '(ιx)(Fx) = (ιx)(Fx . p)' are logically equivalent, which is to say they have the same truth value in every model or possible situation. The justification for this (as we saw in the previous paragraph) is that '(ιx)(Fx . p)' has as its reference the unique object x such that x is F and p: if 'p' is true, this will simply be the unique object such that x is F; but if 'p' is false, there will be no such thing as the unique object such that x is F and p. The identity on line 3 holds, therefore, whenever 'p' is true (because the right hand side designates the same as the left) but does not hold whenever 'p' is false, which means that the expressions which flank the logical equivalence sign have the same truth value in every possible situation. (The justification for line 7 is identical with 'q' substituted for 'p'.)

The remaining inferences occur within the scope of C, and hence their justification requires reference to the additional substitution principles. Line 4 is inferred from lines 2 and 3 by using SUB-LE to replace 'p' in 'Cp' (line 2) with what line 3 says is logically equivalent to it, namely '(ιx)(Fx) = (ιx)(Fx . p)'. Line 6 is inferred from lines 4 and 5 by substitution of definite descriptions: since (by 5) (ιx)(Fx . p) = (ιx)(Fx . q), we may, given ι-SUB, substitute '(ιx)(Fx . q)' for '(ιx)(Fx . p)' in line 4, which yields line 6. Finally, line 8 as inferred from lines 6 and 7 by using SUB-LE to replace '(ιx)(Fx) = (ιx)(Fx . q)' in 'C[(ιx)(Fx) = (ιx)(Fx . q)]' with what line 7 says is logically equivalent to it, namely 'q'.

The only way to evade the Davidson slingshot is to reject at least one of the substitution principles it uses. The sole argument Davidson gives for the principles is that their rejection would make the correspondence connective fully intensional. But that assumes that the connective must set up either a fully extensional or a fully intensional context and, as we saw in section 1.1, there is no reason to accept that.

Barry Taylor sketched out the best kind of defense of the principles when he wrote that "the evident consequences of the traditional conception of the descriptum of a sentence as the complex of entities relevant for its truth" include two claims: first, "sentences so closely connected as to be guaranteed by logic alone to share a truth-value cannot differ in truth-relevant entities, and so must share their descriptum" and, second, "sentences which, like 'Cicero orated' and 'Tully orated', differ merely in the manner they choose to specify the same truth-relevant entity cannot diverge in the complex of such entities they describe" (Taylor 1985, p. 30). The first of these claims speaks in favor of SUB-LE, the second in favor of ι-SUB.

Taylor's defense of ι-SUB would be cogent if the principle concerned only singular terms like the ones he cites, *names* such as 'Cicero' and 'Tully', whose function is solely to refer and which can, therefore, be used uncontroversially in identity sentences. But ι-SUB also applies to definite descriptions and, as we saw in section 1.1, we cannot assume a single substitution principle for all singular terms, but must distinguish between a principle for names and a principle for definite descriptions, which neither Davidson nor Taylor do. I will postpone discussion of his crucial point, however, because it applies to the Gödel version of the slingshot in the same way it does to the Davidson version.

The best known criticisms of Davidson's slingshot have rejected SUB-LE rather than ι-SUB, the most prominent example being Barwise and Perry (1983). They have been followed by John Searle, who wrote in *The Construction of Social Reality* that "my method of investigation is to examine the structure of the facts that make our statements true and to which they correspond when they are true" (Searle 1995, p. 2), which gives him a weighty reason for defending a fact-based correspondence theory. Searle's objection to SUB-LE is that its use entails that true sentences correspond to facts which have constituents which are not matched by any constituents of those sentences. He correctly points out that the inference from lines 2 and 3 to line 4, for instance, would license the inference from:

A The true sentence that Stockholm is a large city corresponds to the fact that Stockholm is a large city

to:

B The true sentence that Stockholm is a large city corresponds to the fact that the unique individual such that he is President of the U.S. is identical to the unique individual such that he is President of the U.S. and such that Stockholm is a large city.

This is completely silly, he contends, because the true sentence that Stockholm is a large city can't possibly correspond to any facts about the President of the U.S.; the President and his identity are quite irrelevant as far as the fact that Stockholm is a large city are concerned. To think otherwise is to fail to "respect the intuitive notions of 'fact', 'truth', and 'correspondence'" according to which "the truth maker for the statement that snow is white is the fact that snow is white" (Searle 1995, p. 224).[15]

The trouble with this is that Searle cannot consistently hold that the only way to refer to the truth maker for 'snow is white' is to use the description 'the fact that snow is white' because that would be to construe the correspondence connective as fully intensional and hence rule out *any* alternative way of referring to a fact. That would deprive the notion of fact of any explanatory power and would render otiose Searle's project of investigating "the structure

---

[15] This is Searle's exact argument but with a different example.

of the facts which make our statements true" (Searle 1995, p. 2). Searle, like anyone who thinks of a fact as an entity in the world, *has* to admit alternative ways of referring to facts, and hence he has to make use of some principles of substitution. Having rejected SUB-LE, it is unclear what principles he does accept, though he appears to give tacit assent to ι-SUB, which, as we shall see, is extremely hazardous to the correspondence theory.

In my view, Taylor's claim that "sentences so closely connected as to be guaranteed by logic alone to share a truth-value cannot differ in truth-relevant entities, and so must share their descriptum" (Taylor 1985, p. 30) is a cogent defense of SUB-LE. The fact that logicians invent fancy alternative ways of constructing sentences which are logically equivalent to sentence 'p' doesn't entail that the fancy new sentences are 'about' something distinct from 'p' (have a different 'descriptum'). Sentence B above is not 'about' the unique individual who is President of the U.S. because, to put it roughly, what permits the use of that predicate to construct a sentence [B] which is logically equivalent to sentence A is that the predicate is being used in B to say that presidents of the U.S. are self-identical, and that is no more 'about' presidents of the U.S. than about anything else.

There is in any case no intuitively clear notion of what a *sentence* is 'about', the only precise notion we have being the model-theoretic one, and from that point of view, SUB-LE is not objectionable. If two sentences 'p' and 'q' are such that there is no model in which they differ in truth value, so that in every *possible* situation in which 'p' is true so is 'q' is, it is difficult to understand what it would mean to say that what makes 'p' true (if anything) is different from what makes 'q' true. I think, therefore, that rejecting SUB-LE is not the way to avoid the slingshot. This deserves more discussion, however, and I will return to it below.

1.3 Gödel and the Slingshot

The Gödel version of the slingshot is based on Gödel's contribution to the *Library of Living Philosophers* volume on Russell (Gödel 1944). Gödel did not state the argument but gave some pointed suggestions about what assumptions were needed and how the argument would go. There have been infrequent discussions of it since, and recently Stephen Neale gave it a rigorous formulation, which I shall use (Neale 1995). But first let me quote the relevant passage from Gödel's paper:

> An interesting example of Russell's analysis of the fundamental logical concepts is his treatment of the definite article 'the'. The problem is: what do the so-called descriptive phrases (i.e., phrases such as, e.g., 'the author of Waverley' or 'the king of England') denote or signify and what is the meaning of sentences in which they occur? The apparently

1.3 Gödel and the Slingshot

obvious answer that, e.g., 'the author of Waverley' signifies Walter Scott, leads to unexpected difficulties. For, if we admit the further apparently obvious axiom, that the signification of a complex expression, containing expressions which have themselves a signification, depends only on the signification of these constituents (and not on the manner in which this signification is expressed), then it follows that the sentence 'Scott is the author of Waverley' signifies the same thing as 'Scott is Scott'; and this again leads almost inevitably to the conclusion that all true sentences have the same signification (as well as all the false ones). Frege actually drew this conclusion ... (Gödel 1944, p. 128)

In a footnote, Gödel gave his suggestion on what the proof should assume (in addition to the "apparently obvious axiom" mentioned in the quotation), namely "that '$\varphi(a)$' and the proposition 'a is the object which has the property φ and is identical to a' mean the same thing". He also noted that "one would have to use the fact that for any two objects a and b, there exists a true proposition of the form $\varphi(a, b)$ as, e.g., $a \neq b$ or $a = a \cdot b = b$", but this is a hint on how to construct the argument and not an assumption it must make. (The hint is embodied in lines 2 and 10 of the proof.)

The assumption that '$\varphi(a)$' means the same as 'a is the object which has the property φ and is identical to a' amounts to the introduction and elimination of the iota sign, for in symbols (with a letter switch) it says that 'Fa' and 'a = (ιx)(x = a . Fx)' "mean the same thing". Gödel didn't say what he meant by "mean the same thing" but Neale interprets it as "signify the same thing" and calls it the "Gödelian equivalence", calling the substitution principle it involves "iota-conversion" (ιCONV) because it involves converting sentences containing names (in my terminology) into sentences containing definite descriptions and vice versa. Put formally, ι-CONV consists of two substitution principles, one for introducing the iota and one for eliminating it:

ι-CONV: $\dfrac{\Sigma[x/a]}{a = (\iota x)(x = a. \, \Sigma[x])}$ $\dfrac{a = (\iota x)(x = a. \, \Sigma[x])}{\Sigma[x/a]}$

This principle plays essentially the same role in the Gödel version that SUB-LE plays in the Davidson version, although ι-CONV is weaker than SUB-LE because the latter entails the former but not vice versa, but also because (to put it informally) whereas SUB-LE introduces new predicates (since the logical equivalence holds between formulae of the form 'p' and '(ιx)(Fx) = (ιx)(Fx . p)'), the Gödelian equivalence holds between formulae of the form 'Fa' and a = '(ιx)(x = a . Fx)' and hence introduces no new predicates (or names) into sentences. It follows that philosophers like Searle, who object to the Davidson version because it assumes SUB-LE, cannot use that objection against the Gödel version, and Neale takes this to be its great strength.

The compositionality assumption mentioned in the quotation from Gödel is a principle of substitution for singular terms. It is clear, from Gödel's examples and from the use to which the argument is put, that singular terms here include definite descriptions and that the principle is ι-SUB – the same principle used in the Davidson slingshot.

Here is the Gödel slingshot set out formally (Table 1.2).

Table 1.2

(1)	Fa	premise
(2)	a ≠ b	premise
(3)	Gb	premise
(4)	a = (ιx)(x = a . Fx)	1, ι-CONV
(5)	a = (ιx)(x = a . x ≠ b)	2, ι-CONV
(6)	b = (ιx)(x = b . a ≠ x)	2, ι-CONV
(7)	b = (ιx)(x = b . Gx)	3, ι-CONV
(8)	(ιx)(x = a . Fx) = (ιx)(x = a . x ≠ b)	4, 5, ι-SUB
(9)	(ιx)(x = b . Gx) = (ιx)(x = b . a ≠ x)	6, 7, ι-SUB
(10)	C(Fa)	premise
(11)	C(a = (ιx)(x = a . Fx)	10, ι-CONV
(12)	C(a = (ιx)(x = a . x ≠ b))	11, 8, ι-SUB
(13)	C(a ≠ b)	12, ι-CONV
(14)	C(b = (ιx)(x = b . a ≠ x))	13, ι-CONV
(15)	C(b = (ιx)(x = b . Gx))	14, 9, ι-SUB
(16)	C(Gb)	15, ι-CONV

This version of the slingshot proceeds in two stages. The first (lines 1 to 9) involves substitutions outside the context of C, the second (lines 10–16) substitutions inside it. The aim of the proof is to show that if S corresponds to the fact that Fa (line 10), it also corresponds to the fact that Gb (line 16), for any 'G' and 'b' for which 'Gb' is true. For example, given that 'the author of Waverley lived in Scotland' corresponds to the fact that the author of Waverley lived in Scotland, it follows that it corresponds to any fact – say, the fact that Stockholm is a large city or that Hesperus is illuminated by the sun. That would mean that the correspondence connective is fully extensional (or truth-functional), so that any true sentence corresponds to every fact.

In the first stage, Gödel's hint about the role of 'a ≠ b' is used in line 2 and then substitutions are made, using ι-CONV and ι-SUB. The inference from line 1 ('Fa') to line 4 ('a = (ιx)(x = a . Fx)') essentially involves, first, substituting for 'a' the definite description '(ιx)(x = a)', so that 'Fa' becomes F(ιx)(x = a) ('the unique x which is identical to a is F') and then rewriting the latter as 'a = (ιx)(x = a . Fx)' ('a is identical to the unique individual x such that x is identical to a and is F). Since no distinction is made between the status of 'a' (a name) and '(ιx)(x = a)' (a definite description), we can use a definite description to interpret line 1 as:

A. The author of Waverley lived in Scotland

and hence interpret line 4 as:

B. The author of Waverley is identical to the unique individual who is (identical to) the author of Waverly and who lived in Scotland.

Reflection on A and B shows that in any possible situation in which A is true, B is also true, and vice versa.

Analogous considerations apply to the inference from line 2 to line 5. The right hand side of line 5 is a definite description which can be read as 'the unique individual x which is such that it is identical to a but not to b'; and that must be 'a', given (line 2) that it is 'a' which is not identical to 'b'. (The inference from line 2 to line 6 is the same except that 'b' has been switched for 'a'.) Since these inferences assume that names and definite descriptions have the same status, we may interpret line 2 as:

C. The moon is not identical to the sun

and hence interpret line 5 as:

D. The moon is identical to the unique individual which is (identical) to the moon and is not identical to the sun.

And, again, reflection shows that in any possible situation in which C is true, so is D, and vice versa.

Lines 8 and 9 use ι-SUB in an obvious way, given that this stage of the proof requires no distinction between the substitution of definite descriptions and the substitution of names. Line 8 follows from lines 4 and 5 (and line 9 from lines 6 and 7) in virtue of the principle that if a = b and a = c, then b = c.

The second stage of the proof uses the results of the first stage, and while these results are entirely acceptable, it does not follow that the substitutions made in them in the second stage are acceptable unless it is assumed that the same principles of substitution hold outside and inside the correspondence connective, which would beg the question. But before considering this point, let me finish my informal account of the proof.

At line 9 the proof assumes 'C(Fa)' in order to show that 'C(Gb)' can be inferred from it, which would establish that any true sentence corresponds to every fact. The proof infers line 11 from line 10 by the same use of ι-CONV as in the inference of line 4 from line 1. It infers line 12 from lines 8 and 11 by a straightforward use of ι-SUB, with '(ιx)(x = a . x ≠ b)' playing the role of 'a' in 'if a = b and a = c, then b = c'.

The proof infers line 13 from line 12 by the use of ι-CONV, now as an elimination rule rather than as an introduction rule. It infers line 14 from line 13 by a use of ι-CONV like its use in the inference from line 2 to line 5. It infers line 15 from lines 9 and 14 by ι-SUB, with '(ιx)(x = b . x ≠ a)' as the formula which plays the role of 'a' in 'if a = b and a = c, then b = c'. Finally line 16 is inferred from line 15 by the use of ι-CONV as an elimination rule, exactly as in the inference from line 12 to line 13.

Since the Gödel version of the slingshot is valid in that, given the two substitution principles it assumes, its premises entail its conclusion, the only way to evade it is to challenge at least one of those substitution principles. Although the principles are acceptable in extensional contexts, to assume they are, therefore, acceptable inside the scope of C would beg the question. I shall show that there are, indeed, good reasons for denying that ι-SUB is acceptable inside C and that attempts to restrict it in order to make it acceptable are ruled out by ι-CONV. Since the Gödel slingshot requires both principles, its conclusion can be evaded. It does not follow that the correspondence theory of truth is home free, for, as I will argue in the final section, evading the slingshot exacts a heavy price.

If ι-SUB were a principle of substitution only for *co-referring* singular terms ('names' in my terminology), there would be, as we have seen, no objection to its use even in non-extensional contexts, but it also applies to definite descriptions whose function in the proof reflects their *attributive* use in assertions. Definite descriptions, that is, function in the proof not simply to *refer* to a particular individual (not to pick out in some way or other a particular individual we want to describe), but to be *true of* whichever unique individual happens to fulfill the description (so that the description itself is essential, not which particular individual it happens to be true of). They function, that is to say, like predicates, except (since they are *definite* descriptions) for the important condition that they be true of exactly one individual (though not of some particular individual however described). This means that ι-SUB is a principle which permits not only the substitution of co-referring singular terms but also the substitution of co-extensive predicates.

That this is the case can be seen if we look carefully at the proof. Consider, for example, line 12, which is inferred from lines 8 and 11 by using ι-SUB to replace '(ιx)(x = a . Fx)' in line 11 with '(ιx)(x = a . x ≠ b)' to get line 12, the justification being the identity expressed in line 8 between those two definite descriptions. The difference between '$(\iota x)(x = a . Fx)$' and what has been substituted for it, '$(\iota x)(x = a . x \neq b)$', is that what follows 'ιx' in the former is '$x = a . Fx$', whereas what follows it in the latter is '$x = a . x \neq b$'. But those are *predicates* (open sentences), which are, indeed, co-extensive, but their substitution means that ι-SUB permits the substitution of co-extensive predicates (and not only the substitution of co-referring terms).

We can reinforce this point by considering line 8, which has the identity sign between the definite descriptions, '$(\iota x)(x = a . Fx)$' and '$(\iota x)(x = a . x \neq b)$'. The question is, what sort of *identity* is expressed here? It is misleading to say that each of these definite descriptions *refers* to the same particular individual; a better answer is that the *extensions* of each of the descriptions is the same – that they are true of exactly the same individuals – though in this case (because they are *definite* descriptions) that means exactly one individual. What these definite descriptions are both true of, however, is not some *particular* individual picked out for description; they are both true of whichever individual happens to belong to the extension of both descriptions (whichever individual both descriptions happen to be true of). ιSUB is better thought of, therefore, not as a principle which permits the substitution of co-*referring* terms but as a principle which permit the substitution of co*extensive* terms, which include co-extensive *predicates*. The identity expressed in line 8, for example,

8. $(\iota x)(x = a . Fx) = (\iota x)(x = a . x \neq b)$

holds only because '$x = a . Fx$' and '$x = a . x \neq b$' are coextensive predicates, and they are coextensive just because both of them are true only of a. '$x = a . Fx$' is true of a and only of a, provided a is F (which it is by line 1 of the proof), while '$x = a . x \neq b$' is true of a and only of a, provided a is not identical to b (which it is by line 2 of the proof). Line 8, therefore, is not an identity sentence in the usual sense: it does not express the identical reference of two names, but rather the sameness of extension of two descriptions.

Another way of showing that ι-SUB permits the substitution of co-extensive predicates is to consider it in the light of Russell's theory of descriptions. Russell held that a definite description must be distinguished from a name because its object may not exist, which he illustrated with the famous example, 'The King of France is bald' (the French monarchy having been abolished when Russell wrote). He further held that this sentence must have a truth value, in which case it must be *false* because there is no King of France. This means that it is misleading to use the iota notation in the usual way (with 'Fx' for 'x is King of France' and 'Bx' for 'x is bald'), that is, $B(\iota x)Fx$, to be read as 'the unique individual who is King of France is bald', because that doesn't make it clear that the sentence is false because there is no King of France. Russell, therefore, treated the sentence as an existential quantification, whose perspicuous paraphrase is "There is a unique individual who is King of France and who is bald", expressed in logical notation, as follows.

(∃x)((Fx . (∀y)(Fy → y = x) . Bx)

Since there is no King of France, the sentence is false (because it is false that (∃x)(Fx)), and as an existential quantification, it includes no singular terms.

Russell argued that definite descriptions should always be treated in this way, so let us apply his theory to the slingshot, this time to the Davidson version; consider the inference from lines 4 and 5 to line 6:

4. C[(ɩx)(Fx) = (ɩx)(Fx . p)]

5. (ɩx)(Fx . p) = (ɩx)(Fx . q)

6. C[(ɩx)(Fx) = (ɩx)(Fx . q)]

Line 6 is inferred from line 4 by substitution in accordance with the identity expressed in line 5: line 6 differs from line 4 in that '(ɩx)(Fx . q)' has replaced '(ɩx)(Fx . p)', which means that the *predicate* 'Fx and q' has replaced the *predicate* 'Fx and p' (the two predicates being coextensive because, in virtue of line 1 in the proof ('p ↔ q'), 'p' and 'q' are coextensive, that is, have the same truth value).

These comments are based, however, on formulations which use the iota notation, which Russell found misleading, so let us see what happens if we rewrite a couple of them using his theory of description:

4* C[(∃x)((Fx . p) . (∀y)((Fy . p) → y = x). (ɩx)(Fx = x))]

6* C[(∃x)((Fx . q) . (∀y)((Fy . q) → y = x) . (ɩx)(Fx = x))]

This rewriting only reinforces the point about the substitution of co-extensive *predicates* because 6* differs from 4* in that 'p' has replaced 'q' twice, with both 'p' and 'q' functioning as predicates.[16] But it also reinforces the point I

---

16 This rewriting presumes that the crucial definite descriptions – '(ɩx)(Fx . p)' and '(ɩx)(Fx . q)' – have what has come to be called "narrow scope", for only if they are interpreted in that way are lines 4 and 6 entailed by their premises. If those definite descriptions are interpreted as having "wide scope", then lines 4 and 6 would be written thus:
4** (∃x)((Fx . p) . (∀y)((Fy . p)   y = x) . C(ɩx)(Fx = x))
6** (∃x)((Fx . q) . (∀y)((Fy . q)   y = x) . C(ɩx)(Fx = x)).

made above that identity sentences like these, which involve definite descriptions, are not *identity* sentences in the usual sense; for when lines 4 and 6 are re-written in accordance with Russell's theory of descriptions as 4* and 6*, neither of them are identity sentences (though they contain identities). This means that on Russell's theory of descriptions, there is a sense in which, strictly speaking, we cannot even *formulate* ι-SUB because the theory rules out the possibility of flanking the identity sign with definite descriptions.

What I just said is misleading, however, in that Russell did permit the formulation of sentences like 4, '(ιx)(Fx) = (ιx)(Fx . p)', but he did so *only* if they were understood as *abbreviations* for sentences like 4*. That entails that substitutions which appeal directly to identity sentences like '(ιx)(Fx) = (ιx)(Gx)' are acceptable *only* in extensional contexts, which means ι-SUB is an acceptable principle of inference only in extensional contexts. (It is, indeed, a principle which can be derived from the standard rules of inference in predicate logic with identity.)[17]

Russell's theory of descriptions makes evident what I take to be independently defensible, namely that ι-SUB permits the substitution of co-extensive predicates and hence that its unrestricted use is acceptable only in extensional contexts.[18] Either version of the slingshot, therefore, can be evaded by refusing

---

The inference from line 4** to line 6** involves no predicate substitution in the context of C, which means that it does not beg the question (by permitting predication substitution in the context of C), but it also means that the argument will not show that C is extensional since all the inferences will be outside the scope of C. This does not constitute a way of *evading* the slingshot, however, because it cannot be claimed that lines 4 and 6 are rightly interpreted as 4** and 6**, the reason being that it is obvious that 4** and 6** do not follow from the premises cited in the proof.

It might be argued that the way to deal with the slingshot is simply to argue that when it comes to C, definite descriptions should, in general, be taken to have wide scope. I am tempted by the idea that the referential use of definite descriptions could be reflected formally by giving them wide scope, and their attributive use by giving them narrow scope. But I have not been able to make sense out of the correspondence connective when definite descriptions are interpreted as having wide scope. (For discussion of the bearing of scope issues on slingshot-like arguments cf. Føllesdal 1969.)

17 Neale made this point when he wrote that Whitehead and Russell demonstrated that, "although descriptions are not genuine singular terms (in their system), if a predicate F applies to exactly one object (i. e. if it has exactly one object in its extension), in truth-functional (i. e. extensional) contexts the description '(ιx)Fx' can be treated *as if* it were a singular term for derivational purposes ... [This] is a derived rule of inference that can be used in truth-functional contexts ..." (Neale 1995, p. 786)

18 Neale recognized this when he wrote that the Gödel slingshot is able to show that the supposedly non-extensional correspondence connective is extensional by employing the fact that "descriptions (as standardly understood) contain *formulae* as proper parts; by permitting the interchange of such devices when their contained formulae are satisfied by the same object, one is

to accept ι-SUB on the ground that permitting its use in the context of the correspondence connective is to assume that the context is fully extensional, thus assuming what was supposed to be proved.

The reason critics and defenders alike tend to miss this point is because 'singular term' is so widely used to apply to both names and definite descriptions, and hence there is a strong inclination to think that since co-referring names can surely be substituted *salva veritate* in the context of C, so can definite descriptions, even when their formal treatment reflects their attributive (and not their referential) use. This is reinforced by speaking of the *extension* not only of definite descriptions but of singular terms generally, or by speaking of what singular terms in general *stand for* or *represent*, terminology which obscures the distinction between using a term referentially and using it attributively, which is a distinction the formal treatment of singular terms must reflect to be relevant to philosophical issues like truth.

The inclination to treat names and definite descriptions alike is made a matter of principle in the Gödel version of the slingshot because of its use of ι-CONV, which sanctions the move back and forth between names and definite descriptions, though its real effect is to treat all singular terms as (attributively used) definite descriptions. It might be possible to formulate a restricted substitution principle for singular terms in the context of C if ι-CONV were rejected, the restriction being that ι-SUB is acceptable for names and for definite descriptions, provided their treatment reflects their referential rather than their attributive role. What ι-CONV does, however, is insure that the treatment of all singular terms reflects their attributive role, and hence if ι-CONV is accepted, ι-SUB has to be rejected to evade the slingshot.

Although Davidson's version does not use ι-CONV, it is also unable to use a restricted version of ι-SUB which would rule out the substitution of co-extensive predicates, the reason being that it must use SUB-LE. While critics like Searle are incorrect in rejecting the use of SUB-LE outside extensional contexts (its use does not entail that a context is extensional), it is like ι-CONV in insuring that the treatment of all singular terms will reflect their attributive rather than

---

essentially permitting the interchange of formulae; and once some weak additional inference principle is assumed (ι-CONV), the formulae in question can be drawn out of their iota-governed contexts to make the purportedly non-truth-functional Sconnectives probably truth-functional." (Neale and Dever 1997, p. 151) His "formulae" refers to open sentences, and his point is that ι-SUB permits the substitution of open sentences provided they "are satisfied by the same object", that is, have the same extension, which is to set up a fully extensional (truth-functional) context. Neale did not make this central to his critique, however, which is both puzzling and unfortunate from the point of view of clarity about the slingshot.

their referential role. We can see this if we examine the use made of SUB-LE in the Davidson slingshot, for example in the inference from line 2, 'Cp', to line 4, 'C[(ɩx)(Fx) = (ɩx)(Fx . p)]'. That makes sense only if the definite descriptions which flank the identity sign in line 4 are not taken to *refer* to the same particular individual, but to set conditions such that whatever individuals meet the one will meet the other (in this case such that exactly one individual will meet them). What is claimed, therefore, is not identity of reference of names but sameness of extension of definite descriptions, which is all that can be claimed in proofs which use SUBLE as this one does. This is why Davidson speaks of the *extension* of singular terms, which reflects their attributive use as being true of objects, rather than their referential use as referring to them.

Neale argues that the Gödel version of the slingshot is to be preferred to the Davidson version because it uses the weaker ɩ-CONV rather than the stronger SUBLE. The latter is, of course, stronger that the former because it entails but is not entailed by it, but as far as evading the slingshot is concerned, there is no difference. Although SUB-LE in itself is not objectionable, it has the same role in the slingshot as ɩ-CONV, namely to insure that all singular terms are treated as having extensions rather than referents. But to treat singular terms as having extensions is to permit the substitution of coextensive predicates, which shows that ɩ-SUB is unacceptable in context C, which means that both versions of the slingshot can be evaded by rejecting ɩ-SUB on the grounds that there is no reason to accept it except in contexts already known to be extensional.

1.4 Consequences for Correspondence

A heavy price has to be paid for evading the slingshot by rejecting ɩ-SUB, namely that definite descriptions (though not names) may not be substituted in the context of the correspondence connective. Thus given that 'Stockholm is a large city' corresponds to the fact that Stockholm is a large city, it does not follow that it corresponds to the fact that the capital of Sweden is a large city or to the fact that the birthplace of Strindberg is a large city. To use another example: although 'Hesperus is illuminated by the sun' corresponds to the fact that Phosphorus is illuminated by the sun (since 'Hesperus' and 'Phosphorus' are names of the same planet), it does not follow that it corresponds to the fact that the evening star is illuminated by the sun (since 'the evening star' is a definite description) even though 'Hesperus', 'Phosphorus' and 'the evening star' all signify the planet Venus.

Defenders of the correspondence theory may well find this constraint on substitution overly restrictive and arbitrary and hence try to evade the slingshot by rejecting SUB-LE and ι-CONV instead of ι-SUB. I argued earlier that rejecting SUB-LE is not the way to evade the slingshot, and there is even stronger reason not to reject it simply to save ι-SUB. The reason is that to reject SUB-LE is to deny that logically equivalent sentences can be substituted *salva veritate* in the context of C, while to accept ι-SUB is to assert that (merely) coextensive predicates can be substituted *salva veritate* in that context, which is to reject a weaker substitution principle in order to save a stronger one. It is true that the Davidson slingshot cannot exploit that fact to prove that ι-SUB sets up an extensional context since the proof also needs SUB-LE, but the Gödel version can, since it needs only ι-CONV, and hence this strategy for evading the slingshot won't work unless ι-CONV is also rejected. But ι-CONV is even weaker than SUB-LE, and while rejecting it evades the Gödel version, it is hard to believe that another formal proof could not be constructed, which uses a principle of inference which functions like ι-CONV and exploits the substitution of coextensive predicates permitted by ι-SUB in order to show that C must be extensional if ι-SUB is used.

The function of ι-CONV (and *a* function of SUB-LE) is to convert sentences with names into logically equivalent sentences with definite descriptions, and vice versa, and its effect is to treat all singular terms as having extensions rather than references, which is the formal reflection of their being used attributively rather than referentially in assertions. Rejecting ι-CONV and SUB-LE would make it *possible* to treat singular terms so as to reflect their referential use, which suggests permitting their substitution in the scope of C if and only if they are being used *referentially*, thus avoiding the substitution of co-extensive predicates, which makes the slingshot a deadly weapon.

The question is whether *principles* could be devised to do this – to permit the substitution of definite descriptions if and only if that does not also permit the substitution of co-extensive predicates. Such principles are implicit in a Russellian theory of facts, which construes facts as composite entities consisting of a particular, referred to by a name, and a universal or property, referred to by a predicate (or consisting of several particulars and properties). The key move here is to construe a predicate not as having an extension consisting of the objects of which it is true, but as referring to a property, so that predicates can be substituted if and only if they refer to the same property. Thus 'creature with a heart' and 'creature with a kidney' have the same extension but they do not refer to the same property (since what it is to have a heart is different from what it is to have a kidney, as transplant surgeons well know), and hence they are not inter-substitutable in the context of C.

What this key move does is to assimilate predicates to singular terms and hence to assimilate the substitution rules for predicates to those for singular terms. Just as one can substitute 'a' for 'b' only if 'a' and 'b' are co-referring (so that a = b), so one can substitute the predicate 'is an F' for the predicate 'is a G' if and only if the predicates are *co-referring*. Against this background, accepting ι-SUB will not load the slingshot because ι-SUB will be applicable only when the substitution of definite descriptions involves the substitution of predicates which refer to the same property; it will not be applicable when it involves the substitution of (merely) co-extensive predicates.

This Russellian way of evading the slingshot, however, exacts at least as heavy a price as simply rejecting ι-SUB. For one thing, it will require a version of the correspondence theory for which correspondence to the facts is a matter of "correspondence-as-congruity" rather than "correspondence-as-correlation" (to use the terms from Pitcher 1964, p. 10) because it requires structural isomorphism between names and particulars and between predicates and properties. This imposes on defenders of the correspondence theory the burden of defending a structural isomorphism between language and reality, which undermines the most common defense of the theory, namely that it is nothing more than common sense whose denial involves extravagant metaphysics.

Davidson always assumes that fact-based versions of the correspondence theory adopt the Russellian point of view, which he views not as a strategy to avoid the slingshot but as the primary reason for rejecting correspondence theories. Thus he wrote in "True to the Facts" that "The failure of correspondence theories based on the notion of fact traces back to a common source: the desire to include in the entity to which a true sentence corresponds not only the objects the sentence is 'about' (another idea full of trouble) but also whatever it is that the sentence says about them" (Davidson 2001b, p. 49), where the latter expresses the notion of a fact as including objects plus properties. He reiterated this 30 years later in his response to Neale in the *Library of Living Philosophers* volume, agreeing that the Gödel slingshot can be evaded "as Russell's semantics did it, by making properties part of facts and so the entities that correspond to predicates" (Hahn 1999, p. 667) but going on to say that "This is a course against which I have argued on the grounds that it cannot be incorporated into a satisfactory theory or definition of truth, and entities that are made up of abstract entities can hardly be thought of as empirical truth-makers." (Hahn 1999, p. 667)

The first objection stated here, which seems to me uncontestable, is that the Russellian idea of treating predicates as referring to properties is not consistent with Tarski's treatment of predicates as satisfied by sequences of objects, which entails that there can be no appeal to Tarski's truth theory in defense of a correspondence theory which uses Russellian facts.[19] The second objection, that Russellian facts are peculiar entities in that they consist not only of particulars referred to by singular terms but also of abstract objects referred to by predicates, can be dealt with only by defenders of the correspondence theory who are prepared to develop it as an elaborate metaphysical theory.

Davidson made another criticism of the Russellian point of view in "True to the Facts" when he mentioned "the well-explored consequence that it becomes difficult to describe the fact that verifies a sentence except by using the sentence itself" ("verifies" here is used in the sense of "make true"). (Davidson 2001b, p. 49) This suggests that the aim of permitting alternative ways of referring to facts without loading the slingshot cannot after all be realized by introducing Russellian facts because taking predicates to *refer* to properties puts an equally severe restriction on the ways we can refer to properties.

The reason is that, although the notion of different predicates having the same extension is straightforward, the notion of their referring to the same property is not, and this raises the question of the conditions under which different predicates refer to the same property. That turns out to be essentially the same question as when different instances of 'the fact that a is F' refer to the same fact. In both cases it can be assumed that *synonymous* expressions refer to the same property or the same fact respectively; but beyond that, the question of whether 'the predicate F' refers to the same property as 'the predicate G' turns on whether those expressions are being used referentially or attributively. But that is the very distinction which motivated the Russellian notion that predicates refer to properties, the idea being that taking facts to include properties insures that singular terms are never substituted in the context of C unless they are functioning so as to reflect a referential use. But now it turns out that the introduction of properties as the referents of predicates cannot insure that singular terms are substituted in the context of C only when used referentially unless the pred-

---

19 This applies, for example, to Ilkka Niiniluto's claim that Tarski's truth theory is "an explicate of the classical (fact-based) correspondence theory of truth" (Niiniluto 1999, p. 91). He argues that Tarski's account needs to be completed (improved?) by adding Carnap's claim (in *Introduction to Semantics*) that sentences designate propositions (rather than truth values), but he says nothing about Church's use of the slingshot to undermine this Carnapian idea. Nor does he consider how Tarski's notion that predicates are true of sequences can be consistent with Carnap's notion that they designate properties, or how Tarski's view that true sentences are satisfied by all sequences can be reconciled with the correspondence claim that true sentences correspond to particular facts. Niiniluoto's view strikes me as a hopeless case of wanting to have your cake and eat it too – of using a Carnapian ontology of properties, propositions and facts but failing to defend it against slingshot-type attacks on the ground that a *Tarskian* truth theory is immune to such attacks.

icates themselves are used referentially and not attributively. That raises the question of what insures that predicates are being used referentially, and to insure that, further entities to be referred to will have to be introduced, the result being an infinite regress, which shows that nothing has been accomplished by the introduction of properties as the referents of predicates.

I conclude, therefore, that the strategy of evading the slingshot by keeping ι-SUB but developing principles which rule out its use to substitute (merely) co-extensive predicates in the scope of C does not yield a better version of the correspondence theory than simply giving up ι-SUB. In either case, the only substitution which can be made for 'q' in 'p corresponds to the fact that q' are substitutions for genuine referring terms which are constituents of 'q'. In practice this will include at most names because there is no way of establishing that a definite description is used referentially rather than attributively in the context of C. Even if it is coherent to take a predicate as referring to a property, it is hopeless to try to distinguish between when a predicate is being used to refer to a particular property and when it is being used attributively to set conditions some particular property might meet. The same is true of the use of definite descriptions in the context of the correspondence connective. There is no way to distinguish between the referential and the attributive use of 'the capital of Sweden' in:

> The true sentence 'Stockholm is a large city' corresponds to the fact that the capital of Sweden is a large city'.

But if 'the capital of Sweden' is not being used referentially, then this claim sets up the slingshot. Hence my conclusion that the slingshot can be evaded but at the price of forbidding any substitutions in the scope of the correspondence connective other than names for names.

This has two consequences which I will state but not develop. One is that the constraints the correspondence theory must meet to evade the slingshot are not met by most fact-based versions of the theory. This is true for any version of 'scientific realism' which takes it to be an empirical matter what the structure of the truthmaking facts are, one example being the influential metaphysical realism once defended by Putnam.[20] It is also true for any version of the theory which tries to establish substantive conclusions about such matters as the nature of mental states, the structure of social reality, or the constituents of action, by inquiring into the structure of the facts which make claims about them true. The reason is that, given the constraints, all that can be said about the structure

---

20 For other examples of what the constraints exclude see Neale and Dever 1997, pp. 156 f.

of the fact which makes p true, beyond that it is that fact that p, would involve the substitution of co-referring names, and that will yield no conclusions which are either substantive or interesting.

The other consequence is that any versions of the correspondence theory which survive these constraints will vary in no significant way from deflationist conceptions of truth, which maintain that all there is to be said about the distinction between what it is to be true and what it is to be false is summed up in the 'Equivalence Principle' – 'p' is true if and only if p – together with various accounts about how to apply the principle to contexts where what is said to be true cannot be expressed but only referred to in complex ways.[21] This does not mean we must stop speaking in terms of true sentences corresponding to the world. The truth of a sentence surely depends on what is said in asserting it (which varies with meaning and context) and on what the world is like, which is to say that its truth depends on correspondence to what the world is like. So 'Stockholm is a large city' corresponds to what the world is like, but if we want to say more precisely to what it corresponds, we can say only that it corresponds to the fact that Stockholm is a large city. Those who try to say anything more substantive than that will find themselves in the company of Goliath and other victims of the fabled slingshot.

---

21 In "Do We Need Correspondence Truth?" (Stoutland 1999a), I have defended such a deflationist conception against those who claim that we cannot get along without correspondence truth.

2 Wittgenstein on Certainty and Truth*

Let me begin by stating the central thought that motivates the discussion in this chapter. I believe that Wittgenstein has given in *On Certainty* a new and deep way of understanding the role of certainty in language, in inquiry, in knowledge, in our life generally – a way of understanding that is essentially correct. The most interesting – and difficult – part of this approach is the idea that we are absolutely certain of the *truth*, of certain propositions, for example, 'The earth existed long before my birth', 'I have never been on the moon', 'Cats do not grow on trees.' "What does this mean", Wittgenstein asked, "the truth of a proposition is *certain*" (Wittgenstein 1969, § 193), and my central thought was that to give an intelligible answer, we must not think of truth in terms of correspondence, coherence, verification, or any substantive concept. This notion of certainty requires what I will call a *minimalist* conception of truth, which is clearly the notion of truth he held in *Philosophical Investigations*. My central aim is to clarify this notion and show its role in Wittgenstein's conception of certainty.

Two questions should be distinguished. The first is whether, when we make explicit the propositions of which we are certain, they must be either true or false. Peter Winch has argued that certainty is not a matter of true-or-false, but is rather what makes possible the very distinction between the true and the false. The second is, given that certainty does involve true-or-false, must what I am certain of *be* true rather than false? If I cannot be *mistaken* about a proposition of which I am certain, does it follow that the proposition is *true*? Norman Malcolm has argued that it does not follow, that "even when you cannot *conceive how* you could be wrong, it is nevertheless not impossible that you are wrong" (Malcolm 1986, p. 232).

I want to reject both of these views, either as interpretations of Wittgenstein or as defensible in their own right, which is a risky business, for there have been no more acute interpreters of Wittgenstein than Winch and Malcolm. In this paper, however, I will discuss only the first question, arguing that Wittgenstein thinks of all propositions as true or false, a point of view which is acceptable provided we think of truth in a minimalist sense.

---

* This paper was first read at a meeting in Minneapolis, in October 1996, where Peter Winch offered several characteristically penetrating and gentle comments in the discussion. Winch also wrote me a long letter some weeks after the meeting, criticizing my paper in detail and suggesting how to improve it. I treasure that letter as a testament of someone who was both and admirable philosopher and human being, and this paper is dedicated to his memory. This version of the paper reflects the changes that were made as a result of Winch's comments.

My paper has two main parts. The first is a brief account of Wittgenstein's conception of certainty as the background for the second, which sets out a view about how and why certainty involves truth.

2.1 Wittgenstein on Certainty

What inspired Wittgenstein to write *On Certainty* was Moore's "A Defence of Common Sense", which he thought was Moore's best paper (as did Moore), and he was much taken by its examples and its underlying aim. He agreed with Moore in rejecting the foundationalist view that unless there are propositions which by their nature are self-evident, we must be skeptics about the possibility of knowledge. He agreed that there are propositions we are certain of, which are not self-evident either to sense or to reason, and which form a motley collection. But he did not think that Moore had a clear view of the topic, and he rejected almost all the claims Moore made in that paper. Here is a summary of what I take to be the main lines of his critique of Moore.

i. Certainty should be distinguished from knowledge. We must have grounds or evidence for what we know, but we do not have grounds or evidence for what we are certain of. What we know must be subject to testing, verification, to making sure, and hence it must be intelligible to doubt what we think we know. But we cannot doubt what we are certain of not because there *is* something we cannot do, but because whatever we do would not be doubting the relevant certainty. Hence there is no room for giving grounds or for making sure of what we are certain of: certainty is groundless (cf. Wittgenstein 1969, §§ 151, 243, 403). This is not a point of terminology. Wittgenstein's point is not that we must never say "I know ..." when we mean "I am certain ..." (cf. Wittgenstein 1969, §§ 8, 591), but that we must not let philosophical habits blind us to situations where our being mistaken is not intelligible, that is, situations for which the usual concept of knowledge leaves no room.

ii. Certainty is groundless but it is not unreasonable. In asserting that "the difficulty is to realize the groundlessness of our believing" (Wittgenstein 1969, § 166) Wittgenstein did not mean that the difficulty is to accept what is unreasonable. There are *reasons* for accepting what we are certain of, but we need not be able to articulate them and they do not constitute *evidence*.

iii. Wittgenstein's topic is objective not subjective certainty. With the word 'certain' we express complete conviction, the total absence of doubt, and thereby we seek to convince other people. That is *subjective* certainty: When is something objectively certain? When a mistake is not possible. But what kind of possibility is that? Mustn't mistake be *logically* excluded? (Wittgenstein 1969, § 194)

We are, Wittgenstein maintains, objectively certain of something when doubting it is unintelligible in such a way as to make it impossible to *understand* what it would be to be mistaken – which is what it is for a mistake to be logically excluded.¹

iv. *Certainty is rooted in action not in cognition.* Giving grounds, however, justifying the evidence, comes to an end; – but the end is not certain propositions' striking us as true, i.e., it is not a kind of *seeing* on our part; it is our *action*, which lies at the bottom of the language-game. (Wittgenstein 1969, § 204)

> The end is not an ungrounded presupposition; it is an ungrounded way of acting. (Wittgenstein 1969, § 110)

This extremely important point is one I can do little more than gesture at. Its crux is that the locus of certainty is not propositions, hence not *what* we judge, but our judg*ings*, which are actions, whose very possibility depends on our not doubting many things. "Doubting and non-doubting behavior. There is the first only if there is the second." (Wittgenstein 1969, § 354) Consider calculating (judging mathematically, as we might say); calculating *is* using certain elementary sums or products without doubt. We *learn* to calculate by being *conditioned* to do elementary sums or products without doubt, indeed, without thought; and only thus is genuine calculating possible. There is no calculating except against the background of these pre-calculative actions which are never called into question. That is what it is to calculate (cf. Wittgenstein 1969, §§ 44 – 47). Note § 232, especially the last sentence. It begins with the interlocutor saying

> We could doubt every single one of these facts, but we could not doubt them *all*,

to which Wittgenstein replies:

> Wouldn't it be more correct to say: 'we do not doubt them *all*.' Our not doubting them all is simply our manner of judging, and therefore of acting. (Wittgenstein 1969, § 232)²

This is surely true of linguistic action: the meanings of signs are rooted in primitive responses to them, which are based not on interpretation but on having been trained to respond unhesitatingly. These primitive responses express the

---

1 Cf. an earlier passage from Wittgenstein: "'I know ...' may mean 'I do not doubt ...' but does not mean that the words 'I doubt ...' are senseless, that doubt is logically excluded." (Wittgenstein 1958a, p. 221)
2 On this point, see Winch's suggestion that the last sentence would be better translated as "Our not doubting them all is simply the way we judge, that is act." (Winch 1998, p. 201)

certainty involved in the use of language and which continues to show itself whenever we speak. For no matter how hesitantly we speak or how carefully we choose our words, the background is always words of whose meaning we are certain. To be a speaker is to have been taught to use words with certainty; we cannot use any words mistakenly if we do not use most words in a way that mistake is ruled out. "Language did not emerge from some kind of ratiocination ... Children do not learn that books exist, that armchairs exist, etc., etc. – they learn to fetch books, sit in armchairs, etc." (Wittgenstein 1969, § 475)

v. Propositions come into the picture only when we make our judgings explicit. Judging is one thing; making judgments explicit in propositions is another. The latter may be helpful in evaluating judgments, but it is not necessary either for there to be judgments or for judgments to be rational. Nevertheless, judgments can, in general, be made explicit (by the agent or about the agent) by articulating the proposition involved in the judgment.

vi. The judgments of which we are certain sometimes can and sometimes cannot be made explicit in propositions. When it comes to judgments of which we are *certain*, making explicit the propositions involved in them is a difficult and delicate matter. When they can be made explicit, we have propositions of which we are certain, and hence, I maintain, ones of whose *truth* we are certain. But there are tangled issues here. One is that when we make explicit a proposition of which we are certain, we seem to *assert* the proposition but, as Dummett puts it, "Part of what a speaker communicates to a hearer by means of an assertoric utterance is that he believes himself to have grounds for what he asserts" (Dummett 1991, p. 167)[3] and we do not have grounds for what we are certain of. Another, more crucial issue is that propositions of which we are certain may be ones it *makes no sense* to doubt, and when that is so, it also makes no sense not to doubt them, the reason being that if 'p' makes no sense, then 'not-p' makes no sense either.

vii. What is objectively certain – stands fast for us – is determined by the language game. A language game constitutes some judgments as grounded and some as ungrounded, gives some judgments the status of certainty, others a different status. Many certainties are shared by every speaker: cats don't grow on trees; tables do not vanish or alter their shape or color when no one is observing them; the earth existed long before we were born. But some are not thus shared, for example, everyone is certain of his or her own name. But in either case it is

---

3 Cf. Brandom: "In *asserting* a claim one commits oneself to vindicate the original claim, showing that one is entitled to make it; ... one accepts responsibility to justify it." (Brandom 1994, p. 173)

not a personal matter whether a judgment or proposition stands fast for me; its certainty is an integral part of the language games in which we participate. (Cf. Wittgenstein 1969, §§ 298, 344, 389, 415, 440.)

viii. There are no rules to determine which judgments are objectively certain. What is certain is a motley collection, defined by no principles. I would emphasize not only that the collection includes both certainties about what our words mean and certainties about the truth of judgments expressed by means of them, but that no principled distinction can be drawn between these two kinds of certainties. "If you are not certain of any fact, you cannot be certain of the meaning of your words either." (Wittgenstein 1969, § 114) "I am no more certain of the meaning of my words than I am of certain judgments. Can I doubt that this color is called 'blue'?" (Wittgenstein 1969, § 126)

ix. Certainty is indispensable. Being certain of the correctness of many judgments is inseparable from inquiry and knowledge (Wittgenstein 1969, §§ 341, 342) as well as from learning (Wittgenstein 1969, §§ 283, 144), understanding or interpreting, hence from there being, a language (Wittgenstein 1969, §§ 80, 81, 114, 126). "We are interested in the fact that about certain empirical propositions no doubt can exist if making judgments is to be possible at all." (Wittgenstein 1969, § 308) "The *questions* that we raise and our *doubts* depend on the fact that some propositions are exempt from doubt, are as it were like hinges on which these turn." (Wittgenstein 1969, § 34) "But one isn't trying to express even the greatest subjective certainty, but rather that certain propositions seem to underlie all questions and all thinking." (Wittgenstein 1969, § 415)

x. What we are certain of is a nest of propositions. Certainty about a single proposition is a matter of the place of the proposition in a nest of propositions. It is held fast by the rest. (Wittgenstein 1969, §§ 144, 152, 225)

2.2 How Certainty Involves Truth

I come now to Wittgenstein's question: "What does this mean: the truth of a proposition is certain?" The question seems to assume that propositions of which we are certain are *true*, but that is what commentators often deny. They appeal to remarks such as Wittgenstein 1969, § 205: "If the true is what is grounded, then the ground is not *true* nor yet false", or Wittgenstein 1969, § 94: "But I did not get my picture of the world by satisfying myself of its correctness. No: it is the inherited background against which I distinguish between true and false." Such remarks, together with others, have led some to the view that certainties are rules which make truth or falsity possible, but which themselves have no truth.[4]

Winch's point of view is more subtle in recognizing different kinds of certainties and rejecting any uniform account of them all. My concern is his claim that Wittgenstein's view shifted from the *Philosophical Investigations* to *On Certainty*. In the former, Winch maintains, Wittgenstein held that "the distinction between truth and falsity can be applied to *all* propositions" (Winch 1988, p. 272) whereas in the latter he held that some propositions are neither true nor false. He did this because he thought, Winch writes, that not only will "I know" not "tolerate a metaphysical distinction" (Wittgenstein 1969, § 482) but that "neither will the distinction between truth and falsity".

My disagreement with Winch does not run deep – as will be clear in what follows – but working through the disagreement can clarify some important issues. I will first lay out what I take to be Wittgenstein's view of truth and of propositions, which will show where I disagree with Winch. Then I will turn to the way *On Certainty* deals with one particular certainty, namely, that the earth has existed long before I was born, which will show why my disagreement with Winch does not run deep.

2.2.1 Wittgenstein on Truth and Propositions

i. Minimalism about truth. Crucial to understanding Wittgenstein's view of what it is for a proposition to be true is *Philosophical Investigations* § 136, a long and difficult passage. I will quote part of it here for what it says about truth and return to it later for what it says about propositions.

> At bottom, giving "This is how things are" as the general form of propositions is the same as giving the definition: a proposition is whatever can be true or false. For instead of "This is how things stand" I could have said "This is true." (Or again "This is false.") But we have
> 'p' is true = p
> 'p' is false = not-p
> And to say that a proposition is whatever can be true or false amounts to saying: we call

---

[4] For one example see Kober 1996, p. 427f. The remarks just quoted do not contradict the claim that propositions of which we are certain are true. § 205 speaks of the *ground* as not true, but a certainty is not a ground. § 94 speaks of a *picture*, but a picture is not a proposition; § 95 speaks of the propositions describing the world picture. As confirmation for my view, consider this from *Remarks on Colour* § 348, written at the same time as *On Certainty:* "There seem to be propositions that have the character of empirical propositions, but whose truth is for me unassailable. That is to say, if I assume they are false, I must mistrust all my judgment." (Wittgenstein 1977, § 348)

something a proposition when in *our language* we apply the calculus of truth functions to it. (Wittgenstein 1958a, § 136)

This is one of a number of passages which show that Wittgenstein has a *minimalist* conception of truth. The crucial idea is that the equivalence thesis is the fundamental or underived fact about the concept of truth: '"p" is true' is equivalent to 'p', and '"p" is false' is equivalent to 'not-p'. 'True', therefore, is *content-redundant:* it is not used to refer to or characterize anything and it expresses no property. Since '"Napoleon was born in Corsica" *is true*' is equivalent to 'Napoleon was born in Corsica', both involve exactly the same objects and properties. Moreover, to *utter* '"Napoleon was born in Corsica" *is true*' is to make an assertion only in a context where 'Napoleon was born in Corsica' would also be an assertion. 'True' is, therefore, also force-redundant: adding it to the utterance of a sentence does not change its force or give it one if it has none.

This does not mean that the concept of truth is redundant; it has a number of indispensable roles to play in our language. One is to enable us to formulate certain generalizations. For instance, I might assert, 'What John just said is true.' Here I don't need 'true', for I could simply *assert* what he just said, since that would accomplish the same purpose. But if I asserted, 'Everything that *follows* from what John just said is true', I do need 'true', for I cannot assert everything that follows from what he said.[5]

Philosophy often involves analogous generalizations. A skeptic claims that our beliefs might be massively false; Wittgenstein claims that we cannot be mistaken about the truth of propositions of which we are certain. If we could list all the instances of such generalizations, we could do without the notion of truth, and clarity is often promoted by trying to do just that as far as possible. But often we simply cannot do without the notion of truth to discuss philosophical claims and arguments.

The danger is to think that a notion so indispensable to philosophical reflection must carry a significant content of its own. To say of a proposition that it is true must be to say that it would be verified, that it coheres with all our coherent beliefs, or that it corresponds to or agrees with reality. Wittgenstein warns against this danger in a number of passages in *On Certainty*, where his special target is the notion of agreement with reality. The crucial passages are these:

> Well, if everything speaks for an hypothesis and nothing against it – is it then certainly *true*? One may designate it as such. But does it certainly agree with reality, with the facts? With this question you are already going round in a circle. (Wittgenstein 1969, § 191)

---

5 The best discussion of these matters I know of is in Brandom 1994.

> The reason why the use of the expression "true or false" has something misleading about it is that it is like saying "it tallies with the facts or it doesn't", and the very thing that is in question is what "tallying" is here. (Wittgenstein 1969, § 199)
>
> Here we see that the idea of "agreement with reality" does not have any clear application. (Wittgenstein 1969, § 215)

As I understand these passages, Wittgenstein does not *deny* that a true proposition agrees with reality; what he denies is that 'agreeing with reality' denotes a determinate relation, which a true proposition bears to something which makes it true. To assert that a proposition is true is not to be committed to that metaphysical claim: truth is not a metaphysical notion.

When we say that a proposition agrees with reality, we say no more than when we say it is true.[6] *How* a proposition agrees with reality is important, but it is not part of what it is for it to be true; it belongs rather to what it is to verify its assertion or to what it is for a judgment involving it to be correct. There are not different kinds of truth, depending on how we determine whether a proposition agrees with reality or how we establish that a judgment involving it is correct. In accepting a proposition as true, we are committed to its agreeing with reality only in the *truistic* sense that a proposition is true (or false) depending on the way the world is. Whether it is *true* that Napoleon was born in Corsica depends on the way the world is and, by the equivalence thesis, it depends on whether Napoleon *was* born in Corsica – that specifies the *relevant* way the world is – but there is nothing substantive about the claim that whether Napoleon was born in Corsica is true depends on whether Napoleon was born in Corsica.

ii. *Correct judgment and true propositions.* I want to deal with two problems that arise in considering this notion of truth. The first is whether it permits an adequate distinction between correct judgment and mistaken judgment (assertion, belief). We do speak of judgments as true or false but only because the term 'judgment' may be used to refer either to *the act of judging* or to *what is judged*. The latter, when made explicit, involves a proposition, and hence is either true or false in the minimalist sense. The *act* of judging, on the other hand, is correct or mistaken (right or erroneous), which is a substantive – because nonnative – distinction. Now the connection between a correct judgment (judging) and a true proposition is surely this: a judgment is correct only if the

---

6 A little later I distinguish two uses of 'proposition'. The one in play here is its use to denote the sense of what is said by the utterance of a sentence in a particular context (rather than its use to denote a meaningful sentence).

proposition judged is true. The problem is how this can be if correctness is substantive while truth is minimal.

The answer is that 'true' is playing its typical generalizing role. The judgment that Napoleon was born in Corsica is *correct* only if it is *true* that Napoleon was born in Corsica but we do not need to use 'true' to state that. We can simply say that the judgment that Napoleon was born in Corsica is correct only if Napoleon *was* born in Corsica. We need 'true' because we cannot spell out all the instances of the generalization that a judgment is correct only if the proposition judged is true. The concept of truth is essential here but not because it carries a significant content of its own.

iii. Minimalist truth and meaningful sentences. The second problem is whether Wittgenstein's conception of truth permits an adequate account of the meaning of sentences, and this will bring me to Wittgenstein's account of *proposition*. A standard truth condition account of sentence meaning cannot be built on Wittgenstein's minimalist notion of truth, for two reasons. The first is that since the concept of truth is content-redundant, it can play no substantive role in *explaining* what it is for a sentence to be meaningful. We cannot, that is, explain the meaning of a sentence as consisting of the conditions which would *make* (render) it true, since 'to make true' means to make it the case that – to explain why – a proposition has the truth property. But on the minimalist account, truth is not a property and hence the notion of what would make a proposition true has neither application nor content.

Some interpreters of Wittgenstein, notably Dummett and Kripke, have argued that he replaced truth conditions with assertibility conditions. On this interpretation, since the meaning of a sentence is not constituted by the conditions which would make it true, it is constituted by the conditions which would make it correct to assert it – for example, the conditions under which asserting it would be conclusively verified. Among the objections to this is that it assumes that we can attach assertibility conditions to sentences considered as meaningless structured noises (or marks), the idea being that the conditions under which a sentence is conclusively verified are supposed to *constitute* the sentence as meaningful. To know the meaning of a sentence is supposed to be to know what my linguistic community would count as conclusive verification of an assertion of the sentence, which apart from that would simply be noise.

That is not Wittgenstein's view, for what he invariably speaks of as assertible or verifiable is a *Satz*, which is (almost always) translated as 'proposition' precisely because Wittgenstein (almost always) thinks of a *Satz* as a meaningful sentence (or utterance), not as mere structured noises (or marks).[7] Assertibility conditions do not *constitute* a proposition from a sentence, for what is assertible must already be a proposition. Moreover, on Wittgenstein's view a proposition is assertible only in a context in which it has a determinate sense, which means a context in which it is determinate what it would be for an utterance of it to be true (or false). We can put that, if we care to, by saying that on his view a proposition is assertible only in a context where it has a truth condition – in the minimalist sense of truth, of course, whereby there are conditions under which the proposition is true but not conditions which would *make* it true.

Wittgenstein thinks of propositions as being in English, German or other natural languages, not as the extra-linguistic objects of the metaphysicians. As he puts it: "We are talking about the spatial and temporal phenomenon of language, not about some non-spatial, non-temporal phantasm." (Wittgenstein 1958a, § 108) But, he continues, "We talk about [language] as we do about the pieces in chess when we are stating the rules of the game, not describing their physical properties." A proposition, that is, is a sentence *qua* having a role in a language (game), just as a chess piece is a physical shape *qua* playing the role of a pawn, a king, or what have you.

When we play chess, we play with chess pieces, not with mere hunks of wood or plastic, for what matters about the pieces is how to move them according to the rules of the game. When we learned chess, we learned how to move rooks and kings, not how to move such and such physical shapes. When playing chess, we do not first see hunks of wood and then conclude that they are rooks or kings and so may be moved in such and such ways; we see rooks and kings and move them accordingly.

So it is with language. When we learned to speak we learned how to utter and respond to propositions, not how to make noises with such and such properties. When we speak, we utter propositions, not mere noises, for what matters about sentences is not what they are but how they are used as propositions. When we listen to speech we do not first hear noises and then conclude that they must have such and such meaning. As speakers, we do not go behind propositions; we use propositions, not some pre-meaningful 'objects' to which we attach conditions of various kinds.

iv. Two senses of 'proposition'. This brings me to the second reason Wittgenstein rejects a standard truth condition account of meaning, namely, because on

---

[7] Occasionally *Satz* is used to denote a meaningless syntactic string, although there is usually warning of the untypical use; the more common term in this context is *Satzzeichen* ('propositional sign').

his view what has a truth condition (in the minimalist sense) is not a proposition taken as a meaningful sentence ('proposition' in the first sense), is not a proposition taken as the sense of the utterance of a (meaningful) sentence by a speaker in a particular context ('proposition' in the second sense). Take an example Wittgenstein used a number of times: "I am here."[8] That is not merely a sequence of sounds or a syntactic string, but a meaningful sentence (a proposition in the first sense) of English. But it does not have a truth value except when (suitably) used in a particular context; only then does it make sense to ask if it has met the condition under which it would be true. Wittgenstein puts this by saying that 'I am here' has no determinate sense except when used in a particular context, its sense depending on the context, where to have a determinate sense is for the proposition to be true or to be false. That last use of 'proposition' refers, therefore, not to the meaningful sentence, 'I am here', but to the sense of an utterance of that sentence in a particular context. Since what has a truth condition is 'I am here' only when used in a particular context ('proposition' in the second sense), it cannot be its truth condition which makes it a proposition in the first sense, i.e. a meaningful sentence.

Wittgenstein held that the concept of 'proposition' is like the concept of 'game' (or number) in that there is no such thing as its essence but only various examples with family resemblances among them (Wittgenstein 1958a, § 135). That means that the two uses of 'proposition' I have just distinguished – one denoting a meaningful sentence, the other the sense of an utterance of a meaningful sentence in a particular context – by no means exhaust the concept. But they are central to the concept and both occur in the crucial Wittgenstein 1958a, § 136, to which I return briefly:

> At bottom, giving 'This is how things are' as the general form of propositions is the same as giving the definition: a proposition is whatever can be true or false … And to say a proposition is whatever can be true or false amounts to saying: we call something a proposition when *in our language* we apply the calculus of truth functions to it … The proposition that only a *proposition* can be true or false can say no more than that we only predicate 'true' and 'false' of what we call a proposition. And what a proposition is in one sense deter-

---

[8] For instance, in Wittgenstein 1969, § 348 or in Wittgenstein 1958a, § 514. Wittgenstein got the example from Russell, who thought there was no distinction to be made between the meaningful sentence, 'I am here', and the sense an utterance of it may have in different contexts. He held, therefore, that it was a sentence whose utterance could not fail to be true (since the one who uttered it could not fail to be where he was) and thus expressed something we knew for certain. Wittgenstein thought that Russell's attempt to express a certainty yielded only non-sense and while there are numerous contexts in which an utterance of 'I am here' makes sense, none of them involve certainty. For a good discussion of this example, see Hertzberg 2001.

mined by the rules of sentence formation (in English for example), and in another sense by the use of the sign in the language-game.

I have quoted selectively in order to focus on the question of the relation of the two senses of 'proposition' to true and false. Both senses are mentioned in the last sentence: a proposition in the first sense (a meaningful sentence) is what is "determined by the rules of sentence formation"; a proposition in the second sense (the sense of an utterance of a meaningful sentence) is what is determined "by the use of the sign in the language-game". The question is what Wittgenstein means by "giving the definition: a proposition is whatever can be true or false". This suggests that propositions in both senses of the term are true or false, which appears to conflict with my claim that a proposition construed simply as a meaningful sentence does not have a truth condition.

The conflict is only apparent, however. "To say a proposition is whatever can be true or false", Wittgenstein writes, "amounts to saying: we call something a proposition when *in our language* we apply the calculus of truth functions to it." That is something we can do with 'I am here' (or 'This is how things are') construed as a proposition in the first sense: we can easily construct negations, conjunctions, disjunctions, or conditional propositions containing it, and then make inferences which involve modus ponens, modus tollens, or other valid inference forms, which, as we say, preserve truth. We do not do that with expressions that are not well-formed sentences, nor with interrogatives, imperatives, and so on, where the 'and so on' can be specified as what in our language we *do not* apply the calculus of truth functions to.

'True' is not being used here, however, to specify the condition under which a proposition would be true. Knowing the result of applying the calculus of truth functions to 'I am here' tells us nothing about the condition under which it would be *true* since it will not be true nor will it be false except as used in a particular context, and when no context is supplied for 'I am here', none is supplied either for the truth functions of that proposition. As Wittgenstein said about 'This is how things are', "to say that this proposition agrees or does not agree with reality would be obvious nonsense" (Wittgenstein 1958a, § 134) – 'proposition' here being used in the first sense.

Consider another example, one Putnam has used: "There is a lot of coffee on the table."[9] That is a proposition of English, and hence one to which the calculus of truth functions may *be* applied, permitting all sorts of inferences to proposi-

---

9 I got the example from James Conant, who says Putnam got it by modifying an example (about butter) from Charles Travis.

tions which would be true if that one were true. But there are here no truth conditions, for apart from its use on a particular occasion, there are no conditions under which that proposition would be true (or be false). A speaker may use it in a context where its sense is that there are many cups of coffee on the table, or that a lot of coffee has been spilled, or that there is a big bag of coffee beans, etc., etc., and whether it is true or false depends on *which* of these propositions – here understood as the sense of an utterance of the sentence in a particular context – is the one it is being used to express. Apart from a particular context, the proposition (in the first sense), 'There is a lot of coffee on the table', simply has no truth condition.[10]

We may therefore "predicate 'true' and 'false' of what we call a proposition" in either sense of 'proposition'. This does not mean that 'true' functions in different ways but that it functions with respect to propositions in different senses of the term. In either case it functions, for instance, to enable the kind of generalizations discussed above, whether they involve propositions as (only) meaningful sentences, where the notion of truth *conditions* has no place, or propositions as the sense of the utterances or propositions, where the notion of truth conditions is used to specify what that sense is.

We might say, therefore, that Wittgenstein has a truth conditions account of sense but not of meaning, provided we take truth in a minimalist way. That means that the notion of truth conditions plays no substantive role in explaining what *constitutes* sense; we use it only to *specify* the sense of a proposition by expressing in our language what would be true if and only if the proposition were true. Thus if someone utters 'There is a lot of coffee on the table', we can specify the sense of what she said in that context by saying it would *be* true if and only if a lot of coffee had been spilled on the table. "For how a sentence is *meant* can *be* expressed by an expansion of it and may therefore be made part of it." (Wittgenstein 1969, § 350)

I do not think, therefore, that the Wittgenstein of *On Certainty* had changed his mind from what he said about truth in the *Investigations*. Winch is right that "if the claim to know will not support a metaphysical emphasis, *neither will the distinction between truth and falsity*". I take that to be what minimalism about

---

10 Note that this is not a matter of ambiguity; none of the words in the sentence is ambiguous (like 'bank' or 'top'). Nor is it a matter of indexicality: eliminating the indexical expressions would not fix its truth conditions. Nor is the phenomenon rare; it is ubiquitous because, with sufficient imagination, we can devise situations in which any proposition can be made to have a truth condition different from the one we instinctively think it has, Wittgenstein also holds that for *any* proposition we can, given enough imagination, construct a situation in which it has a sense (cf. Wittgenstein 1958a, § 622). No proposition is *inherently* with or without sense.

truth is all about: there need be no metaphysical emphasis in the true-false distinction, and that view Wittgenstein also held in *On Certainty*. But if so, then Winch is wrong in saying that "Questions about truth and falsity go with: expressions of doubt, investigation of hypotheses, etc." (Winch 1988, p. 273) That is the case for questions about *knowledge*, but not for questions about *truth*. Indeed, I take it to be a basic thrust of *On Certainty* that it is possible to pry the true-false distinction out of contexts of investigation, evidence or making sure. We cannot pry knowledge out of such contexts but we can pry truth out of them. The claim that propositions of which we are certain are true, is, therefore, a *metaphysical* claim only if *true* is given a metaphysical emphasis. And that is exactly what is denied by Wittgenstein's minimalist notion of truth and the notion of propositions as 'whatever can be true or false' that goes along with it.

2.2.2 One Example of Certainty

The question remains, however, *which* of the claims to certainty Wittgenstein discusses involve propositions (in the second sense), and here I am largely in agreement with Winch.[11] I shall discuss only one example, which can be generalized but by no means universally, namely, certainty about the earth's having existed long before I was born. One's instinctive reaction is that here we surely have a judgment about the age of the earth which we have made explicit by using a proposition in a context where it has a determinate sense and which, since the judgment is certain, is true. Is that so?

There is this difficulty. Wittgenstein wrote that "If someone doubted whether the earth had existed a hundred years ago, I should not understand, for *this* reason: I would not know what such a person would still allow to be counted as evidence and what not." (Wittgenstein 1969, § 231) By "I should not understand", Wittgenstein means that the speaker's utterance fails to make sense in the context and hence is nonsense. In spite of what the skeptic may think, Wittgenstein maintains, she has failed to give sense to her utterance, failed to express a proposition with a truth condition.

For Wittgenstein, early and late, there is nonsense when a sentence is used in a context in which the speaker's utterance fails to have a determinate sense. The sentence may be meaningful; that is, it may be a proposition in the first

---

[11] I agree in particular with the way he characterizes judging as acting, for example when he writes that Wittgenstein puts the "emphasis on *action* as the primitive response to the world of which language is a 'refinement'..." (Winch 1988, p. 270).

sense, and hence there may be familiar contexts in which it does have a sense. But the speaker has used it in such a way that it has no determinate sense, hence where no condition under which it would be true has been determined.

> ... The words 'I am here' have a sense only in certain contexts, and not when I say them to someone who is sitting in front of me and sees me clearly, – and not because they are superfluous, but because their sense is not *determined* by the situation, yet stands in need of such determination. (Wittgenstein 1969, § 348)[12]

This is what the skeptic does in saying things such as 'I doubt whether the earth existed long before I was born.' What is the sense of 'The earth existed long before I was born', as used in this way in *this* context? What proposition is being uttered by the skeptic here? If his expression of doubt has a determinate sense, we must know what it would be for it to be true that the earth has *not* existed long before we were born. Indeed, we just know what would count for or against such a claim. Does the skeptic think people might lie about such things, that historians might be mistaken in claiming that Charles I or Napoleon existed, or that Uppsala's cathedral is several hundred years old? Does he think extraordinary mutations might account for our collective illusion about the age of the earth or that some explosion might account for the earth's coming into existence so recently? The more such questions are multiplied, the less there seems to be sense in what he was trying to say.

But can we who reject the skeptic give sense to an utterance which attempts to express the *negation* of what he was trying to say, namely, 'I do not doubt that the earth existed long before I was born'? As a simple denial of what the skeptic attempted to say, that can have no more sense than his utterance, and if he failed to say anything, this utterance must also fail to express a proposition with a sense or a truth condition.

So of what propositions (in the second sense) are we certain? What propositions make explicit the judgments of which we are certain in this case? They must be propositions like 'Napoleon was born in Corsica over a hundred years ago' or 'Uppsala has had a cathedral for several hundred years'. Of each of these we might have doubts in *some* context, but there is (no?) context in which we would have doubts about all of them; such general doubt would be senseless. So in being certain that the earth existed long before we were born, we are certain of a nest of propositions which support each other, and this we may express by saying that we are certain that the earth existed long before

---

12 Anscombe's translation of 'Sinn' has been changed from 'meaning' to 'sense'.

we were born.[13] But that is not the denial of 'I doubt whether the earth existed long before I was born' for that does not have sense in the way the skeptic wants it to have sense. Its sense could only be that there are circumstances under which any specific historical claim can be doubted, but that is not what the skeptic wants to say. He wants to express doubt about whether the earth existed before he was born, not doubt about specific claims. The latter, he thinks, can be salvaged in some sense, or don't really matter.

What follows Wittgenstein 1969, § 231, where Wittgenstein writes that he would not understand someone who doubted whether the earth had existed a hundred years ago, is the passage I discussed earlier: "We could doubt every single one of these facts, but we could not doubt them *all*." "Wouldn't it be more correct [Wittgenstein replies to the interlocutor] to say: 'We do not doubt them *all*.' Our not doubting them all is simply our manner of judging, and therefore of acting." He continues:

> If a child asked me whether the earth was already there before my birth, I should answer him that the earth did not begin only with my birth, but that it existed long, long before. And I should have the feeling of saying something funny. Rather as if the child had asked if such and such a mountain were higher than a tall house that it had seen. In answering the question I should have to be imparting a picture of the world to the person who asked it. (Wittgenstein 1969, § 233)

Wittgenstein's point is that to get a child to *understand* what we mean by saying that the earth existed long before my birth would require giving the child a *picture* of the world – in the sense in which a picture is worth a thousand words – as a substitute for what goes into our manner of judging and therefore of acting, which are things a child will learn how to do only through education and culture but which we now attempt to communicate through some kind of picture. Thus he continues in Wittgenstein 1969, § 234: "If I wanted to doubt the existence of the earth long before my birth, I should have to doubt all sorts of things which stand fast for me." Those things don't *yet* stand fast for the child, and hence he cannot yet understand what it is for the earth to have existed long before his birth, unless we can somehow get across a picture. But those things *will* stand fast for him, and then he will understand what it is for the earth to exist long before he was born, but by that time he will *not* be able to understand what it would be to doubt it.

---

[13] Cf. Wittgenstein: "I do not explicitly learn the propositions that stand fast for me. I can *discover* them subsequently like the axis around which a body rotates. This axis is not fixed in the sense that anything holds it fast, but the movement around it determines its immobility." (Wittgenstein 1958a, § 152)

Where then is the truth in certainty? Winch is wrong in thinking that truth can figure in these contexts only if it is given a *metaphysical* emphasis. He is right in thinking that certainty and truth have a complex and indirect relationship, but not because Wittgenstein separates propositions from truth. It is rather because he separates certainty from a denial of the skeptic's doubts. Certainty is not a matter of denying the truth of what the skeptic says but of showing that he fails to say what he wants to say because his utterances fail to make the sense he thinks they do.

This is not a view new to *On Certainty*, though it was articulated there in a new and striking way, but one which goes back to the *Tractatus* (6.51): "Skepticism is not irrefutable, but obviously nonsensical, when it tries to raise doubts where no questions can be asked. For doubts can exist only where a question exists, and an answer only where something *can be said*."[14]

---

14 In addition to Minneapolis, I read versions of this paper at Uppsala and Stockholm Universities and learned much from the discussions. Lilli Alanen has read several versions of it and nourished its development in indispensable ways. It reflects the criticisms James Conant made of it when it was first read in Minneapolis as well as what I have learned from his important papers on the role of nonsense in Wittgenstein's work. The latter include "Wittgenstein on Meaning and Use", read in Minneapolis (Conant 1998), and "The Method of the *Tractatus*" (Conant 2002).

3 Putnam on Truth

Hilary Putnam's work has been original, technically proficient, relevant to broad human concerns, widely influential – and subject to unexpected sharp turns. He invented the computational functionalist view of the mind, showed how to make it precise, related it to wider issues, saw it become the received view – and then turned against it, eloquently urging its rejection. He put forward a new conception of scientific realism, worked out technical details, suggested its wider significance, helped make it prominent in epistemology and philosophy of science – and then became its foremost critic. If Putnam's work did not have so many virtues, such sharp turns in his thought (of which these are only two examples) would suggest a philosopher unable to develop a stable view or unwilling to be serious. But the radical shifts in Putnam's thought are not signs of instability or frivolity, nor of carelessness or faddishness. They rather manifest a sensitivity to underlying shifts in the intellectual and philosophical climate of our time, rooted in an acute sense of when and how fashionable ways of thinking have gone wrong and are leading nowhere.

It is, therefore, worth the effort to pay attention to changes in Putnam's views for what they can teach us about which ways of thinking are likely to be philosophically rewarding and which are likely to be unproductive and ephemeral. The best way to do this is to consider his views about *truth* because major changes in his philosophical point of view have always centered on changes in his conception of truth. These changes can be bewildering to those whom Putnam has convinced, only to find that he himself is no longer convinced by what they found so convincing. But many of us simply find it difficult to make overall sense of his numerous essays, which were written for diverse occasions, and which mingle the technically esoteric with the everyday and move from an historical aside to a memorable example to a witty label for some doctrine.

This paper is an attempt to make overall sense of Putnam's views about truth by giving a kind of world-historical survey of their development. The thesis in Putnam's work is *metaphysical realism*, an influential view which continues to have many devoted defenders. The antithesis is *internal realism*, which has been much discussed but seems not to have had a lasting impact. The synthesis is Putnam's current view, for which he prefers the name *commonsense realism*. It rejects both the correspondence truth central to the thesis and the epistemic truth central to the antithesis, on the ground that both try to give illicit metaphysical substance to everyday concepts. It offers instead an understanding of truth which represents a clear turn to work in the spirit of Wittgenstein.

Let me first give a brief overview of Putnam's relevant publications. The main source for metaphysical realism is his John Locke Lectures (1967) and the paper "Reference and Understanding", both in *Meaning and the Moral Sciences* (Putnam 1978). There are also relevant papers in his *Philosophical Papers*, volumes 1 and 2 (Putnam 1975a, 1975b). The rejection of metaphysical realism came with two papers: "Realism and Reason" (1976; in Putnam 1978) and "Models and Reality" (1977) in *Philosophical Papers*, volume 3 (Putnam 1983), but the main development of internal reason is *Reason, Truth and History* (Putnam 1981) and *Representation and Reality* (Putnam 1988). *Realism with a Human Face* (Putnam 1990) is a transitional work, although internal realism dominates it. The turn to commonsense realism is prominent in *Words and Life* (Putnam 1994a) and even more so in Putnam's "Dewey Lectures", published as "Sense, Nonsense, and the Senses: An Inquiry into the Powers of the Human Mind" in *The Journal of Philosophy*, September, 1994 (Putnam 1994b).[1]

3.1 Metaphysical Realism

Fundamental to metaphysical realism is a version of the correspondence theory of truth and a correlative theory of reference. The correspondence theory holds that the concept of truth denotes a property which statements[2] possess in virtue of their corresponding to the states of affairs they are about or represent. The point of the theory is not to *define* the concept of truth; that is taken in its ordinary sense as conforming to such platitudes as that a statement is true just in case it says what is really the case, or says of what is, that it is, and so on. Such platitudes[3] can be usefully expressed in terms of what I shall call the

---

1 James Conant edited both *Realism with a Human Face* and *Words and Life*, and his introductions are very useful surveys of how Putnam's point of view has changed.

2 I will use 'statement' throughout this paper as the default term for what is said to be true (or false), which means that the term will vary in sense depending on the context. The context will usually make it clear whether the term is used to refer to a declarative sentence (which may or may not be meaningful), to an assertible sentence (which may not be declarative), or to what is (or would be) stated by the assertive utterance of a sentence in a particular context (which is my own view of what is properly said to be true or false). I will be explicit about which sense of 'statement' is in play only when something crucial turns on it.

3 I am assuming that defenders of different *conceptions* of truth share a *concept* of truth, which is to say they agree in accepting such platitudes as these. A conception of truth is an explication of what the concept of truth is, how it is related to other concepts, what it is to have such a concept, and so on. Among the matters on which conceptions of truth disagree is whether the con-

Equivalence Principle [EP], according to which any instance of the following schema is true:

> S is true if and only if P

where for 'S' we put a specification of a statement and for 'P' we put that statement itself or one which means the same. One instance of the schema is the statement Tarski made famous as the paradigm of a T-sentence:

> "Snow is white" is true if and only if snow is white.

For such instances, EP functions as a disquotational principle, but EP is broader than that, permitting instances like the following, which specify the statement not by quoting it but by using a that-clause:

> It is true that neutrinos have mass if and only if neutrinos have mass.

The point of the correspondence theory is not to defend EP – that is taken for granted as a platitude – but to establish that the concept of truth denotes a *substantive property*[4] and to give an account which *explains* why a (true) statement has that property (an account of what *makes* it true), namely because it corre-

---

cept of truth denotes a (substantive) property and if so what is its nature. To share a *concept* of truth, therefore, is not to share a view about the *property* of truth.

4 By a *substantive* property (or relation), I mean one which is not merely the correlate of a predicate, but one which plays an essential role in a unified explanatory account of a range of phenomena. The property of being an elm, for example, is substantive because it plays a unified explanatory role in botany: it is *because* a sapling is an elm that it will develop a specific shape and type of bark, etc., and it is because it is an elm that its development can be explained in the same way as any other elm. Being an elm, we can say, is an explanatorily relevant way of classifying objects. The property of being a square table with two scratches, on the other hand, is not substantive: there is no explanatory scheme in which it plays a role, and whatever might explain why *this* object is a square table with two scratches will not explain why any other object is so. Being a square table with two scratches is not an explanatory way of classifying objects. 'Being an elm', we might also say, denotes a natural or substantive property, whereas 'being a square table with two scratches' denotes an artificial or insubstantial one. We might also say that a substantive property is one which *determines* it instances, unlike a non-substantive property, which is *determined by* its instances just as a set is determined by its members. This notion of a substantive property resembles one suggested by Putnam in "On Properties", where he writes that "The concept of a property is intimately connected with the notions: nomological, explanation, cause, etc., and even comes close to being definable in terms of those notions." (Putnam 1975a, p. 321) As far as I know, Putnam has not followed up on this suggestion.

sponds to the state of affairs it represents. If we specify what a statement represents as the state of affairs whose existence *would* make it true (its truth condition), then a statement *corresponds* to what it represents just in case the state of affairs which would make it true exists, where a state of affairs which exists is *a fact*.[5]

We can distinguish *realist* from *nonrealist* versions of the correspondence theory. Realist versions hold that there is no necessary connection between a statement's being true and its being warranted to assert it. A statement which we are warranted in asserting may not be true, and a statement may be true even if we are not warranted in asserting it. The conjuncts in that sentence are logically independent of each other, and hence a realist could accept one without accepting the other, just as a nonrealist could reject one without rejecting the other. Putnam made acceptance of the *first* conjunct a criterion of metaphysical realism when he wrote, "What shows that one understands the notion of truth realistically [is maintaining that] a statement can be false even though it follows from our theory (or from our theory plus the set of true observation sentences)" (Putnam 1978, p. 34), where "our theory" refers to one which meets all our criteria for being warranted. That he understood metaphysical realism as also accepting the second conjunct is clear, however, by his explicit rejection of any view that makes truth "a version of warranted assertibility" (Putnam 1978, p. 108).[6]

The theory of reference correlative to this theory of truth maintains that reference is a substantive relation which holds between terms and the objects in the world (particulars, properties, functions, or what have you) to which the terms refer. Again, the point of the theory is not to *define* 'refers', which is taken in its ordinary sense: a term refers to an object just in case it is about it, designates it, is true of it, applies to it, is satisfied by it, or what have you. The point of the

---

5 Arthur Prior calls this, in his excellent "Correspondence Theory of Truth" (Prior 1967), the 'existence version' of the correspondence theory. Prior dislikes that version, but nothing in this paper turns on his objections to it.

6 Dummett emphasizes the rejection of the *second* realist conjunct in arguing that we cannot assert that a statement is either true or false unless we know there is a procedure we could apply to establish either that it is warranted to assert it or warranted to deny it. If it is Dummett's view that truth and warranted assertibility are mutually entailing (which I take to be compatible with a *nonrealist* correspondence theory of truth, which is what I think Dummett's view amounts to), he of course rejects *both* realist conjuncts; but I know of no place where Dummett explicitly rejects the first conjunct, that is, denies that a statement we are warranted in asserting may not be true. I mention this because Putnam says he was much influenced by Dummett's anti-realism, in spite of the fact that what was crucial for him in rejecting metaphysical realism was rejection of the first, not the second, realist conjunct.

theory is to establish that the *concept* of reference denotes a substantive relation and then to give an explanatory account of why terms bear that relation to the objects to which they refer. Such an account will both explain the nature of the reference relation – show that it is causal, physical, intentional, etc. – and explain why any term bears the relation to its referents. This is *correlative* to the correspondence theory of truth because the objects to which terms *refer* must be the constituents of the states of affairs (or facts) to which statements constituted by those terms *correspond* when they are true. Indeed, 'true' can be defined in terms of reference in a standard truth-theoretical way, which generalizes on an example like this one: 'Snow is white' is true just in case 'snow' refers to snow, 'is white' refers to the set of white things, and snow is a member of the set of white things.

Putnam's realist version of the correspondence theory of truth departed from standard versions in two novel and interesting respects. First, its account of truth (and reference) played no role in his account of what it is to *understand* (be competent in) a language: "The implicit knowledge of truth conditions", he argued, "is not *presupposed* in any way by the understanding of a language." (Putnam 1978, p. 110) He rejected the view that understanding a statement consists in knowing its truth conditions (which for a metaphysical realist means knowing which state of affairs would make it true) for the same reason Dummett did, namely on the ground that such a view would entail the absurd conclusion that we must know the truth conditions of a statement before we can understand any statement which has those truth conditions.[7] He also rejected the view that understanding a term consists in knowing which objects it refers to, arguing instead that to understand either a statement or a term is to know how to use it, that is, to know how to use it in accordance with the way speakers of the language in general use it.

His view, more precisely, was that to understand a statement in a given language is to know how to use it in accordance with the degree of warrant speakers of that language would (implicitly) assign assertions of it under various conditions, and to understand a term is to know how to use it in statements one un-

---

[7] The argument is that if we maintain that understanding a statement consists in understanding its truth conditions, then we are committed either to the absurd claim that we could understand the truth conditions of statements in a language without understanding the language or to an infinite regress whereby we understand the truth conditions of a statement by understanding a statement describing them, which we understand by understanding its truth conditions, etc., etc.

derstands in that sense.⁸ For example, to understand 'The sun is shining' is to know that English speakers are rightly warranted in uttering those words when they see a bright, round object in the sky, less warranted when they notice that it is light outside but do not see the bright object, unwarranted when they see no light, etc. The view was like Dummett's in being verificationist, but unlike it in not appealing to *conclusive* verification (or warrant) to mark out a distinctive kind of *linguistic* use connected with shared meaning as opposed to shared belief (which would presuppose an illegitimate use of the analytic-synthetic distinction). It assumed a *contrast* between a statement's truth conditions and its assertibility conditions (the conditions under which it would be warranted to assert it) and identified understanding with practical knowledge of the latter.⁹

"Nothing in this account of 'use' says *anything* about a correspondence between words and things, or sentences and states of affairs" (Putnam 1978, p. 99), but that did not mean, Putnam went on, that terms do not refer to objects or that statements are not true in virtue of their correspondence to states of affairs. It meant that knowing how to use a statement does not require knowing which state of affairs would make the statement true, and that knowing how to use a term does not require knowledge of the object to which it refers. "One does not need to know there is a correspondence between words and extra-linguistic entities to learn one's language. But there is such a correspondence none the less ..." (Putnam 1978, p. 111)

This separation of use from correspondence presupposed the distinction, made in model-theoretic studies of formal languages, between characterizing a language and specifying its interpretation (or its semantics). Putnam's idea was that the distinction applies also to the language of science and everyday

---

8 Cf. Putnam 1978, p. 97 f. Note that 'statement' is being used here in the sense of 'sentence': the view is that a sentence – as a set of noises – is a meaningful statement just in case a community of speakers has come to regard it as warranted to utter it under various specific conditions, namely conditions in which the community counts that sentence as warranted.

9 This verificationist account of understanding and use (which is also integral to internal realism) should not be confused with the positivist 'verifiability theory of meaning', which Putnam has always rejected. Indeed, he characterizes volume 2 of his *Collected Papers* as "largely concerned with the development of ... a nonverificationist theory of meaning ..." (Putnam 1975b, p. viii). The latter presumes a distinction between meaning (which he took to be "largely determined by reference" (Putnam 1975, p. ix)) and use, but Putnam's verificationism is about use rather than meaning. His view also differs from positivism in emphasizing the holist character of understanding to the point of denying any special status to observation statements. It should also be noted that the main target of Putnam's metaphysical realism was not a view like his own internal realism but the positivist reduction of theoretical statements to observational statement, which he has always opposed.

life because to characterize what it is to understand that language in terms of how expressions are used is, on his view, to leave it open how to interpret the expressions of the language. The difference is that in the case of formal languages, expressions are merely *assigned* an interpretation in accordance with the requirements of a formal scheme, whereas in the case of the language of science and everyday life, expressions already *have* an interpretation, which has to be discovered. Speakers can *use* expressions of the latter, however, without having discovered what that interpretation is – that is, without having acquired knowledge of what states of affairs true statements correspond to or to which objects terms refer.

How then do we come to know the (correct) interpretation of expressions in science and everyday life? This brings us to the second respect in which Putnam's correspondence theory departed from standard versions. It grounded its account of truth and reference, not in an *analysis* of the concepts of truth, reference, and related concepts (like meaning, assertion, belief, evidence), but in an empirical theory intended to *explain* why the ways we use expressions in science or everyday life are *successful* in various respects.

Putnam's idea was that human behavior is reasonably successful in dealing with the contingencies of life and that a major factor in that overall success is the contribution *linguistic* behavior makes by enabling us to do such things as predict and explain a wide range of phenomena in both everyday life and science. Our using language in such success-furthering ways does not require knowing *why* it is so successful, but there is an explanation nevertheless, whose principal claim is that a large majority of the statements we accept are *true* and a large majority of the terms we use *refer* to real things. Putnam argued further that this explanation *requires* that truth and reference be construed in terms of the *realist* version of the correspondence theory, and that claim constituted his central argument for metaphysical realism.[10] At the same time, it explained how we acquire knowledge of the correct interpretation of the expressions of the language of science and everyday life: their (correct) interpretation is the one which assigns states of affairs to statements and objects to terms in accordance with the requirements of that theory which best explains the success of our use of the language, and that theory is metaphysical realism.

Two things about this require further discussion. The first is the question of why we cannot explain the success of our language use by appealing to the fact

---

10 "Reference and truth are so construed that [given ordinary circumstances] sentences will tend to be accepted in the long run if and only if they are *true*, and predicates will be applied to things if and only if those things have the properties *corresponding* to those predicates." (Putnam 1975b, p. 289)

that the great majority of the statements we accept are simply *true*. Why do they have to be true in the metaphysical realist sense? If I succeed in finding my way to the city library, one reason is that the beliefs I have about where it is and what streets to take to get there are true. But that doesn't require that those beliefs be true in the metaphysical realist sense; it is enough that they are warranted and hence (if that is a sense of 'true') that they be *true* in that sense.

Putnam granted this point (Putnam 1978, p. 102) but argued that it leaves out a crucial dimension of success, namely our success in acquiring *new* beliefs, which are on the whole true: "A satisfactory account of truth ought to ... *account for the reliability of our learning*", ought, that is, to account for the fact that "certain sorts of learning are *reliable* – in the sense of leading to a large number of true beliefs." (Putnam 1978, p. 103) Such an account, he argued, has to "understand that reliability as a fact of nature" (Putnam 1978, p. 103), which means that it cannot be *a priori* but must provide an empirically based, causal explanation of why certain ways of acquiring belief yield mostly true beliefs. Putnam used as an example the theory of vision, which gives a causal explanation of why persons with normal vision generally acquire true beliefs (or accept true statements) about such things as the color of objects, just by seeing them under normal conditions. He took this as an instance of a whole range of such causal theories, which explain not only the success of perceptual capacities, but also the success of various experimental techniques which yield mostly true beliefs because of the causal interaction they set up between persons and the phenomena they are investigating.[11]

But, again, what is so special about such causal explanations that they support metaphysical realism's conception of truth? Why isn't warranted assertibility enough? The reason, Putnam argued, is because it is the very nature of such explanations to allow for serious error. The explanation of reliability given by the causal account of vision, for example, entails that I may have good eyesight and be observing an object from a proper distance but still be mistaken about its color. "In the case of seeing what color a rug is, it is part of the causal explanation that there is *room for error* – it is *physically* possible that one seems to see a green rug, etc., and the rug not be green." (Putnam 1978, p. 108) I may, therefore, be warranted in asserting that the rug is green even though it is not true that it is green, and Putnam took this to be sufficient both to undermine what he took to be the central claim of nonrealism – that truth is equivalent to warranted assertibility – and to establish that the conception of truth required to explain the

---

[11] These explanatory theories are not themselves theories of truth, but are elements of an 'overarching metatheory' which does function as a theory of truth. Cf., for example, Putnam 1994a.

overall success of our language meets the realist criterion, which is that any statement we are warranted in asserting might not be true. Indeed, Putnam generalized this last point so that not only *any* warranted assertion but *every* warranted assertion (or almost every), might be false.

> The most important consequence of metaphysical realism is that *truth* is supposed to be *radically non-epistemic* – we might be 'brains in a vat' and so the theory that is 'ideal' from the point of view of operational utility, inner beauty and elegance, 'plausibility', simplicity, 'conservatism', etc., might be false. 'Verified' (in any operational sense) does not imply 'true', on the metaphysical realist picture, even in the ideal limit. (Putnam 1978, p. 125)

The other matter that requires discussion has to do with EP, which, Putnam agreed, is a requirement any adequate conception of truth has to meet. There is, however, reason to worry whether metaphysical realism meets it, which is best seen by returning to the distinction between a language and its interpretation, which grounded Putnam's distinction between the capacity to use a language and knowledge of what it corresponds to. I noted above that Putnam's view was that the correct interpretation of our language is the one which assigns states of affairs to its statements in accordance with that theory of truth which best explains the success of the language, and we now have his argument that such a theory must be an empirically-based causal theory. But that means it will be a matter of empirical fact which states of affairs are assigned to which statements, and hence that states of affairs could be assigned to statements (as their truth-conditions) in ways that conflict with EP.

Some philosophers seem not to worry about this. Noticing that a statement like 'Heat is proportional to the amount of caloric fluid present' has been falsified but was nevertheless very useful in its time, they argue that early scientists who spoke in terms of caloric fluid were really talking about kinetic energy. They go on to claim that the correct *truth condition* for 'Heat is proportional to the amount of caloric fluid present' should be 'Heat is proportional to the amount of kinetic energy of the molecules.' Whatever merit there may be to the thought behind such paraphrases, however, it is gross confusion to put it in terms of *truth conditions*, for the latter have to meet EP – as Putnam would agree.

Those versions of the correspondence theory which, unlike Putnam's, do not distinguish an account of use from an account of truth conditions, have no problem with meeting EP. Such versions do not characterize a correspondence theory as holding that what makes a statement true is that it corresponds to *a* state of affairs, but rather that it corresponds to the state of affairs *which it represents*, for even false statements correspond to some state of affairs or other. They are false because they do not correspond to the right state of affairs – that is, the state of affairs which they represent. This point is built into standard versions of the correspondence theory inasmuch as they link their account of understanding and use with their account of truth by holding that to understand a statement *is* to understand its truth conditions, which entails that what a statement represents is the state of affairs which would make it true, and that is precisely what EP claims.

Putnam was aware that he had to find some other way of insuring that metaphysical realism about truth meets EP – of insuring, as he puts it, that "The correspondence involved in the causal story is exactly the correspondence set up by the truth definition." (Putnam 1978, p. 105) He did this in two ways. One was by simply stipulating that "the realist accepts some standard truth definition for the language" so that the theory explaining the reliability of our learning consists of the "causal theory of perception and language use *plus* semantic theory of truth" (Putnam 1978, pp. 104–105). The other appealed to the fact that deductive logic requires EP (since it preserves truth only if it conforms to EP) and that "it is part of our explanation of speakers' reliability that one of the ways in which they acquire new beliefs is the use of deductive logic" (Putnam 1978, p. 107).[12]

Before turning to the way Putnam dismantled most of this in his internal realist period, I want to make a few comments on metaphysical realism's conception of *reality*. The core idea was that reality consists of a vast, determinate and unique collection of objects of various kinds – some concrete, some abstract; some particulars, some properties, some events, some continuants, etc.[13] – and that all referring terms refer to objects from this vast collection. Terms refer in diverse ways, depending on the language or scheme of reference they belong to, because, for example, they group or classify the objects in quite different ways. Such grouping will typically be layered: what is referred to collectively by 'A' may be a group of B's, and each B may be a group of C's; or 'D' may refer to C's directly without referring to B's, each of which is a group of C's, and so on, depending on the language (or scheme) to which the terms belong.[14] But, and

---

12 This may, of course, make it seem less "miraculous" (as Putnam puts it) that "the relation between states of affairs and sentences described by the causal theory of perception, language acquisition, etc. is *also* the one specified by the truth definition for the language" (Putnam 1978, p. 106), but the connection between these two relations remains *external*, a point Putnam emphasizes in his own later criticism of metaphysical realism.
13 The details will vary with the versions of the view.
14 For example, 'opening a can' may refer to one thing I did this morning, while 'certain movements of my arm and hand' refers to the many bodily motions that, taken collectively, went on in my opening that can, while in turn 'various neuro-muscular changes' refers to events that, taken collectively, went on in each of the movements of my arm and hand. In one sense, each of these terms refers, on this occasion, to the same things, namely neuro-muscular changes, but because

this is what is crucial for metaphysical realism, *what* is referred to in these diverse, layered ways are ultimately members of the same determinate and unique collection of objects – the *ultimate* objects – and it is these objects which constitute reality. Equally important, that they *are* the ultimate objects – that there are no objects more fundamental of which they consist – is independent of whatever language or conceptual scheme the terms which refer to them belong. Hence what referring terms refer to always consist, in the final analysis, of these ultimate objects, which are also the ultimate constituents of the states of affairs which make any (true) statement true.

To clarify this conception of reality, consider an alternative, for example, Putnam's (Putnam 1987, p. 18) example of a famous dispute about the 'ontological status' of points in a Euclidean plane: are the points in the plane *parts* of the plane (Leibniz) – i.e., concrete objects – or are they "mere *limits*" (Kant) – hence abstract objects? Metaphysical realists insist that there must be a correct answer to whether they are parts or limits; for if 'points' is a referring term, the objects it refers to must (in the end) belong to the determinate and unique collection of ultimate objects, and the objects in that collection to which 'points' bears the reference relation will be either concrete or abstract, hence will make it true either that points are parts of the plane or that they are merely limits of the plane.

An alternative view is that points are parts of a plane in one way of conceptualizing geometry and limits in another, so that there is no such thing as *the* correct answer to the question, "What are points?" The answer depends on which conceptual scheme we are using in posing the question. This is a genuine alternative because it rules out any such things as *the ultimate objects* of which every real thing consists and to which, in the last analysis, every referring term refers. What is an ultimate object depends on the scheme: in one way of conceptualizing geometry, points are ultimate objects; in another way, planes are ultimate and points are mere limits of planes. The question of what objects are *really* ultimate has no answer independent of a particular scheme, and different schemes will yield different answers.[15]

Metaphysical realists object because such an alternative makes the answer to the question of what is ultimately real depend on the language to which terms belong, which they regard as making reality (and truth) dependent on language or thought. This objection rests on a *metaphysical* distinction between what is

---

the terms belong to different kinds of discourse, they refer to them in different ways in that they group or classify them in different ways.

15 The metaphysical realist, Putnam wrote later (Putnam 1987, p. 20) "makes the mistake of supposing that 'which are the real objects?' makes sense *independently of our choice of concepts*".

independent of language (or mind) and what is not independent. This distinction is not the one we use when we must decide on empirical grounds if marks on a stone were made by humans or by the sea, or whether a fire was started by arsonists or by lightning. It is an *a priori* distinction intended to draw a sharp and principled line between what is real in 'itself' and what is real only because we 'count it' as real or because it 'appears real' to those who share our sense organs and conceptual capacities.[16] Those who accept it reject the notion that a point is really a part of a plane in one scheme and really a limit in another, since that makes what is ultimately real depend on which geometrical language we use. Metaphysical realists maintain that what is real must be completely independent of language and thought: an object must be ultimate or non-ultimate, abstract or concrete, an individual thing or a collection of things no matter how we refer to it. It is precisely because correspondence theories of truth and reference appear to render such a conception of language-independence intelligible that they are fundamental to metaphysical realism.

Putnam characterizes these features of metaphysical realism in a well-known passage.

> The world consists of some fixed totality of mind-independent objects. There is exactly one true and complete description of 'the way the world is'. Truth invoices some sort of correspondence relation between words or thought signs and external things and sets of things.[17] (Putnam 1981, p. 49)

---

[16] One version of this is Searle's distinction between "those features of the world that exist independently of us and those that are dependent on us for their existence" (Searle 1995, p. 10), which he takes as fundamental to any plausible account of truth and reality. Another version is Bernard Williams' notion of the "absolute conception of the world" (Williams 1978, p. 241f.). John McDowell objects to the distinction on the ground that it illicitly assumes that "the world is fully describable in terms of properties that can be understood without essential reference to their effects on sentient beings" (McDowell 1998b, p. 114). What is real in itself is more or less what Kant meant by a thing in itself, about which McDowell recently wrote: "Considering things as things in themselves is considering the very things that figure in our knowledge but in abstraction from how they figure in our knowledge." (McDowell 1998b, p. 469) Whereas Kant saw the futility in trying to do that, metaphysical realists do not, and hence they characterize what is achieved when we do not consider things as things in themselves as knowledge of what we merely count as, or merely appears to be, real.

[17] Here are other formulations of the same point. "The scientific realist picture is that there is a certain domain of entities such that all ways of using words referentially are just different ways of singling out one or more of those entities. In short, the picture is that what an 'object' of reference is, is fixed once and for all at the start and that the totality of objects in some scientific theory or other will turn out to coincide with the totality of All the Objects There Are." (Putnam 1978, p. 120) Metaphysical realism holds "that there is – in a philosophically privileged sense of 'object' – a definite Totality of All Real Objects and a fact of the matter as to which properties of

Three claims were made here, which critics have wanted to pry apart, but which Putnam thought were inseparable; the best way to see why he thought so is to put them in terms of the physicalism he held at that time.[18]

For a physicalist, the world consists of elementary physical particles and forces,[19] and hence any description of what there is will be a description of such physical elements. While it does not follow that all such descriptions are in physicalist terms – they may be functionalist or even irreducibly mentalist terms – *what* are described must be the physical elements, and it is these Putnam refers to as a 'fixed totality of mind-independent objects' (which I have called the 'ultimate objects'). Given the physicalist claim that 'the way the world is' is fixed by the physical elements and their arrangement (by supervenience, for instance), any description of the way the world is must ultimately be a description of the arrangement of those physical elements, and any 'true and complete description' of them must be equivalent to any other 'true and complete description' of them. Finally, what makes any such description true will be 'some sort of correspondence relation' between it and the state of affairs described – thus the connection of all three claims.

3.2 Internal Realism

Internal realism was the antithesis of metaphysical realism in that it not only rejected its conception of truth but adopted an epistemic conception which made truth *equivalent* to warranted assertibility – not, indeed to what we *are* warranted in asserting but to what we *would be* warranted in asserting in *ideal* circumstances. "To claim of any statement that it is true", Putnam wrote, "is, roughly, to claim that it could be justified were epistemic conditions good enough." (Putnam 1990, p. vii) The basic motivation for this shift was Putnam's rejection of metaphysical realism's conception of reference and hence also of the conception of truth which is inseparable from it.

His argument against metaphysical realism's notion of reference rested on the way it applied the model-theoretic distinction between a language and its interpretation, giving a use theory of the former and a realist-correspondence theory of the latter. He appealed to results from model theory to argue that, given the

---

those objects are the intrinsic properties and which are, in some sense, perspectival" (Putnam 1994a, p. 303).
18 Although the point does not require physicalism; dualism would do as well.
19 Cf. Searle's oft-repeated claim that "the world consists entirely of physical particles in fields of force" (Searle 1995, p. xi).

way this distinction was applied, use can in no way determine reference, which means there can be no such thing as a correct (or incorrect) interpretation of the language in the sense of 'interpretation' required for metaphysical realism. His claim was that no matter what constraints our use of expressions meet, even if our theories are ideal in every respect and the statements we assert are fully warranted, there are any number of ways of assigning objects to terms, no one of which is any more correct (or incorrect) than another. This means that the very notion of a reference relation which explains why a term refers to a particular set of objects makes no sense, for there is no particular set of objects to which *any* term refers. The point is not that we do not know which (ultimate) objects terms refer to but that there is no such thing as their referring to one object rather than to any number of others.

> [The argument] begins by showing – that one can show this is, today, an undisputed result of modern logic – that if there is such a thing as 'an ideal theory', then that theory can never implicitly define its own intended reference relation. In fact, there are always many different reference relations that make I true, if I is a consistent theory which postulates the existence of more than one object ... One can always find a reference relation that satisfies our observational constraints and also satisfies such theoretical constraint as simplicity, elegance, subjective plausibility, and so on, under which such a theory I comes out true ... [A metaphysical realist] must insist that it is something other than operational and theoretical constraints that singles out the right reference relation. But this is an incoherent idea. (Putnam 1994a, p. 353)

The conclusion here is a variant of Quine's doctrine of the indeterminacy of reference (also called 'ontological relativity'), which also held that there can be no such thing as a reference relation and no such thing as a term referring to one set of objects rather than any number of others. Quine held not only that reference depends on the reference scheme of a language but that there are unlimited ways of applying a reference scheme – of 'mapping' it unto the world – no one of which is any more correct (or incorrect) than another. For example, in the statement 'That apple is red', 'that apple' can be taken to be a singular term which refers to an apple, and 'is red' to be a predicate which denotes the property of being red. But Quine argued that the statement will retain its truth value (and its truth conditions) if we shift the reference so that 'that apple' refers to the object to the left of the apple and 'is red' denotes that property anything possesses just in case the object to its right is red. Any number of further shifts ('permutations'.) can be devised (in accordance with what Quine called "proxy functions"), all of which leave both the truth values and truth conditions of the statements unchanged. This kind of shifting of the reference of terms is possible for *any* statement, provided we also shift the terms in other statements in a systematic way. Reference, that is to say, is indeterminate: there is no fact of the matter as to which object(s) any term refers.[20]

Putnam differs sharply from Quine, however, in *rejecting* the indeterminacy of reference, whereas Quine accepts it as a "trivial and indisputable" result (by contrast with the indeterminacy of *translation*, which he thinks is "serious and controversial"). In the passage I quoted earlier, Putnam's assertion that we can always find a reference relation that satisfies observational and theoretical constraints was not a statement of his own view, but what he took to be an unacceptable consequence of metaphysical realism. The model-theoretic argument and the appeal to the indeterminacy of reference, that is to say, were not meant as part of an internal realist account but as a *reductio* of metaphysical realism. "What I argued was that metaphysical realism leaves us with no intelligible way to refute ontological relativity, and concluded that metaphysical realism is wrong. And I still see ontological relativity as a refutation of any philosophical position that leads to it." (Putnam 1994a, p. 280)[21]

Metaphysical realists have responded to this critique in a number of ways, most notably by trying to develop a *causal* theory of reference, according to which reference is determined, not by the use we make of the expressions in a language, even when that use meets every relevant constraint, but by causal relations between users of the terms and what those terms refer to (so that a reference relation is a kind of causal relation), which amounts to the view that reference determines use rather than the other way around. Although Putnam is famous for his twin earth thought-experiments, which are intended to show that a speaker's causal relations to her environment are essential in fixing the reference of her terms, he does not use the thought-experiments to support this kind of a causal theory of reference (or, indeed, any *theory* of reference).[22] In any case, he argues that no such theory could save metaphysical realism because the kind of

---

20 Putnam discusses Quine on this matter in 1981, p. 33 f., in a section which gives his clearest statement of this critique of metaphysical realism.
21 I emphasize this point because it is not *obvious* in the publications of Putnam's internal realist period (as opposed to such later ones as *Words and Life*) that the model-theoretic argument was meant as a *reductio* of metaphysical realism rather than as a support for some of the relativistic aspects of Putnam's own internal realism. Putnam is, of course, not claiming that Quine derived the indeterminacy of reference from metaphysical realism but only that the doctrine can be so derived. Putnam does write, however, that "Quine writes as if there were a noumenal reality, and what his model-theoretic argument shows is that our terms have an infinite number of ways of being modeled in it." (Putnam 1994a, p. 362)
22 An account of what is required to *fix* reference is not an account of what (if anything) *constitutes* the reference relation.

causation needed for a causal theory of reference is causal *explanation*, which is inescapably interest-relative and irreducibly intentional, and hence no more capable of fixing reference than language itself (something even an ideal language cannot do).

If metaphysical realism is wrong about reference, it must also be wrong about truth. If referents can be shifted indefinitely while preserving truth conditions, then there is nothing to the claim that states of affairs whose constituents are ultimate objects of reference *make* statements true. For if referents of terms can be shifted at will, then the states of affairs statements are about can be shifted in the same way, so that any number of different states of affairs would make the same statement true, and that would be to evacuate the correspondence notion of *making true* of any intelligible content.[23]

But why replace metaphysical realism with an *epistemic* conception of truth? Putnam did so primarily because he *could* see no other way of bringing together a conception of understanding and a conception of truth and reference in a way that avoided the deep problems he saw in metaphysical realism's use of the distinction between language and its interpretation.

> To adopt a theory of meaning according to which a language whose whole use is specified still lacks something – namely its 'interpretation' – is to accept a problem which can only have crazy solutions ... Either the use already fixes the 'interpretation' or nothing can ... We need, therefore, a standpoint which links use and reference in just the way that the metaphysical realist refuses to do. (Putnam 1983, p. 241)

To get such a standpoint, Putnam did not *reject* the distinction between a language and its interpretation – that is, between use and reference. What he did was change his conception of truth, and hence of reference, in order to bring it in line with his conception of understanding as use.

He continued to hold the view that understanding consists "in the fact that speakers possess (collectively if not individually) an evolving network of verification procedures" (Putnam 1983, p. 22), which are what *constitute* sentences as meaningful. But in order to align his conception of truth with this verificationist conception of understanding, he identified truth itself with verification, not with actual verification but with what would be verified (or warranted) by speakers were they in an optimal epistemic situation.

---

23 This paragraph gives an intuitive account of what Putnam usually puts in model-theoretic terms, for example, in "Realism and Reason" (Putnam 1978, pp. 125–126). The argument is analogous to Frege's 'sling-shot' argument against the correspondence theory.

> A statement is true of a situation just in case it would be correct to use the words of which the statement consists in that way in describing the situation, [which means] that a sufficiently well placed speaker who used the words in that way would be fully warranted in counting the statement as true of that situation. (Putnam 1978, p. 115)

The model here was Dummett's anti-realist conception of truth, although Putnam extended verifiability (beyond what Dummett would) to cover epistemic situations which are so ideal that speakers may not even be *able* to occupy them because they lack the requisite powers of observation or intellectual capacities. The advantage of this extension was that it yielded a notion of verifiability or warrant which was stable over time (what would ideally warrant a statement at one time would do so at any other time).[24]

The conception was not intended as a *definition* of the truth concept; it took our ordinary concept for granted but presumed that truth was a substantive property and then gave an *explanation* of why true statements have the property, namely because their assertion would be warranted under ideal conditions. It was, therefore (like metaphysical realism), a substantive-explanatory conception of truth, though of course it differed decisively in being an epistemic conception.

It was the latter which eliminated the dichotomy between understanding a statement and knowing its truth conditions (in this case *epistemic* truth conditions). Since, on the one hand, to understand a statement in a language is to know (implicitly) what the speakers of that language count as the conditions under which it would be warranted to assert it, and since it is true just in case it would be warranted to assert it under *ideal* conditions, to understand a statement is to know (implicitly) the conditions which, if idealized, would make it true. In other words, to know how to use a statement is inseparable from knowing the conditions under which it would be true (in the epistemic sense), and hence Putnam's claim that "The essence of 'internal realism' is that truth does not transcend use." (Putnam 1978, p. 115)

If truth does not transcend use, then neither does reference: an epistemic conception of truth requires an epistemic conception of reference. The latter aims not to define 'refers', but to explain why a term refers to such and such ob-

---

[24] "I avoided strong anti-realism by identifying a speaker's grasp of the meaning of a statement not with an ability to tell whether the statement is true now, or to tell whether it is true under circumstances the speaker can actually bring about, *as* Dummett does, but with the speaker's possession of abilities that would enable a sufficiently rational speaker to decide whether the statement is true in sufficiently good epistemic circumstances." (Putnam 1994b, p. 462; cf. Putnam 1981, p. 55; Putnam 1983, pp. 3, 85) Internal realism was committed to conceptual relativism, but it rejected any relativism about truth.

jects. The answer, roughly, is that a term, say 'cat', refers to objects X, just in case we are warranted (in the ideal case) in asserting of X's that they are cats. This means that the claim that 'cat' refers to cats is a truism: anyone who understands English – who knows how to use English expressions – knows that 'cat' refers to cats. Indeed, Putnam calls it a tautology (Putnam 1978, p. 128), though it is a tautology that can be understood only by understanding large parts of the language. To understand it, one must understand how English speakers use 'cat' and 'refers to', which in turn requires understanding many other expressions, and that requires knowledge of the conditions under which it is warranted to assert numerous statements of the language.

> We understand 'refers to' *not* by associating the phrase 'refers to' with a 'correspondence', but by learning such assertibility conditions as the following:
>
> (2) 'Cat' refers to an X if and only if X is a cat.
>
> Interpreted as an assertibility condition, what (2) tells us is to assert 'That sentence refers to (contains a word that refers to) cats' when and only when a sentence has been used which contains the word 'cat' or some word W such that one is prepared to assert:
>
> (3) Something is a W if and only if it is a cat.
>
> [On this view of reference] the understanding of our language is through the internalization of assertibility conditions, and not through the learning of truth conditions in the realist sense. (Putnam 1983, p. xv)

For internal realism, therefore, knowledge of the reference of 'cat' comes with knowing how to use statements containing the term, that is, knowing under what conditions it would be warranted to assert statements which involve a referring use of the word 'cat'. If those statements are warranted, then we have referred to cats. It is beside the point to appeal to a meta-theory about the success of language and learning in order to establish what our terms refer to. Metaphysical realists needed such an appeal because of their assumption that there is a determinate and unique collection of objects whose status as ultimate objects of reference is independent of language or reference scheme. But internal realists reject that assumption in favor of the notion that the status of the objects to which terms refer – whether they are abstract or concrete, properties or particulars, individuals or groups – depends on the language to which the terms belong. This means that it is determinate to which objects our terms refer: 'cat' refers to cats because the objects to which 'cat' refers are individuated by the reference scheme of the English speakers whose use of 'cat' determines what the interpretation of the term is.

> A sign that is actually employed in a particular way by a particular community of users can correspond to particular objects within the conceptual scheme of those users ... We cut the world into objects when we introduce one or another conceptual scheme of description. Since the objects and the signs are alike internal to the scheme of description, it is possible to say what matches what. (Putnam 1981, p. 52)

Reference, that is to say, is determinate precisely because it is dependent on a language or scheme of reference. There is a fact of the matter about which objects terms refer to just because there is no (language-independent) fact of the matter about which objects are ultimate or how ultimate objects are individuated.[25]

To illustrate this point, consider ordinary talk about human action. We say that someone is repairing a window or driving from Providence to Boston, each of which is an individual action performed at a given time. Individuating actions in this way has no echo in physics or physiology, which cannot count 'repairing a window', for example, as referring to an individual action but at best as referring to a miscellany of events inside and outside the body (events which in turn cannot be referred to by ordinary action talk). An internal realist would put this point by saying that 'Repairing a window' refers to an action within the reference scheme of ordinary English talk about action (and so is an ultimate object of reference for that scheme) but not within the reference scheme of physics (for which particles and fields are ultimate objects). Putnam put the point by writing that "*What objects does the world consist of?* is a question that it only makes sense to ask *within* a theory or description." (Putnam 1981, p. 49)

All this clearly rules out the metaphysical realist's notion that even the claims of an ideal science might be massively mistaken. Indeed, a further reason why Putnam rejected metaphysical realism was that its use-transcendent notions of truth and reference were not essential to any explanation of the success of our language use, including the reliability of our learning. He argued that we could explain that success in terms of truth and reference even if they are conceived in terms of warranted assertibility. Internal realism, he wrote, "is all the realism we want or need ... Metaphysical realism collapses at just the point where it claims to be distinguishable from Peircean realism – i.e. from the claim that there is an

---

[25] Quine's use of the term 'ontological relativity' to refer to his doctrine of indeterminacy of reference obscures this point. For Quine, there is no fact of the matter about reference at all, even relative to a language, and this is what Putnam objects to. For internal realism there is a fact of the matter about reference, but one which is relative to a language. Although it is relative to our conceptual scheme which objects there are to be referred to by terms from the scheme, we can refer determinately to any of them.

ideal theory ..." (Putnam 1978, p. 130) There were two main reasons for this conclusion.

One was the model-theoretic argument discussed above, which Putnam took to show that any distinction between truth and warranted assertibility was unintelligible. According to that argument, a theory which is warranted in the ideal sense is, like any consistent theory, one whose expressions can be given an interpretation under which all statements come out true, from which it follows that all the statements of an ideally warranted theory must be true. Metaphysical realists will object that such a result is irrelevant because what is required is that the statements of an ideally warranted theory come out true, not under *some* interpretation, but under the correct (intended) interpretation of the theory's expressions. But, Putnam argued, that is an empty objection because, given that the theory is ideal, there are no reasons left to distinguish one interpretation as more correct than another. Any consideration that might bear on choosing the right reference relation has already been incorporated into the ideal theory[26] and hence, "The supposition that even an 'ideal' theory (from a pragmatic point of view) might *really* be false appears to collapse into unintelligibility." (Putnam 1978, p. 126)

The other was his rejection of the argument that because theories of learning entail that we may be wrong even about warranted assertions, we must distinguish truth from warranted assertibility. This argument is correct in presuming that an assertion which is warranted, for instance by direct undistorted perception, may be false, but it does not establish that an assertion may be false even if it belongs to an ideal theory. For from the standpoint of an ideal theory, one could distinguish those assertions warranted by undistorted direct perception which are true from those which are false, because the former but not the latter would belong to the theory which is warranted in the ideal (Peircean) sense. That any process of learning is going to lead to our having beliefs which we take to be warranted but which are false is, as metaphysical realists agree, an *empirical* truth, but that means it must belong to the very theory which enables us in the long run to determine which of the beliefs we took to be warranted were in fact not warranted and hence were false.

There is a final point I want to make about internal realism, which is about the term 'realism'. I have noted the internal realist claim that which objects of reference are ultimate objects and how they are individuated depends on the lan-

---

[26] "An epistemically ideal theory would necessarily have models ... and, in fact, models that satisfied all operational and theoretical constraints (and *thus – were intended models* [my emphasis]). [Hence] metaphysical realism – the view that truth outruns even idealized justification – is incoherent." (Putnam 1983, p. 85)

guage or reference scheme, which implies that reference is relative to a reference scheme and that only within a scheme is reference determinate. None of this implies the ontological claim that the existence of objects depends on a language or reference scheme, and there was no such claim in "Models and Reality" or in "Realism and Reason". But in *Reason, Truth and History*, Putnam wrote that "'Objects' do not exist independently of conceptual schemes" (Putnam 1981, p. 52), and he went on to develop the idea that both metaphysical and internal realists are committed to a correspondence view of truth, the difference being that whereas metaphysical realists holds that truth is "correspondence with mind-independent or discourse-independent 'states of affairs'", internal realists conceive of truth as consisting in its "fitting the world as the world presents itself to some observer or observers ..." (Putnam 1981, p. 50). Where metaphysical realists held that we can think and talk about things as they are independently of our minds, internal realists hold that we cannot, which explains the correspondence between statements and states of affairs: the statements themselves constitute the character of the states of affairs to which they conform.[27]

This idealist way of construing internal realism presumes the intelligibility of a metaphysical distinction between mind-dependent and mind-independent realities. That distinction is, as we saw, fundamental for the metaphysical realist claim that the states of affairs which make statements true and the objects to which terms refer must (except when we are talking about language) be mind-independent. But it is also fundamental for the idealist claim that states of affairs and objects of reference are mind-dependent because they can play no role in truth or reference except as conceptualized by us. If metaphysical realism is the view that we can think and talk about things as they are independently of our minds, this idealist version of internal realism is the view that this is something we cannot do because we can think and talk only about things as concep-

---

[27] I remarked earlier that, on my view, Dummett's conception of truth is really an anti-realist version of *correspondence* truth, since Dummett seems to think of statements as made true by states of affairs, with the proviso that we know we could put ourselves in a position to determine whether they exist. Although Putnam's claim that for internal realism truth is correspondence seems to reflect this way of reading Dummett, Dummett never spoke in an idealist way about the states of affairs that make statements true. I suspect that Putnam's idealism originated in an attempt to bring together the traditional epistemic conception, that statements are made true by other statements, with enough of a correspondence theory to ground EP, the result being the notion that statements which are true in virtue of being warranted satisfy EP because true statements correspond to the world "as the world presents itself to some observer" (Putnam 1981, p. 50).

tualized by us.[28] But if this metaphysical distinction between mind-dependent and mind-independent reality is itself rejected, then we need not choose between a metaphysical realist and an idealist internal realism, and the way is open for a third alternative.

3.3 The Turn to Wittgenstein

Putnam's rejection of internal realism was a more radical change in his point of view than his rejection of metaphysical realism, for he thereby rejected an assumption made by all the traditional views, namely that the concept of truth denotes a substantive property. His present view, 'commonsense realism', transcends both the thesis of correspondence truth and the antithesis of epistemic truth, and it is a view I share. It is not always as clearly developed in his work as I would like, however, and hence my discussion in this section will often veer toward what I think he *ought* to say.

Both metaphysical and internal realism had a verificationist account of understanding, and while the linkage of such an account with a correspondence view of truth was an inessential novelty, verificationism was at the heart of internal realism, and hence to reject the former was to reject the latter. Crucial to Putnam's verificationism was the view that mere sounds (or marks) are constituted as meaningful statements in virtue of the fact that members of a linguistic community have come to count their assertive utterance as correct only under specific conditions which they take to warrant their assertion. For example, the marks 'il pleut' mean (in French) that it is raining because one is warranted in uttering them assertively just when one sees drops of rain, feels water falling, etc. (just when one is warranted in asserting the English marks 'it is raining'). To understand a statement, then, is to know (implicitly) the conditions under which members of one's linguistic community take it to be warranted to assert it, and it was this conception of understanding that Putnam came to reject in principle.[29]

His main objection was that it is not possible to attach conditions of warranted assertibility to mere marks or sounds and thereby constitute them as meaningful statements: only already meaningful statements – not meaningless marks or sounds – can have degrees of warrant or similar conditions of assertibility. Philosophers (like Dummett) are driven to such a mistaken view because

---

[28] In his Dewey Lectures (Putnam 1994b, 448n) Putnam noted his: regret at "having myself spoken of 'mind-dependence' in connection with these issues in *Reason, Truth and History*".
[29] There is a useful discussion of different assertibility conceptions of understanding in 1994a, p. 204 f.

they think, correctly, that an account of understanding must permit public knowledge of what speakers say or mean, but they mistakenly construe that as knowledge accessible to persons regardless of their language, which requires that an account of understanding describe sounds as what anyone can hear, and then add on an account of how states or processes, which are over and above the sounds but also accessible regardless of language, constitute such sounds as meaningful. Putnam rejects such a view: "The use of words in a language game cannot, in most cases, be described without employing the vocabulary of that game or a vocabulary internally related to the vocabulary of that game" (Putnam 1994b, p. 458), which means that language is public, not in the sense that speakers who do not know the language can recognize what is going on, but rather in the sense that anyone who understands the language (and is not deaf) can *hear* it as meaningful.

The use of words in this sense is normative from the start, and hence an account of understanding should not include descriptions of words as mere marks or sounds, nor should it be an account of how "we get from the physics to the semantics" (Searle 1983, p. 27), as Searle puts it, and which is what the functionalist Putnam thought it was. It is Putnam's rejection of functionalism which is the wider context for his rejection of this view of understanding. Functionalism attempts to identify a scientific account of what goes on in the head when we understand with a philosophical account of what it is to understand, and that is a project Putnam now rejects. "The difference between the scientistic and the Wittgensteinian purport of the slogan 'meaning is use' is stark", he wrote in his Dewey Lectures. The former involves a utopian notion of scientific psychology, which at its worst "... lowers the level of philosophical discussion to that of popular 'scientific' journalism" (Putnam 1994b, p. 494).

The latter would say simply that "Understanding is having the abilities that one exercises when and in using language" (Putnam 1994b, p. 459), and it is this non-verificationist notion of understanding which is integral to commonsense realism.

Another way of putting Putnam's objection to internal realism is that he came to see it as no less metaphysical than the metaphysical realism to which it responded. He has almost always used 'metaphysical' as a term of reproach – he used the term 'metaphysical realism' only after giving up the view – but he has used it in different ways.[30] His current use is Wittgenstein's, according to

---

30 Cf. 1983, p. 208: "Metaphysics [is] the enterprise of describing the 'furniture of the world', the 'things in themselves' apart from our conceptual imposition ...", and also p. 227, where he speaks of "the kind of 'absoluteness' the metaphysician aims at".

which no statement is inherently metaphysical; what is metaphysical is the use we make of a statement in a specific context. To use a statement metaphysically is to take a statement which is used to make an intelligible claim (factual, ethical, logical, etc.) in one context and use it in a different context where it fails to make a claim of any kind because the context fails to fix a sense for the statement as used in that context. Strictly speaking, therefore, there are no metaphysical claims, but rather utterances of statements which only give the illusion of making claims.

A primary reason for such illusion is that we take a word which has a use, and hence a meaning (reference), in one context and use it in another context, thinking that we can export its meaning (or reference) to the new context. We think, Wittgenstein wrote, "as if the meaning were an atmosphere accompanying the word, which it carried with it into every kind of application"[31] (Wittgenstein 1958a, § 117). So it is with terms like 'true' or 'understand'; we use them without difficulty in many contexts where their meaning is clear, but as philosophers we are prone to abstract them from such contexts and attempt to theorize about what their essential meaning is independent of any contexts which could fix their sense. Hence Wittgenstein's warning: "When philosophers use a word – 'knowledge', 'being', 'object', 'I', 'proposition', 'name' – and try to grasp the essence of the thing, one must always ask oneself: is the word ever actually used in this way in the language-game which is its original home?" (Wittgenstein 1958a, § 116) Putnam thinks that both metaphysical and internal realists ignore this warning in their accounts of 'true' and 'understand', and that to get an adequate account of them we must bring them "back from their metaphysical to their everyday use"[32] (Wittgenstein 1958a, § 116).

Metaphysical realists were metaphysical in thinking they could make sense out of the notion of truth as a substantive property by speaking of the correspondence between a true statement and a state of affairs, which gives a substantive explanation of why the statement is true. Internal realists responded with another metaphysical theory: what explains why statements are true are the states of affairs which, insofar as they could present themselves (under op-

---

31 I have altered the translation of *Bedeutung* from "sense" to "meaning".
32 This is nothing like the positivist verifiability doctrine of cognitive meaning, for there is no general doctrine about as to when an expression does and does not make sense. The claim that a certain (attempted) use of a statement fails to make sense (that the statement as used in that context fails to have a sense) is one that must be made out in each case; it must be shown that the speaker has failed in context to use a statement to say anything. That can be a difficult and often indirect task. It is a matter of showing that one's linguistic skill (know-how) has failed one, which may require more than saying what has happened. On this point, cf. Conant 1998.

timal conditions) to some observers, would warrant assertion of the statements. Metaphysical realists insisted that the states of affairs which make statements true must be independent of mind or language; internal realists replied that, on the contrary, they are dependent on mind or language. Both were committed to the intelligibility of a metaphysical distinction between mind-independent and mind-dependent reality, and hence to the intelligibility of a context-free, principled distinction between mind and world. While metaphysical and internal realists disagreed about truth, both maintained that it was substantive enough to play an essential role in a causal-explanatory theory of the success of science, a theory which explained, not the specific success of a particular scientific theory but the success of scientific theories generally. Both shared a verificationist theory of understanding, which was metaphysical in trying to give an account of what understanding consisted in by reference to the way in which attaching conditions of assertibility to mere marks or sounds *constituted* them as meaningful expressions.

If both correspondence and epistemic conceptions of truth are rejected, what alternative is left? One ready alternative in the present situation is some version of deflationism. By that I mean any view of truth which asserts that the concept of truth does not denote a substantive property and that there cannot, therefore, be a substantive explanation of what makes a statement true or any substantive role for truth in an explanatory (rather than an interpretive) theory. The fundamental fact about truth is the Equivalence Principle, although it must be added immediately that on any plausible version of deflationism, truth will play a much more complex role than EP taken by itself shows, the reason being that the concept of truth is not redundant or eliminable, as we know from a statement like 'Everything that follows from a true statement is true.' The crucial role of the truth-concept is precisely to permit generalizations like that, which are particularly prominent in philosophy, where we make such statements as 'Skeptics claim that our beliefs might be massively false' or 'Davidson claims that most of our beliefs must be true', statements which we could not make without a concept of truth.

I believe that commonsense realism can be nothing other than a version of deflationism, but Putnam has vehemently maintained that of all the accounts of truth, deflationism is the worst. He gives three main arguments. The first is that deflationism is itself a metaphysical view in that it assumes that truth has no significance if it has no metaphysical content, but having no such content, it is a pointless concept which we should drop. This is Putnam's formulation of his differences with Rorty in the face of Rorty's puzzlement over where they disagree,[33] and I think he is right concerning a number of things Rorty has written, which do show signs of disillusionment stemming from an unsatisfied yearning after metaphysics.

Deflationism need not, however, be rooted in disillusion with attempts at metaphysical theories of truth, and if what it rejects is nothing but "houses of cards" (Wittgenstein 1958a, § 118), then it is not nihilist either. Nor need it be the view of someone who "has bought into a physicalist or phenomenalist, or ... cultural relativist picture of reality"[34] (Putnam 1990, p. 32). We can (and should) be deflationists without being metaphysicians, disillusioned or otherwise, and without being nihilists or cultural relativists. It depends on what the view is, what it rejects and what it accepts, and what the arguments for it are.

Putnam's second argument is that deflationism has a verificationist conception of understanding, which he now takes to be "the most disastrous feature of the antirealist view, the very feature that brings about the loss of the world (and the past)" (Putnam 1994b, p. 500). This objection can be met, of course, by adopting a different conception of understanding, and Putnam has given no arguments why deflationists *must* be verificationists. He is no doubt right that they generally have been, presumably because their main target has been the correspondence theory of truth, and in rejecting that they have also rejected a truth conditions conception of meaning (where the notion of truth conditions is understood in the realist-correspondence sense), concluding, as Putnam himself once did, that verificationism is the only alternative.

But there are other accounts of understanding – Putnam's current view, for example, or Brandom's, or McDowells's or Davidson's for that matter – which are not verificationist and which do not construe understanding a statement as knowing its assertibility conditions *as opposed to* knowing its truth conditions. That kind of contrast arises when philosophers, attempting to give a metaphysical theory about what has to be added to noises or marks to constitute them as meaningful statements for a linguistic community, recognize that it makes no sense to attach correspondence truth conditions to mere noises but think that it does make sense to attach socially agreed on assertibility conditions. The latter, however, makes no more sense than the former: noises cannot be constituted

---

[33] Cf., for example, Putnam 1994a, p. 300 or Conant's introduction (Putnam 1994a) on p. xxiv.
[34] Here is the whole passage: "The only reason that I can think of for denying that truth is a property is that one has bought into a physicalist or phenomenalist, or, in the case of some philosophers; a cultural relativist picture of reality which leaves no room for such a property. Having adopted such a picture, the philosopher feels compelled to say either that there is no such thing as truth, or, more commonly today, to 'save' the word true by offering a disquotational picture."

as meaningful statements no matter what we attach to them. We can, if we wish, describe a warranted assertion in terms of the noises the speaker made, but there is nothing left over which could, as it were, be reattached to constitute those noises as a warranted assertion.

If we recognize that there can be no metaphysical theory about what constitutes noises as meaningful statements, and if we refuse to accept the correspondence theory's attempt to give metaphysical substance to the notion of truth conditions, then we need not *oppose* truth conditions to assertibility conditions. To understand the meaning of a statement is to know what it can be used to assert; and to know what it can be used to assert is to know the conditions under which whatever is asserted would be true. For example, to understand the English statement, 'Neutrinos have mass', is to know that it can be used to assert (in whatever language) that neutrinos have mass, and to know that is to know that it is true if and only if neutrinos have mass. Such understanding presupposes knowing a lot of physics, of course, but what one knows in understanding the statement is just what it can be used to assert.

To take another example: to understand the English statement, 'There is a lot of coffee on the table' is to know that if it is used, in a given context, to assert that there are a lot of coffee bags stacked on the table, then it is true if and only if there are a lot of coffee bags stacked on the table. It is also to know that if, in a different context, it is used to assert that there is a lot of coffee spilled on the table, then it is true if and only if there is a lot of coffee spilled on the table, and so on for other possible uses of the statement. In all these cases, one has to know a great deal to know what assertion is being made in the particular context, but what one knows are the conditions under which the statement, as asserted in that context, would be true.[35]

The third objection to deflationism is that it excludes the possibility of any normative account of truth. In one sense, of course, this is correct: if truth is not a substantive property, it cannot be a normative property. The problem, as Putnam sees it, is that if truth is not a normative property, neither is assertion, judgment, or meaning, which would eliminate normativity from language altogether, which is absurd. "To say that truth is a normative property", he wrote, "is to emphasize that calling statements true and false is evaluating them; and evaluation presupposes standards, among them the laws of logic." He went on, "Our standards of truth are extendable and revisable; they are not a

---

[35] For discussion cf. Essay 2 in Gustafsson and Hertzberg 2002. The point of view is defended at length in Charles Travis, *The Uses of Sense: Wittgenstein's Philosophy of Language* (Travis 1989), a book to which Putnam often refers.

collection of algorithms. But for all that, there are statements that meet them and statements that do not; and that is what makes truth a 'substantive' notion." (Putnam 1992b, p. 436)

Assertion, judgment, and meaning are surely normative notions,[36] but it doesn't follow that truth is, where truth is opposed to *falsity*. 'Truth' is also opposed to *error* (or mistake), but that contrast is distinct from the true-false contrast. The truth-error contrast applies to assertion or judgment (and belief) *as* asserting or judging, not to *what* is asserted or judged considered in abstraction from it being asserted or judged (though of course the latter must be described or identified in terms of *what* is asserted or judged). What is asserted or judged is true or false; asserting and judging are truthful or erroneous, correct or incorrect, right or mistaken.[37]

The contrast between truth and error, applying as it does to assertion and judgment, is explicitly a normative contrast, but the contrast between true and false is not – or so deflationists argue. Normativity is explicit only when statements are asserted or denied, the reason being that there would be nothing wrong with false statements if we never asserted (or accepted) them, just as there would be nothing right with true sentences if we always denied (or rejected) them. I take this to show that although the truth-error contrast is normative, the contrast between true and false is not. We can, therefore, agree with Putnam that "truth is a *normative* property" (Putnam 1992b, p. 436), if that is taken to refer to the truth (correctness) of an asserting or judging, while at the same time accepting the deflationist notion that the truth of *what* is asserted or judged is not normative.

This does not, however, speak to the question of the *ground* or source of the normativity we ascribe to assertions or judgments in evaluating them as correct or incorrect. Defenders of the correspondence theory maintain that its ground must be that *what* is asserted is true, which is a primary reason they reject the deflationist denial that 'true' denotes a substantive property. They maintain that just as there must be something that makes statements true, so there must be something that makes it correct to assert those statements, and that can only be that the statements asserted have the substantive property of correspondence truth.

---

[36] They are normative in some important sense, though not in the way many philosophers think. The topic is complex and I will not pursue it here.

[37] On this see Josiah Royce's article "Error and Truth" (Royce 1951) from the 1913 *Encyclopedia of Religion and Ethics* – interestingly, the only article on truth in this famous old encyclopedia. For some of the complications about that to which the true-false contrast applies, see Essay 2 in Gustafsson and Hertzeberg 2002.

This account of the ground of the normativity of truth is not open to Putnam, of course. At one point he characterized the correspondence theory as holding that "to say a sentence is true is not to make a normative judgment at all: it is just to say that the sentence 'agrees' with something ('the facts') or that it 'corresponds' to something ('a state of affairs')" (Putnam 1992a, p. 78). If this is correct (as I think it is for all but theologically based versions of the correspondence theory), then the normativity of assertion or judgment cannot be grounded on the correspondence truth of what is asserted, since that is non-normative. Moreover, it is implausible to think that, given the diversity of the assertions speakers make, they could all be made correct simply by being instances of the correspondence relation. Hence even if the correspondence theory could be defended against the sort of objections Putnam has made, it would be no help in accounting for the normativity of truth.

Epistemic theories of truth do not argue that the normativity of assertion or judgment is grounded in what is asserted or judged being true; they ground it on a normative notion of what we are warranted in asserting. Their strategy is to define what it is *correct* to assert in terms of what we are warranted to assert under ideal conditions, and then to define truth (as opposed to *falsity*) as what it is correct to assert. This strategy is the converse of the correspondence theory, for it requires defining correct assertion without reference to truth, the reason being that it would be circular to use truth in defining correctness and then to go on and use correctness in defining truth.[38]

Epistemic theories are not subject to the criticism just made of the way the correspondence theory attempts to ground the normativity of assertion or judgment, and I think they are essentially right in grounding that normativity in a normative notion of *warrant* or – which is better – a normative notion of reasons for asserting what we do. Assertion, judgment and belief are normative because they are inseparable from our having, giving, and receiving reasons for what we say and think. But epistemic theories are wrong in defining what it is to be true (or false) in terms of what it is to be correct (or incorrect) to assert something, and hence they are wrong in taking the notion of what it is to be true to be normative. We do not need and we do not want such a normative conception of what it is to be true. If it is true that neutrinos have mass, then they do, whether or not we have good reasons to assert that they do, and we may have the best of reasons to assert that they do even if it is not true that they do.

---

[38] Peirce is an example of this strategy. He characterized *a correct* belief as one which the community of inquirers would settle on in the long run, and *then* identified such a belief with a *true* belief. For Peirce, belief is a nonnative notion not because it aims at what is true; rather what is true is normative because it is what *warranted* belief gets to in the long run.

An adequate deflationist view, therefore, will maintain that the contrast between *truth* and *error* is a non-native contrast, but that it is not grounded in the contrast between *true* and *false* since the latter contrast is neither substantive nor normative. It is rather grounded in the reasons we have for what we assert or believe, and those are both extraordinarily diverse and dependent on the variety of contexts in which assertions and judgments are made and beliefs formed and changed. There are, as Wittgenstein wrote,

> Different kinds of use of what we call 'symbols', 'words', 'sentences'. And this multiplicity is not something fixed, given once for all; but new types of language, new language-games, as we may say, come into existence, and others become obsolete and get forgotten. (Wittgenstein 1958a, § 23)

We may be able to formulate interesting generalizations about our reasons for assertion, judgment, or belief but those generalizations will often be imprecise and apt to mislead, and they will in any case depend for their explanatory force on the instances they generalize over.

It does not follow that the true-false contrast plays no role in the truth-error contrast. Indeed, it plays a crucial *expressive* role in this sense: it is correct to assert that P only if P is true. That P is true, in other words, is a necessary condition for an assertion of P to be correct.[39] But that does not mean that P's being true is itself part of what makes an assertion of P correct, which would return us to a metaphysical conception of truth. What is at work here rather is the role of 'true' in enabling certain generalizations, which, as we have noted, is precisely the role which shows the indispensability of a concept of truth. The general claim that it is correct to assert that P only if P is true, cannot be formulated without the truth concept, but we can formulate instances of it without that concept. For example, the claim, 'it is correct to assert that neutrinos have mass only if it is true that neutrinos have mass', can be reformulated without loss as 'it is correct to assert that neutrinos have mass only if neutrinos have mass'. To generalize that requires the concept of truth, but it does not follow that the generalization refers to some property which makes its instances correct; on the contrary, the content of the generalization is derived wholly from its instances.

The crucial point is that although assertion is normative, its normativity is not grounded in truth (as opposed to falsity). While there must be something substantive which makes an assertion correct (or incorrect), it is not that what

---

39 It is not a sufficient condition because someone may assert P and P may be true, but he may assert it for reasons that are very bad or irrelevant so that his asserting the truth was sheer accident. *What* was asserted was true, but his asserting it did not meet norms of correctness.

is asserted is true (or false), for the latter has no substantive content of its own. Putnam rightly notes that a deflationist conception of truth will have to assume a "suitably 'thick' sense" of assertion and hence must recognize that "asserting is guided by notions of correctness and incorrectness". But he is mistaken in thinking that "the problem of truth reappears when we ask for an account of what it is for an assertion to be correct and what it is for it to be incorrect" (Putnam 1983, p. xiv). Ramsey was right that "the problem is not as to the nature of truth and falsehood, but as to the nature of judgment or assertion" (Ramsey 1990, p. 39)[40] which sets the task of giving an account which makes no use of a substantive truth concept.

It must be admitted that this distinction between the true-false contrast and the trutherror contrast is not as straightforward as all this suggests.[41] The distinction corresponds roughly to the distinction between the sense of an utterance and its force, the true-false contrast applying to the sense of what is uttered and the truth-error contrast applying only to an utterance as having assertive force. But the sense-force distinction is neither unproblematic nor simple. There are no conventions or rules determining the force of an utterance, and hence the distinction between sense and force has to made by discerning many, often complex, facts about the speaker and the context of her utterance. Assertion itself is a complex kind of speech act, which comes in diverse forms, and therefore evaluation of it is complex and multi-faceted. It may be simplistic to think that we can invariably and cleanly separate out from an utterance that aspect (its sense) to which the true-false contrast applies from that aspect (the asserting) to which the truth-error distinction applies, and hence simplistic to characterize the former as non-substantive and the latter as normative.

I agree that it is often difficult to make the distinction in any sharp or even clear way and therefore difficult to distinguish the use of 'true' as governed by EP from its use as governed by normative considerations. Indeed, this may account for the widespread conviction that the true-false contrast must be normative: we might say that in practice it is: But it doesn't *follow* that the distinction is not a useful – indeed necessary – one to make, if for no other reason than that EP applies to true (versus false) but cannot apply to truth (versus error) because the former is not a matter of degree whereas the latter is. But the distinction also helps unmask the pretensions of metaphysical theories both about what makes-true and what makes-correct. What makes an assertion correct is not that what we assert is true in the correspondence sense but that we have adequate reasons

---

[40] "Facts and Propositions", from which this comes, was written in 1927.
[41] This paragraph responds to a criticism pressed by Martin Gustafsson.

for the assertion *and* that we have met the ideal set by EP: it is correct to assert that F only if P is true.

So what, then, is commonsense realism about truth? I think it is a defensible deflationist conception which makes EP the fundamental fact about the truth concept, and that means three things. 1) The concept of truth (as opposed to falsity) does not denote a property with a nature which determines its instances: the generalizations the truth concept permits have no more content than the sum of their instances. 2) There is no substantive account of what makes a statement true. There is an ordinary sense of 'making true' which is unobjectionable – what makes it true that Putnam is so cheerful is his genes, his happy marriage, his good health, and so on – but that is not what defenders of substantive conceptions of truth mean by the notion. 3) Truth has no substantive role to play in explanatory schemes (to say nothing of causal-explanatory schemes), whether they aim to explain the success of inquiry, the meaning of statements, the content of the attitudes, and so on. We can specify what it is to understand a statement (or belief) in terms of its truth conditions, but they play no role explaining what understanding consists in or why thoughts have content.

Because of the fundamental role of EP, commonsense realism will resemble the correspondence theory and may be mistaken for it. If we deflate the correspondence theory in the right way, we get commonsense realism; if we inflate the latter, we may get the correspondence theory. Commonsense realism is like the correspondence theory (and unlike epistemic conceptions) in holding that truth transcends knowledge (or recognition), something which should be seen as an immediate consequence of the Equivalence Principle. As Putnam wrote, speaking of whether Lizzie Borden really did kill her parents with an ax, "the recognition transcendence of truth comes, in this case, to no more than the 'recognition transcendence' of some killings" (Putnam 1949b, p. 511). Furthermore, commonsense realism ought to be like the correspondence theory in making truth univocal. There are not different kinds of truth (as opposed to falsity) but only different ways to justify assertions, different kinds of attitudes we take toward statements, different contexts in which we affirm or deny them, and so on, all of which are compatible with a single concept of truth.[42]

---

[42] I think what I say here is better than Putnam's view as expressed in 1994b, p. 515: "On the one hand, to regard an assertion or a belief or a thought as true or false *is* to regard it as being right or wrong; on the other hand, just what sort of rightness or wrongness is in question varies enormously with the *sort* of discourse. 'Statement', 'true', 'refers', indeed 'belief, 'assertion', 'thought', 'language' ... have a plurality of uses, and new uses are constantly added as new forms of discourse come into existence ..." I think there are a lot of reasons for taking 'true'

This does not mean that the contrast between the correspondence theory of truth and commonsense realism is insignificant. There is a great difference between aiming at a metaphysical theory of a substantive property and trying to understand the role of the concept in our lives. "Giving up on the funny metaphysical somethings does not require us to give up on concepts that, whatever our philosophical convictions, we employ and must employ when we live our lives." (Putnam 1949b, p. 517) This holds as well for reference, which is also a concept commonsense realism should not reject, even while denying that it is a substantive relation and hence construing it in a deflationary way.

Internal realism made a beginning toward a deflationary understanding of reference by maintaining that reference does not transcend use and that the fundamental fact about it is a kind of equivalence principle:

(R) 'Cat' refers to an X if and only if X is a cat. (Or simply: "'Cat' refers to cats.")

But internal realism inflated that principle by taking our understanding of 'R' to consist in knowing the assertibility conditions of 'R', thus construing the truth of 'R', and hence of reference, in epistemic terms. The internal realist conception of reference, therefore, faced the same difficulty as its conception of truth: it rested on a notion of assertibility conditions which are *contrasted* with truth conditions and taken to be specifiable from a neutral point of view by one who need not understand the language.

A consequence of this was that internal realism failed to deal adequately with what Putnam regarded as objectionable about the indeterminacy of reference. Although framed to deal with this, internal realism was developed most fully in *Reason, Truth and History*, which defended the essentially idealist view that reference was determinate because the objects of reference were constituted by the scheme of reference itself. This presupposed a metaphysical distinction between mind-independence and mind-dependence, which Putnam came to see as unintelligible. Moreover, internal realism did not come to terms with the root of the problem of indeterminacy, namely that the truth conditions of a statement, however construed, are not enough to fix the reference of terms.

Commonsense realism recognizes that the key to determinate reference is an adequate conception of understanding and use, namely the one sketched above, which is what Putnam did not have in his internal realist period. The new insight

---

to be univocal and that reasons to the contrary lose their force when 'true' and 'correct' are adequately distinguished.

was that "there is another, fundamentally different, way to conceive of 'use'" (Putnam 1994a, p. 283).

> On this alternative picture, which, I believe, was that of the later Wittgenstein, the use of words in a language game cannot, in general, be described without employing the vocabulary of that very game. If one wants to talk of the use of the statement, 'There is a coffee table in front of me', one has to talk about seeing and feeling coffee tables, among other things. In short, one has to mention perceiving coffee tables.
> The answer to Quine's argument [for indeterminacy] seems to me, then, to be as simple as this: when we use the word 'Tabitha', we can refer to Tabitha and not to the whole cosmos minus Tabitha [that is, to a permutation of the reference scheme], because after all we can see the cat, and pet her, and many other things, and we can hardly see or pet the whole cosmos minus Tabitha. (Putnam 1994a, pp. 283–284)

The crux is to recognize that issues about perception and about reference are at bottom "the same issue, the issue of the relation of thought to the world" and that both require rejecting an 'interface' notion of that relation – one which denies that our capacity to perceive and our capacity to refer "reach all the way to the objects themselves" (Putnam 1994a, pp. 281–282). If we reject the interface notion, then the use of words is thought of, not as an activity which has to be hooked up to the world, but as an activity which, like Wittgenstein's language game, is a "whole, consisting of language and the actions into which it is woven …" (Wittgenstein 1958a, § 7). Language and perception are interwoven[43] and because both involve contact with the objects themselves, there is no place for the permutations and switchings which undermine the determinacy of reference. Reference too is brought back from being "a funny metaphysical something standing behind our talk" to being a concept "we employ and must employ when we live our lives" (Putnam 1994b, p. 571).

I have used Hegelian terms to characterize Putnam's passage from metaphysical realism to internal realism and then to the commonsense realism which supplanted them both. Hegel thought of a synthesis as taking up into itself the best of both thesis and antithesis and hence as being by far the richer view. It may appear that commonsense realism does not fit this description – that it is impoverished compared to the metaphysical richness of the thesis and antithesis from which it grew. This is a common reaction to the Wittgensteinian turn exemplified by Putnam's recent thought. It is thought to be a destructive turn, whose vitality is parasitic on others continuing to do work that those

---

[43] "Our ability to refer is not one ability but a whole complex of abilities, including our perceptual abilities." (Putnam 1994a, p. 289)

who know better can then undermine. It is unlike Hegel's synthesis in being dismissive and impoverished, though it is like it in being arrogant.

This reaction may be understandable, and it surely fits those who, as Wittgenstein noted, have appropriated his results "variously misunderstood, more or less mangled or watered down" and who have therefore used his writing "to spare other people the trouble of thinking" rather than to be stimulated to thoughts of their *own* (Wittgenstein 1958a, Preface). But the reaction does not fit Putnam nor does it fit others who have taken this same turn, provided their work meets three conditions.

First, what is destroyed must, on reflection, not be worth saving – above all because it fails to make intelligible claims. Thus Wittgenstein:

> Where does our investigation get its importance from, since it seems only to destroy everything interesting, that is, all that is great and important? (As it were all the buildings, leaving behind only bits of stone and rubble.) What we are destroying is nothing but houses of cards and we are clearing up the ground of language on which they stand. (Wittgenstein 1958a, § 118)

Putnam has by no means convinced everyone that what has been destroyed is nothing but houses of cards, but he has made the right kind of effort to show that – by examining positions in detail, by showing how they do no explanatory work, by saying how they fail to be intelligible.

Second, it must be manifest in the work that what is being undermined is not the result of stupid, inattentive, or superficial thinking. The illusion of intelligibility is one that grips even the most intelligent, attentive and deep thinkers, and only arrogance or self-deception permits serious philosophers to think that they themselves are not subject to that illusion or to other obsessions which cloud our understanding. Wittgenstein wrote that "The problems arising through a misinterpretation of our forms of language have the character of *depth*. They are deep disquietudes; their roots are as deep in us as the forms of our language and their significance is as great as the importance of our language." (Wittgenstein 1958a, § 111) Philosophy, he said, is a "battle against the bewitchment of our intelligence by means of language" (Wittgenstein 1958a, § 109), a battle he never took himself to have won. Nor did he ever make "the real discovery [which] is the one that makes me capable of stopping doing philosophy when I want to" (Wittgenstein 1958a, § 133). Putnam's work manifests his continuing struggle to break free above all from his own illusions – illusions without which he would not have reached his present point of view.

Finally, philosophical investigation ought to aim at what Wittgenstein called "a perspicuous representation", which produces "just that understanding which consists in 'seeing connections'" (Wittgenstein 1958a, § 122) and which is the best way to think of commonsense realism. Unlike a Hegelian synthesis, a perspicuous representation is not metaphysically richer than the thesis and antithesis out of which it emerges, but that is what one would expect if our task is "to bring words back from their metaphysical to their everyday use" (Wittgenstein 1958a, § 116). Nor is it richer in yielding a more complicated theory of the phenomena, which is again what one would expect if "There must not be anything hypothetical in our considerations." (Wittgenstein 1958a, § 109) But it is richer in the sense of giving us more of what we can expect from philosophy when it aims, not to compete with science, art, or religion, but to have a work of its own: to free us from the philosophical illusions which infect science, art, and religion, as well as philosophy, and to give us intellectual clarity about how our ways of speaking and thinking grow out of and yet determine our lives as human beings.

4 Do We Need Correspondence Truth?

By correspondence truth, I mean a conception of truth which takes 'true' to be (a) a genuine predicate, which (b) denotes a property which a truth bearer possesses (c) in virtue of its relation (correspondence) to what it is about, (d) independently of our knowledge of what it is about. Truth is a property but it is so constituted by a relation as to be itself a kind of relation. It is like being a father, which is a property constituted by a man's fatherhood relation to others.

While this has been the dominant conception of truth from Plato to recent analytic philosophy, my view is that its claims should be rejected and that we should accept the resulting *deflationist* conception of truth. In this chapter, I support that view by arguing that correspondence truth serves no legitimate needs.

On a deflationary view of the kind I have in mind, there is no such thing as a truth property because 'true' is not a predicate, except on a superficial syntactical level, the level, for example, on which 'nobody' (as in 'Nobody passed me on the road') is a singular term. Indeed, 'true' does not affect either the sense or the force of an expression in which it occurs, for it is not used to refer to or characterize anything. 'It is true that Harry is in bed' and 'Harry is in bed' have the same *sense* (involve exactly the same objects and properties) in every context – whether they occur freestanding or embedded in other expressions (for instance, conditionals), whether they are asserted or denied, questioned or commanded. Utterances of them also have the same *force:* to *assert*[1] 'It is true that Harry is in bed' is just to *assert* 'Harry is in bed'. The same holds for every kind of force: to ask if Harry is in bed is also to ask if it is true that Harry is in bed, and so on. We might put the general point by saying that 'true' has no substantive content of its own. The equivalence thesis follows immediately; since 'p is true' has the same substantive content as 'p', 'p is true' is equivalent to 'p'. Hence believing 'p' is equivalent to believing that 'p is true', doubting 'p' is equivalent to doubting that 'p is true', wondering whether 'p' is equivalent to wondering whether 'p is true', and so on.[2]

---

[1] 'Assert', not 'say': to *say* 'It is true that Harry is in bed' is not necessarily to *assert* 'Harry is in bed'.

[2] The equivalence thesis does not entail that sentences must have a truth value. 'Is Harry in bed?' has no truth value, unless it is being used to make an assertion. 'Harry is in bed' has a truth value, *unless* it is being used to give a command (for instance). Declarative sentences are presumed to have truth value because they are presumed to be assertible; if that presumption is mistaken for some reason in some context, then the sentence lacks a truth value in that context. This presumption must be taken for granted in using the equivalence thesis; the thesis does not apply to sentences which do not meet it.

This does not mean that the equivalence thesis tells us all there is to know about truth; if it did, 'true' would be eliminable (redundant), which it is not. Expressions can play an essential role – can express a concept – even if they have no role in referring, predicating, or indicating force. 'Either-or' and 'if-then' are examples, and so is 'exists', which looks like a predicate, but, as Kant pointed out, is not. Like these examples, 'true' is not eliminable, even though it does not express a property or indicate force, and like them, it plays a structural role in sentences. Unlike them, it makes no contribution *of its own* to the sense of sentences in which it occurs because unlike them, it has no substantive content of its own. What, then, is its role and what kind of concept is it?

The deflationist account of truth I favor is the pro-sentential account.[3] It holds that 'true' is an anaphoric expression, that is, one whose role is to articulate (or institute) connections between expressions and which derives (or inherits) its content from an antecedent expression. Pronouns are the most familiar kind of anaphoric expressions: they articulate connections between expressions referring to things or people and inherit their content entirely from antecedent nouns. E.g., in 'John is sick, and he cannot come', 'he' derives its content entirely from the antecedent 'John' and refers only to whomever 'John' refers to. Although 'he' has no content of its own, it is not eliminable, for if we simply said 'John is sick and John cannot come', it might not be clear whether both occurrences of 'John' refer to the same person.

Another case where pronouns are not eliminable is their *quantificational* (or *generalizing*) use, as in 'If a number is prime, it is not divisible by two'. Here 'it' articulates a connection between expressions and derives its content entirely from its antecedent expression, which in this case determines a class, any member of which may be the antecedent of 'it'. Since the members of the class cannot be listed, there is no way of eliminating the 'it'. Pro-nouns generally have this role of connecting expressions, a role which is conceptual and bears on the content of sentences, even though their own content derives only from antecedents.

A pro-sentence is an anaphoric *sentence*, which derives its content, not from an antecedent noun but from an antecedent *sentence*. The pro-sentential account claims that the essential role of 'true' is to enable us to form pro-sentences, which articulate (or institute) connections in our discourse. For example, 'What John said is true' is a pro-sentence; that whole sentence derives its content from an antecedent sentence, namely, one which John uttered earlier. It asserts

---

[3] Developed by Dorothy Grover and first published in the classic paper she wrote with Belnap and Camp (Grover, Camp, and Belnap 1975). For more discussion see Grover 1992.

just what John asserted without repeating it.[4] 'It is true that Harry is in bed' is another example: the whole sentence is a pro-sentence, formed by the use of 'it is true' and deriving its content from the contained sentence ('Harry is in bed').

Many pro-sentences play an inessential role in that they can be eliminated in favor of sentences which do not contain 'true'. 'It is true that Harry is in bed' derives its content from the contained sentence, 'Harry is in bed', and uttering the latter is as good as uttering the former. The same may hold for 'What John said is true': if John said, 'Today is Thursday', we can do without 'is true' by saying, 'John said that today is Thursday and today is Thursday', which suffers only from repetition. But if we do not know exactly what John said but nevertheless want to endorse it, 'is true' is not eliminable. Pro-sentences are ineliminable in quantificational (generalizing) contexts, where we say things like 'An omniscient being believes only what is true'; 'is true' is essential to that sentence because we cannot formulate all the sentences an omniscient being believes. The same holds for sentences like 'All the logical consequences of a true sentence must be true' or 'Not all true sentences in arithmetic are provable'. Such pro-sentences function like pro-nouns of quantification, and they (and the truth expressions which make them possible) are ineliminable for the same reasons.[5]

I shall not spell out the details of an anaphoric account of 'true' nor shall I defend it. I want only to put on the table an account according to which 'true' plays an essential role but not one which is predicative, force-indicating, or involves any substantive content of its own, in order to sharpen the question of whether we need correspondence truth. I shall discuss and criticize four arguments that we do need it.

The first is that correspondence truth is just common sense and its rejection is paradoxical. A deflationary account, it is argued, denies that truth-bearers have

---

[4] Note that 'What John said is true' is a *pro-sentence* which contains a pro-noun ('what'); as a pro sentence, it is the whole sentence which is connected anaphorically with an antecedent sentence, not the pronoun in it. The analysis is not that 'what John said' anaphorically refers to John's earlier utterance and says of it that it is true; that would be to take the anaphoric expression as a *pro-noun*. Rather 'What John said is true' is what anaphorically refers to his earlier utterance; the anaphoric expression is the whole *pro-sentence*. Note too that it is not the presence of 'is true' which makes the utterance assertive; 'What John said was silly' is also assertive. 'Is true' does in this context *endorse* what John said, but it does not do that in many other contexts, for example, 'If what John said is true, then he is in trouble.'

[5] Generalizations of this kind are of particular interest to philosophers, which is one reason why they tend, rightly, to resist claims that 'true' is eliminable or redundant. The burden of this paper, however, is that it is a mistake to think that a notion so indispensable to philosophical reflection must carry a substantive content.

a truth-relation to the world, which is a radical proposal for a *new* concept of truth. Surely, we say such things as the following: 'Whether your assertion about when the train arrives is true *depends on* when the train arrives.' 'If you think Oswald shot Kennedy, your belief *about* that tragedy is true.' Such everyday expressions imply that 'true' denotes a relation between truth-bearers and the world, and to deny it is to cut language and thought off from the world. The response to this is that a deflationary account of truth does not deny such truisms; what it denies are *theories* about them. Every true belief or assertion is related to a correlative state of affairs, namely, the one spelled out in the equivalence thesis. That my assertion that the train arrives at 8 is true if and only if the train arrives at 8 is guaranteed by the equivalence thesis. We might even sum it up by saying that whether my assertion that the train arrives at 8 is true depends on whether the train arrives at 8 – just because the anaphoric conception of truth holds that the content of 'it is true that p' depends on the content of 'p'. But these elaborations of the equivalence thesis do not imply a correspondence theory.

On the anaphoric account, to assert that it is true that the train arrives at 8 is a way of asserting that the train arrives at 8, and hence the truth claim must depend on the claim about when the train arrives, and hence on when the train arrives, since that is what the claim is about. The correspondence theory puts it differently; its view is that to assert that it is true that the train arrives at 8 is to assert (or imply) that the assertion (or proposition) that the train arrives at 8 corresponds to what it is about. That way of putting it goes far beyond the truisms we started with. The different ways these truisms are construed can be illustrated by considering interpretations of Tarski's work on truth. Tarski's 'semantic conception of truth' is best viewed as a formal systematization of a deflationary account of truth, not as a correspondence theory. Tarski gave as the definition of 'true sentence', "satisfied by all sequences" (Tarski 1956, p. 111), which, if we read 'satisfied by' as 'correspond to', would mean that a true sentence *corresponds* to *all* sequences. That is hardly a correspondence theory, for it would mean that all true sentences correspond to the same thing. Davidson, who made this last point, also argued at one time that Tarski's theory can be called a correspondence theory because it sees truth as constituted by a relation between words and the world – not, indeed, a relation between *sentences* and the world, for the reason just mentioned – but a relation between *predicates* and the objects that satisfy them (Davidson 1984). Since a predicate is not satisfied by all objects but only by a specified set, there is room for the claim that satisfaction is a relation between predicates and objects in the world. Given Tarski's definition of truth in terms of satisfaction, there is room for the claim that truth itself is a relation between language and the world. Satisfaction is not, however, the kind of relation needed for a correspondence theory.

Tarski did not define 'satisfaction' by a general formula nor did he specify criteria for its application. He did not say, for example, that what satisfies a predicate is the set of things it is true of (which would be question-begging in a definition of 'true'). All he did was give a list: objects x satisfy (in a given language) predicate 'y' if and only if: (1) 'y' is 'red' and x's are red; (2) 'y' is 'green' and x's are green; (3) 'y' is 'barn' and x's are barns, and so on for every predicate in the language. 'Satisfaction' is 'defined' by such a list, by writing down a name of each predicate and matching with it an expression that denotes a set of objects, and *all* we know of satisfaction for a language is such a list. This means that Tarski does not treat satisfaction as a relation with a nature which constitutes its instances, which truth must be according to the correspondence theory. There is for each predicate a set of objects to which it is related, but the fact that this is merely set out in a *list* shows that for a predicate to be satisfied by a set of objects does not require that satisfaction be a relation which determines its instances. Indeed, it is rather the other way around: the instances determine the relation because there is nothing more to satisfaction than the pairs of predicates and objects in the list for a given language.[6]

Hartry Field has argued that on this interpretation, Tarski fails to realize his goal of reducing semantic notions to non-semantic ones (Field 1972). Field wants to make a correspondence theory out of Tarski's results and then show that correspondence is a physical relation on the basis of satisfaction being physical. But that requires treating satisfaction as a constitutive relation, which Tarski didn't do. If we take seriously a deflationary approach, we can see how Tarski reduced semantic notions to non-semantic ones: he reduced truth to satisfaction, and

---

[6] Quine explains this point very elegantly in Quine 1995, pp. 65 ff. My claim that Tarski does not treat satisfaction – or truth – as a relation with a nature which constitutes its instances is a useful way of saying that he does not treat 'true' as designating a property. It undermines the objection that 'true' must designate a property since every set of objects determines a property, and so the set of true sentences must determine a truth property. That objection can be granted (assuming it is not paradoxical to speak of the set of true sentences) since properties in that sense come free, and any set of sentences will have an infinite number. In the sense of property in which *having been uttered in Helsinki in December* or *containing the letter 'n'* are properties of sets of sentences, a deflationist conception can grant that truth is a property. But that is not relevant to what a deflationist conception denies (and what a correspondence theory affirms), namely, that truth is a property constituted by the correspondence relation and which constitutes as true any sentence which is true.

then defined 'satisfaction' by a list which correlated names of predicates with names of sequences of objects, none of which are semantical notions.[7]

The second argument that we need correspondence truth is that the concept of truth has to be used to explain various things, which is not possible if we accept a deflationary account like the anaphoric one. One version holds that we need correspondence truth to explain why if we act on true beliefs, we get what we want much more often than if we act on false beliefs. The claim that truth furthers success has been challenged, but that isn't necessary to undermine the need for correspondence truth. Say that the reason I have success in the stock market is because I have true beliefs about the profitability of companies like GE or MCI. One can say as well that the reason for my success is because (a) I believed that GE would be profitable and GE was profitable, (b) I believed that MCI would be profitable and MCI was profitable, and so on. To avoid listing the beliefs, we can use 'true' to formulate generalizations about them (use it 'quantificationally'), which is just what the anaphoric conception takes to be a central role for the concept. We need 'true' to make a generalization about why I am successful but that doesn't require that it be a predicate.

Another version of the argument is that we need a concept of truth to give an explanation of the meaning of sentences or the content of thoughts. "What [our thoughts] are about", writes Nagel, "depends ... on what has to be referred to in any explanation of what makes them true." (Nagel 1986, p. 69) But only correspondence truth gives us the explanatory kind of truth conditions needed here. It is correct that an anaphoric conception of truth does not allow for such an explanatory use of truth conditions, for it holds that the role of 'true' is to form pro-sentences, which derive their content only from antecedents. These antecedents cannot (on pain of infinite regress) all be pro-sentences, and those which are not must have their content explained without reference to a concept of truth, the reason being that we cannot use a concept of truth (or of truth conditions) to explain content, if the concept of truth requires antecedents which already have content. To put the point in other words: truth conditions cannot account for the content of sentences generally since there are no truth conditions unless there are already sentences with content. It doesn't follow that *understanding* a sentence cannot be characterized as understanding its truth conditions, for, given the equivalence thesis, to understand p is to understand what it is for p to be true, that is, to understand the truth conditions

---

[7] There are, that is, no semantical terms in the list following the 'if and only if', which is the definition of 'satisfies' – e.g., 'name' is not in the definition (only the names of predicates and objects).

of *p*. But this concept of truth conditions has nothing to do with correspondence truth; it does not refer to what would make a sentence true, to the property whereby a sentence would be made true, or to the state of affairs we have to grasp to understand a sentence. Rather, to understand the truth conditions of a sentence is to understand what it could be used to assert, hence to understand its assertible content, the content it has even when not being used assertively but with the force of a question, a request, and so on.

The question remains whether we need correspondence truth to explain meaning and content. It must be noted that this is not the same as asking whether we can do without notions of meaning or content to explain language or intentional behavior generally.[8] To think it is the same is to assume that only correspondence truth conditions can yield an acceptable notion of meaning and content. But there are lots of other ways to develop such an account. Peirce's definition of belief, for example, makes no use of a concept of truth. Coherentists always define judgment without reference to truth. Wittgenstein, of course, famously characterized meaning in terms of use. Sellars gave an account of meaning in terms of the inferential powers of sentences plus language-entry and language-exit transitions. While Davidson appeals to the notion of truth in his theory of meaning and attacks a deflationary conception, his theory of meaning makes no use of correspondence truth as a relation which constitutes a truth property. On his view, meaning is essentially a matter of inferential connections among sentences, and the point of a theory of meaning is to articulate these connections recursively.

The third argument that we need correspondence truth is that truth is the sort of thing which must be explained: there must be something which makes a true belief (or assertion) true, something in virtue of which it is true. Correspondence truth can be explained in this sense, but truth on the deflationary conception cannot, for there is nothing to explain. Russell once wrote in defense of the correspondence theory that if truth is not "a property wholly dependent on the relation of the beliefs to outside things", then it would have to be an intrinsic property, in which case "we could discover whether a belief was true just by attending to the belief itself" (Russell 1912, p. 123 – he is criticizing a view Moore once held). Russell's point is a truism in recent analytic philosophy. Here is Dummett: "The correspondence theory expresses one important feature of the concept of truth which is not expressed by [the equivalence thesis] ... that a statement is true only if there is something *in virtue of which* it is true (emphasis in original)." (Dummett 1964, p. 106) The alternatives are that 'true' denotes a prop-

---

8 As is claimed by 'eliminativists' in the philosophy of mind.

erty for which there is no explanation, so that truth is arbitrary, which is absurd, or that it is a property intrinsic to the belief, which might hold for necessary truth but surely not for contingent.

From the point of view of a deflationary account, however, this argument simply begs the question, for it assumes that truth is a property. If 'true' denotes a property, then there *must* be something which makes a belief true rather than false, for the alternatives – that the property is arbitrary or intrinsic – are unacceptable. But if truth is not a property, then it is question-begging to require an explanation why a belief has it. There can be nothing in virtue of which a belief has the truth property if 'true' does not function as a property-ascribing predicate. The anaphoric account holds both that 'true' has an essential role and that there can be nothing which makes a belief true. Even critics of the correspondence theory find this difficult to accept, for they worry that something essential is missing if we just *drop* the making-true idea. The worry should be taken seriously, and to do that we cannot simply suppress the question of what makes a belief true; we have to reformulate it in a way consistent with the denial that 'true' denotes a property. To do so, we should attend not only to the distinction between the true and the false to what makes a belief true *rather than false* – for the distinction between *p*'s being true and *p*'s being false is, on a deflationary account, just the distinction between *p* and not *p*, and what worries us here is not how to explain negation. We should also attend to the distinction between *correct* and *incorrect* belief (or assertion), that is, to the distinction between *true* and *erroneous* (or *mistaken*) belief – and hence to what makes a belief true *rather than erroneous*. Whereas the distinction between the true and the false applies to *what is believed* (asserted), the distinction between the true and the erroneous (between truth and error) applies to *our believing* (or asserting)[9] and it is this distinction which is the real source of the worry that a deflationary conception of truth leaves out something essential in rejecting the notion of making-true.

The worry persists because of three assumptions. The first is that there must be something in virtue of which a belief is *correct* – something which *makes* a belief true rather than erroneous. The second is that what makes a belief (our believing something) *correct* must include that what is believed is true, what makes it incorrect (erroneous) must include that what is believed is false.[10]

---

9 This point might be put by saying 'true' is ambiguous in that it expresses one concept in a context where it is contrasted with falsity and another in a context where it is contrasted with error. I argue below that these two concepts are necessarily connected.
10 For an assertion to be correct, more is required than that what is uttered be true, for even madmen may utter what is true without having made a correct assertion if their madness pre-

The third is that the second assumption *requires* a non-deflationary conception of truth, in particular, a correspondence conception. Together these assumptions amount to the claim that since there must be something in virtue of which a belief is true *rather than erroneous*, there must also be something in virtue of which a belief is true *rather than false*. That is the claim that should be rejected – we don't need a concept of making-true in order to have a concept of making-correct – but that requires rejecting at least one of these three assumptions.[11] The first should not be rejected; the distinction between correct and incorrect belief is substantive and normative, and hence there must be something which makes a belief correct rather than incorrect. Nor should the second. The concepts of correct and incorrect (of truth and error) must not be confused with the concepts of truth and falsity, but they are necessarily connected in that what makes a belief (assertion) correct must include that what is believed (asserted) is 'true', and what makes it incorrect must include that what is believed (asserted) is false.[12] To believe truly rather than erroneously requires believing what is true rather than what is false. It is the third assumption which is problematic, namely, that a deflationist conception of truth can play no role in accounting for the distinction between correct and incorrect belief.

This brings us to the final argument that we need correspondence truth. Defenders of the correspondence theory claim that the distinction between truth and error *must* be made in terms of correspondence truth. Since that distinction is substantive, it must, they argue, be defined in terms of truth understood as having a substantive content of its own. I reject that claim, first, because using correspondence truth to define the distinction raises more problems than it solves and, second, because an acceptable account of the distinction can be given in terms of a deflationist (e.g., anaphoric) conception of truth. I shall gesture briefly at only one problem raised by the use of correspondence truth in this context. If correctness is defined in terms of correspondence truth, then reasons for thinking a belief is *justified* will not be reasons for thinking the belief is *correct*, unless they are also reasons for thinking the belief is true in the correspondence sense. Typical reasons for thinking a belief is justified include its explanatory power, simplicity, congruence with other beliefs, accept-

---

vents their utterance from being an assertion at all. An analogous point can be made about beliefs: a madman may say he believes such and such a true claim but it does not follow that he has a correct belief: he would not have a correct belief if his madness has undermined his capacity for having genuine beliefs.

11 The points quoted above from Russell and Dummett, while they do not apply to the true-false distinction, do apply to the truth-error distinction.

12 Or at least not true (if the sentence is not assertible in the context).

ance by the best authorities, etc. But none of these is a reason for thinking a belief is true in the correspondence sense,[13] and hence, since correct belief requires correspondence truth, none is a reason for thinking the belief is correct. The result is an unacceptable gap between a belief being justified and its being correct to believe it. To overcome the gap, it must be maintained that the correspondence truth of a belief is *itself* a reason for thinking we are *justified* in the belief since only such a reason would also be a reason for thinking the belief is correct. But the idea of a belief whose correspondence truth can itself be a reason for our believing it commits us to truths which self-evidently correspond to the world, which is a foundationalist thesis we should reject.

If correspondence truth (without foundationalism) is not adequate to distinguish correct from incorrect belief, must we turn to a deflationary conception? A possibility I have not discussed, which I shall mention briefly, is *epistemic* conceptions of truth – the coherence theory, pragmatism, contemporary anti-realism – substantive conceptions which are distinguished by their defining *true* (versus false) in terms of *correctness* (rather than the other way around): a true belief is just one it would be correct to believe. These normative conceptions of truth eliminate because, given that truth is what it would be correct to believe, they are free to take the gap the correspondence theory opens up between justification and correctness because, given that truth is what it would be correct to believe, they are free to take as a criterion of correctness ideal justification. Clearly there need be no *gap* between justification and ideal justification: our being justified in believing '*p*' is *a* good reason for thinking we may be ideally justified in believing it.

The difficulty with using an epistemic conception of truth to distinguish correct from incorrect belief is that it trivializes the second assumption mentioned above, namely, that what makes a belief correct must include that what is believed is true. This is so because on the epistemic claim that a true belief is one it would be correct to believe, the assumption reduces to the notion that what makes a belief correct is that it is one it would be correct to believe, which is entirely empty. That leaves the concept of truth understood anaphorically (or in some other deflationary sense) as the only one we can use in distinguishing correct from incorrect belief and still preserve the claim that what makes a belief correct must include that what is believed is true. Bur perhaps the concept of truth is not adequate. Perhaps we must characterize the cor-

---

[13] The arguments clearly needed here are left out for lack of space. There is surely no *direct* connection between these factors and correspondence truth; the connection would require extensive epistemological and metaphysical commitments, all of which I regard as dubious.

rect-incorrect distinction entirely without the concept of truth, or take the route of rejecting the concept of correctness altogether and get along only with concepts of *true* and *justified* belief.[14] What makes these alternatives seem attractive is the thought that if one uses truth understood in a deflationary sense in characterizing the correct-incorrect distinction, then the latter can be neither substantive nor normative; consequently, the notion of what makes a belief correct will be as empty as the notion of what makes a belief true. But the thought should be resisted. Although on a deflationary conception, truth is neither substantive nor normative, *belief* is (and so is *assertion*), and that accounts for the substantive and normative character of the distinction between correct and incorrect belief (or assertion).

Truth understood in a deflationary sense cannot be used to characterize or explain belief or assertion, and so another concept – a normative one, like inferential role – must play the key role in characterizing and explaining them.[15] As a result, they are construed as inescapably normative.[16] But it is not truth which makes belief and assertion normative, nor is it what makes the distinction between correct and incorrect belief a normative distinction. What the concept of truth does is *mark* the presence of what is necessary for a belief (or assertion) to be correct. It does this, not by designating a truth relation in which the belief stands – there is no such thing – but by connecting in discourse the (content of the) belief with the particular factors which make that belief *correct*. That is why we can say that what makes a belief correct must include the truth of what is believed. What lies behind this is the crucial point that on an anaphoric conception, the really significant role for a truth concept is to link up discourse so as to enable certain kinds of generalization. If we are content (and if it is possible) to spell out the *instances* of a generalization in a given context, we do not need the truth concept in that context. Thus the claims being considered here – it is correct to believe '*p*' only if '*p*' is true, and '*p*' being true must be a part of what makes the belief that '*p*' is correct involve a generalization, and *that* is why 'is

---

[14] Epistemic conceptions of truth illustrate both alternatives. Peirce defined correct belief without any reference to truth, as what the community of inquirers would settle on in the long run (which he *then* used to define truth). Many relativists simply do away with correctness in favor of justification, arguing that since justification is relative, so is truth.

[15] For discussions of this point (and much else related to this paper), see Brandom's 1994, esp. chapter 5.

[16] Much more so than when they are characterized in terms of correspondence truth: believing '*p*' is accepting '*p*' as true; asserting '*p*' is uttering it so as to show one intends it to be taken as true. Since correspondence truth may not be construed as normative at all (as it is not by physicalists like Field), the characterization may leave the correct-incorrect distinction without its normative character.

true' turns up in them. If we spell out the instances of the generalization, we do not need to use a truth locution. The following, for example, says all we have to say about the correctness of the beliefs involved: It is correct to believe that today is Thursday only if today is Thursday, and today's being Thursday must be part of what makes that belief correct. It is correct to believe that Harry is in bed only if Harry is in bed, and Harry's being in bed must be part of what makes that belief correct. The concept of correct belief in those sentences is normative, and what the instances of the truth generalization do is show that a necessary condition for satisfying the particular norms for the beliefs in question is that the world is a particular way. The concept of truth simply enables us to say that in a general way; it does not enable us to ascribe any properties or relations other than the ones there already are in the world.

5 Making True

In an article in the *Routledge Encyclopedia of Philosophy*, Michael Tye discusses the 'adverbial theory' of mental states.

> According to the adverbial theorist, there are no pains, itches or visual images, conceived of as objects people have. Instead to have a terrible itch is just to itch terribly, to have a throbbing pain is to hurt … in a throbbing manner … Now the problem for physicalism supposedly disappears. There are no phenomenal *objects* as such, and so there is no question of trying to accommodate their necessary privacy and ownership in the physical world. (Tye 1998, p. 315)

Whether such physicalism about mental states is acceptable turns, as Tye sees it, on what it is that *makes true* the things we say about our pains, itches, or visual images. "If there are no phenomenal objects, then just what is it that makes phenomenal talk true? If, when I have a terrible itch, it is really true that I itch terribly, then what exactly is it about me which *makes* this true?" (Tye 1998, p. 315)

The notion that such philosophical issues can be resolved by asking about various statements what makes them true ("in virtue of what they are true") is a commonplace in recent analytic philosophy and has led to a flourishing revival of metaphysical theories about the nature of this and that. Many more instances of this use of making true as a philosophical tool could be cited but I will mention only one, namely John Searle's use of it in his book, *The Construction of Social Reality*. "My method of investigation is to examine the structure of the facts that make our statements true and to which they correspond when they are true." (Searle 1995, p. 2) This book, he writes, "investigates the status of the facts in virtue of which our statements about social reality are true" (Searle 1995, p. 199).[1]

This sense of making true is supposed to denote a relation between facts, understood as states of affairs in the world, and what facts make true. The latter are construed in different ways, as sentences, assertions, beliefs, propositional contents, and so on, but since it won't matter for my argument how they are construed, I will use the term 'statements', which is conveniently ambiguous between declarative sentences, assertions, the contents of assertions or beliefs, and so on. It does matter how 'fact' is construed, and I will come to that, but let us first consider the making-true relation itself.

---

[1] An interesting (complex though confused) instance which I will not discuss is Dennett's early book *Content and Consciousness* (Dennett 1969).

There are (at least) two philosophically relevant contexts in which making true is not problematic. One is *causal-explanatory*. We claim, for example, that what makes it true that Mars is so cold is that it is far from the sun, or that what makes it true that John is depressed is that he has lost both his job and his wife. The other is *logical*, where what makes a statement true is some other statement(s). An example is a truth table, like the table for disjunction, which displays how any statement of the form 'p ∨ q' is made true by either 'p' or 'q' being true.[2] Neither of these sense of making-true, however, is the notion which philosophers use to investigate the nature of mental states or social reality. That sense – the 'philosophical sense' – is supposed to denote an explanatory relation between statements and facts, whereas the causal-explanatory sense denotes a relation between facts and other facts, and the logical sense denotes a relation between statements and other statements. The philosophical sense is supposed to explain why a statement is true, but it relates the wrong terms to be explanatory in either a causal or a logical sense.

The distinctive sense in which making true is supposed to be explanatory is important for philosophers like Tye and Searle because, on their view, it makes it possible to investigate the nature of mental states or social reality simply by reflecting on the true statements we make about them. They maintain that if these statements are true, they are made true by facts, and hence the structure of the facts which make them true will be manifest in the structure of the statements they make true. This opens up a uniquely philosophical mode of investigation, which asks not what statements are true, what the evidence for them is, or how they are logically related, but what is the structure of the facts which make them true. Such investigation is intended to bear on such metaphysical questions as how mental states can exist in a purely physical world (Tye) or how there can be social phenomena like money, property or marriage "in a world that consists of physical particles in fields of force" (Searle 1995, p. xi). It is an investigation which proceeds from the structure of language (or thought) to the structure of facts, thus restoring legitimacy to the traditional task of metaphysics as the quest for knowledge of the structure of reality based wholly on reflection on the structure of language and thought.

---

[2] This is the original notion of 'truth condition', introduced by Wittgenstein in the *Tractatus*, which referred to the truth conditions *only* of complex propositions which (unlike elementary propositions) were made true by logical relations to other propositions. The *Tractatus* (cf. 4.41 and 4.431) referred to the truth *possibilities* of elementary propositions not to their truth conditions. Russell shared this sharp distinction between the truth of elementary and the truth of complex propositions, though he took 'elementary' epistemologically.

The philosophical sense of making true derives from the correspondence theory of truth, whose many versions are united in taking a statement to be true *because* it adequately represents some feature of the world. What gives the correspondence theory its distinctive stance is the emphasis it puts on the 'because', which it takes to be explanatory: adequate representation *explains* why a statement is true. Versions of the theory differ in the way they spell out the notion of adequate representation, in particular how they spell out what it is for a statement to represent some particular feature of the world. This is essential because while any statement adequately represents some feature or other, to be true it must adequately represent that feature it is about – of which it is a representation.

Earlier versions of the theory took statements to represent *things* of various kinds: statements were true because they adequately represented the things they were about. In this century the notion developed that statements were better thought of as representing *states of affairs*,[3] and thus adequate representation became *correspondence* between statements and the states of affairs they represented or were about. This calls for a notion of what it is for a statement (whether true or false) to represent a state of affairs in such a way that if it corresponds to the state of affairs it represents it is true, and if it does not correspond to that state of affairs, it is false. This call is met by the notion of *truth conditions*, taken not as involving logical relations between statements and statements, but as involving a relation between statements and what they would correspond to if they were true – the conditions under which they would be true. The idea was that statements, whether true or false, represent the conditions under which they *would* be true.

The notion of *fact* comes into the picture as denoting the state of affairs which a *true* statement not only represents but to which it corresponds.[4] Making true is the reciprocal of correspond – a statement which corresponds to a fact is made true by the fact –, and both notions refer to the sense in which facts are supposed to explain why statements are true.

It is crucial to note how the correspondence theory construes the notion of truth conditions. The point of that notion is to use the concept of truth to specify what a statement represents, the thought being that statements, but not terms or

---

3 This was due largely to Frege, who dropped the subject-predicate form in favor of argument-function. As Hans Sluga put it in his book about Frege: "'All men are mortal' is not a statement about all men, but one about the function 'if a is a man then a is mortal', saying of it that it is a fact whatever we substitute for 'a'." (Sluga 1980, p. 87)

4 A complicated story can be told about this, which has been told very well by Arthur Prior (Prior 1967).

concepts, can be true. False statements also represent, however, and hence the notion of a truth *condition:* a statement, true or false, represents the conditions under which it would be true. What this amounts to depends, however, on the conception of truth involved. In the case of the correspondence theory, truth conditions are not merely the conditions under which a statement would be true – since such conditions need play no role in explaining *why* a statement is true – but are the facts whose existence would make it true.

There is general agreement, at least nominally, that any adequate conception of truth must conform to what I will call the *equivalence principle* (henceforth EP), according to which any instance of the following schema is true ('iff' means 'if and only if'):

S is true iff p

where for 'S' we put some specification of a statement and for 'p' we put the statement itself or a statement equivalent to it (for example, a translation). One instance of the schema is the statement Tarski made famous as the paradigm of a T-sentence:

'Snow is white' is true iff snow is white.

Another instance is this:

'John has a pain' is true iff John has a pain.

The statement 'It is true that snow is white iff snow is white' is not strictly speaking an instance of the schema but I will count it, along with similar paraphrases, as an expression of EP.

By EP I mean something much stronger than Tarskian T-sentences, for those are material biconditionals, hence true just in case the statements which flank the iff have the same truth value (so that "Snow is white' is true iff coal is black' is true). Since an adequate conception of truth must conform to EP, so must an adequate conception of truth *conditions* (since a truth condition just is a condition for truth), and that requires something stronger than a material biconditional. The latter might specify the conditions under which a statement is *true* but it cannot specify the conditions under which it *would be* true since the truth value of a biconditional depends on the *actual* truth value of its constituents. The content of EP, that is to say, is not simply that it is true that snow is white iff snow is white; its content is that it would be true that snow is white iff snow were white (or to take an equally legitimate example: it would be true that snow is black iff snow were black).⁵ That is what EP intends as a criterion of adequacy for a conception of truth.

If we consider T-sentences not in isolation but in the context of Tarski's truth theory, they also function as specifying truth *conditions*. For although a T-sentence is a material biconditional, Tarski required that the statement used on the right hand side (henceforth RHS) must either be the statement referred to on the left hand side (LHS) or a translation of it, and this rules out deviant cases ("Snow is white' is true iff coal is black') while admitting only correct specifications of truth conditions. If we generalize beyond formal languages, we can say that what Tarski required of a T-sentence expresses the essential point of EP: the same words, or words with the same meaning, must be used to specify what is true (on the RHS) and the conditions under which it is true (on the LHS).

Another reason for EP is that it is required for any coherent truth conditions account of what it is for a statement to represent a state of affairs. To know what state of affairs a statement represents is just to understand it. Thus English speakers know that 'Snow is white' represents snow as white just by understanding English. On the truth conditions account, a statement represents the conditions under which it would be true, which means that any speaker who understands a statement also knows the conditions under which it would be true. To make sense of that idea we require EP, for only its claim that it is true that to understand the one is to understand the other.

Finally, EP is essential because what distinguishes the conditions for truth from other kind of conditions is that the former exemplify EP whereas the latter do not. Take, for example, the conditions for winning a 1500 meter foot race, which we could express (incompletely) in terms of a biconditional something like this:

> S is a winner of a 1500 meter race iff S starts when the other runners do, keeps in the lane, pushes no competitors, and finishes before the others.

This exemplifies nothing like EP because the RHS must be different from the LHS to specify in any intelligible way the conditions for winning a race. This is not so for truth conditions, however, which must be spelled out in this way:

> It is true that S is a winner of a 1500 meter race iff S is a winner of a 1500 meter race.

---

5 Perhaps the point should be made by saying that 'It is true that snow is white is true iff snow is white' must be law-like and hence support counterfactuals.

What distinguishes 'it is true that' from other expressions is precisely that the biconditionals in which it figures exemplify EP; if they do not, then they are specifying the conditions for something other than truth.

I come now to the central and motivating thesis of this paper: because EP is fundamental to any adequate conception of truth, there is no notion of making true which can justify any philosophically useful inferences from the structure of statements to the structure of facts. Whatever justification there may be for a distinctively philosophical investigation into the structure of facts, it cannot be by appeal to a conception of truth, for an adequate conception rules out any notion of making true which grounds claims about the structure of facts which go beyond EP itself. That is to say, EP allows us to infer, for example: from 'It is true that John is in pain' to 'John is in pain' but not (as the adverbial theory of mental states would have it) to 'John is feeling painly', for the latter is not licensed by EP. Call the RHS a description of the fact correlative to the true statement: my thesis is that a conception of truth justifies no description of a fact correlative to a true statement which is not an instance of EP.

This thesis undermines the use of making true in philosophical investigation because such investigation bases its conclusions about the structure of facts on analysis of the structure of true statements. The only possible justification for doing that is that there is a conceptual connection – an internal connection, if you will – between a true statement and the correlative fact. I agree that there is such a connection – it is implicit in the truth conditions account of what a statement represents – but since that account rests on EP, so does the very notion of a conceptual (or internal) connection between statement and fact. Indeed, the fundamental point of EP is to articulate the internal connection between true statements and facts.

But if the only justification for inferences from the structure of true statements to the structure of facts is EP, then philosophical investigations into the structure of the facts which make statements true are pointless. To have a point, such investigations must assume that facts are complex objects whose structural features have to be discovered and articulated by philosophers skilled in conceptual analysis. Whatever structural features facts may have, however, cannot be discovered or articulated by any appeal to making true, for there is no legitimate notion of making true which goes beyond EP, and EP yields only truisms about the structure of facts. It permits the claim that 'it is true that John has a pain iff John has a pain' but not the claim that 'it is true that John has a pain iff John is feeling painly'.

It must be admitted immediately that EP does not always require that the statement referred to on the LHS be the same as the statement used on the RHS. The latter can, of course, be a translation of the former as in:

> 'Schnee ist weiss' is true iff snow is white.

In the case of indexicals we need to paraphrase in order to express truth conditions in a relatively context-free way. It is legitimate to express the truth conditions of 'I am ill' simply by the statement that I am ill, but only the person who says 'I am ill' can express the conditions in that way. Hence a less context-bound expression is useful:

> 'I am ill' is true iff the person speaking is ill.

Indeed, some kind of paraphrase will be the general rule for statements in ordinary language since they typically have context-bound truth conditions.[6]

Paraphrases aimed at making the expression of truth conditions less contextbound do not, however, go beyond EP, but are rather governed by the intent to keep it intact. For these paraphrases aim not at any kind of analysis but at formulating a statement whose utterance by speakers in general would express what an utterance of the LHS by a particular speaker expresses. Doing that is useful for various purposes but it has no significance for analyzing the structure of truth conditions or facts; its utility is semantical, not metaphysical.

This objection to making-true as a philosophical tool invites a number of responses, of which I want to discuss two, one made by John Searle and one which uses Davidson's account of truth conditions but which Davidson himself would reject. The latter response is an extension of the point just discussed about how EP may require paraphrases of the LHS in order to give adequate expression of a statement's truth conditions. Davidson has a famous argument about how articulation of the truth conditions of certain statements about change shows that if those statements are true, then we are committed to the existence of events as particulars rather than as properties or states of affairs.

> If I am right, we cannot give a satisfactory account of the semantics of certain sentences without recognizing that if any of those sentences are true, there must exist such things as events and actions. Given this much, a study of event sentences will show a great deal about what we assume to be true concerning events. (Davidson 2001a, p. 146)

This argument is in part responsible for the proliferation of the use of making-true as a philosophical tool. Tye's discussion of the adverbial theory of mental states, for example shows clear evidence that he has been influenced by David-

---

6 Since the RHS must also be in ordinary language, it follows that such paraphrase will seldom result in a completely context-free expression of truth conditions.

son's discussion of the logical form of event statements, which he takes to involve an appeal from the structure of such statements to the structure of the facts which make them true.

Davidson's work, however, when properly understood, not only lends no support to using making-true in this way but actually rules it out. In his early writings, he did say he had a correspondence theory of truth but it was, at best, an eccentric one, for his reason for calling it a correspondence theory was that it involved a satisfaction relation between terms and objects which was posited only to enable derivation of truth conditions, where the latter were explicitly said to exclude any correspondence relation between statements and facts. Davidson appealed to Fregean considerations (in what has come to be known as the 'slingshot argument') to show that if a true statement corresponded to any fact, it must correspond in the same sense to every fact, which clearly excluded any making-true relation usable as a philosophical tool.

Davidson's argument that there must be events if certain statements about change are true is tied up with his distinctive way of specifying truth conditions as part of a theory of meaning for a language. The theory uses Tarski's theory of truth and keeps the requirement that an adequate theory must entail a T-sentence for every sentence in the language. But unlike Tarski, he cannot specify a T-sentence by requiring that the sentence on the RHS either be or be a translation of the one referred to on the LHS because a theory of meaning cannot *assume* but must rather show that the RHS and the LHS meet such a requirement. That, however, raises the problem of deviant T-sentences, which (like "Snow is white' is true if and only if coal is black') are true but cannot be taken to specify truth conditions and cannot be ruled out by appeal to translation. Davidson argues that deviant T-sentences can be ruled out by requiring of a theory of meaning that every T-sentence be a logical consequence of axioms which both specify satisfaction conditions of the basic terms in a language and which entail true T-sentences for every sentence. Davidson insists, for various reasons, that such a theory of meaning should not use a logic stronger than first order predicate logic, and it is this which accounts for the kinds of paraphrase he uses in his account of events, their point being to show how inferences generally acceptable to persons who understand the language can be articulated in predicate logic.

Thus to take his well-known example: everyone agrees that 'Jones buttered a piece of toast in the bathroom at midnight' entails that Jones buttered a piece of toast, but to show that predicate logic sanctions the entailment requires, he argues that we paraphrase the claim using an existential quantifier which ranges over events. The latter shows that event terms are names, not predicates or sentences, and hence that events must be particulars rather than properties or states of affairs. This kind of paraphrase gives what Davidson calls the 'logical form' of a sentence, which simply means that it articulates in the language of predicate logic the logical relations it has with other statements. The only connection this has with ontology is that it shows that events terms are singular terms and hence range over particulars. It does not go beyond EP, for Davidson's quantificational paraphrases do not analyze the structure of the facts which make statements true; they simply *articulate* the logical form of the statements for which EP holds, which means that both the LHS and the RHS should have the same articulation. That is to say, a Davidsonian T-sentence is *not* this one:

> 'Jones buttered the toast in the bathroom' is true iff [Ex] (x is a buttering of toast & x was in the bathroom).

but rather this one:

> '[Ex] (x is a buttering of toast & x was in the bathroom)' is true iff [Ex] (x is a buttering of toast & x was in the bathroom).[7]

Searle's response is that there is no conflict between commitment to EP and commitment to a conception of truth which grounds the use of making-true as a philosophical tool because, given obvious assumptions, EP entails the correspondence theory of truth. I quote his argument verbatim.

1. Assume disquotation
   For any s, s is true iff p.
2. Given the appropriate replacements for 's' and 'p' in the above formula, the right-hand side of a T sentence specifies a condition that is satisfied if and only if the sentences specified on the left-hand side is true.
3. We need a general name for those conditions when satisfied, and that name, among others, is 'fact'.
4. We need a verb to name the variety of ways in which sentences, when true, relate to facts in a way that makes them true; and that verb, among others, is 'correspond.'
5. With these understandings, from the disquotational criterion we get a version of the correspondence theory:
   For any s, s is true iff s corresponds to the fact that p. (Searle 1995, p. 203)

Much of this argument is unexceptionable. The first step appeals to an acceptable (if sloppy) formulation of EP. The second introduces the notion of (truth) condition to refer (as I have done) to what the RHS of EP specifies. The third introduces 'fact' to refer to truth conditions which are actually satisfied. It is the fourth step which is problematic, for it defines the notion of 'correspond' in

---

7 See Davidson 2001a, pp. 143–145.

terms of facts making statements true, and it is only if that is granted that it is reasonable to draw the conclusion in step 5.

The problem is what is meant by the notion of facts making statements true. If it means no more than that sentences are true if their truth conditions, as specified by the RHS of EP, are satisfied, then the notion is merely a reformulation of EP. In defending his point of view, Searle often implies that that is precisely what he has in mind. This is clear when he considers statements which usually call for special treatment by advocates of the correspondence theory, disjunctions, negations, or conditionals, for example, which are typically dealt with in stages[8] in order to avoid having to posit disjunctive, negative, or conditional facts. Such facts do not trouble Searle in the least, and he simply dismisses Russellian worries about strange kinds of facts.

> The true statement that the cat is not on the mat corresponds to the fact that the cat is not on the mat. What else? And what goes for negative statements goes for all the rest. If it is true that if the cat had been on the mat, then the dog would have had to have been in the kitchen, then it must be a fact that if the cat had been on the mat, then the dog would have had to have been in the kitchen. For every true statement there is a corresponding fact, because that is how these words are defined. (Searle 1995, p. 214)

I have no objection to this, which strikes me as a commendable way of showing how EP works. But if this were all there were to Searle's account of facts making statements true, there would be no room for what he claims to be his philosophical method, namely investigating the structure of the facts in virtue of which our statements about social reality are true. Given that view of facts, there would be nothing more to do than write out (true) statements about social reality.

Searle has another view of facts, however, which grounds his notion of philosophical method. This more expansive view is at odds with the view just quoted (the latter is essentially the view that 'fact' is simply a name we apply to truth conditions when they are satisfied) although Searle seems to think the two views of fact amount to the same thing. He clearly wants to have his cake and eat it too. On the one hand he argues that a correspondence theory of truth is no more than an articulation of EP and that facts are not objects but ways of referring to satisfied truth conditions. But he also argues that a correspondence theory licenses substantive inferences from true statements to the structure of the facts which make those statements true. Here is the way he tries to justify holding both views.

---

8 In the case of disjunction, by first giving the truth conditions of each disjunct and then using something like a truth table to specify the truth conditions of the disjunction itself.

> Wherever there is disquotation, there are also alternative ways of describing or specifying the facts. Thus the true statement "Sally is the sister of Sam" corresponds to the fact that Sally is the sister of Sam, but there are further things to be said, e.g., that Sally is female, and that Sally and Sam have the same father and mother. Many philosophical disputes are about the structure of facts, and in general these issues go far beyond disquotation. For example, the philosophical disputes about color, and other secondary qualities, are about the nature of the facts that correspond to such claims as that this object is red, and the analysis of such facts requires more than disquotation. (Searle 1995, p. 221)

The reference to disquotation expresses commitment to EP, but the rest of the quotation articulates a conception of facts which goes far beyond the notion of truth conditions involved in EP. If there are alternative ways of describing facts, then facts must be objects, since an object is just what has alternative descriptions. These alternative descriptions are not at all like the paraphrases Davidson gives, but analyses which, as Searle notes explicitly, "require more than disquotation" and hence more than EP. No appeal to EP could possibly resolve "the philosophical disputes about color, and other secondary qualities", and if such disputes are "about the nature of the facts that correspond to such claims as that this object is red", 'fact' is clearly not being used simply as a name for truth conditions "when satisfied".

Consider other contexts in which an analogous notion of conditions is used. We speak, for example, of the conditions for being a legitimate law, for being an eligible voter, for winning a race. Take the case of winning a race: the conditions for winning a 1500-meter foot race include that one have started with the other runners, have kept in the lanes, did not push a competitor, and reached the finish line first. These are conditions under which one would win a race (loosely speaking, since they are not sufficient conditions). We can speak of them, if we wish, as conditions that make a person a winner.

But this sense of 'make a winner' is not explanatory: it does not explain why anyone won the race but specifies the conditions that have to be met to win the race. The explanatory sense of 'make a winner' would specify such things as how the runner trained, how she paced herself during the race, how she got psychologically prepared, and so on, which help explain why she won. None of these factors is a condition for winning a race in the sense of the conditions under which a race would be won.

The parallel to truth conditions is very close. The conditions under which a statement is true do not explain why the statement is true any more than the conditions under which someone won a race explains why she won the race. The main difference is just that there is no EP for winning as there is for truth, and that means that, in one sense, the conditions for truth are even less informative than the conditions for winning. At the same time, truth conditions are important since one has to know them to understand a statement, and *that* may be an achievement. But the achievement is in understanding what a statement meant when expressed in a particular context, which is to understand what it would be for the statement to be true. Such understanding is not philosophical, and it is not a philosophical achievement, nor does it give any clue to how to analyze statements about mental states or social reality. How to do the latter and what the point of doing so may be are not questions which can be answered by appeal to any adequate conception of truth.

6 A Mistaken View of Davidson's Legacy: Reading Lepore and Ludwig

Ernest Lepore and Kirk Ludwig's *Donald Davidson: Meaning, Truth, Language, and Reality* (2005) is a critical discussion of Davidson's philosophy of language and the philosophical themes connected with it, which means that it touches on much of his work. The authors have read almost all of Davidson's writings, and there are over 300 footnotes. It is well written and well organized, with a wealth of intricate expositions and arguments. Parts of the book are technical and very intricate and may be difficult for many readers, although help is provided by an introductory overview of the whole book and by an introduction and summary to each of the three main parts, and there is a large bibliography and index. With over 400 pages, the book represents a great deal of hard work, and a review cannot deal with all the manifold arguments, analyses, and critical judgments it contains.

It is, however, a deeply unsympathetic study of Davidson's work, not because it is highly critical, but because it gives an exceedingly uncharitable reading of his writings. Rather than trying to see if his major claims might fit together into an account of the interrelation of language, mind, and world that is at least initially plausible, they take the claims piecemeal, construe them to fit their notion of how a philosophical claim should look, and then argue that Davidson's arguments fail to meet their standards of proof. They ascribe to Davidson views he explicitly rejected or that are clearly at odds with what he has written, and when they ascribe a view he did hold, their account of it is often off key, missing the central point. The first part of the book, which is about Davidson's theory of meaning, suffers from their imposition of their own view on Davidson; the two latter parts are wholesale rejections of his philosophical claims for not measuring up to their conception of how philosophy should be done.

Although I remain critical of a number of Davidson's claims and would like more argument for others, I regard him as an immensely insightful, creative, and acute philosopher, who can be obscure but is seldom confused or inconsistent, and who developed an impressive overall conception of mind and world that is largely correct. My aim here, however, is not to defend Davidson's views but to show how Lepore and Ludwig give a distorted interpretation of his work and then sharply criticize what they mistakenly take to be his views, the result being an impoverished Davidson who hardly counts as a philosopher of the first rank.[1]

I shall document these assertions by focusing on three themes that I take to be crucial: the role of compositionality in a theory of meaning; the role and status of radical interpretation; and the nature of theoretical concepts.

The first part of the book gives an extensive and detailed exposition of Davidson's early work in developing a meaning theory for natural languages. My objection is not primarily to their exposition, which is useful in a number of ways, but to the philosophical views that lie at the back of it and which are obscured by the technical apparatus they employ. In particular, they fail to note the philosophical significance of Davidson's central point that meaning is *truth-based*, which means that truth was a central concept in all his work.

Davidson regarded meaning as a matter of truth conditions, and hence something that relates to the world directly and not through the mediation of a third thing, as it did in the Lockean idea that words signify ideas that signify things in the world, or in the notion that words signify representations that refer to things in the world. He held that the meaning of a sentence *is* the conditions in the world under which it is true – objectively true. This already challenges the Cartesian skepticism that Lepore and Ludwig bring to bear on their discussion of radical interpretation, and it leads directly to Davidson's later externalism, which denies that "what someone means by what he says depends only on what is in or on his mind, and that the situations in which words are learned merely constitute evidence of what those words mean, rather than conferring meaning on them" (Guttenplan 1994, p. 233).

The point is that in claiming to accept Davidson's theory of meaning, Lepore and Ludwig are committed to others of Davidson's claims that they later reject as implausible. It is not clear, however, if they really do accept the theory of meaning. While they accept the technical apparatus and constraints Davidson puts on an acceptable theory, including the project of fitting English idioms into it, they reject what follows immediately from Davidson's emphasis on truth, namely, the crucial centrality of *sentences* in a meaning theory. "Words have no function",

---

[1] This may surprise some who know that Ernie Lepore was a good friend of Davidson's who helped edit his collected works. However, while Davidson said of Lepore that "No one has been as assiduous and productive in working with truthconditional semantics" (Hahn 1999, p. 716), by which he meant Lepore's work in extending a Tarski-type meaning theory to natural languages, his approval of Lepore's work did not extend to his critical interpretation of Davidson's philosophical work in general. See, for instance, his reply to Fodor and Lepore in "Radical Interpretation Interpreted", which speaks of how "they have most woefully misunderstood and misread me" (Davidson 1994a, p. 124).

Davidson wrote, "save as they play a role in sentences: their semantic features are abstracted from the semantic features of sentences, just as the semantic features of sentences are abstracted from *their* part in helping people achieve goals or realize intentions." (Davidson 1984, p. 220) That is reflected in the meaning theory in that its *theorems* specify the meaning – the truth conditions – of *sentences*, theorems we verify by observing a speaker's linguistic behavior. The meaning of *terms*, by contrast – what they refer to or are true of –, is specified by the *axioms*, which are verified only insofar as they yield verified theorems.

Davidson emphasized this point early and late. He wrote this, for instance, in "Reality without Reference":

> A general and pre-analytic notion of truth is presupposed by the theory [of meaning]. It is because we have this notion that we can tell what counts as evidence for the truth of a T-sentence. But the same is not required of the concepts of reference and satisfaction. Their role is theoretical, and so we know all there is to know about them when we know how they operate to characterize truth. We don't need a general concept of reference in the construction of an adequate theory. (Davidson 1984, p. 248)

In "The Structure and Content of Truth" he wrote that "Reference and related semantic notions like satisfaction are, by comparison [to truth], theoretical concepts." (Davidson 1990, p. 300)

Davidson is here talking not about language per se but about a theory of meaning that aims to specify what, if we did know it, would be sufficient to interpret every utterance of speakers of a language. That is not something speakers of the language need to know in any form, nor does it explain how they are able to speak a language or what goes on when they understand. Davidson emphasized that it must exhibit a language as *learnable*, and since a speaker has learned to understand novel utterances without limit, a theory of meaning must permit an unlimited set of meaning-giving theorems. Such a theory must have a finite base, which implies that it be compositional and hence able to yield an infinite set of theorems from a finite set of axioms. For Davidson, however, compositionality is not a requirement on language but on a *theory* of language, since what language must be like to be learnable is not a question to be answered by philosophy.

Lepore and Ludwig, however, take compositionality to be a requirement on language itself.

> The requirement of a compositional meaning theory is not primarily motivated by the infinitude of sentences formulable in our languages. It is motivated by the fact that our languages are compositional, i.e., by the fact that we understand utterances of sentences in

our language on the basis of mastering how their elements can be used systematically to produce sentences with different meaning. (Lepore and Ludwig 2005, p. 32)

Unlike Davidson, they think that a meaning theory should *explain* our capacity to understand sentences: we understand their meaning on the basis of understanding the meaning of their terms and their semantic structure. While recognizing Davidson's restricted appeal to compositionality in what they call his 'initial project', they argue that he also (should have) had an 'extended project' that provided "insight into what it was for any of the terms of a language to have the meanings they do" (Lepore and Ludwig 2005, p. 207).

One reason, in their view, for the extended project was to provide the constraint on a meaning theory that would sort out T-sentence theorems that actually give the meaning of a sentence from those that are merely true (like "snow is white' is true iff coal is black'). They reject Davidson's assertion that a *complete* extensional meaning that is established by a radical interpreter will yield only meaning-giving theorems, claiming that what is required is that the *axioms* be interpretive. "That [the theory] be interpretive is the requirement that its axioms be interpretive. Thus, not any theory that issues in T-sentences is adequate. It must issue in them from the right axioms. And there is a fact of the matter about which axioms are correct." (Lepore and Ludwig 2005, p. 124)

They tie this in with their view that a meaning theory should explain our capacity to speak and understand a language, and they think that Davidson should (perhaps did) agree. They admit that he did not believe (as Dummett thought he should) that "speakers had explicit or implicit *propositional* knowledge [of a meaning theory] that they deployed in understanding others" (Lepore and Ludwig 2005, p. 121). But they quote his statement that a theory aims to capture "the structure of a very complicated ability – the ability to speak and understand a language" (Davidson 2001b, p. 25), on which they comment that, "Irrespective of whether Davidson has continued to endorse the requirement that the truth theory capture in some more robust sense the structure of a speaker's ability to speak and understand his language, we believe it is both defensible and important for Davidson's program." (Lepore and Ludwig 2005, p. 122) Indeed, they contend that "The requirement that the theory capture the structure of a speaker's ability to speak and understand his language, and that it be interpretive, amount to the same thing." (Lepore and Ludwig 2005, p. 124) On their view, "the truth theory serves by being a vehicle for deriving interpretive T-sentences from axioms which are interpretive, in a way that shows how understanding complexes [sentences] depends on understanding their parts and their mode of composition" (Lepore and Ludwig 2005, p. 146).

They even argue that a meaning theory should be compositional *because* linguistic competence is compositional:

> We can note that mastery of the use of each semantical primitive in a language must be encoded in our nervous system separately from each other, and that our capacities for encoding uses of semantical primitives are finite. It *follows* that our mastery of a language with infinite resources must rest on mastery of a finite number of semantical primitives and rules that enable us to understand complex expressions on the basis of the primitives they comprise. (Lepore and Ludwig 2005, p. 31, my italics)

At another point they suggest that the fact that a meaning theory has an interpretive axiom for each primitive expression "corresponds to a disposition in a competent speaker to use the word in accordance with its semantic role and reference or application conditions" (Lepore and Ludwig 2005, p. 124). Such a psychological fact is sufficient, they claim, to undermine the indeterminacy of reference which Davidson thinks is inseparable from his meaning theory: "There is a fact of the matter about which axioms [of a meaning theory] are correct *because* there is a fact of the matter about the structure of speakers' dispositions to use words." (Lepore and Ludwig 2005, p. 124, my italics)

There is abundant evidence that Davidson rejected this construal of his theory of meaning. He was explicit that such a theory is not a psychological explanation of linguistic competence or of our understanding of language. A meaning theory for a learnable language must be compositional in a sense that is consistent with (indeed derivative from) its being holistic, but whether the structure of what goes on in our mind/brain is compositional is not a question for a meaning theory but for science. He also was explicit in rejecting a "building-block theory" in favor of "a version of the holistic approach" that means "we must give up the concept of reference as basic to an empirical theory of language" (Davidson 1984, p. 221). Lepore and Ludwig's assertion, however, that an interpretive meaning theory must have the right axioms that are themselves interpretive makes reference basic. Moreover, it contradicts Davidson's insistence that we know all there is to know about reference and satisfaction (which is what the axioms are about) "when we know how they operate to characterize truth" (Davidson 1984, p. 223).

One consequence of construing reference as basic is to open the way for Cartesian skepticism. If reference is taken to be the connection between words and things on which truth depends, then referential connections can swing free of the truth of the sentences in which referential expressions occur, which yields the conception that speakers can grasp the meaning (reference) of words in the context of largely false beliefs. If Davidson's theory is construed in that way, it is not surprising that Lepore and Ludwig find his later rejections of Cartesian skepticism implausible.

Lepore and Ludwig contend that Davidson's work is a philosophical edifice that rests on two fundamental premises. "The first is that speaking requires being interpretable by any possible speaker in any possible environment. The second is that the basic concepts of interpretation theory have their content exhausted by their role in tracking behavior." (Lepore and Ludwig 2005, p. 388) They call the latter concepts, which include meaning, belief, intention, etc., 'theoretical'. They continue: "It looks as if these theses will stand or fall together" (Lepore and Ludwig 2005, p. 388), their view being that they fall together, and hence so does Davidson's philosophical edifice, with the exception of his meaning theory (if properly interpreted).

This section of my review is about the first premise, although most of their discussion concerns a related claim that, given that there are speakers, is entailed by that premise:

> (P): One can come to know something sufficient to interpret a speaker from the evidential position of the radical interpreter.

As it stands, (P) is a reasonable formulation of something central to Davidson's point of view, which he took to follow from Quine's oft-repeated claim that meaning is public and observable. Both Quine and Davidson thought that claim was not a philosophical thesis requiring proof but a commonplace that, properly understood, would be acceptable to all. Quine, wrote Davidson,

> Revolutionized our understanding of verbal communication by taking seriously the fact, obvious enough in itself, that there can be no more to meaning than an adequately equipped person can learn and observe; the interpreter's point of view is therefore the revealing one to bring to the subject. (Davidson 2005a, p. 62)

The point is that to understand what it is for expressions to mean what they do, we should consider how they function in communication, since there is no more to their meaning than the use to which speakers put them in their behavior. What we inwardly mean by an expression does not determine what it means, since "What people mean by what they say derives from occasions of successful communication" (Davidson 1994a, p. 127), which is to consider meaning from the point of view of an interpreter. To ensure that we do not import alien assumptions, Davidson urged that we take the point of view of a *radical* interpreter who thinks of herself as interpreting a hitherto uninterpreted language. Hence the claim that there can be no more to meaning than what is accessible from the point of view of radical interpretation. That claim remains a commonplace because, although radical interpretation is a philosopher's invention, it is an idealized and purified version of the ordinary interpretation we might engage in, for instance, to justify a claim about what someone difficult to understand is really saying.

Davidson's primary concern was not to argue for this claim but to elucidate it and use it to articulate crucial features of language but also of thought, since we cannot impose on a speaker a distinction between language and thought prior to understanding her. Hence his claim that "What a fully informed interpreter could learn about what a speaker means is all there is to learn; the same goes for what the speaker believes." (Davidson 2001c, p. 148) The point of view of the radical interpreter is crucial, then, to understanding the nature of beliefs, desires, and intentions, and hence the nature of intentional behavior generally. It is central to his work, not as a foundational premise but as a background assumption justified by its value in dealing with philosophical problems.

Lepore and Ludwig, however, insist that Davidson must *establish* that radical interpretation can succeed for any possible speaker in *any* possible environment, which means that they treat (P) not as a commonplace but as a complex philosophical thesis. To clarify what they contend to be Davidson's attempt to establish (P), they distinguish between a modest and an ambitious project. The *modest* project takes (P) as an *a posteriori assumption* and then asks what must be the case about meaning, belief, etc. *if* it is true. This will yield only conclusions that are conditional on (P) and that are *a posteriori*, since (P) is. The *ambitious* project gives arguments for (P) that they hold must be *a priori*, the reason being that *a posteriori* arguments cannot work since they depend on identifying successful cases of radical interpretation, which assumes that we already have a justified interpretation theory and thus begs the question. An *a priori* argument entails that (P) must be *a priori*, and hence that "anything we discovered the radical interpreter must assume to succeed at interpretation would be not just true, but necessarily true" (Lepore and Ludwig 2005, p. 167).

The immediate objection to this is that it construes Davidson's work in terms he explicitly rejects. (P) concerns interpretation of a language from the outside, a point where Davidson firmly rejects the analytic-synthetic distinction and the allied distinction between the *a priori* and the *a posteriori*. While he does think that successful radical interpretation is part of the *nature* of meaning, belief, and other attitudes, he does not classify claims about the nature of something as *a priori* necessary, or as merely empirical. He wrote that "erasing the line between the analytic and synthetic saved philosophy of language as a serious subject" (Davidson 2001a, 'A Coherence Theory of Truth and Knowledge', in Donald Davidson, Subjective, Intersubjective, Objective (Oxford University Press, 2001) p. 145) and later that "I know of no clear way of distinguishing metaphysical or *a priori* knowledge from other forms of knowledge." (Hahn 1999, p. 620) Lepore and Ludwig admit that Davidson said such things, but they seem to think he did not take them seriously. That is just not true, and it is foreign to his intellectual world to assume that a claim like (P) must be either *a priori* or *a posteriori*, necessary or empirical.

Waiving this point, let us consider whether radical interpretation is indefensible no matter how (P) is construed. Lepore and Ludwig's objection to the *modest* project, which *assumes* that (P) is contingently true, is that it is in fact false: "We cannot confirm anything knowledge of which (we would be justified in believing) would suffice for interpretation from the radical interpreter's standpoint." (Lepore and Ludwig 2005, p. 222) Their argument is that since (in their view) only one interpretation of a speaker can be correct, and since the available evidence is always consistent with alternative interpretations, we are never in a position to determine the correct interpretation. They insist that this is genuine *under*determination because we cannot construe alternative interpretations as different ways of specifying the same facts. The latter would be indeterminacy, and although that is Davidson's view, they reject it:

> the evidence available to the radical interpreter, together with the constraints he can legitimately bring to bear on his task, genuinely underdetermine the theories he can confirm, and the appearance of underdetermination cannot be accounted for by appeal to the indeterminacy of interpretation. (Lepore and Ludwig 2005, p. 222)

On Davidson's view, while we can acquire knowledge sufficient for radical interpretation, this does not rule out alternative specifications of what a speaker's expressions mean or the content of her beliefs. These, like alternative specifications of temperature in Fahrenheit or centigrade scales, specify in different ways the same underlying facts of the matter. In the case of meaning and belief, the underlying facts of the matter are the invariant inferential and evidential relations among them and to the speaker, which we can know through radical interpretation.

In arguing that such knowledge is not possible, Lepore and Ludwig make three assumptions Davidson would reject. In the first place, they set a very high standard for the success of radical interpretation, insisting that it must succeed for *any* speaker in *any* possible environment, which enables them to construct outré thought experiments that exhibit situations in which it is not possible for radical interpretation to succeed. But this is irrelevant to Davidson, who wrote in reply to Fodor and Lepore:

> I do not think that I have ever argued for the claim that radical interpretability is a condition of interpretability. Not only have I never argued that every language is radically interpretable; I have not even argued that every language can be understood by someone other than its employer, since it would be possible to have a private code no one else could break. I don't think, and have not argued, that radical interpretation of natural languages *must* be possible; I have argued only that it *is* possible. (Davidson 1994a, p. 121)

Secondly, they have an overly narrow view of the evidence available to the radical interpreter. They say that it must be "purely behavioral" (Lepore and Ludwig 2005, p. 159), which they think means that it must be describable without psychological terms (although they note that Davidson rejects behavioristic reductionism) (Lepore and Ludwig 2005, p. 414, n. 307). That is not Davidson's view:

> What I have tried to do is to give an account of meaning (interpretation) that makes no essential use of unexplained *linguistic* concepts ... In saying what an interpreter knows it [may be] necessary to use a so-called intentional notion – one that consorts with belief and intention and the like. (Davidson 1984, p. 176)

The prime example is describing a speaker as holding true a sentence, but it can also include "adding another dose of sympathy or imagination or ... learning more about the things the subject knows about" (Guttenplan 1994, p. 232), which though not behavioristic are legitimate instances of behavioral evidence.

Thirdly, they give a distorted account of the procedure of the radical interpreter by construing it as like the traditional scheme for verifying a scientific theory (Lepore and Ludwig 2005, p. 196). For Davidson, however, interpreting a speaker is nothing like verifying a scientific theory, since, while both are third-person, the concepts of interpretation must be sharply distinguished from scientific concepts. Radical interpretation, like interpretation generally, does not follow a fixed order. It is holistic in that no claim to knowledge is inextricable from other claims, no sentence is meaningful independently of other sentences, there are no attitudes except in the context of many others. Moreover, the criteria for correct interpretation are part of what must be discovered in the interpretive process, which must itself also conform to those criteria. Marcia Cavell wrote of how Davidson described "the chasm between an exchange in which the participants have clear concepts and an exchange in which concepts themselves come into focus, are refined, and developed" (Davidson 2005a, p. xviii). The latter is what goes on in interpretation, and, indeed, in much of Davidson's philosophical work. Lepore and Ludwig miss this because of their anti-interpretive model of radical interpretation, which makes Davidson's procedure look to them like begging the question.

Lepore and Ludwig maintain that, in spite of their argument that the modest project is a failure, it remains open whether the *ambitious* project, which construes (P) as an *a priori*, necessary truth, can succeed. They contend that a plausible *a priori* argument for (P) would show that radical interpretation *must* succeed in spite of the empirical evidence that it cannot. While this involves a strange notion of modality, it *is* their view: "the evidence available to the radical interpreter ... genuinely underdetermines the theories he can construct [and hence] radical interpretation is not possible ... [But] our argument is still hostage to the possibility of providing an *a priori* argument for (P)." (Lepore and Ludwig 2005, p. 222) In their opinion, the *a priori* argument also fails.

To illustrate the way they deal with Davidson's views, I quote their formulation of what they take to be his main *a priori* argument (Lepore and Ludwig 2005, p. 399):

(E1) Necessarily, every thinker is in communication, or has been in communication, and potentially is in communication, with others.

(E2) Therefore, necessarily, every thinker is interpretable in any environment in which he is located, by any other speaker.

(E3) Therefore, radical interpretation is possible, and the only content that can be given to psychological and linguistic concepts is provided by their role in accounting for behavior, in the context of a theory of interpretation formulated from the third-person standpoint. [I will discuss here only the claim about radical interpretation; I come to the rest below.]

As noted earlier, this is contrary to Davidson's view about the status of *a priori* necessary claims, but let's waive that in order to consider their evaluation of the argument. They regard it as acceptable only if its premises are entailed by further *a priori* necessary arguments. The crucial premise is E1, for which they consider three further arguments.

The first is the argument from the concept of error. It proceeds from the premise that "To have the concept of belief, one must have the concept of error, or, what is the same thing, of objective truth" (Lepore and Ludwig 2005, p. 397) through four further premises to the conclusion that "To have the concept of belief, one must have a language and be (or have been) in communication with others" (Lepore and Ludwig 2005, p. 399), which entails E1. They object to a number of these premises. They maintain, for example, that because it is "easy to specify contexts in which there would be a point to deploying the concept of error which do not involve communication" (Lepore and Ludwig 2005, p. 402), it follows that Davidson is wrong about the relation between the concept of belief and objective truth. But that does not follow, since his view is that communication is necessary to master the concept of belief and error but not to apply it in every situation.

They maintain further that when our seeing a dog barking up the wrong tree leads us to say 'he thinks the cat is up there', we must be "taking the dog to have false beliefs [in order to] restore his sanity [!] and our sense of order" (Lepore and Ludwig 2005, p. 402). This is supposed to show that there is "scope for the application of objective truth" (Lepore and Ludwig 2005, p. 402) quite independently of communication, which would imply that dogs have the concept of objective truth. In any case, they believe that the most Davidson is entitled to is that "we must *think* of ourselves in communication with others in order to have the concept of belief, truth, and objectivity" (Lepore and Ludwig 2005, p. 403, my italics) and hence "a gap remains between thinking of ourselves in communication with others and actually being so" (Lepore and Ludwig 2005, p. 403). Such a claim ignores the basic thrust of Davidson's anti-Cartesian point of view and the central role which objective truth had even in his early writings.

The second argument they consider is from triangulation. It claims that "it is only if a subject is in communication with another that we will be in a position to identify on *third person or objective grounds* what the object of his thoughts are" (Lepore and Ludwig 2005, p. 406). They object that this begs the question because it *assumes* that radical interpretation is possible and cannot be used to support it. That objection, however, ignores the distinctive holistic character of interpretation, which allows for tentative conclusions to support claims that can in turn be used to support the tentative conclusion, and so on. They also object on the ground that thought experiments show that it is *possible* that speakers are radically wrong about the common cause of their responses; but that mistakenly assumes that because one can *imagine* conditions under which triangulation fails, triangulation has no essential role to play in an account of the nature of meaning and belief. The fact that we can misidentify the content of a speaker's belief does not entail that we do not generally get it right, nor does it rule out the point that getting it generally right is a precondition for making the kind of sense of each other that is required for having a coherent mental life.

The third argument is from knowledge of other minds (Lepore and Ludwig 2005, p. 414).

(G1) Necessarily, speaking a language is having the capacity to interpret other language speakers and being interpretable by other language speakers [a priori truth].

(G2) We never have direct epistemic access to the thoughts of other speakers or to the meanings of their utterances [a priori truth].

(G3) Therefore, from (G2), the only evidence available for interpretation is third person evidence, that is, evidence equally available to every potential interpreter of a speaker.
(G4) From (Gl) and (G3), any language speaker can be interpreted on the basis of third person evidence in any environment by any other language speaker.
(GS) From (G4), radical interpretation is possible ... [which is what the 'ambitious project' aims to establish]

Their first objection is that (Gl) is *plausible* only if it is read as 'Every speaker is interpretable in *some* environment by *some* speaker', but to get (G4) we need 'Every speaker is interpretable in *every* environment by *every* speaker.' That is relevant, however, only if (G4) specifies the nature of radical interpretation, which (as noted above) is not Davidson's view.

Their second objection is that (G3) is simply false, the reason being that "we know the contents of our own thoughts independently of observing our behavior". We can, they continue, "establish correlations between our thoughts and our behavior, and then project these correlations to the case of others. This is a version of what has been called the argument from analogy." (Lepore and Ludwig 2005, p. 415) Note that (G3) asserts that "the only *evidence* available for *interpretation* is third person evidence". Davidson accepts that, but it does not contradict their claim that "we know the contents of our own thoughts independently of observing our behavior", which Davidson also accepts. His view is that *interpretation* should be based on evidence but that knowledge of our own (present) thoughts is based on *neither* interpretation *nor* evidence.

Their appeal to the argument from analogy shows how different Davidson's intellectual world is from their Cartesian world. They think, for instance, that a main objection to the argument is that it is weak inductive reasoning, to which they reply as follows:

> The mistake is to represent the reasoning as if it took place in isolation from our broader knowledge of the causal order. Human beings fall within a single biological kind ... Granting that psychological features of ourselves are biologically based, skepticism about other minds reduces to skepticism about induction in general, but presents no special problems. (Lepore and Ludwig 2005, p. 415)

This objection either assumes knowledge of other minds, which begs the question, or it accepts the fantasy that someone without knowledge of other minds could have knowledge of the causal order, including knowledge that human beings (identified without reference to having a mental life) belong to a single biological kind and have psychological features that are biologically based.

They cite Davidson's criticism of the argument for simply assuming "that what we call the mental states of others are similar to what we identify as mental states in ourselves" (Lepore and Ludwig 2005, p. 415). They reply, first, by repeating the point about the strength of inductive reasoning, and then claiming that Davidson assumes "an unappealing operationalist conception of how meaning is determined, which has long been discredited in the philosophy of science" (Lepore and Ludwig 2005, p. 416). That schoolroom reprimand, however, misses the point entirely, which is that the argument from analogy assumes that we can grasp the meaning of *terms* independently of being able to use them in sentences that there is non-linguistic access to the reference of terms. Indeed, it assumes that one can grasp the meaning of psychological terms simply by immediate awareness of their objects, for example, by merely *having* a sensation or feeling (their example is embarrassment). Those assumptions are inconsistent with all Davidson's work, including his truth-based theory of meaning.

What these arguments that Lepore and Ludwig ascribe to Davidson fail to do is establish that "Every speaker is interpretable in every environment by every speaker on the basis of third person evidence." (Lepore and Ludwig 2005, p. 414) The question is why, given Davidson's explicit rejection of such a strong criterion for the success of radical interpretation, they insist both on the criterion and on the necessity of proving that it can be met.

The answer has to do with what they call Davidson's second fundamental premise that "the basic concepts of interpretation" are purely theoretical, "whose purpose is to enable us to systematize and keep track of behavior neutrally described" (Lepore and Ludwig 2005, p. 387) and whose content, therefore, "is to be understood wholly in terms of their role in accounting for the behavioral evidence available to us from [the third-person] standpoint" (Lepore and Ludwig 2005, p. 418). Their content, that is to say, "is exhausted by their application in the domain of evidence in such a way that results in the content of the theories' theoretical claims not transcending their predictions about facts in the domain of evidence" (Lepore and Ludwig 2005, p. 225).

What Lepore and Ludwig intend by these formulations of Davidson's view goes considerably beyond Davidson's claims about the essentially public and observable character of thought and language. They ascribe to him the view that the procedure of the radical interpreter in systematizing behavioral evidence *constitutes* the content of linguistic and psychological concepts, so that where there is no evidence, there is no language or thought. Given this construal of Davidson, it is understandable why they require proof that a very strong sense of radical interpretation can succeed. On their view, the concepts of interpretation have determinate objects, each of which has its own intrinsic nature. Hence an adequate procedure for determining what a speaker's words mean and what his attitudes are *must* return a *determinate* account of both. Radical interpretation, on the one hand, must yield a verifiably correct account of the meaning of the *terms* in a speaker's language since, on their version of compositionality, that is necessary for the meaning theory to specify determinate meanings for the *sentences* of the language. On the other hand, interpretation must yield a verifiably correct account of the content of a speaker's individual beliefs and other attitudes since each is a determinate object that has an intrinsic content as a matter of fact.

Failing to meet the requirement is particularly urgent given their claim that Davidson holds that behavioral evidence constitutes the content of the concepts of interpretation. That makes it necessary for radical interpretation to succeed for *any* speaker in *any* environment since there cannot be speech and thought where evidence is lacking. Moreover, only if the evidence is sufficient to establish *determinate* content for a speaker's utterances and beliefs can they have the content required to be determinate objects. "What must be done", they contend, "is to show that the third person standpoint can yield acceptably determinate assignments of contents to beliefs and interpretations to sentences." But "they have no idea how this could be done", because "the central difficulty [of Davidson's account] lies in the apparent underdetermination of the content of our thought about meaning and thought content by behavioral evidence" (Lepore and Ludwig 2005, p. 418).

Lepore and Ludwig are doubly mistaken about this requirement: Davidson holds neither that the concepts of interpretation are determinate objects in their sense nor that evidence constitutes their content. I have given reasons for denying that he construes *terms* as having determinate reference and satisfaction conditions. A similar point applies to his view of beliefs and other psychological states. A belief is a state of a whole agent, not an entity in her mind or brain. In ascribing the belief that a rabbit ran by, we use the sentence 'A rabbit ran by' to identify the state, but the sentence is not the object of her belief. We can, therefore, say about beliefs something similar to what we say about sentences: what is invariant is their relation to a speaker, to each other, and to the conditions which (in part) cause a speaker to have them. But since there are alternative ways of specifying their content, interpretation will yield alternatives about which there is no fact of the matter, which means that they are not determinate objects.

Davidson did hold that evidence constitutes the content of certain concepts, notably reference and satisfaction, which are "theoretical constructs [whose] role is theoretical, and so we know all there is to know about them when we know how they operate to characterize truth" (Davidson 1984, p. 223), truth being the point where evidence bears on the meaning theory. These concepts are also theoretical in that we do not need them to be competent speakers but to have a theory about language. But he did not claim that behavioral evidence *con-*

stitutes the content of other linguistic and psychological concepts, those that are required to be a competent speaker.

He wrote that "Meaning is entirely determined by observable behavior, even readily observable behavior. That meanings are decipherable is not a matter of luck; public availability is a constitutive aspect of language." (Davidson 2005a, p. 56) But the claim that public availability is a *constitutive aspect* of language means, not that it constitutes language, but that it is *of the nature* of language and thought to be publicly available, and hence of their nature to be interpretable. "As a matter of principle ... meaning, and by its connection with meaning, belief also, are open to public determination" (Davidson 2001c, p. 148), and hence, "Thoughts, desires, and other attitudes are in their nature states we are equipped to interpret; what we could not interpret is not thought." (Davidson 2004, p. 88) This is why radical interpretation is basic to understanding language and thought: the essential features of meaning and belief are those that can be established from that point of view. That is not the case, for instance, with neural states, whose essential features are not accessible from the point of view of interpretation but require extensive scientific investigation and instrumentation. Although holding that beliefs and other mental states are identical with states characterized in the natural sciences, Davidson insists that there is a deep divide between the description and explanation given in the natural sciences and those given from the point of view of interpretation.

But the claim that beliefs and other mental states are interpretable *in their nature* is not the claim that the evidence yielded by interpretation *constitutes* them. Although rationality is constitutive of mental states, interpretation is not; where there is thought there need not be interpretation. That is not to say that beliefs and other mental states only happen to be interpretable. They are interpretable in their nature that is a 'constitutive aspect' of mental states – but that does not mean that they are interpretable under *any* circumstances, since what obtains in the nature of things need not always obtain.[2] On Davidson's view, given what speakers and our world are like, it is not intelligible that mental states should be uninterpretable in principle, a view he holds along with an unequivocal assertion of their reality:

> Our mental concepts are as essential to our understanding of the world as any others; we could not do without them. The propositional attitudes, such as intentions, desires, beliefs, hopes, and fears, are every bit as real as atoms and baseball bats, and the facts about them are as real as the facts about anything else. (Davidson 2005a, p. 316)

---

[2] For this point see Thompson 1995, pp. 290f.

Lepore and Ludwig argue that Davidson's view of the role of radical interpretation is inconsistent with "our having access to our own mental states independent of our observing our behavior" (Lepore and Ludwig 2005, p. 222). Their argument assumes that Davidson regarded concepts of mental states as purely theoretical, an assumption I believe is false. It also assumes that "the standpoint of interpretation [is] the sole standpoint from which to understand our beliefs, and other attitudes" (Lepore and Ludwig 2005, p. 389), which is also false. Davidson did not assume that the interpretive standpoint was the only one from which to understand language and thought. Indeed, he regarded it as a necessary feature of language and thought that we have first-person authority about them, which means that we are in general right in what we take them to be, although not by interpreting them, since the idea of interpreting our present selves is not intelligible.

The latter gives the nub of his (cryptic) account of the asymmetry between the third and the first person, an account meant to illuminate the asymmetry but not to explain why it exists since that it does is constitutive of being a speaker and thinker. Lepore and Ludwig criticize Davidson for not having such an explanation. Their own account is that

> The real source of first person authority is first person knowledge [for] which there is little hope of a philosophically illuminating explanation [and hence it must be recognized] as something we can appeal to in explaining other things, as an end point of explanation. (Lepore and Ludwig 2005, p. 367)

But this is to accept a Cartesian account of knowledge of one's own mental states as the point at which explanations come to an end while rejecting Davidson's own view of that point and, moreover, unlike Davidson, simply to assert the view.

Two other points to note. One is that a primary aim of interpretation – the third-person point of view – is to determine what things are like for the speaker from her point of view. Interpretation aims to know what a speaker believes, desires, or intends, and that is to know, from a third-person point of view, how (in part) the world presents itself to someone from a first-person point of view. The other point is that Davidson's considered view was that the third-person point of view was not the only basic point of view: there were three – the first, the second, and the third – and they were on a par.

> If I did not know what others think, I would have no thoughts of my own and so would not know what I think. If I did not know what I think, I would lack the ability to gauge the thoughts of others. Gauging the thoughts of others requires that I live in the same world with them, sharing many reactions to its major features, including its values. So there is

no danger that in viewing the world objectively we will lose touch with ourselves. The three sorts of knowledge form a tripod: if any leg were lost, no part would stand. (Davidson 2001c, p. 220)

One might see Ludwig and Lepore's work on Davidson as illustrating what often happens when an uncommonly good philosopher leaves the scene, namely, the rise of divergent interpretations of his writing. In the case of Davidson, a struggle is shaping up between those who see his work as continuing a certain tradition of analytical philosophy and those who see it as going beyond that tradition in decisively new ways. Lepore and Ludwig's work is of the first kind; it amounts to a passionate and opinionated defense of the view that Davidson's work is squarely in the tradition of analytical philosophy as they understand it.

Davidson was, of course, an analytical philosopher in many ways. He said that he got through grad school by reading Feigl and Sellars' anthology, which in 1950 defined the canon of analytical philosophy. He used the idiom of analytical philosophy, and his work is not intelligible to those unfamiliar with it. But at the same time, he rejected many traditional claims of analytical philosophy: the unity of science, the non-cognitive character of ethical discourse, the idea that beliefs and desires are things in the head, the distinction between sense content and scheme, the need for a theory of truth, the utility of the analytic-synthetic distinction in an account of language, the need to define basic concepts in terms of necessary and sufficient conditions, and much else. His arguments were seldom like those of traditional analytical philosophy: they were typically brief and sweeping, they were embedded in interpretations and hence often very circuitous, they frequently aimed less at proving a conclusion than at suggesting a strategy, getting across a point of view, or making plausible a new way of seeing things.

Analytical philosophy is no longer a well-defined school, but Lepore and Ludwig show their allegiance to one version of it, best exemplified in the work of John Searle and Jerry Fodor. It is a conservative version that takes seriously the analytic-synthetic distinction and the parallel distinctions between *a priori* and *a posteriori* knowledge and between meaning and belief. It is suspicious of holism about meaning and the attitudes, it is sympathetic to the epistemic primacy of the first person, it construes the distinctive claims of Davidson's later philosophy as parts of a large-scale metaphysical theory, and it requires that those claims be proved by deducing them from premises that must either be proved or shown to be self-evident. It is in many ways a reassertion of the (so-called) Cartesian framework in philosophy.

Because Lepore and Ludwig take that framework as a kind of default position, they require that any alternative to it requires stringent proof. That is another reason why they insist that Davidson prove that radical interpretation can succeed, for they recognize that to give radical interpretation the status Davidson does is to dismantle that framework. Showing that speaking requires being interpretable *only* in *some* circumstances "leaves open the possibility of radical error about one's environment [as well as] the possibility of taking the first person standpoint as epistemically basic" (Lepore and Ludwig 2005, p. 388), leaves open, that is to say, the *possibility* of a Cartesian framework. To show that an alternative is preferable requires establishing that the latter is not even possible, which is not something Davidson aimed to do. His aim was to undermine that framework by showing how it was a mistaken philosophical reconstruction of the conception of ourselves and our world that constitutes our life in a shared world.

6.1 Postscript – Radical Misinterpretation Indeed: Lepore and Ludwig Revisited

Ernest Lepore and Kirk Ludwig have claimed that my review of their massive book on Davidson is hostile because it gives an incomplete account of their treatment of certain issues. My review is not hostile in the dictionary sense of 'feeling or showing enmity or ill will'. I have no enmity against them, and my response was motivated not by ill will but by an attempt to give an honest evaluation useful to serious students of Davidson. My review is harsh, but not more than Davidson's criticism of philosophers like Quine, Strawson, Dummett, Grice – or Fodor and Lepore – and it was constrained, but only because of the inevitable limitation in dealing with a 440-page book packed with intricate arguments within a single discussion. In this chapter I aim to revisit some of the issues in that review with an eye to clarifying what was said there at the same time as I also aim to address some of the criticisms raised in Lepore and Ludwig's response.

Lepore and Ludwig think that Davidson is a philosopher of the first rank, and although writing a book about him is not proof, I do not doubt that they so think. My claim was that Davidson *as presented in their book* is not a philosopher of the first rank (something true of Kant as often presented). My objection was not that their book is highly critical but that it gives a distorted and exceedingly uncharitable reading of his writings. It is absurd, given my published criticisms of Davidson, to suggest that I think criticism threatens his status as a philosopher.³

Unfortunately, Lepore and Ludwig's response to my review is as deficient as their book: it imposes their own philosophical categories and assumptions on the text and then attacks the result as if it were the text. Consider what they write about my discussion of the centrality of truth in Davidson's work. I wrote, not that they misunderstand the meaning theory, but that they fail to grasp the *philosophical* significance, for Davidson's larger project, of his claim that the meaning of a sentence *is* the conditions in the world under which it is objectively true. They claim that this cannot be Davidson's claim because it entails that there are no false sentences. But Davidson made that very same claim in writing of "an effective method for determining what every sentence means (i.e., gives the conditions under which it is true)" (Davidson 1984, p. 8), and he, of course, meant what I did: 'the conditions under which a sentence *would be* true'. Philosophers often use the less precise expression, something charitable critics would recognize.

Lepore and Ludwig contend that I am committed to the existence of (reified) truth-conditions or of such entities as possible facts, but I am no more committed to such metaphysical excesses than Davidson was. I know that Davidson had no use for facts,⁴ but also that he had no use for representations, urging us to give up talk of "linguistic utterances representing reality (or anything else)" (Davidson 2005a, p. 130). Lepore and Ludwig ignore the latter in their discussion of radical interpretation by assuming what Davidson called "a Cartesian, individualistic conception of meaning and the intentional" (Davidson 1994a, p. 127). Had they grasped the philosophical significance of Davidson's claim that the meaning of sentences is given directly (unmediated by representations) by their truth-conditions, they would have recognized that this Cartesian conception was ruled out already in his earliest work.

I do know and so stated that a sentence of the form 'S is true iff p' does not give the truth-conditions of 'S' merely because it is true, but I did not state that Davidson requires that "the sentence that replaces '*p*' in the metalanguage *translates* the sentence 'S' refers to" (Lepore and Ludwig 2007, p. 559) because that doesn't apply to natural languages; moreover, 'translates' here only means that the T-sentence belongs to "a systematic account of truth-conditions" (Davidson 2001a, p. 144). Davidson claims that a T-sentence that gives the truth-condi-

---

3 I now think, however, that many of these criticisms were misplaced.
4 I have published a paper on the slingshot argument that implies endorsement of Davidson's rejection of facts.

tions of a sentence should be a *theorem* of a truth theory that meets convention-T and is law-like. By 'truth-conditions', Davidson sometimes means 'canonical theorems of a truth theory for a language', but truth-conditions were not confined to a meaning theory because "a general and pre-analytic notion of truth is presupposed by the theory. It is because we have this notion that we can tell what counts as evidence for the truth of a T-sentence" (Davidson 1984, p. 223).

I do admit to a misunderstanding on my part in relation to Lepore and Ludwig's claim that the axioms of a truth-based meaning theory should be *interpretive*. They meant that the axioms should yield as theorems T-sentences that meet convention-T, which Davidson, of course, accepts. Here I was misled by 'interpretive', a term Davidson applies not to the axioms of the theory, since their character is *internal* to the theory, but to the use of its theorems in interpreting a speaker, which is *external* to the theory. Davidson makes this distinction in discussing the 'dilemma of reference'. On the one hand, the meanings of sentences depend on the meanings of words, but that leads to the hopeless building-block theory of meaning.[5] On the other hand, the meanings of words are only abstractions from the meanings of sentences, but that holistic approach seems unable to account for the semantic features of the words that make up sentences:

> What is needed to resolve the dilemma of reference is the distinction between explanation *within* the theory and explanation *of* the theory. Within the theory, the conditions of truth of a sentence are specified by adverting to postulated structure and semantic concepts like that of satisfaction or reference. But when it comes to interpreting the theory as a whole, it is the notion of truth, as applied to closed sentences, which must be connected with human ends and activities. (Davidson 1984, p. 221)

Issues about axioms concern explanation *within* the theory:

> Words, meanings of words, reference, and satisfaction are posits we need to implement a theory of truth. They serve this purpose without needing independent confirmation or empirical basis ... We must treat [satisfaction and reference] as theoretical constructs whose function is exhausted in stating truth-conditions for sentences. (Davidson 1984, pp. 222–223)[6]

Seen from within, the theory has a building-block appearance, but that is a feature of the theory, not of the language theorized about (which is what I meant by

---

[5] The building-block theory is a 'picture of how to do semantics' and not only a theory of language acquisition. In any case, Davidson denies that "the situations in which words are learned merely constitute evidence of what those words mean, rather than conferring meaning on them" (Guttenplan 1994, p. 233).
[6] This yields the 'inscrutability of reference'.

'language itself'). When it comes to explanation *of* the theory and its role in interpretation, the building-block approach is rejected: "The theory can be supported by relating T-sentences, and nothing else, to the evidence ... Reference drops out. It plays no essential role in explaining the relation between language and reality." (Davidson 1984, pp. 223, 225)

Lepore and Ludwig's distinction between an initial and an extended project may look like this, but it is different. In the initial project, they write, we "grant the meanings of words, and show how we can understand complex expressions on their basis" (Lepore and Ludwig 2007, p. 564). On my view, this belongs to explanation *within* the theory, except that we do not *grant* the meaning of words but posit axioms to yield theorems about complex expressions. The extended project concerns "what it is for primitive expressions to mean what they do" (Lepore and Ludwig 2007, p. 564), which Lepore and Ludwig appear to identify with Davidson's explanation *of* a theory. But if 'primitive expressions' means 'sub-sentential expressions', Davidson has no such project since he thinks that an account of the meaning of such expressions is *internal* to a meaning theory. But only by thinking of such an account as *external* could Lepore and Ludwig write that "with each semantical primitive of the language, there will be associated a distinct ability, knowledge of how to use that semantical primitive" (Lepore and Ludwig 2005, p. 123). For Davidson, that is speculation about "arcane empirical matters that neither philosophers nor psychologists know much about" (Davidson 1994b, p. 3).

If Lepore and Ludwig's remarks about meaning are taken to be *only* about the inner structure of the theory, then I agree with many of them. For example, nothing I wrote contradicts their remarks about indeterminacy *within* the theory. What I objected to was their claim that "there is a fact of the matter about which axioms are correct because there is a fact of the matter about the structure of speakers' dispositions to use words" (Lepore and Ludwig 2005, p. 124), which surely appears to deny indeterminacy on grounds *external* to the theory. One *might* construe their remark as claiming that indeterminacy of *interpretation* is harmless (like the choice of a Fahrenheit or Celsius scale) and that what is constant ('the fact of the matter') underneath the diverse interpretations is a speaker's dispositions to use words. But for Davidson what is constant is the *pattern* of sentences held true and the speaker's psychological attitudes, and that yields no fact of the matter either about axioms or about dispositions to use words.

Another example concerns rules. A meaning theory requires internal rules attached to the semantical primitives, but Davidson denies that linguistic competence requires rules. Lepore and Ludwig refer to a passage in which Davidson talks of "rules already mastered", but this is from one of his earliest pieces on meaning theory (Davidson 1984, p. 8), and the idea is one Davidson later rejects.

"Language is not an ordinary learned skill; it is, or has become, a mode of perception" (Davidson 2005a, p. 135), and hence not a matter of mastering rules. "I am against the idea that we understand speakers by appealing to, or applying, rules, conventions, or a theory." (Davidson 2005a, p. 315) "Conventions and rules do not explain language; language explains them." (Davidson 2005b, p. 58)

Davidson writes that a meaning theory gives the structure of an ability, but he denies that it accounts for linguistic competence or its exercise. A theory specifies "what it is about the structure of thought, emotion, and desire that makes understandings and communication possible" (Davidson 2005a, p. 294), but not what goes on when we understand or communicate.

> It is the philosopher, trying to understand understanding, who needs the theory in order to say what it is that the interpreter knows if he understands a speaker ... This does not suggest that the flawless interpreter knows such a theory. (Davidson 2005a, p. 324)

> [My] approach to the problems of meaning, belief, and desire ... is not ... meant to throw any direct light on how in real life we come to understand each other, much less how we master our first concepts and our first language. I have been engaged in a conceptual exercise aimed at revealing the dependencies among our basic propositional attitudes at a level fundamental enough to avoid the assumption that we can come to grasp them – or intelligently attribute them to others – one at a time. My way of performing this exercise has been to show how it is in principle possible to arrive at all of them at once. (Davidson 2004, p. 166)

Kant undertook in the *First Critique* a similar project in giving an account of what it is about the structure of intuition and judgment that makes empirical knowledge possible, but that account was silent about the psychological processes of cognition. Davidson attempted no more in articulating logical form: that is to give "the truth-conditions of a sentence in the context of a theory of truth that applies to the language as a whole ... [and] outside [the] theory, the notion of logical form has no clear application" (Davidson 2001a, p. 143). Since it "need never feature in the transactions of real life" (Davidson 2001a, p. 145) it is not "responsible to the speaker's disposition to use words" (Davidson 2001a, p. 137).

Two questions arise about Lepore and Ludwig's fevered response to my review of their discussion of radical interpretation. Did they interpret Davidson correctly, and can his view, interpreted charitably, be defended? I said no to the first and yes to the second, and their response gives me no reason to reconsider either answer, nor is it relevant to the things I wish I had said differently. The issues are too complicated, however, to deal in the space available, with their misinterpretations of what Davidson or I wrote, or to defend my views. That would require going through quotations taken out of context and misused, citing pertinent passages they failed to quote, showing how they have provided

Davidson with arguments he would reject, and more. I can reply to only a few of their criticisms here, and what follows are my replies to some of the more salient.

I wrote that Davidson regards the claim that meaning is public and observable as a commonplace rather than a philosophical thesis and that their (P) ("One can come to know something sufficient to interpret a speaker from the evidential position of the radical interpreter" (Lepore and Ludwig 2005, p. 166)) "as it stands ... is a reasonable formulation of that commonplace". I went on to say that "it is *central to his work* ... as a background assumption", which does not mean that it is "beyond appropriate critical attention" or cannot be construed as a controversial thesis. Lepore and Ludwig do the latter because they think Davidson's project requires that (P) be construed as "Speaking requires being interpretable by any possible speaker in any possible environment." (Lepore and Ludwig 2005, p. 388) That *is* controversial, but Davidson rejects it, for instance, in a passage (criticizing Fodor and Lepore) we both quote, though 'astonishingly' I failed to mention their discussion of it. I did so because their labored attempt to interpret a passage directly criticizing their construal of (P) was so distorted and self-serving I thought it better not to mention it.

Davidson roots the commonplace in "language [being] necessarily a social affair" (Davidson 2001c, p. 117), a point he also made about the psychological attitudes and developed in his work on triangulation. But his aim was not to *prove* the commonplace by appeal to the social character of language or to the triangular nature of our knowledge. His concern was to clarify what it is for meaning and the attitudes to be public and observable, for language to be social, for knowledge of oneself, other persons, and the material world to be interrelated, and how these various claims relate to each other.

Davidson often writes of what is necessary, in principle possible, essential, or by nature, of what is constitutive, of conceptual ties, and he would distinguish constitutive truths from truths about the number of planets (though a committee recently altered the latter). My complaint was not that Lepore and Ludwig took Davidson to use such concepts and distinctions but that they were insensitive to his use of them and construed them in their own terms. In particular, they took truths about what is essential, conceptual, by nature, constitutive, etc. to be *a priori* as opposed to *a posteriori*.

What Lepore and Ludwig take that distinction to be is unclear, and the passage they cite – "These terms could be replaced with *any* pair that captures the difference between the kind of ground involved in establishing truths constitutive of a subject-matter, and in establishing truths which are not" (Lepore and Ludwig 2005, p. 173 n. 139) – is not helpful, for it does not clarify the difference. In any case, Davidson would reject the way they actually use the *a priori*, for instance, in their 'ambitious project', which determines their understanding of the constitutive-non-constitutive distinction (rather than the other way around) because it assumes a sharp distinction between *a priori* and *a posteriori* and is inconsistent with rejection of the analytic-synthetic distinction.

Spelling out Davidson's own understanding of concepts like necessary, constitutive, or conceptual is essential to interpreting his work, which Lepore and Ludwig don't do. A metaphysical system (Kripke's, for example) should not be imposed because Davidson thought that metaphysical construction raised more problems than it solved. The task is to articulate their relations to each other and to other fundamental concepts, accepting them for what they are and not forcing them into external forms.

My writing that Davidson's account of first-person authority is "meant to illuminate the asymmetry but not to explain why it exists" is defensible. Davidson holds that first-person authority is a *constitutive* feature of the mental, and hence so is asymmetry, and since constitutive features are not contingent in the usual sense, they cannot be explained in a substantive sense. Davidson does speak of explaining this asymmetry, but he does so by saying that *it makes no sense* to interpret ourselves, which is no substantive explanation. Moreover, to explain the asymmetry between authority about our own and others' intentional states is not to explain why we have first person authority in the first place; that is a point at which "questions come to an end" (Davidson 1994c, p. 233).

Lepore and Ludwig's argument that the underdetermination of radical interpretation ruins Davidson's project seems to me utterly wrong-headed. A claim (or theory) is *underdetermined* if all relevant evidence is insufficient to determine whether to accept it or an *incompatible* alternative, whereas it is indeterminate if no amount of evidence will determine whether to accept it or an empirically equivalent *compatible* alternative. Davidson insisted that interpretation is *indeterminate*, but "a harmless consequence of the fact that there is more than one way of describing what is invariant" (Davidson 2005a, p. 319). It's like different descriptions of the same area in hectares or acres, which applies also to interpretation provided that distinctions between analytic and synthetic and meaning and belief are rejected. Lepore and Ludwig's objection that this assumes that "the interpreter's language marks more distinctions than can be marked in the language of the speaker being interpreted" (Lepore and Ludwig 2007, p. 569) presupposes that there is such a thing as *the* language of the interpreter and of the speaker, each being able to mark a determinate number of distinctions, which Davidson, if he found it intelligible, would reject.

Davidson's view of *underdetermination* is distinct and more complex.

First, what underdetermination *is* depends on what evidence is *relevant*. If a claim about the attitudes is underdetermined because there is no "correct answer to the question whether or not someone has a certain attitude", and if that means that there are no "objective grounds for choosing among conflicting hypotheses" (Davidson 2001c, p. 82), then Davidson does *not* think that interpretation is underdetermined since he maintains that there are such objective grounds. These grounds are, however, internal to interpretation because there can be no 'common standard of interpretation' that we use in interpreting others, "for mutual interpretation provides the only standard we have" (Davidson 2001c, p. 83). Lepore and Ludwig would not accept this because they think that the only evidence relevant to radical interpretation is "behaviour neutrally described", which means that evidence grounded on mutual interpretation is irrelevant. This badly misinterprets Davidson, as I argue below.

Second, Davidson is not committed to underdetermination on the ground that "public availability is a constitutive aspect of language" (Davidson 1990, p. 314) *unless* the latter means that "Speaking requires being interpretable by any possible speaker in any possible environment." (Lepore and Ludwig 2005, p. 388) Davidson explicitly rejects that, holding that "the correct interpretation of one person's speech by another must *in principle* be possible [emphasis in original]" (Davidson 2005b, p. 56), which means that it might sometimes fail and hence that claims of a radical interpreter might be underdetermined. But even if they were, it would not follow that the intentional attitudes are unreal; "they are every bit as real as atoms and baseball bats" (Davidson 2005a, p. 316).

Rather than respond to what Lepore and Ludwig take to be the many errors in my discussion of theoretical concepts, I shall reformulate what I view as their basic misinterpretation of Davidson. They claim that Davidson's most fundamental assumption is that:

> We can properly treat psychological and linguistic concepts as theoretical concepts whose purpose is to enable us to systematize and keep track of behavior neutrally described – or, to put it in another way, the assumption that the third person stance, as embodied by the stance of the radical interpreter, is conceptually basic in understanding meaning and psychological attitudes. (Lepore and Ludwig 2005, p. 387)

The main difficulty here is the notion of 'behavior neutrally described', which Lepore and Ludwig understand in an austere way as excluding the intentional attitudes, and they take 'publicly observable' to apply only to such behavior. On their view, Davidson held that the reality of intentional attitudes consists in the role they play in systematizing and keeping track of – explaining – behavior in this very austere sense.

This misunderstanding of Davidson's view accounts for many of the wrongheaded things they say about his conception of the attitudes. Davidson contends that the behavior explained by psychological and linguistic attitudes is intentional under some description, and although it may also be neutrally described, the attitudes do not explain it *as such*. When he writes that the intentional attitudes are constituted by their role in systematizing and keeping track of behavior, he means behavior described not neutrally but *as* the action of agents.

Lepore and Ludwig get this wrong because they misdescribe what goes on in radical interpretation. They are right that the initial evidence for radical interpretation cannot be what the interpreter knows about the speaker's linguistic behavior *as* intentional (*as* her saying or believing such and such) because not knowing that makes interpretation *radical*. The initial evidence must, therefore, be behavior neutrally described – typically the speaker's utterance of a sentence she holds true whose meaning the interpreter does not know. But her utterance can (in general) be relevant to interpretation only if there is a description under which it *is* intentional (that the interpreter does not initially know). To understand the sentence uttered, the interpreter must discover what the speaker means by it and what belief she expresses – and hence discover a description under which it is intentional. But he can do that only if the speaker's utterance *is* intentional, and it is only relative to *that* that the speaker's psychological and linguistic attitudes play a role in her behavior, linguistic or otherwise. Although radical interpretation must *begin* with behavior neutrally described, it does not investigate how the intentional attitudes systematize and keep track of behavior *thus described*. The purpose of the attitudes – the role that constitutes their reality – is to systematize and keep track of behavior *described as intentional*. That is a consequence of the autonomy of psychology.

The notion that the third-person stance is conceptually basic in understanding the intentional attitudes must also be understood in these terms. If 'third-person stance' means the stance of the radical interpreter, then it is *not* a stance open to anyone with normal senses but only to agents who can identify other agents and can understand and perceive their behavior *as* intentional action. Being able to perceive behavior as neutrally described is a necessary (although artificial) first step in radical interpretation, but what is conceptually basic in understanding the attitudes is what that first step leads to, namely, the interpretation of the behavior of speakers *as* intentional and *hence* explicable in terms of their intentional attitudes.

This is the sense of behavior Davidson had in mind when he wrote that "Meaning is entirely determined by observable behavior, even readily observable behavior" (Davidson 2005b, p. 56). That does not mean that the radical interpreter can simply *observe* what a speaker is saying or doing; he has put himself in a situation where such observation is ruled out initially. But as interpretation proceeds, he will learn how to *observe* what the speaker is saying or doing (language is "a mode of perception" (Davidson 2005a, p. 135)), which means, not that he gives up the third-person stance, but that he is now able to make, on the basis of observation, knowledgeable claims about the speaker's intentional attitudes.[7]

My remarks about Davidson and analytical philosophy were intended to situate the major differences between Lepore and Ludwig's interpretation and mine. We agree that Davidson was an analytical philosopher in many ways and that his arguments are "frequently aimed less at proving a conclusion than at suggesting strategies, getting across a point of view, or making plausible a new way of seeing things". The latter is, of course, consistent with his papers being "full of intricate, subtle, extended, and detailed argumentation" (Lepore and Ludwig 2007, p. 584), something I do not deny but that Lepore and Ludwig take to be (apart from the meaning theory) largely a failure. In my view, they think so poorly of that argumentation – or lack thereof – because they do not take seriously enough his seeing things in a new way. That requires arguments that do not use premises that are standard, received, or obvious to philosophers because it is precisely such premises that Davidson challenges. If the task is not primarily constructing arguments to support conclusions but rejecting premises philosophers are prone to use[8] and finding and supporting new premises, then novel strategies and argumentation have to be devised, something for which Lepore and Ludwig have little patience or charity.

I wrote that analytical philosophy is no longer a well-defined school. It was when it began, although no *doctrines* unified the work of Frege, Russell, and Moore. Now, however, doctrines unify the work of Searle and Fodor, along with Lepore and Ludwig. and many contemporary analytical philosophers. I chose Searle and Fodor as exemplars of 'a shared *version*' of analytical philosophy precisely because, from Lepore and Ludwig's point of view, they share little. From a Davidsonian perspective, however, they share important assumptions – some of which I noted in my review[9] – whose rejection distinguishes him from much recent analytical philosophy.

---

7 My reference to triangulation (see Chapter 6 above, ●p. XXX● Please ensure that page number will be added in final (PDF) version. ●) as showing that "the third-person point of view [is] not the only basic point of view" was not directed at the methodologically fundamental status of radical interpretation and the third person (*properly understood*) in an account of the attitudes. Its point was that the three points of view are so interconnected that none of the 'varieties of knowledge' can be regarded as a basis for the others.

8 Lepore and Ludwig do not deny that their point of view represents the "(so-called) Cartesian framework" in philosophy, although rejecting it is surely central to Davidson's work.

9 Showing that I am right or wrong about the items I listed would require considerable discussion.

This is less evident to those who use Davidson's early work on meaning to interpret his later than to those who read his early work in the light of the later. There are no seismic changes in his work, but some points are developed in more detail or in different directions, while others are down-played or re-expressed. Because he did not write a synoptic book, it is not always evident how the points he made in his papers fit together or which points are crucial and which are dispensable or need reformulation. A really useful study of Davidson would clarify these matters. That would call for criticism that aims to improve rather than undermine his claims and that is set in the context of an interpretation as charitable as careful reading permits. The result would be a Davidson who avoids unproductive scholastic disputes while retaining the virtues of analytical philosophy. What is important is not whether he is *called* an analytical philosopher but whether his work is understood and criticized in its own terms rather than in terms of external categories, distinctions, and doctrines.[10]

---

10 I am grateful for helpful suggestions in the writing of this response from Lilli Alanen, Antti Kuusela, Jeff Malpas, Paul Needham, and Frans Svensson.

7 Davidson and Dewey: A Critical Comparison

It was Rorty who argued most influentially that Davidson should be seen as a pragmatist. Evaluating this argument is complex because we have three claims to consider: that Rorty's account of pragmatism is adequate to the great pragmatists such as Dewey; that Davidson's work meets Rorty's criteria for being a pragmatist; that Davidson's work is pragmatist in Dewey's sense. Although there is truth in each of these claims, in a deeper sense I think we should reject them all. The interesting claim is the last, which is my focus here.

The fundamental idea of pragmatism is that the primary relation of subjects to world is practical rather than theoretical or cognitive: we are knowers only in being doers. This is the basis of Rorty's claim that that the aim of thought and inquiry is being able to cope with the world rather than to get true views about it, which means, he thought, that knowledge and rationality are not a matter of our relation to the world but of our relation to our peers. "Solidarity, not objectivity" was his slogan. This was grounded in what he took to be the result of the rejection of Aristotelian science, namely, that our world is physicalist, devoid of conceptual structure, whose effect on us is brutely causal. Such a world cannot warrant beliefs that correspond to it; we do not represent it but cope with it as best we can. There are, therefore, no metaphysical or epistemological distinctions between different kinds of descriptions of the world. Each kind, whether from physics, natural history, sociology, or poetry, enables us to cope in its own way. To think some kinds describe the real world, while others describe a merely constructed world or only express our attitudes, assumes the discredited notion that there is a such a thing as a true description of the real world.

This can be seen as a quick sketch of Davidson, who wrote that "the concept of action is central to many of the perennial concerns of philosophy" (Davidson 2005a, p. 277). It appears to fit his account of language, which, given his rejection of the analytic-synthetic distinction, "… erased the boundary between knowing a language and knowing our way around the world generally" (Davidson 2005a, p. 107) and implied that "the interpretation of speech must go hand in hand with the interpretation of action generally" (Davidson 2001b, p. 154). He accepted the legitimacy of diverse descriptions of the world, holding that psychology is autonomous and hence that mental descriptions are irreducible to physical ones and that explanations of mental events, including intentional actions, are distinct from yet as legitimate as explanations in physical science.

He also shared the view that we live and move in a physicalist world, and, like the pragmatists, he rejected the 'myth of the given' – that any natural objects are themselves reasons for belief or action. What we know of the world is by the beliefs it *causes* us to have. But he did not accept solidarity rather than objectivity: beliefs are objective thoughts about the world, whose truth is not a matter of coping with it.

While there are pragmatic features in Davidson's great work, I do not think he is a pragmatist, not only because he takes objectivity over solidarity and rejects pragmatist accounts of truth, but for even deeper reasons. He holds that our primary relation to the world is not practical but causal, a causality mediated by thought – primarily belief – and hence theoretical rather than practical. Perception is thought caused by the world; action is bodily movement caused by thought. Neither are practical in the pragmatist sense, which, as Dewey put it, stresses not causes but consequences. Davidson's taking action to be a central concept may appear to make him a pragmatist, but because his conception of action is theoretical rather than practical, this is misleading: he is not a pragmatist in any significant sense, or so I shall argue.

I will first consider Dewey's conception of experience, then Davidson's, then draw some evaluative comparisons, and finish with a brief consideration of further respects in which Davidson's view suffers from not being pragmatist.

7.1 The Natural World

I want first to say something about the scientific revolution's rejection of Aristotelian science, which meant that the natural world, *insofar as it is described by the physical sciences and made intelligible by their methods*, is physicalistic. Descartes was the first great philosopher of the scientific revolution, arguing that it showed, not only that the natural world as conceived in the physical sciences is devoid of teleological structure and associated normativity, but that *the natural world itself* is devoid of such structure. He took this to be true also of living beings, which he regarded as mere mechanisms governed entirely by the laws of physics, as well as of human beings, though not of human souls, which were distinct from the natural world.

Although denying teleological-normative structure to the natural world, he thought it has logical structure: it is a world of objects and properties, of facts and propositions, of modalities and mathematical structures, and its denizens can, therefore, in principle, serve as reasons for beliefs about its physical structure. But they cannot serve as reasons for beliefs about what is good, as motivations to act, or as reasons for acting. The natural world, though logically structured, was devoid of what I shall call 'conceptual structure', hence evaluatively blank, motivationally inert, and not a space of reasons.

Something like that view of the natural world has persisted. It was Frege's view, the view of Carnap and other positivists, and it is the view underlying current analytic metaphysics. A critic of it was Quine, who argued not only that the natural world itself is physicalistic, but that it is devoid even of logical structure. On his austere view, the natural world contains no properties, facts, propositions, or modalities. If any sense can be made of those notions, it is in language, which unlike the world has logical structure.

That is also Davidson's (and Rorty's) view of the natural world, inherited from Quine. It is Dewey's too but with one decisive change: for Dewey, Quine's austere view is not true of the natural world *as such* but only insofar as described by and made intelligible in terms of the physical sciences. Dewey counted living creatures as natural, and while admitting that the physical sciences can treat them as physicalistic, he held that the world of living things is not *as such* physicalistic. It is a distinct realm of nature that is not intelligible *as* a realm of living things in terms of the concepts and methods of physics and chemistry. It no doubt evolved from a physicalistic world but it is now not reducible to it.

The world of living things is not physicalist, but it is not conceptually structured either. Because non-human animals need nourishment, they have a reason to eat food, but they do not eat food because it is food; as brute animals, they have no concept of food or of anything else being a reason to act. The questions remains whether there is such a thing as a conceptually structured world – a world that yields reasons for thought and action and is normatively and motivationally significant. If so, what is its ground and origin, and how is it related to the natural world as conceived in the physical sciences?

One answer is that the latter is all there is, that talk about conceptual content and normative rationality can be reformulated in physicalist terms or done without. This is physicalism like Quine's and many of our contemporaries. Another answer is neo-scholasticism, which puts conceptual structure back into the natural world and makes it a space of reasons. A third alternative is Cartesian dualism, which adds a mental world of inner events and states that are by nature conceptually structured and causally related to the physicalist world.

Finally, there is a broadly Kantian response, which holds, not that there is another world in addition to the physicalist, but that the latter, in some sense, becomes a conceptually structured space of reasons as the result of human thought or practice. Projectionism is one version of this response: we project our attitudes on the world, which becomes, insofar as we take them into account, a 'quasi-conceptual' world. Another is John McDowell's view – a version of Kant's own – that the natural world affects our senses only inasmuch as those "states or episodes of sensibility ... are themselves actualizations of conceptual capacities" (Smith 2002, p. 271). The world we experience and in which we act and think is, therefore, a conceptually structured world just because it would not be a world we experience and respond to did it not affect us by actualizing the conceptual capacities we have come to possess.

Davidson and Dewey's view are also Kantian in this broad sense in that both hold that there is conceptual structure only because of human thought and practice. Both also hold that there is *logical* structure in the world for the same reason, but to keep this manageable I will talk only about conceptual structure. Their views of that are very different. For Davidson it involves the causal role of human thought in perception and action. For Dewey it is because our experience is essentially a matter of practice that constructs the conceptual structures of our everyday world.

7.2 Dewey on Experience

Dewey's conception of experience is central to his pragmatism and a natural starting point for a comparison of his view with Davidson's. He defined experience as "an affair of intercourse of a living being with its physical and social environment" (Dewey 1980, p. 6). This can apply to any living being if we take 'social' in a very broad sense, but I shall consider only human experience, which is interaction between *subjects* and *world*. Paradigm examples, which he thought were like Aristotle's, are visiting a friend, writing a paper, repairing a car, going to summer camp, buying a suit, watching a game. Each of these is *an* experience. We might ask, 'Have you had an experience of buying a suit?' or 'Have you had much experience fixing a car?'

These are clearly practical matters – 'ways of doing and suffering' – not instances of knowing. Our fundamental relation to the events and things in our world, Dewey held, are practical, not theoretical. Knowing is "a connection of things which depends on other and more primary connections between a self and things ...", and hence it is wrong to think that "... No qualities or things are present in experience except as objects of some kind of apprehension ..." – that they are "either totally absent from experience or else [are] objects of 'consciousness' or knowing" (Dewey 1916, p. 3). On the contrary, "Things and qualities are present to most men most of the time as things and qualities in situations of prizing and aversion, of seeking and finding, of converse, enjoyment and suffering, of production and employment, of manipulation and destruction." (Dewey 1916, p. 3) This means that "The one who knows things also stands in other connections with them [and hence] it is possible to make an intelligible contrast between things as known and things as loved or hated or appreciated, or seen or heard or whatever." (Dewey 1916, p. 273)

Dewey *contrasted* being known with being seen or heard because he denied that seeing a color or hearing a sound constitutes knowledge. Brute animals also see colors and hear sounds but they do not have knowledge of them. He did not deny that experience includes colors seen, sounds heard, and other sense impressions, but held that these are "simply natural events having, in themselves (apart from a *use* that may be made of them), no more knowledge status or worth than, say, a shower or a fever" (Dewey 1916, p. 253).

> The plain man ... does not regard noises heard, lights seen, etc., as mental existence; but neither does he regard them as things *known* ... His attitude to those things *as* things involves their *not* being in relation to him as a mind or knower. He is in the attitude of a liker or hater, a doer or an appreciator. (Dewey 1916, pp. 257–258)

Experience encompasses both sense awareness and action. Colors seen, sounds heard, textures felt, etc., brought about by things and events affecting our senses, are always present in experience. But their presence is practical not cognitive: to be aware of them *is* to respond, use, suffer, enjoy them. Sense awareness and actions are mutually dependent and not easily disentangled, if at all.

Dewey held that knowledge in the strict sense requires judgments that are inferentially warranted. He described the acquisition of knowledge, which he called 'inquiry', in a Peircean way as moving from a confused, unsettled situation of doubt to one that is unconfused, settled, and warranted by data. Inquiry is itself an experience that, unlike ordinary experience, is cognitive, but it is rooted in non-cognitive experiences, which are the source of the data necessary for warranted judgment. Data requires objects seen, heard, felt, etc., which in themselves are merely natural objects. But we make such objects into data by *using* them to *indicate* something else. They thereby acquire conceptual structure, becoming what Dewey called 'signs'. The natural event of a noise heard, for example, can be used to indicate that a train is approaching, thereby becoming a sign and hence, if a train *is* coming, a datum for inference.

Using a noise heard as a sign of a train assumes having the concept of a train and presumably some knowledge. While Dewey thought that experience is primarily practical, he also thought it presupposes, indeed, is permeated with, the *results* of inquiry. In the first instance, we deliberately *use* a noise to indicate a train, but as we do that over time, we come to be able simply to *hear* the noise as the sound of a train. This is a kind of non-inferential knowledge that is made possible, not by a natural capacity for immediate knowledge, but by our giving conceptual structure to natural events. "*For practical purposes*", Dewey wrote, "many perceptual events are cases of knowledge; that is they have been *used* as such so often that the habit of so using them is established as automatic."

(Dewey 1916, p. 165) "... Their nature as evidence, as signs, [comes to overshadow] their natural status." (Dewey 1916, p. 164)

Their becoming signs can be an everyday occurrence. "We go about with a disposition to identify certain shapes as tables, certain sounds as words of the French language, certain cries as evidence of distress, colors as woods in the distance ...." (Dewey 1916, p. 23) Or it may be more complex, as in the case of a physician who "has acquired certain habits in virtue of which certain physical qualities and events are more than physical, in virtue of which they are signs or indications of something else" (Dewey 1916, p. 21). Getting data for scientific investigation is still more complex because they have to "discovered by physical manipulations which detach them from their ordinary setting" (Dewey 1916, p. 27).

The notion that natural events *acquire* conceptual structure is crucial because Dewey took the world, *considered in abstraction from experience*, to consist of brute objects and events. But when we encounter such events in experience that has been enriched by previous experience, especially by prior inquiry, they are conceptually structured and hence can be data for inference and reasons for belief or action. Such experiential encounters are not cognitive in the strict sense if they do not involve inference, but they are conceptual because of *prior* cognitions. The point I quoted earlier, that things and qualities are present in experience, not as objects of apprehension but typically in "situations of prizing and aversion, of seeking and finding, of converse, enjoyment and suffering" (Dewey 1916, p. 273), does not mean that these situations, though practical and not cognitive, are brute; they are conceptually structured, and hence what is encountered is evaluatively relevant and motivationally significant.

I do not mean to suggest that natural objects and events acquire conceptual significance for single individuals on particular occasions. For Dewey, the fact that human experience, unlike that of brute animals, has conceptual content, is partly due, of course, to our having inborn capacities that brutes do not. But the decisive point is that these capacities make possible the creation of the cultural environment in which we have been brought up and in which we live, think, and act. Human experience is what it is because of a common culture and the numerous cultural artifacts it has created – architecture, agriculture, industry, commerce, schools, the arts, science, and technology, and so on.

> To a large extent the ways in which human beings respond even to physical conditions are influenced by their cultural environment ... [Human] activities are encompassed in an environment that is culturally transmitted, so that what man does and how he acts, is determined not by organic structures and physical heredity alone but by the influence of cultural heredity, embedded in traditions, institutions, customs and the purposes and beliefs they both carry and inspire. (Dewey 1938, pp. 42–43)

Everyday experience, he wrote, "is saturated with the results of social intercourse and communication" (Dewey 1925, p. xiii).

The essential condition of this is language, which Dewey understood as extending beyond speech to include "not only gestures but rites, ceremonies, monuments, the products of industrial and fine arts" (Dewey 1938, p. 51). He recognized that language is an indispensible means of communication, which he took to be primarily practical – a way of getting "agreement in action" (Dewey 1938, p. 51). But he thought it also has a more basic role, namely, making human experience *as such* – not on a particular occasion, not mine or yours – conceptually structured and rationally significant.

It fulfills this role in virtue of two fundamental functions: "... It is the agency by which other institutions and acquired habits are *transmitted* and it *permeates* both the forms and the contents of all other cultural activities." (Dewey 1938, p. 45) To have these functions, a language must be common to and widely shared by members of a society who create and preserve cultural institutions and participate in cultural activities. Indeed, Dewey maintained that the acquisition of a language meant changes in the physical structure of human beings.

> The acquisition and understanding of language with proficiency in the arts (that are foreign to other animals than men) represent an incorporation within the physical structure of human beings of the effects of cultural conditions, an interpenetration so profound that resulting activities are as direct and seemingly 'natural' as are the first reactions of an infant ... This modification of organic behavior in and by the cultural environment ... is the transformation of purely organic behavior into behavior marked by intellectual properties ... (Dewey 1938, p. 49)

Dewey's view that the events, qualities, and things that are present even in non-cognitive experience are conceptually structured means that the world in which we live, think, and act is not physicalistic. It contains qualities we enjoy, suffer, disparage, things we appreciate and use, actions we perform for various reasons. These are not physicalistic objects on which we project our attitudes or that cause us to have beliefs or other thoughts about them. Nor are intentional actions the bodily movements of neuro-physiology caused on the occasion of acting by beliefs and desires. As animals, we can move our bodies and limbs in intricate and skilled ways; as human beings, we can move them intentionally in response to reasons as such. No special causality is required either to act intentionally on an occasion or to give conceptual structure to our moving our bodies.

What lies back of this view is Dewey's conviction that we cannot allocate the qualities, things, and events of everyday experience to the mind rather than to the world, or to the world rather than to the mind. Experience involves both mind and world, subject and object, mental and physical. Neither can stand alone in experience, and we cannot separate out the distinctive contribution each makes. "Any experience in all its non-reflective phases is innocent of any discrimination of subject and object." (Dewey 1916, p. 86n)

Dewey granted that mind and world, subject and object, can be distinguished for various purposes when we engage in inquiry, particularly in the physical sciences. What he denied is that any such distinction applies generally or that what is thus distinguished exists in experience as distinguished – that mind and world are externally related. Such a distinction requires abstracting from or suppressing important features of experience in order to focus on features that belong to world rather than to mind or vice versa, and it will be in the service of some particular inquiry: it will be, as Dewey put it, functional and not ontological.

Consider what it would be to focus on the world – on the objects of an experience. "… The presentation of objects as specifiably different things in experience is the work of reflection [and hence so is] the discrimination of something experience*d* from the modes of experienc*ing*." (Dewey 1916, p. 86n) "… In actual experience … *an* object or event is always a special part, phase, or aspect of an environing situation." (Dewey 1938, p. 66) How objects and events are discriminated in this holist situation is relative to various factors and cannot always be done.

> The terms distressing, perplexing, cheerful, disconsolate … do not designate specific qualities in the way in which *hard*, say, designates a particular quality of a rock. For such qualities permeate and color *all* the objects and events that are involved in an experience. (Dewey 1938, p. 69)

When we say a picture has a Rembrandt quality, we refer, not to a property of an object but to something "that affects and modifies all the constituents of the picture and all of their relations" (Dewey 1938, p. 75). The notion of an object functions differently in an aesthetic experience than in, say, a situation where we repair a picture or fit it in a frame.

Consider what it would be to focus on the mind – on the subject of an experience. We must not, Dewey wrote, think of "the 'me' or knowing self, as a separate thing within which experience falls (instead of its falling in a specifiable place within experience)…" (Dewey 1916, p. 71). The reference here to 'knowing self' means that Dewey thinks we focus on the 'me' primarily in inquiry and should not think, therefore, that the 'me' is outside experience rather than a feature of it. In fixing my car, for example, my success depends indifferently on whether I'm a competent mechanic, whether I have good tools, or whether I'm dealing with a well-designed car. But if I have a problem, I will have to make inquiry as to its source, thus distinguishing between me, the tools, and the car to determine if it is *my* lack of competence or something else that is the problem.

Dewey held that inquiry in the physical sciences requires making a particularly sharp distinction between mind and world and focusing only on world. The particles and forces of physics are reached by such inquiry, which abstracts from the complexity and flux of everyday experience in order to construct mathematical descriptions of the non-obvious but stable *relations* between the elements of everyday experience. These relations are necessary conditions of experience, both brute and human, but they do not, he wrote, disclose "... the inner nature of things but only those connections of things with one another which determine outcomes and hence can be used as means" (Dewey 1925, p. xii). The intrinsic nature of things "is revealed in experience as the immediately felt qualities of things" (Dewey 1925, p. xii), and hence the abstract and idealized descriptions of physics do not describe the essential nature even of the physical world. Dewey was not, he wrote, "a materialist about matter" – not a physicalist about the physical.

Dewey took the *object* of knowledge to be *that* such and such. His claim that we *construct* the *object* of knowledge can be understood, therefore, as meaning that knowledge requires constructing novel descriptions of the world – that is, ways of saying *that such and such* that are not given in everyday experience. He also held that experimental manipulation, which is the decisively new element in post-medieval science, requires constructing instruments to create new situations that do not exist naturally (dramatically illustrated by giant accelerators), and it is for these constructed situations that inquiry aims to construct new descriptions.

Dewey thought Cartesian dualism arose by taking the distinction between mind and world to be an ontologically basic fact rather than an abstraction from experience. It took the physical world to be exhausted by what the physical sciences describe, assigning what is left over to the mind: to make the world physicalistic is to make the mind mentalistic. Descartes tried to bring them together with his notion of the mind-body union, but what he tried to bring together had been so conceived that the closest union possible was causal, which is inconsistent with a physicalist view of the physical and cannot account for salient features of human experience. Dewey's view was the reverse: he started with experience as mind and world together, and construed the distinction between them as secondary.

7.3 Davidson on Experience

Davidson took experience to be sense perception, which he regarded as essentially cognitive and hence theoretical rather than practical. Like Dewey, he held that sense impressions are merely natural objects or occurrences that we share with brute animals and have no conceptual structure, and hence are not reasons for beliefs or actions. They are nevertheless necessary conditions for empirical knowledge because the world affects our sense in cognitively relevant ways by causing us to have sense impressions.

The latter are cognitively significant, however, not in our using them as signs but in causing us to have perceptual beliefs, which having conceptual content, can be reasons for further beliefs. Sense impressions, that is, are *causal* intermediaries between a subject's beliefs and the world but not *epistemic* intermediaries. But beliefs are *epistemic* intermediaries between subjects and the world because our relation to the world either as knowers or as agents is always mediated by them. "Nothing can supply a reason for a belief", he wrote, "except another (or many another) belief" (Davidson 2005a, p. 136), nor can anything be a reason for an action that does not include a belief.

Back of this is Davidson's conviction that conceptual structure requires propositional thought, of which belief is the primary instance. Whatever else has conceptual structure derives it from thought, typically in virtue of causality. Thus action has conceptual structure – is performed for reasons – because it is caused by belief, and the same is true of attitudes like pride or joy. This is 'rational causality', which includes belief and other thoughts: rationality is "whatever involves propositional thought" (Davidson 2001c, p. xiv).

Davidson's conception of sense perception appears to generate skepticism about the senses: if only a belief can be a reason for a belief, our beliefs must, on pain of infinite regress, rest on beliefs for which there are no reasons and hence are unwarranted. But Davidson contended that "general skepticism of the senses is unintelligible" (Davidson 2004, p. 5). He held that beliefs that are not warranted by reasons nevertheless *are* reasons if they are apt to be true, and, indeed, he held that "beliefs are by nature generally true" (Davidson 2001c, p. 153), for which he gave two arguments.

The first is his holist view that "… a belief owes its character in part to its relations to other, true, beliefs" (Davidson 2004, p. 15), and hence "the possibility of error depends on a generous supply of truths; indeed, the more numerous our errors, the more we must have right in order to give substance to our mistakes" (Davidson 2004, p. 5). If our beliefs were massively false, they would be so disconnected from the world that they would cease to be about the world, and hence what is in the world would be irrelevant to their being *either* true or false.

The other is his *externalism* – the view that the content at least of perceptual beliefs, is constituted not by what subjects think or do, but by things in the world that cause them to have those beliefs. The argument presumes that "what a fully informed interpreter could learn about what a speaker means is all there is to learn; the same goes for what a speaker believes" (Davidson 2001c, p. 148), which implies that meaning is "open to public determination" (Davidson 2001c, p. 148) and, since meaning and belief are intertwined, so is belief. Both are knowable because

> Sentences and the thoughts they may be used to express, are causally tied to what they are about. For in the plainest cases we can do no better than to interpret a sentence that a person is selectively caused to hold true by the presence of rain as meaning that it is raining. (Davidson 2004, p. 36)

That is, in interpreting a sentence that expresses a speaker's perceptual belief, we assume that the content of her belief is about what we believe to have caused it, and hence we must assume that her belief, like ours about what causes it, is true. We could be wrong but we cannot believe we are, for to identify her belief requires our believing it is true.

These arguments are directed against skepticism about knowledge, but a more fundamental skepticism is about intentionality – "how beliefs are possible in the first place" (Davidson 2004, p. 5) – that is, how they are connected to the world so as to be *either* true or false, *either* warranted or not. Davidson called this the problem of *objective purport:* how we are "to account for our having the concept of objectivity – of a truth that is independent of our will and attitudes" (Davidson 2004, p. 7). Objective purport was pretty much assumed in the two arguments just discussed, but in his later work Davidson thought it needed defense, hence his doctrine of triangulation.

Triangulation involves an interrelation of two creatures with each other and with the world that impinges on them. Since triangulation is intended to explain how beliefs (or thoughts in general) are possible, it is pre-conceptual. "Triangulation is not a matter of one person grasping a meaning already there, but a performance that (when fully fleshed out) bestows a content on language." (Davidson 2001c, p. xv) The problem is to show how externalism of content is possible: how it is that an interpreter can have a belief about an object that he believes causes another person to have a belief about that same object. Davidson thought we cannot just help ourselves to such beliefs: they arise rather from a more primitive triangulation that is pre-conceptual.

Consider teaching a child the word (or one-word sentence) 'table' by rewarding it when it utters 'table' in the presence of a table. Why, Davidson asked, take the child to be responding to a table instead of to the visual impressions (or stimulations in the brain) that enable her to see the table. The table, the visual impressions, and the stimulations in the brain are all causes of her response. The problem is not how we can *tell* to what the child responds, but what it would *be* for her to respond to one rather than another.

Davidson's answer was to recognize that there are *three* factors in this situation: the child, the teacher, and the stimulus. The stimulus is not merely what causes the child to utter 'table' in the presence of tables, it is also what can cause the teacher to do the same. But in addition there is a relation between teacher and child in that the teacher observes that her response to tables is similar to the child's. This is triangulation:

> One line goes from the child in the direction of the table, one line goes from us in the direction of the table, and the third goes between us and the child. Where the lines from child to table and us to table and us to child meet, 'the' stimulus is located ... It is the common cause of our response and the child's response. (Davidson 2001c, p. 119)

Davidson went on:

> Enough features are in place to give a meaning to the idea that the stimulus has an objective location in a common space; but nothing in this picture shows that [any participants] have this idea ... [Nevertheless, triangulation] is necessary if there is to be any answer at all to the question what its concepts are concepts of. If we consider a single creature by itself, its responses, no matter how complex, cannot show that it is reacting, or thinking about, events a certain distance away rather than, say, on its skin. (Davidson 2001c, p. 121)

The point of triangulation, then, is to explain how to get from a situation where a creature's response to a stimulus is merely causing his reaction to a situation where a subject's response to an object is a matter of his acquiring a belief about that object rather than about the occurrences between his belief and its object. Perhaps Davidson is right about pre-conceptual triangulation: for something to *be* the cause of a creature's response, it must also cause a similar response in another creature. But that is independent of what either creature *observes* (fortunately, because observation is not pre-conceptual), which undercuts the extension of triangulation to the object of a *belief*. Davidson's claim is that something is the object of a subject's (perceptual) belief only if she is in contact with another subject who *observes* which object causes the belief, which is surely not in general true. Moreover, even if the object of a perceptual belief is usually its cause, it doesn't follow that its cause constitutes it as its object, if for no other reason than what belief is caused by an object affecting our senses depends on other beliefs. The presence of a hedgehog affecting my senses will not cause my belief that a hedgehog is in the road if I believe hedgehogs are porcupines; in that case I believe there is a porcupine in the road.

My concern here is not to criticize the triangulation project so much as to consider its presuppositions. It assumes that the physical world – the world we perceive, respond to, and change – is essentially physicalistic, an austerely Quinean world devoid of logical structure, but more to my interest here, devoid of conceptual structure and hence motivationally inert and normatively blank. Conceptual structure and the rationality it makes possible require thoughts – in particular beliefs – which are states distinctive to human beings who, themselves physicalist, have acquired over time the capacity to entertain them. Thought itself is conceptually structured, but whatever else is so structured is so because of its causal relation to thought.

The things we perceive, for instance, are typically perceived *as* such and such, which is due to their causing us to have perceptual beliefs about them. We perceive a hedgehog *as* an animal with distinctive qualities because it has caused sense impressions that have caused us to have beliefs that are structured in terms of the qualities of living animals. The hedgehog as an inhabitant of the physical world is not conceptually structured; only our perceptual beliefs about it are. Similarly, the actions we perform are essentially the brute bodily movements of neuro-physiology that acquire conceptual structure only in being caused by beliefs and desires that constitute them as actions. The bodily movements as such are not conceptually structured, but when and as they are caused by our beliefs and desires, they acquire a derived conceptual structure and are intentional under a description.

Davidson was explicit about the centrality of causation in his point of view. The essays in *Actions and Events*, he wrote,

> are unified in theme and general thesis. The theme is the role of causal concepts in the description and explanation of human action. The thesis is that the ordinary notion of cause which enters into scientific or common-sense accounts of non-psychological affairs is essential also to the understanding [of action]... (Davidson 2001a, p. xi)

He generalized the point in claiming that "Cause is the cement of the universe; the concept of cause is what holds together our picture of the universe, a picture that would otherwise disintegrate into a diptych of the mental and the physical." (Davidson 2001a, p. xi) The mental and the physical – world and mind – are separate spheres held together by causality.

This is intertwined with his view of the world as essentially physicalist. He took the *concept* of cause to be interest-relative and hence to be avoided in physics. The cement of the universe, nevertheless, consists of causal *relations*, which are natural *relations* that do not, therefore, obtain in virtue of any laws, causal or otherwise. But they *entail* that there are strict laws – hence laws of physics – covering the events, which means that causally related events have physicalistic descriptions and hence are physicalist.

He had a sophisticated view of the physicalist and the mental as two different kinds of descriptions or properties, holding that this dualism has no ontological significance, his view being ontological monism. His monism, moreover, is not physicalist in the ordinary sense because he held that mental descriptions are irreducible to physicalist ones and that, although all events have physicalist descriptions, those involving thought also have mental descriptions. Nor was he a dualist because he denied that the mental is a domain of inner states of which we are immediately aware. He was nevertheless a physicalist about the essential nature of the physical world: it consists of a vast network of physicalistically describable events devoid of conceptual structure and connected by natural relations of causality. "Beyond the skin", he wrote, "there is mindless causality." (Davidson 2005a, p. 136)

The crucial point about Davidson's conception of the physical world is that, apart from thought, which is conceptual by its nature, nothing else – for instance, objects as perceived or bodily movements as intentional – acquires conceptual structure except if, when, and as causally explained by thought on a particular occasion. He does not have the view that although the world, if considered in abstraction from human experience, can be conceived as physicalist, the world that we perceive as subjects and in which we act as agents is already conceptually structured and does not become so only on the occasion of the causal exercise of thought.

On this alternative view, the world has become, over a long period of interaction with human activity, evaluatively and motivationally relevant, and we have acquired the capacity to move our bodies intentionally, a capacity that does not consist in our thoughts causing our bodies to move but simply in our intentionally moving them. That we can under normal circumstances move them intentionally, does not call for special explanation, whereas the occurrence of such movements without our intentionally moving our bodies does.

7.4 Some Critical Comparisons

What I have just done is criticize Davidson in the light of Dewey's insights, and I shall conclude with more along that line. Dewey's view that the objects and events in the experienced world are conceptually structured independently of what subjects do on an occasion rests on two points. One is that human beings have, over a long period of time, created cultural institutions, above all languages, that are conceptually structured and that preserve and transmit that structure to persons who live in and among those institutions. The other is that "even the neuro-muscular structures of individuals are modified through the influence of the cultural environment upon the activities performed" (Dewey 1938, p. 43).

Davidson's view has none of this. His view of language as an instrument of communication of thoughts, which as such requires no common language and no more than two speaker-interpreters, does not give language its fundamental role as creator and transmitter of the culture that is embedded in social institutions and makes distinctively human experience possible. The latter view requires a shared common language intertwined with a shared culture in which children are brought up to perceive and respond to the world as others do. As McDowell put it, echoing Gadamer: "Shared languages matter for the constitution of subjects of understanding ... [They] give a normative shape to our lifeworld, in a way that is not reduced to the activities of subjects." (McDowell 2009, p. 98)

Davidson's conception of language is not, in spite of his taking it to be a mode of action, practical or pragmatist, because his view of *action* is basically theoretical: to move my body *is* for its movements to be caused by beliefs and desires. Action consists of physicalist bodily movements caused by my thoughts, which are states that I am caused to have. That presupposes a sharp distinction between the purely physical aspect of an action – the movements of the body (and what they cause) and the mental aspect – the thoughts that cause the movements, a distinction that requires taking a physicalist-theoretical stance that abstracts from the complexities of action as understood by agents.

In walking my dog, for example, I move my body, thereby pulling on the leash, avoiding slippery ice, being alert to the traffic, strengthening my legs, obeying doctor's orders to move around, and enjoying the fresh air – all descriptions under which my acting is intentional. There is no relevant distinction here between what I do and what I perceive, or between moving my body, pulling on the leash, and walking my dog. My bodily movements do not *cause* but *are* my pulling on the leash, and walking my dog: exercising my capacity to move my body *is*, in this context, pulling on the leash and walking my dog. Moreover, walking my dog in this context also *is* strengthening my legs and obeying doctor's orders, and if asked *why* I am walking my dog, I reply, because I am strengthening my legs, which I am doing because I am obeying doctor's orders, thus specifying factors that are internal to my acting. If I am asked *why* I am acting in a way so richly described, I may or may not be able to give an explanation – one that is external to the acting – but any such explanation will not constitute but will assume that what I am doing is intentional. To isolate mental causes and physical effects from such complexity and regard them as the fundamental constituents of my acting would be to substitute for a practical understanding of action, a highly theoretical and abstractive conception that suppresses its intentional features.

Davidson's insistence on truth conditions as essential to interpreting language yields an account that is also essentially theoretical. He wrote that "if we could not often fathom from his linguistic behavior when a speaker holds his sentences true, we could not interpret his speech" (Davidson 2001c, p. 190). That may be true for much speech but certainly not for all, and not for what we might call primary speech – as used by Wittgenstein's builders or in Dewey's non-cognitive experiences, where subjects are not knowers but doers, who suffer, enjoy, respond, manipulate, destroy, and so on, activities that are directed to objects and can be said to be correct or mistaken but do not presume a conception of objective truth. Dewey's view that objective truth becomes significant only when language is an agent of inquiry restricts it applicability too much, but surely there are many instances of using and understanding speech where truth conditions play no role.

Davidson's theory of meaning requires truth conditions, the "Davidsonian project" being to show how speech of all kinds can be represented in terms of combinations of truth conditions. He required the latter in order to use Tarski's truth theory as a general theory of meaning. It would be wrong to take Davidson as thinking that language as such must have *all* the properties of a *theory* of language. Nevertheless, his attempt to articulate the *conceptual content* of any sentence in terms of the conditions under which it would be true, assumes that all conceptual content is a matter of truth conditions, which is to attribute a feature of a theory of language to language itself. Suffering, enjoying, responding, and seeking have conceptual content, as do sentences that express, direct, or prescribe these activities, but there is no reason for thinking such content is a matter of those activities or sentences having truth conditions.

The contrast I have been making between Dewey and Davidson is reflected in their conceptions of the role of the physical sciences. Dewey's view, as I noted earlier, is that the aim of the physical sciences is to give mathematical descriptions of the underlying stable *relations* that obtain between the transient and qualitative events and objects of everyday experience. This requires a severe abstraction from and suppression of the complexities of ordinary experience, since there is in such experience no clear distinction between perception and action, nature and culture, mind and world. The physical sciences articulate necessary (not sufficient) conditions of the things of ordinary experience, conditions knowledge of which is vital for the enhancement of that experience and for the perpetuation and increase of what is valuable in life. But they do not describe the world as it really is – its essential or intrinsic nature. The particles and forces of physics are *intellectually* superior to the objects of everyday experience, and knowledge of them enables us to do and perceive things otherwise impossible, but they are not more real or ontologically more fundamental.

Davidson's view is that the aim of the physical sciences is to construct descriptions of the essential nature of the physical world and formulate the fundamental laws of physics that connect them. These physicalistic descriptions apply to all events, including mental events, although not to the latter *as* mental (because mental *kinds* of events are different from physical *kinds*) but *as* physicalistic. Physics, therefore, characterizes the fundamental nature of all events because mental descriptions are supervenient on physicalist descriptions.

Supervenience is not, for Davidson, an explanatory relation, and hence rational descriptions and explanations of belief and action are not derivable from or replaceable by physicalistic descriptions and explanations. His account of supervenience as the claim that every mental difference implies a physical difference could be taken to mean that mental differences result in physical ones (which is, very crudely, Dewey's position) or simply that some physical difference or other is a sufficient condition for a mental difference, which is Davidson's view. The latter means that the things and qualities of everyday experience consist of physicalistic objects and events that have mental descriptions, rather than the physicalistic consisting of the elements that are necessary conditions for, and abstracted from, everyday experience. I think the latter is the more plausible but I cannot argue the point here.

I conclude by briefly considering the objection that Dewey's view is an indefensible form of idealism, that is, of the notion that what the world is like is not independent of human thought and experience. It is, of course, not independent of human action, which constantly intervenes and changes the world, and that is central to Dewey's view.

To ask whether what the world is like is independent of human thought and experience is not to ask what the world is like 'as it is in itself', which is not an intelligible question. It is to ask *either* what the world would be like if there *had never been* human thought and experience, *or* what the world would be like *now* if we abstracted the 'contribution' of human thought and experience. Physicists are interested in the first question, for instance, what the world was like shortly after the big bang, and they have constructed giant accelerators to create conditions like those that apparently obtained when the universe was new. But answering that question does not answer the second, even though what existed after the big bang still exists in some form. Physicists are also interested in the second question in abstracting from the qualitative flux of experience in order to construct mathematical descriptions of law-like relations. The world as thus described does exist *now* independently of human experience (although we would know nothing about it without experience and thought).

But what of the world of human experience – the conceptually structured world I have been discussing. I have argued that the world of physics is not more real than that world, even though the latter would not exist had human beings never existed. But that does not mean it is dependent on human thought and experience in the way idealists have claimed because, on Dewey's view, the practical nature of experience implies that the conceptually structured world persists independently of the activity of thinkers and the experiences of individual subjects.

This is due, in the first instance, to the evolutionary process having produced a *life* world, a world of living things, which is characterized by what Dewey called 'feeling' – "a name for the newly actualized quality acquired by events previously occurring upon the physical level, when those events come into more extensive and delicate relationships of interaction" (Dewey 1925, p. 267). This world contains food and creatures who eat, mates and creatures who copulate, enemies and creatures who fight or flee. Living creatures and an animate environment evolved together, and thus changed the world in permanent ways that call for new kinds of description and explanation that are not physicalist but animate.

Human beings are living creatures who developed new innate powers that enabled them to acquire conceptual capacities and create culture and the institutions that embody and transmit it. The world in which they live, think, and act is, therefore, unlike the world of physics and unlike the animal world, not independent of human experience. But what is crucial in human experience as Dewey conceived it, is not thought but action in and interaction with the world, and it is such action and interaction over long periods of time that has created our world. To recognize that role for human experience is not to support idealism.

8 Common Sense Psychology and Physical Science

In a recent book (Sehon 2005), Scott Sehon defends a teleological account of explanations in common sense psychology[1] (henceforth: CSP) against the current orthodoxy that such explanations of behavior are causal. He has a particular interest in the relationship of explanations in CSP to explanations in physical science. There are, he argues, three options: 1) CSP and physical science contradict each other; 2) physical science entails CSP or vice versa, or they entail each other; 3) CSP and physical science are logically independent. The first two he regards as versions of 'strong naturalism' and rejects in favor of the third option, which he accepts, although reluctantly, because it entails that the success of CSP is not explained by physical science. The latter, as Sehon admits, assumes that *any* explanation of why CSP is successful would come from physical science (including neuroscience and cognitive science), and since it yields no such explanation, Sehon concludes that we have to accept the success of CSP as a kind of mystery.

> ... In the end the most basic teleological facts and concepts are irreducible and primitive. In and of itself this is not so embarrassing, for all theories ... will leave some basic facts unexplained. However, a theory of the world that managed to subsume [the basic principles of CSP] by showing they followed from more basic physical science would, all things being equal, be superior to one that left [those principles] as brute, irreducible facts. (Sehon 2005, p. 219)

Since we cannot show that the principles of CSP follow from physical science, their holding "reliably of human beings and other agents is left as a brute, irreducible fact with no further explanation" (Sehon 2005, p. 219).

Sehon's discussion of CSP and its relation to physical science is illuminating, and I agree with many of his criticisms of various views, particularly of physicalist attempts either to reduce CSP to physical science or to show that superve-

---

[1] This is a good enough term for the constitutive understanding that underlies human interactions with each other and the world. It is much better than 'folk psychology', which wrongly suggests that this understanding is some kind of proto science that might be undermined by scientific theories. The term 'common sense psychology' can be misleading if it suggests that such understanding consists of explicit knowledge or that its claims have the foundationalist status 'commonsense philosophers' have given it. I take it to be a kind of practical know-how required for competent human agency whose propositional commitments can be made explicit only by hard work.

nience establishes explanatory links between them. I do not, agree, however, with a number of his central claims, and in what follows I shall try to show how I think they go wrong. I do not do this because I think Sehon has written a bad book but precisely because he has written a good one, which nicely formulates the issues so as to invite useful criticism and has enabled me to articulate my own views more clearly and coherently.

I shall focus my discussion on three claims that Sehon defends at some length:
1. The explanations of behavior in CSP are teleological; causal explanations belong to the domain of physical science.
2. Causal explanations in physical science are the fundamental kind, not least because it is intelligible to think they could explain the success of CSP explanations but not the other way around.
3. The success of CSP is, nevertheless, unexplained because only physical science could explain it and only if CSP were reducible to it, which it is not.

I agree with the final point that CSP is not reducible to physical science, but I reject the other claims, and hold instead the following:
1. Explanations of behavior in CSP are often causal.
2. Causal explanations in physical science are not the fundamental kind of explanation: what is fundamental depends on the context.
3. CSP explanations do not need and cannot have an external foundation. Their success is no mystery for it is intelligible apart from external support.

The first claim has two parts: explanations in CSP are essentially teleological and causal explanations belong to the domain of physical science. The heart of Sehon's book is the first part, which deserves considerable discussion, but it is not my main interest here, so I will be somewhat quick in addressing it before moving on to the second part.

8.1 CSP and Teleological Explanation

Sehon characterizes a teleological explanation as explaining an agent's behavior "by citing the *purpose* or *goal* of the behavior in question …". Such explanations "cite a future state of affairs toward which the behavior was directed, rather than an antecedent state that caused the behavior" (Sehon 2005, p. 13). Consider, for example, Joan's going to the kitchen in order to get a glass of wine. Although we might express that by saying 'Joan went to the kitchen because she wanted to get a glass of wine', its form in 'explicitly teleological language' is 'Joan went to the kitchen in order to bring it about that her desire for wine was satisfied.' The 'paradigmatic form' of a teleological explanation, he writes, is "A φd in order to ψ." (Sehon 2005, p. 149)

Underlying such explanations are two principles whereby "the agent is rational and her behavior makes sense" (Sehon 2005, p. 139) that must apply when an agent's behavior is irreducibly teleological:

> R-1: Agents act in ways that are appropriate for achieving their goals, given the agent's circumstances, epistemic situation, and intentional states.
>
> R-2: Agents have goals that are of value, given the agent's circumstances, epistemic situation, and intentional states. (Sehon 2005, p. 139)

These principles enable us to determine whether an agent is really directing her behavior and, if so, to what state of affairs, enabling us to rule out inanimate objects, plants, and various kinds of animals as engaging in behavior that requires a teleological explanation. Although we can characterize the behavior of the latter in what appear to be teleological ways ('A heat-seeking missile turns toward the north', 'A plant turns toward the sun'), "we would want to resist any attribution of agency" (Sehon 2005, p. 161) to them because in such cases teleological explanation can be reduced to causal explanation. The two principles do not apply, for example, to the wasp, whose behavior can be adequately explained in terms of its evolutionary niche. (Sehon 2005, p. 162) It is highly unlikely that "the wasp has a system of values and directs its behavior ... to achieving appropriate goals [and hence it] is not an agent directing its behavior". Cat behavior, by contrast, "seems sufficiently rich and sophisticated to warrant attribution of a relatively complex set of goals. Moreover, we can get a grip on the idea that various kinds of states of affairs are of value from the cat's perspective: eating, being fed, being let outside ... etc." (Sehon 2005, p. 166)

Human beings are, of course, the paradigm of rational agents, and the two principles apply fully to them. The principles imply that a wide variety of counterfactuals hold of the agent, and this enables us to distinguish between an agent's merely having a goal and her having a goal *and* acting in order to achieve it. We can establish that A φd in order to achieve X rather than Y by asking such questions as 'Would A still have φd if circumstances were such that φing would achieve X but would be detrimental to achieving Y?' We look, that is, "at counterfactual situations to see what account of the agent's behavior makes the most rational sense" (Sehon 2005, p. 158). Thus Sehon counters Davidson's defense of a causal account of action explanation by appealing to counterfactuals that in his view are grounded on teleology and are not causal.

There are two objections I shall make to this teleological account of CSP explanations. The first is that it assumes that all CSP explanations of intentional action cite a goal toward which the action is a means. In my view, this is not the case: what is essential to CSP explanations is that they cite the reason for which an agent acted – they are *rational* explanations – not that they cite the purpose or goal of the action.

We typically make what Sehon calls 'rational sense' of an agent's behavior by determining the reason for which she acted intentionally as she did, and that *may* require explaining her action as her taking a means toward an end. For example, we may explain why Joan went to the kitchen by saying she did so in order to get a glass of wine, which is the reason for which she acted. But rational explanations are often not like that. I wave at a friend across the street not as a means to an end, not to fulfill some goal, but simply as a friendly act. My behavior was not directed at a future state of affairs but was a response to a present one: the reason for which I waved was that my friend waved at me. I comfort a child who has fallen off her bicycle not as a means to an end but simply as someone who needs comforting and that I am in a position to provide. My swimming in the morning is not directed at a future state of affairs; I swim just because I enjoy it. Although one might be able to reformulate these rational explanations in means-ends terms, doing so would distort them because we often act intentionally without aiming to fulfill a goal.

The second objection is that Sehon confounds a teleological *description* of an action with a teleological *explanation* of it. Explanations in general depend on how the explanandum is described, a point crucial to CSP because giving an adequate description of behavior can be as difficult as explaining it. A description of behavior that permits a rational explanation of it is invariably teleological: it describes what the agent intended or meant by his behavior. When I waved at a friend, I moved my body and limbs in many ways that could have been my doing diverse things, but the crucial thing is what I *intended by* the movements I made – what I *intended* in moving my body and limbs.

To specify what I intend is to give a teleological *description* of my behavior – not to explain it but to describe it so it can be explained. The teleological *description* is that I was waving: by moving my body and limbs I intended to be waving. The explanation is that I did so in response to my friend's waving at me, which is not a teleological *explanation*. At another time when I intended my behavior to be waving, the explanation itself might be teleological in form: I was waving in order to get a taxi. The general point is that a rational explanation requires a teleological description but not vice versa.

Sehon writes that "if we want to make rational sense of an action, we want to know what the agent was trying to accomplish" (Sehon 2005, p. 177). That is true but what is thus characterized is not the *explanation* of an action but its teleological *description* as what the agent intended. An explanation specifies an additional point, namely, *why* she acted as she did, *why* she was trying to accomplish whatever it was. This is not necessarily something we only know *after* we know what the agent intended to do: making rational sense of an action requires knowing *both* what she was intending to do and why she was doing it, and we often do not know either without knowing both.

Sehon's account of reasons for action conforms largely to the belief-desire model except that he denies that beliefs and desires play a *causal* role. While I think that model of reasons for action is deeply mistaken,[2] I won't discuss it here except to note that Sehon's treatment of Dancy's alternative to the model also confounds description with explanation. Dancy's view (which I largely share) is that reasons for action are not psychological states but states of affairs in the world to which agents respond. Sehon discusses Dancy's example of a man whose action is explained in terms of someone's having lied to him, which Dancy formulates as "The ground on which he acted was that she had lied to him." (Dancy 2000, p. 132) Sehon comments that "citing a previous state of affairs in the light of which the agent acted doesn't by itself make rational sense of the action ... That she lied to him may be one part of the story behind what the agent is doing, but doesn't yet tell us what the agent is trying to accomplish." (Sehon 2005, p. 177) But Dancy's citing the fact that she had lied as the reason for the man's action *assumes* that he knows what the agent was trying to accomplish; knowing the latter *is* knowing what he did intentionally. Knowing that is, of course, part of what it is to make rational sense of the man's action but it doesn't explain his action – it doesn't specify the reason for which he acted. Even if knowing the reason for which he acted were necessary to know what he was trying to accomplish, it does not follow necessary to know what he was trying to accomplish, it does not follow that the latter explains why he acted.[3]

---

2 See my "Responsive Action and the Belief-Desire Model" (Stoutland 2001).
3 Sehon's view of reasons is somewhat obscure. The clearest statement of it is this: "... If the agent φd in order to ψ, then we might say that the agent's reason for φing was whatever made ψ valuable from the agent's perspective. In other words, the agent's reason will be whatever explains the value of ψ." He goes on to argue that, although a desire can be a reason in this sense, it often is not. I think this puts reasons on the wrong level. To say that S φd in order to ψ is to say that the reason S φd was that φing was a means to ψing. But we can go on to ask why he took that to be a reason – not only why he took it to be true that φing was a means to ψing but why he took that to be a reason for him to φ, which may very well be that he took ψing to be valuable (with there being a further explanation of that). The reason he took ψing to be a reason for him to ψ is not, however, itself a reason for him to φ.

8.2 Causal Explanation and Physical Science

I come now to Sehon's claim that causal explanations belong essentially to the domain of physical science, which he takes to be a major reason for regarding explanations in CSP as teleological and not causal. I agree with his general way of distinguishing between explanations in CSP and in physical science. He maintains that CSP explanations are *normative* in that they involve considerations we take to favor (or disfavor) our acting, which is not the case in the physical sciences where phenomena are never explained (or described) in terms that favor (or disfavor) their occurrence – that take them to be appropriate, justified, or correct (or the reverse). CSP explanations are also normative in that ascribing propositional attitudes to an agent "involves an irreducibly normative element" (Sehon 2005, p. 62) in the sense Davidson spelled out.[4] Davidson noted further that this implies that there are no strict law-like generalizations in CSP connecting intentional actions with psychological states since ascribing such actions and states presumes that the agent is rational, which entails that any generalizations we formulate will have to be given up if required to preserve the rationality of the agent – something we could not do if the generalizations were strict and law-like. CSP explanations do not involve precise generalizations (not even probabilistic ones) but at most rough generalizations about actions, reasons, and circumstances.

That CSP explanations are normative means they are also *agent-centered* in that they require identifying both what the agent took herself to have done and what she took to be a reason for her to have done it. An agent cannot always articulate what she did, for 'taking' denotes a stance that may be implicit, and others may (in certain situations) be better able to articulate what she did (or her reason for doing it) than she can. What others articulate should, nevertheless, be an articulation of what the action was from the agent's point of view. CSP explanations can, therefore, also be characterized as *first-person*, which does not mean the agent has introspective or infallible knowledge of her own actions and reasons or that the latter cannot be known by others, but that the agent's point of view on the world is central to a CSP explanation.

The reason for this is that the normative significance of states of affairs for an agent – their practical significance as reasons that might explain her actions – manifests itself only to those who are able to view them from that agent's point

---

4 This does not mean that a CSP explanation must justify an action or provide a reason that really favors it; it means rather that it uses terms (appeals to considerations) that could justify the action or be a reason for it.

of view. This is not the case for physical science, which, whether it requires a 'view from nowhere', certainly does not require the agent's own point of view since its explanations may be quite unintelligible to the agent herself. To understand what an agent responds to as a reason for her action, however, requires grasping the agent's own point of view, not to agree with it but to understand how the world and its normative significance would appear from that point of view.

This implies that CSP explanations are *interpretive*. Their ascription is holistic in that our criteria for establishing the reason that explains why an agent acted is not independent of establishing what she did, and neither is independent of what she took to be a reason for her to do it, which may require establishing what she believed or desired, which may require finding out what she did, and so on. We cannot, therefore, simply use our own concepts and distinctions in describing and explaining an agent's action but must *interpret* how she understands it. This supports Sehon's claim that "the behavioral evidence available to the interpreter will generally allow for indefinitely many attributable states of beliefs and desires" so that she must "choose the set that maximizes the rationality of the agent" (Sehon 2005, p. 60).

A final feature distinguishing CSP explanations is that they are *constitutive* in that a human agent who is capable of acting intentionally must also be capable of giving and receiving reasons for the actions of himself and others.[5] Such explanations are not in the domain of experts but are essential to human thought and action, a point that figures in Sehon's rejection of eliminativist views of CSP.

Sehon says rather little about the nature of the physical sciences other than that CSP is not one of them. In my view, he underestimates the complexity of the physical sciences and the unlikeness of being able to reduce either biology or chemistry to physics. He is too quick, therefore, to accept the completeness of physics, is too speculative about "the propositions ultimately put forward by a completed physical science" (Sehon 2005, p. 9), and is mistaken in claiming, for instance, that biological explanation "no longer involves anything above and beyond the mechanistic principles of physical science" (Sehon 2005, p. 153). I will return to this, although it does not bear on his general character-

---

5 This is not inconsistent with the claim that there are autistic persons who suffer from 'mind-blindness' – typically understood as an impaired capacity to ascribe mental states to others. An *impaired* capacity does not mean *no* capacity, and the impairment is much more a matter of articulating various claims about other persons than about interacting with them in linguistic and non-linguistic ways. The latter is what is constitutive about CSP explanations, which, as noted above, may be implicit without being articulated.

ization of physical science, which he takes to be centered on explanations of phenomena in terms of natural laws[6] that often enable causal explanations of phenomena, in particular of the behavior of organisms, including human beings. With all of this I agree.

But I do not agree that causal explanations play no role in CSP. Sehon gives no analysis of the concepts of causality and explanation, and although he does not discuss whether we should distinguish 'cause' from 'causally explain', he assumes that 'cause' means 'causally explain' and that the latter involves causal laws, which he takes to be law-like, universal generalizations in the standard sense. This is the concept of causality that underlies the notion that causal claims are founded on our ability to intervene in nature to bring about an effect, the point of such intervention (or manipulation) being to verify a necessary connection between cause and effect.[7]

I agree that explanations in CSP are not causal in *that* sense: they are not grounded in law-like universal generalizations, which is what philosophers (including my past self) usually mean when they deny that rational explanations of action are causal. I now think, however, that to confine the term 'causal explanation' to that sense is to invite serious misunderstanding and that we should take it as only a species of a more general notion of causal explanation.

What is this general notion of causal explanation? I would argue that the generic sense of 'explain' is 'render intelligible' and that there are numerous ways to render phenomena intelligible. One might specify their parts or the whole of which they are parts, spell out their function or articulate the role they play in a narrative, clarify what to think or say about them, perhaps by analyzing terms, elucidating various claims, or redescribing them. One might show that the puzzle or mystery that motivated the search for an explanation was not really puzzling or mysterious, or trace out what claims about them imply or follow from, or what it would be for them to be true. Or one might construct a causal explanation of the phenomena.

What, then, is required for an explanation to be *causal?* The dictionary defines 'cause' as "something that produces an effect, result, or consequence" (*American Heritage Dictionary* 1982). Anscombe formulates the basic idea as follows: "Causality consists in the derivativeness of an effect from its causes ... Effects derive from, arise out of, come of, their causes." (von Wright 1974, p. 136)

---

[6] What a natural law is and how it functions in explanation is a controversial question. The controversy has been renewed by Nancy Cartwright's claim that, taken in the traditional sense, the laws of physics are false, which requires reconstruing them in a quasi-Aristotelian sense as natural capacities.

[7] This is von Wright's view of causality as developed, for instance, in von Wright 1971.

The essential thing, I suggest, is that causal explanation makes it intelligible *why* a phenomenon begins to be when it would otherwise not be, ceases to be when it would otherwise continue to be, or continues to be when it would otherwise cease to be. Call effects of that kind *events* or *processes*; what causally explains such effects *produces* them. If a cause produces an effect – if the effect *derives from*, *arises out of*, the cause – it's not mere luck that there is an effect: the effect would not have been had the cause not been. The latter makes the account causally *explanatory*, provided it describes the cause in a way that makes it intelligible why the effect came to be.[8]

This characterization allows for different types of causal explanation. One type is based on law-like, universal generalizations, but another type is consistent with the features that are distinctive to CSP. The latter is exemplified by rational explanations that are best characterized as causal because their effects, intentional actions, are events or processes, and because citing the reason explains why the agent acted. It not only describes what he did or what his intention or goal was, but it explains *why* he did it: what his acting derived from or arose out of, what produced it. Explaining why someone opened a door, stopped the car, or continued to climb the hill by citing the reason for which he acted says what each action derived from – what produced it.

Sehon denies that explanations in CSP are productive: "When we give a genuinely teleological explanation of a piece of behavior,… we are seeking to know the state of affairs toward which the agent's behavior was directed" (Sehon 2005, p. 153), but we do not thereby "gesture at some sort of mysterious noncausal means of bringing about behavior" (Sehon 2005, p. 153). On his view, behavior has causes that bring it about, but they are *physicalistic* "with brain states playing a central role. Teleological explanations simply do not purport to be identifying the cause of a behavior."[9] (Sehon 2005, p. 218) To explain, for example, why someone is walking to the cooler, we cite the purpose of her action – to get a beer – which is the goal "toward which her behavior was directed". But that CSP explanation does not tell us what produced or causally explained her behavior; for the latter "we can surmise that a sensory stimulus triggered a

---

[8] I agree with Davidson that causes and effects can be described in purely extensional ways and hence in explanatorily empty ways, but I do not find his distinction between "cause" and "causally explain" to be helpful in an account of CSP explanations.
[9] Cf. Sehon 2005, p. 203: "… If mental states can causally explain behavior, then mental states must be brain states."

chain of events in her brain and nervous system, with the ultimate result that she walked to the cooler" (Sehon 2005, p. 137).[10]

On my view, although we should not rule out physicalistic causal explanations of the behavior involved in our intentional action, that does not rule out causal explanations from CSP.[11] The latter typically appeal to reasons for action, that is, to considerations that *favor* an agent's acting in a certain way. Of course, rational explanations frequently appeal to considerations that do not *actually* favor the action. Klaus gave money to a beggar because she is poor, but she may in fact be rich, her begging being a kind of theater. Although the reason he gave the money did not actually favor his doing so, it nevertheless explained it, something we come to know by understanding his point of view – how the situation presented itself to him, namely as a poor woman who needed money.

I contend this is a causal explanation of why Klaus acted because it goes beyond saying what he did, what goal he had, or the intention with which he acted, to explaining why he acted – what his acting derived from. It explains his acting by specifying the reason without which there would have been, on this occasion, no such acting, which is to explain it *causally*. But the explanation presumes no generalizations, not even such a cautious one as, 'Whenever persons of a certain type encounter, in these circumstances, a beggar they take to be in need, they give her money.' We may be able to *predict* that Klaus would give a beggar money because we've seen him doing so many times, but that rough generalization does not *explain* why he does so, certainly not why he gave money to *this*

---

[10] I don't think Sehon is consistent in arguing that teleological explanations, as he understands them, are not productive. He argues (Sehon 2005, p. 159) that, although teleological claims support counterfactuals, they support different counterfactuals than causal claims do. But his example compares 1) "A φd in order to ψ", the teleological claim, with 2) "A's desire for ψ caused her to φ", which he takes as the *causal* claim. 1) supports 3) "Ceteris paribus, if A had not had the goal of ψing, A would not have φd", while 2) supports 4) "Ceteris paribus, if A had not desired ψ, then A would not have φd" which, he concludes, shows that what the *teleological* claim supports is different from what the *causal* claim supports. But, I would argue, the reason 1) and 2) support different counterfactuals is because *in-order-to* claims are not equivalent to *desire* claims, not because 1) is teleological and 2) is causal. *Both* are *causal* in making claims about what would not have happened had not such and such not happened, which are surely productive claims. Sehon here treats "A φd in order to ψ" as not merely stating the goal of A's action but as stating that A would not have φd if he had not had the goal to φ, which is surely a productive claim about A's φing. Further evidence of this is his discussion of counterfactuals in CSP when he writes of our knowing "what Joan would have done had she *believed* that there was no wine in the kitchen" (Sehon 2005, p. 225). His claim that this is teleological and not causal is not credible.
[11] I deal with objections to this compatibility claim below.

beggar. What explains that is that she, as he saw it, needed money. That is the reason for his having given – its cause, but not its necessitating cause.

Anscombe's arguments that causes need be neither necessitating nor nomological I find convincing. If an event occurs that was not necessitated by law, it does not follow that it occurred by chance; its occurrence may be explained and hence not a matter of chance, and yet not a matter of necessity. That C causally explained E on this occasion does not entail that when C occurs again, E must, as a matter of law, also occur – even if the situations are the same. The claim that C was sufficient for E means that C was *enough* to bring about E – that it was a sufficient condition in *that* sense – but it need not be a sufficient condition in the logico-philosophical sense of *whenever* C occurs, then E occurs. "Sufficient condition", Anscombe wrote, "sounds like 'enough', and one certainly *can* ask: 'May there not be *enough* to have made something happen – and yet it not have happened?'" (Anscombe 1981, p. 135) Rational explanations are like that: the presence of a beggar was, on this occasion, sufficient (enough) reason for Klaus to have given her money – it explained why he did so – but it doesn't follow that if he were to encounter a beggar again, he would give her money, even if the circumstances were the same.[12]

Davidson is credited with having resurrected from the Wittgensteinian tomb the claim that reasons are causes, and his "Actions, Reasons, and Causes" was undoubtedly immensely influential in making the standard causal story the orthodox view. While I continue to be highly critical of that standard story, it is important to note that it is not in the spirit of Davidson's own account of rational explanation, which is heavily indebted to Anscombe's *Intention* and hence to Wittgenstein's observations on action. Most versions of the standard story ignore Davidson's claim that rational explanations are not reducible to explanations in physical science but belong to CSP, which he takes to have the distinctive features I sketched out above. Many overlook his claim that causal *relations* obtain *only* between *events*, and since beliefs and desires are not events, they are not causally *related* to actions. His view is that desires and beliefs causally *explain* actions but are not instances of causal *relations* connecting desires and beliefs with actions. The real explanatory force of a rational explanation, on his view,

---

[12] Kant wrote in the *First Critique* (Kant 1998, A 549/B 577): "Every cause presupposes a rule according to which certain appearances follow as effects; and every rule requires uniformity in the effects. This uniformity is, indeed, that upon which the concept of cause (as a faculty) is based ..." I accept this if it means same cause-same effect: if cause C brings about effect E, it will, whenever it brings about an effect, bring about E. But I do not accept it if it means that whenever C occurs, it is necessary that E occur.

turns on the conceptual and normative principles implicit in our *interpretation* of the actions of rational agents in the light of their reasons.[13]

When Davidson is construed in this way, his view is not so very different from the one I would defend. We agree that rational explanations of action are causal but not in the sense in which physical explanations are. Where we differ is, first, in the role of beliefs and desires. I agree that they are reasons for action only in virtue of their content, but I think that *only* their content – worldly states of affairs – constitutes them reasons for action and that such content is not confined to beliefs and desires but is that to which agents can respond directly (see Stoutland 2001). Secondly, I disagree with his claim that when a reason causally explains an action, there must, first, be an event *associated* with the reason that is causally *related* to the action and, second, there must be a law that connects a *physical* description of the *associated* event with a *physical* description of the action – hence a law of physics. While Davidson denied that laws of physics play a role in CSP itself, he held that they underlie CSP explanations: the latter *entail* the existence of correlated physical laws of which we may have no knowledge.

Although I do not accept this audacious claim, I will not spell out my objections here. I do not think it commits him to epiphenomenalism since that would require that a rational explanation is valid only *in virtue of* such a physical law, which Davidson denies in holding only that a rational explanation *entails* that there is such a law (see Davidson 2005a). Nor do I think it supports Sehon's assumption that to account for the success of CSP we must appeal to physical science, a point to which I return below.

8.3 CSP and Causal Explanation

Sehon's main defense of his claim that CSP explanations are not causal is that if they were, CSP would be reducible to physical science, a defense he makes a number of times. For example, he defends the claim that "If beliefs can causally explain behavior, then beliefs are brain states" (Sehon 2000, p. 67) by arguing for its contrapositive: "If beliefs are not brain states, then they cannot causally explain behavior." (Sehon 2000, p. 68) He then argues that beliefs can neither be reduced to nor be token identical with brain states, which, given the contrapositive, entails that beliefs cannot *causally* explain behavior. But since beliefs *do* explain behavior, they must do so non-causally. (Sehon 2005, p. 75) Later he argues against the view that an agent's behavior might have two different

---

[13] I have spelled out this claim in Stoutland 1999b.

causes – a physical cause and a mental cause such as a desire. His main objection is that "if human physiology ultimately gives a gapless causal history of bodily motions, either mental states are identical to the physiological cause or they are not causes of behavior" (Sehon 2005, p. 202), but since mental states are not identical to physical states, they are not causes of behavior.

This defense of the non-causal nature of CSP explanations assumes that causal explanations are found only in physical science – that only physical explanations are productive. Why that assumption? Some make it because they think that only in physical science do we get the true knowledge required for genuine explanation. Steven Pinker, for example, writes that CSP "has so much power and precision in predicting, controlling and explaining everyday behavior ... that the odds are high that it will be incorporated in some form into our best scientific theories" (Sehon 2005, p. 216). But Sehon does not accept this reductionism because "there are truths of common sense psychology that are logically independent of, and hence not explained, by the truths of physical science" (Sehon 2005, p. 216).

He does, however, accept (without defending) the causal completeness of physics, which he takes to be decisive for his view. He accepts, that is, the claim that all physical effects are due to physical causes or, as David Papineau puts it, "All physical effects are fully determined by law by a purely physical prior history." (Papineau 2002, p. 250) While many who accept this (empirical) claim think it entails reductionism of some kind, Sehon does not. He maintains that there are truths of CSP (along with terms, properties, and entities) that are not reducible to physical science. While he does contend that "we are constituted by elementary physical particles [as is] anything that is capable of having effects", which is everything except "numbers and many other abstract objects" (Sehon 2005, p. 133), he does not count that as reduction. What he thinks does follow from the causal completeness of physics is that whatever causally explains our behavior must be physical. Physical science "will ultimately provide a gapless causal history [of behavior], a history that appeals only to physical states of the agent" (Sehon 2005, p. 201), which he takes to entail that there are no causal explanations in CSP.

But the latter does not follow from the causal completeness of physics. What does follow is that causal explanations in CSP are not a part of physical science – that such causes do not function to fill in gaps in the causal histories the latter constructs. Papineau argues that what made the causal completeness of physics so plausible in our time is that physics was able to establish that "there is one quantity, energy, preserved in all natural interactions whatever" (Gillett and Loewer 2009, p. 23), and which rules out any non-physical forces (vital, mental, etc.) that do not reduce to "fundamental conservative forces" (Gillett and Loewer

2009, p. 22) and hence enables physics to "uphold the universal conservation of energy" (Gillett and Loewer 2009, p. 28). If this argument is decisive, it follows that explanations in CSP do not appeal either to the fundamental forces of physics or to any special forces over and above them.[14] But it does not follow that such explanations are not causal; causal explanations in CSP are not a matter of special forces, whether or not they are reducible to "a small stock of fundamental forces" (Gillett and Loewer 2009, p. 30). Even if physics is causally complete, there may be causal explanations of a quite different type.

My view is, therefore, that two different types of causal explanation of human behavior are acceptable, one belonging to and serving the purposes of physical science, the other belonging to and serving the purposes of CSP. Two main objections will be raised to this view. One is that it is not consistent with the completeness of physics, the other that there cannot be two causal explanations of the same behavior.

The first contends that if one accepts the claim that all physical effects are due to physical causes, then a CSP causal explanation outside physical science entails either that some physical effects are due to non-physical causes or that CSP explains non-physical effects. In either case, one appears committed to the kind of dualism ruled out by the completeness of physics – a dualism between the observable physical and the introspectable mental.

This argument, however, equivocates on 'physical'. The claim that physics is complete uses the term in a *physicalistic* sense: it does not mean by 'physical effects' the middle-size observable phenomena that are part of our everyday world (including human behavior) but the carefully described phenomena that figure in the experiments designed to test the theories of physics. The same holds for 'physical causes', which are not the observable states of affairs that agents cite as reasons in giving rational explanations of why they act but the theoretically characterized physicalistic entities and processes of physics. The explanations of CSP, therefore, appeal to non-physical causes only if that means non-*physicalistic* causes, and they explain non-physical effects only if that means non-*physicalistic* effects. But those explanations do not appeal to causes and effects that are non-physical in the sense of being immaterial, not in space, or not knowable on the basis of observation. We do not, therefore, have to choose between physicalism and dualism.

---

14 I do not accept the causal completeness of physics and hence do not agree that arguments like these establish it. The main problem is that these arguments mistakenly assume that the *interaction* of the fundamental forces of physics conform to the same laws as the forces taken separately.

This distinction between the technical physicalistic and the everyday physical does not mean they exist in different worlds since it is a *conceptual* distinction between two ways of describing (conceptualizing) phenomena – either as in physics or as in CSP. The two ways of describing phenomena yield two corresponding types of explanation since explanation is always of phenomena *as* described. Explanation, that is to say, is intensional: from the fact that E explains x and x=y, it does not follow that E explains y. This is generally recognized in the case of intentional action: that the beggar needed food explains Klaus's action described as 'intentionally giving her money' but not as 'causing a small riot in the street', even though both descriptions are true of the same act. It is often overlooked that this point also applies to explanation generally. Something falls from a high window: physics explains the phenomenon *as* a falling object by appealing to the law of gravity, but it does not explain that same event *as* someone jumping out of a window, for the latter description is not part of any natural law.

This distinction is especially pertinent to the explanations of behavior that Sehon discusses. He makes the point that "notions like *purpose*, *goal direction*, *belief*, and *desire* have no role in physical science" (Sehon 2005, p. 222) but he does not make the corresponding point about the behavior these notions are supposed to explain, namely, that *as described in terms of CSP*, human behavior has no role in physical science. 'Human behavior' is like 'physical' in having a technical sense in physical science *and* an everyday sense in CSP. A neuroscientific account of human behavior does not explain behavior *as* described in CSP, *as* walking to the kitchen or waving to a friend; it explains it described *as* 'colorless movements', which are specialized and abstractive descriptions that leave out distinctive CSP features of behavior. Sehon's assertion that a "brain scanner will be [relevant] only when our concern is directly related to the person's motor behavior and its physical causes" (Sehon 2005, p. 225) is correct if 'motor behavior' is used as neuroscientists use it and 'physical causes' means 'physicalistic causes'. But CSP is also concerned with motor behavior *when* it is described *as* an agent's moving her body and limbs and thereby intentionally doing various things, for that puts motor behavior in the domain of CSP, not as colorless movements but as an agent acting.

The second objection to my claim about two types of causal explanation of human behavior concerns cases where the same (motor) behavior is explained in CSP (someone moves her body and limbs in order to pull a rope) and in neuroscience (her bodily behavior described as 'colorless movements'). Jaegwon Kim puts the objection as follows:

A 'purposive' explanation of human action in terms of the agent's 'reasons' and a 'mechanistic' (e.g. neurobiological) explanation of it in terms of physiological mechanism must be regarded as incompatible and mutually exclusionary – *unless* we accept an appropriate reductive relationship between intentional states and underlying biological processes. (Kim 1993a, p. xiii)

His objection appeals to what he calls the "principle of explanatory exclusion": "[T]here can be no more than one 'complete' and 'independent' explanation for any single explanandum." (Kim 1993a, p. xiii)

I believe Kim is mistaken. Let us assume that the two types of explanation are *independent*, and hence that explanations in CSP cannot be reduced to 'underlying biological processes'. Let us also assume that each is *complete* in that one makes it intelligible why the agent acted intentionally as he did, the other why his physicalistically described bodily movements occurred as they did. My view does not violate Kim's 'principle of explanatory exclusion' since if we have two such independent and complete explanations of the same behavior, the explanations will be of different types. This implies that, although we explain the same behavior, we do not have, as far as Kim's principle is concerned, a single *explanandum* because (as argued above) in giving an explanation of behavior, we must explain it *as* described, which in this case means either *as* described in CSP or *as* described in neuroscience. These different types of description of an agent's behavior are compatible, and since explanation is of behavior *as* described, the explanations are also compatible.[15]

8.4 CSP and Physical Science

My contention that causal explanations of a distinctive type are central to CSP is often admitted by philosophers who, granting that CSP explanations are distinctive, nevertheless think they cannot stand by themselves but must be supported by external explanations from physical science. While Sehon does not think CSP explanations are causal, he also thinks they cannot stand by themselves.

---

[15] The notion of 'same behavior' calls for more reflection since the two types of description do not, in general, *individuate* in the same way. But if what is differently described is not in the strict sense the *same* behavior, then Kim's principle is preserved at another level. The best thing to say, however, is that there is no behavior over and above what is described in one way or another: 'the *same* behavior' is not a determinate description of behavior but a determinable description made determinate only by descriptions from CSP, neuroscience, etc.

> ... If teleology is irreducible, then we have no explanation for why teleological explanation works ... If we had a causal analysis of teleology ... we would expect that cognitive science would find the causal story underlying the cognition of humans and other animals, and that this causal story would explain the applicability and legitimacy of teleological concepts. (Sehon 2005, p. 172)

Sehon simply takes it for granted that CSP needs support from physical science, as do most philosophers who agree with the claim. The most explicit attempt to defend it that I know of is Hartry Field's paper on "Physicalism" (Earman 1992). Field begins his paper by asserting that "I take it as beyond serious doubt that there is an important sense in which all facts depend on physical facts and all good causal explanations depend on good physical explanations." (Earman 1992, p. 271) That is a rough statement of what he means by 'physicalism', which he does not give a great deal of argument since he regards it as beyond serious doubt. His main defense is that "some such doctrine has played an important methodological role in guiding the development of science" (Earman 1992, p. 271). He spells that out as follows:

> The methodological role of the doctrine of physicalism is double-edged. On the positive side, the doctrine tells us that when we have a putative body of facts and causal explanations that we are quite convinced are basically correct, we need to find a physical foundation for them ... For instance, the implicit acceptance of the doctrine of physicalism on the part of most scientists has led to the successful search for the molecular foundations of genetics and the quantum-mechanical foundations of chemical bonding. The other, negative, aspect of the doctrine of physicalism is that when faced with a body of doctrine (or a body of purported causal explanations) that we are convinced can have no physical foundation, we tend to reject that body of doctrine (or of purported causal explanations). I think this is the attitude that most of us take toward astrology or telepathy: even if there were positive evidence for telepathy that we did not know how to refute, most of us would tend to disbelieve the telepathic claims (and presumably suspect the evidence) simply because it seems so difficult to conceive how such claims could fit in with a physicalistic worldview. (Earman 1992, pp. 271–272)

There are two main objections to this argument. The first is that, whether or not physicalism has played an important methodological role in guiding the development of physical science,[16] CSP is not a physical science, and it is absurd to

---

[16] I do not think that the doctrine of physicalism has played the guiding role in the physical sciences that Field assigns to it. Chemists and biologists seek explanations from physics for various chemical and biological phenomena, but many of them reject the reductionism that Field takes to be integral to physicalism. They reject it because they think a robust sense of the reality of distinctively chemical and biological phenomena is essential for guiding the quest for under-

think of its developing by finding a physical foundation for its claims. Theories about dreaming, mental illness, personality disorders, and other psychological phenomena have developed over time, but it is no part of CSP to articulate such theories. Field thinks it is because he thinks CSP is a 'special science' whose "first explanatory task is simply to explain in terms of an underlying science like physics why generalizations of this theory should hold" (Earman 1992, p. 283). But CSP is not a special science, and since its rational explanations of intentional action are not based on generalizations, it is irrelevant to seek a physical explanation of why they hold. The essential task of CSP is to describe and explain intentional action, which is something that does not depend on knowledge that has developed over time in any relevant sense.

A second objection is to what Field calls the negative aspect of physicalism: to accept causal explanations that have no physical foundation would be like accepting the claims of astrology or telepathy. We disbelieve the latter, he holds, "simply because it seems so difficult to conceive how such claims could fit in with a physicalistic worldview" (Earman 1992, pp. 271–272), so that rejecting physicalism would open the door to all sorts of pseudo-scientific claims and theories.

But one surely does not have to accept physicalism to maintain that astrology and telepathy are contrary to the knowledge provided by physical science. It might be true, as Field suggests, that we are unable to *refute* such pseudo-sciences unless we appeal to physicalism, but we may also be unable to *refute* clever flat-earth believers, and they can be ardent physicalists. Moreover, the strongest objections to such pseudo-sciences are provided by special sciences, and they are irreducible to physics – irreducible, that is, unless one accepts strong physicalism, which would beg the question at issue. In any case, CSP, unlike astrology or telepathy, does not purport to be a science. Sane human beings may, of course, give astrological or telepathic reasons for their behavior. But to reject them as normatively justified reasons is not to deny that an agent's acceptance of them may be integral to a causal explanation of why he acted as he did.

Field's skepticism about the validity of the latter type of causal explanations – that "we tend to reject ... purported causal explanations [that] have no physical foundation" (Earman 1992, p. 272) – assumes that, absent a physical foundation, we are unable to distinguish acceptable from unacceptable rational explanations. Establishing a causal explanation in CSP is, of course, different

---

lying physical explanations. The quantum mechanical explanation of chemical bonding, for example, presupposes the notion of a chemical kind, which is a macroscopic phenomenon not reducible to physics. See, for example, Needham's discussion of reductionism in Needham 2005.

from establishing one in physical science: appeal to generalizations or experimental manipulation is irrelevant, and while appeal to scientific data is often relevant to whether a reason is normatively acceptable, it is not usually relevant to whether a reason is explanatorily acceptable. Indeed, the CSP explanations an agent gives of her own behavior are not based on observation or evidence of any kind. Such explanations are not, however, incorrigible, and they may be challenged by other agents, who do appeal to evidence of various kinds. The latter may be based on observation of what the agent did before or after the action in question, on her character and what she could or could not have done, on the situation in which she acted, on her past life, and so on. Considerations of that sort are, in general, quite sufficient to distinguish acceptable from unacceptable rational explanations of an agent's behavior.

These are *interpretative* considerations of the kind that are essential to the ascription to an agent of actions, mental states, and reasons, which means their ascription is holistic. While explanations in physical science may be holistic in the Duhemian sense of involving complex trade-offs between theory and observation in the explanatory process itself, they are not holistic in having to take account of the complex trade-offs in *what* is being explained, where an explanation of the agent's action is validated by showing that it makes maximum coherent sense of her actions, mental states, and reasons for acting. That open-ended process is necessary for confirming a causal explanation in CSP, and it may involve indeterminacy in our conclusions. There is nothing like this in physical science where, however tentative a conclusion may be, the aim is to articulate it determinately by giving a precise statement of how things are.[17] CSP explanations may occasionally leave it open whether an agent acted for one reason rather than another, not because we do not know enough to decide but because there is no answer to the question. It does not follow that rational explanations are defective, only that they are different.

Field offers a further argument for the necessity of a physical foundation for CSP, namely, "not to explain the laws of the special sciences themselves but simply to explain why the application of the special-science laws never comes into conflict with the application of the underlying laws" (Earman 1992, p. 284).

> This is in effect a demand that we explain why our neurophysiological laws and our psychological laws never come into conflict. Or, to introduce a convenient phrase, it is a demand that we show that our neurophysiology and our psychology "mesh." It seems to me that whenever we employ laws at different levels, there is a prima facie possibility of

---

[17] Even when the conclusion is probabilistic in form, the aim is a precise quantitative statement of the probabilities, not a statement whose indeterminacy means there is no fact of the matter.

their coming into conflict, and it is eminently reasonable to want an explanation of why such conflict does not arise. I take it that a main advantage of reducing psychology to lower-level science ... is that doing so one would be able to explain the mesh between psychology and the lower-level sciences. (Earman 1992, p. 285)

In putting this point, Field assumes that CSP is a special science that aims to establish general laws, an assumption I have rejected. But let us waive that and modify his point so that it asks for an explanation of why neurophysiological and CSP explanations never come into conflict – why they 'mesh'.[18]

I have discussed this point at length elsewhere[19] and hence will only summarize my view here. Given the modified point, what Field calls 'mesh' (which I call 'congruence') concerns the relation between a rational explanation of an agent's intentional behavior and a neurophysiological explanation of the bodily movements that are involved in that behavior. Field thinks we need a substantive explanation of that relation and suggests reduction of CSP to a lower-level science. On my view, a substantive explanation is simply out of place. What is supposed to be explained is why the movements of, say, Mary's right arm in her intentionally moving it (for example, to pull on a string) mesh with the movements of her arm as described in neurophysiology. But there is neither need nor place for giving a substantive explanation of *that* because those are the same movements, although differently described – in terms of CSP, on the one hand, in terms of neurophysiology, on the other.

If Mary moved her right arm to pull on the string, then a neurophysiological explanation of her arm movements *could not fail* to be an explanation of the movements involved in her having intentionally moved her right arm since the arm movements explained (in CSP) by her intentionally *moving* her arm *are* the movements we explain neuroscientifically. The movements are described differently, but what neurophysiology describes in a specialized and abstractive way *are* the movements Mary made in moving her arm in order to pull on the string.

The movements of an agent's body and (what we take to be) her intentional action *can* fall apart. If Mary had set out to turn on the lamp but her upper body had (unknowingly) become paralyzed, she would have been unable to move her body so as to pull on the string. But the issue of mesh would then be moot, be-

---

18 Sehon (2005) raises a similar problem on p. 216, which he seems to resolve by his claim that teleological and causal explanations are logically independent and answer very different questions. This, however, overlooks the point that CSP does not simply describe behavior in teleological terms but also explains what produces it.
19 See "The Problem of Congruence" in this volume.

cause her behavior would not be her intentionally pulling on the string, or even her intentionally moving her arm. It might have presented itself as having the *form* of intentional action but it could be explained *only* as bodily movement in neurophysiology.

Consider Mary as unable for some reason to move her right arm and hence unable to pull the string as she usually does. She would then use her left arm, and a CSP explanation of her acting would refer to her moving that arm to pull the string. The movements she thus made could also be described in terms drawn from neurophysiology and (let us assume) be given a neurophysiological explanation. But what the latter explained would clearly have to be the same movements Mary intentionally brought about in moving her left arm. The explanations drawn from CSP and from neurophysiology would mesh, therefore, because the movements each explained would be the same movements differently described.

In explaining an agent's behavior, therefore, there is *necessarily* a mesh between the two types of explanation. If Mary failed to act intentionally as expected because she could not move her limbs in the way required for *that* action but was able to act in *another* way by making different movements, then the movements that resulted from her intentionally moving her body and limbs would also be different. But so would the neurophysiological descriptions of her behavior since they describe those same movements (in neurophysiological terms), and their neurophysiological explanation would be adequate only if it yielded the movements as thus described.

Field would likely reject this account of meshing because it takes CSP explanations as basic and requires that neurophysiological explanations conform to them. That gives CSP explanations priority over neurophysiological ones, which is unacceptable, it will be objected, to anyone sympathetic to the achievement and status of physical sciences like neurophysiology.

My response is that neither type of explanation is basic in an *overall* sense because which type has priority depends on the context and the questions being asked. When the question concerns their mesh CSP explanation takes priority. The reason is that to consider the mesh between the two types of explanation of the movements of the body involved in acting, we must identify which movements they are. When an agent acts, his body moves in all sorts of ways, many of which are not relevant to what he is doing intentionally. To identify the movements that are relevant, we must identify his intentional act, and that requires putting his acting in the context of CSP and, typically (for holistic reasons), identifying the reason for which he acts. It is *those* movements, the ones identified by their role in a CSP explanation, that we also aim to explain (though described differently) neurophysiologically.

There are other contexts in which neurophysiological explanations are prior, for instance, explaining why agents are *incapable* of certain actions. CSP explanations cannot explain such incapacity because they presuppose that the agent is *capable* of acting and hence that he is normal. To the extent that he is normal, however, rational explanation takes priority, which means that there will *necessarily* be a mesh between his behavior as action and as mere movements. We can, therefore, say that while abnormality can be substantively explained, normality cannot. It does not follow that we cannot explain why beings with the potential to become normal agents have come to exist – because of evolutionary considerations or more short term explanations that might belong either to physical science or to CSP.

Of course, such beings might never have come to exist, and then there would have been no behavior to be explained in CSP. Such an impoverished world illustrates another context in which neuroscientific explanations are basic, namely, what would have been explained had there been explainers can exist without normal agents, but not vice versa. That is one way of expressing *global* supervenience of CSP on physical science: destroy the physicalistic and you destroy everything else, while the contrary is not true. I accept that, but it has no consequences for the nature and function of CSP.

Davidson's view of whether CSP explanations need a physical foundation is subtle and merits further discussion. It is widely thought that his "Principle of the Nomological Character of Causality" is his way of providing such a foundation. That principle means, not that causal explanations are in terms of general laws (which Davidson denies), but that any causal explanation entails that there is a causal *relation* between events related to the explanation, which in turn entails that those events have descriptions that are instances of a strict law, hence a law of physics. This conception of the relation of causes and laws was thought to be Davidson's way of grounding CSP explanations in physical laws because he was construed as holding that causal explanations in CSP had their causal force *in virtue of* the laws of physics they entailed. But Davidson denied ever claiming that: on his view, a causal relation between two events *entails* that there is a physical law connecting physical descriptions of the two events but this does not mean they are causally related *in virtue of* such a law.

Davidson gave no arguments for his "Principle of the Nomological Character of Causality" until his 1995 paper on "Laws and Causes". He argued there that causal explanations explain only changes (events) and that what is a change is relative to how a situation is described (which he illustrates with Goodman's points about green, grue, blue, and bleen). Since descriptions of what is a change must involve law-like predicates, it follows that there are causal explanation only when there are laws. That is sufficient, he maintains, to show that "singular causal statements ... entail the existence of strict laws" (Davidson 2005a, p. 219).

That description does not do justice to his subtle paper but it is enough to show that he asserted the cause-law connection because of conceptual relations between laws, changes, and causes, not because the connection provides a physical foundation for CSP explanations. This reinforces the point that Davidson's view is that causal explanations *entail* the existence of physical laws, not that they are valid in virtue of them, which means that Davidson, unlike Field, does not think that "all good causal explanations depend on good physical explanations" (Earman 1992, p. 271). The fact, moreover, that we need not know what physical laws causal explanations entail also bolsters the point that they do not support CSP, for laws of which we are ignorant cannot increase the power of a causal explanation to render intelligible why an agent acts as she does.

In the final part of this discussion, I want to defend the claim that CSP explanations can stand alone without external support. I agree with Sehon that it is "a brute, irreducible fact with no further explanation" that the principles of CSP "hold reliably of human beings and other agents" (Sehon 2005, p. 219) *if* that means that CSP requires no *external* support, but not if it means that the success of CSP is unintelligible, inexplicable, or a mystery. Reflection on the nature of CSP itself can show why it works, and hence we need not leave unanswered the question of why its explanatory claims are true and its explanations successful.

We should first consider the background to this question – the assumptions made in posing it. Sehon quotes Steven Pinker as writing that: "... Scientific psychology will have to explain how a hunk of matter, such as a human being, can have beliefs and desires and how the beliefs and desires work so well." (Sehon 2005, p. 216) This is a very misleading way of posing the question about why or how CSP works, and, although Sehon rejects Pinker's answer, he accepts his way of posing the question.

> We are constituted by material particles, and these material particles don't suddenly cease to follow the laws of nature just because they are embedded in the body of an agent ... How can it even be possible that there are nonphysical facts about physical objects? Given that we are physical objects, how is it even consistent to maintain that there are facts about us that do not reduce to physical facts? (Sehon 2005, p. 231)

To ask, "How can it even be possible that there are nonphysical facts about physical objects?" is to ask "How is it possible that there are CSP facts about *physicalistic* objects" since the latter are what hunks of matter or physical particles are. However, while there are true descriptions of human beings as hunks of matter or physical particles, it is misleading to say that is what human beings *are* (or *are constituted by*), since it misses completely what is distinctive about them. Moreover, many facts of CSP are physical in an everyday sense since they are about human behavior, which is quite physical; they are nonphysical only in the sense of being non-*physicalistic*.

Physicalistic descriptions of human beings characterize them in an idealized sense since they ignore the concrete contexts in which they live and act, and they describe them abstractively in that the physical forces involved are characterized in abstraction from the innumerable ways in which the latter interact.[20] To ask how there can be facts from CSP that are about hunks of matter or physical particles is, therefore, to begin with idealized and abstractive descriptions of human beings and then ask how described in *that* way, they can also be described as CSP does. In one sense, the answer is obvious since what CSP describes in its own concrete (normative and agent-centered) ways just *is* what physical science describes in its idealized and abstractive ways. But Pinker or Sehon do not want an *obvious* answer; they want to know how what is described *only* as hunks of matter or physical particles can also be described as CSP does and successfully explained in its terms. There is no answer to *that* because it is not a good question. The agents whose behavior (thoughts, feelings) we explain in CSP do not *consist* of hunks of matter or physicalistic particles, since that is at best a *physicalistic* way of describing them. Of course, such agents *are* physical but in the everyday sense that is not identical with the physicalistic. They also exist in a world that is physical in that everyday sense, and they have many causal powers that are not adequately characterized in physicalistic terms. It is facts about agents in *that* sense 'that do not reduce to *physicalistic* facts', and it is the success of CSP explanations of the behavior of agents in *that* sense that we are trying to understand.

We can ask why there are such agents at all, a question that has an initial Darwinian answer: there are clear survival benefits to beings that evolve so as to be increasingly capable of behavior that can be explained in CSP. We can then explain how individual beings, who are born of parents that have thus evolved, themselves become mature human agents: they have, relative to other animals, a long maturation period, which permits their being trained and edu-

---

[20] Nancy Cartwright writes that "the rules of composition [of laws of nature] are empirically supported ... only so long as nothing *interferes* ... Our first order principles and our principles of composition support only claims about what happens so long as all relevant factors can be correctly described with the theory ..." (Cartwright 2002, p. 243) 'Interference' is, of course, central to CSP, which has many relevant features that cannot be correctly described within physicalistic theory.

cated in and by the human community to give and receive reasons for their action. This capacity to act for reasons is sustained and further developed by the fact that reasons for acting are embedded in various practices, institutions, and artifacts and by the fact that participation in the latter affects the structure of the brain and nervous system.

What is thus explained is the existence of beings with the capacities of intentional agents. While that does not explain why CSP explanations are successful, it shows that what is to be explained is not how hunks of matter or physical particles are able to give successful CSP explanations of each other but how *human agents* can do so, which is the way the question should be posed.

Pinker speaks of CSP as having "so much power and precision in predicting, controlling, and explaining everyday behavior", which he illustrates by describing two persons who agree to meet at a bar in Chicago at a certain time two months hence and do just that: "That is amazing! In what other domain could laypeople – or scientists for that matter – predict, months in advance, the trajectories of two objects thousands of miles apart to an accuracy of inches and minutes?" (Sehon 2005, p. 216) This is, however, the wrong way to characterize the success of CSP predictions because it uses the terms of physical science. CSP predicts, not the trajectories of two objects thousands of miles apart, but the intentional actions of two agents who have communicated with each other. It predicts what each will do intentionally and the reason why, but it makes only very vague predictions about the movements of their bodies and limbs, which can vary widely as long as they are sufficient for their actions. The 'power and precision' that CSP has must be characterized in the language of CSP itself, and while it falls far short of physical science in predicting the trajectories of bodies, it far exceeds it in predicting what agents will do intentionally (or at least try to do).

At the same time, there are many actions that CSP cannot predict if for no other reason than that agents often change their minds. Moreover, even if an agent does not change his mind and we can predict that he will be at a bar at a certain time and place, not only can we not predict the movements of his body and limbs except very vaguely, but we cannot predict how he will get there or what his going will lead to. Indeed, predicting what an agent will accomplish is often less important than explaining what he is trying to do and why. Pinker speaks of our controlling everyday behavior, which we can, of course, often do, but we do so on a very different basis than we control the trajectory of a missile, the course of a river, or color of a substance. We cannot control an agent's *intentional* behavior by forcing his action or deceiving him, for what we thus control he does not do intentionally. To control what he does intentionally requires that we link up with the reasons that explain why he acts, and that requires that we explain his behavior in terms of CSP.

The deepest measure of success for CSP explanation is that it enables us to deal with each other as human beings. It enables us to evaluate agents and their actions and to hold them responsible for what they do, crediting them, if we wish, for what they do well, blaming them, if we must, for what they do badly. It enables us to recognize the range of emotions people express in their actions, to know when they are suffering or when they are pleased, to respond to what they are feeling and intending and not merely to their external movements. It enables us to work together, to respond intelligently to needs and desires, to cooperate in making the space and objects in which we live. The success of CSP, in short, is not specifiable apart from accounts of what it is to live a human life.

The first reason I suggest for why CSP explanation is successful in this way is that it is constitutive: to be a human agent capable of acting intentionally *is* to be capable of giving and receiving successful CSP explanations of the actions of oneself and others. As an account of the success of CSP this is, admittedly, very thin because what is to be accounted for – the success of CSP explanations – is identical with what accounts for it – namely, an agent's capacity to act intentionally. It is a kind of elucidation, however, since its point is that to give an account of why CSP explanations are successful is, in part, just to give an account of what it is to live a human life. CSP explanations are not successful because they meet an external standard; they are successful because there would otherwise be no such thing as human existence. Some may argue that human existence itself has an external purpose; even if that is the case, it is not the standard by which to judge the success of CSP explanations. They enable us to live as human beings, not to fulfill some external end of human existence.

To alter the character of CSP explanations in a fundamental way would be, therefore, to alter the character of human life itself. Proposals to reform CSP that are based on external standards would also be proposals to change the nature of human life, changes that are based on external standards. Such a deep reform of human life is not impossible but it would have to come from within human life itself and hence from within CSP. Proposals from physical science for such a fundamental reform could conceivably be accepted, but only to the extent that they managed to effect a change not only in CSP but in human existence itself.

The second reason I suggest is that CSP explanation is successful in that it works *among us*. The capacities we have acquired as agents through evolution, culture, and education are capacities to coordinate our lives so that we can act, feel, and think together. Crucial to this are the commitments we give and acquire in making intentions or giving promises, in fulfilling roles (as parents, teachers, workers, friends, etc.), in making contracts, in borrowing and lending, and so on. Such commitments enable us to predict what others will do, to plan what we will do, to settle matters so that we do not constantly have to make new decisions or deal with the always new decisions of others. CSP works so well because we constantly engage, explicitly or implicitly, in making these commitments. (It explains, of course, why Pinker's two men were able to meet in a bar two months after a conversation.) If it is asked why we make them, various answers may be proposed: we were brought up that way, that is the way life goes on in our society, that is the very fabric of human existence. If it is asked why we keep such commitments, similar answers are relevant, along with the fact that to understand what it is to make such commitments is to understand that one will fulfill them – except under certain conditions that are also mutually understood.

One may push deeper, however, and ask what underlies the success of these commitments in enabling us to act, feel, and think together, especially given that it was such success that enabled us to acquire the capacity to give and receive them in the first place. The basic answer is that we live in a common world that provides common reasons for our action that we can perceive in common. This obvious truth rules out the notion that we are in touch with the world only through getting information about it – that what we encounter directly is a virtual reality that is in each of our heads and needs to be coordinated. If that is ruled out, then our encounter with the common world (however that is explained) is sufficient to explain our ability to make and keep the mutual commitments that support our common acting, feeling, and thinking.

This shows that CSP's primary virtue is not truth but its enabling us to live and cope with each other and with the world in which we are embedded. It is, if you will, a way of being in the world. But that does not mean there are no truths in CSP. I agree with Sehon that "There are truths of CSP that are logically independent of, and hence not explained by, the truths of physical science", but I disagree with his going on to write that "accordingly, these truths will apparently not be susceptible of further explanation; thus in addition to whatever mysteries physical science leaves, CSP will introduce further inexplicable mysteries." (Sehon 2005, p. 215) "By virtue of what are [the principles of CSP] true of us?", he asks, answering that "Part of what it is to have a nonreductionist theory of mind is to have questions like these left unanswered." (Sehon 2005, p. 231)

The notion of 'that in virtue of which a proposition (or principle) is true' in the sense of what *explains* why it is true – *makes* it true – seems to me confused. The question 'in virtue of what is a proposition true?' can be answered only in Tarskian fashion: "'p' is true if and only if p'", which is not an *explanation* of why 'p' is true (or what makes it true) but an account of what it is to be true. The reason we cannot explain why the principles of CSP are true is not that they are irreducible; the Tarski point applies to any proposition, not only to those that belong to a nonreductionist theory.[21] There would be, in any case, no explanatory force in saying they were made true by physicalist facts since that would just be a way of saying that they are physicalist truths (which Sehon denies).

This does not mean that the truths of CSP are to be construed in an anti-realist, perhaps instrumentalist, way. There are intentional actions, reasons for action, beliefs, desires, and intentions, all of which are just as real as any physicalistic entities. The same is true of the everyday physical world, whose macro-entities do not have second class reality compared to the particles of micro-physics.[22]

We can, of course, specify what makes the claims of CSP true if that means what *evidence* there is for them. Claims of CSP are false if they specify the wrong reason for an agent's action, misdescribe what she has done, or ascribe to her a belief she does not hold or a desire she does not have. But there is typically, in principle, sufficient evidence to determine when such claims are false and to correct them because, as Sehon puts it, "CSP is constrained by its own internal principle …" (Sehon 2005, p. 231) We can distinguish between the reason for which an agent acted and what merely appears to be her reason, between what she really did and simply claims to have done, between what she did and did not believe. These are interpretive and not scientific claims, but that is what we want and what we get from the explanatory truths of CSP.

---

21 This point is defended by Frege and Davidson, and I defend it in Chapter 1 of this volume: "What Philosophers Should Know about Truth and the Slingshot".
22 I agree with Cartwright's claim that "concepts from macrophysics and from various branches of technology and engineering are required *in conjunction with* those of 'microphysics' to obtain true law statement …" (Cartwright 2002, p. 278).

9 Philosophy of Mind with and against Wittgenstein*

What in 20th-century philosophy of mind, as practiced in the analytical tradition, is likely to be taken seriously by philosophers in, say, the 23rd century? In addressing this question, it seems to me that there are three points in 20th-century philosophy of mind that stand out as especially relevant and significant, namely Wittgenstein, physicalism, and Davidson. I consider Wittgenstein the preeminent philosopher of the century, whose work will be more and more appreciated and assimilated as time goes by. I consider physicalist philosophy of mind to be a noteworthy continuation of the Hobbesian tradition that will always be with us, but I doubt that any of its individual practitioners will stand out as more historically significant than such 19th-century physicalists as Jean Cabanis or Ludwig Buechner (whose 1855 work, *Force and Matter*, went through 16 editions). I consider Davidson a splendid example of how to do philosophy of mind in a manner inspired by Wittgenstein without being a Wittgensteinian, someone history may remember as the most important analytical philosopher of mind.

Before continuing, I want to say a word about analytical philosophy itself, whose boundaries are becoming less and less clear. Wittgenstein differed from paradigm analytical philosophers in such fundamental ways that historians of philosophy will probably cease to regard him as an analytical philosopher. Nevertheless, he surely belongs to the analytical *tradition* because of his philosophical education (Frege and Russell), his influence on analytical philosophers (however much it rested on misunderstanding), and the fact that he worked in Cambridge when it was the center of analytical philosophy. Ever since logical positivism ceased to be influential, physicalists have constructed the same kind of metaphysical theories philosophers like Moore thought it was the task of analytical philosophy to stamp out; what makes such metaphysics analytical is that it is done by philosophers who were trained in the analytical tradition. Davidson rejected such metaphysical theorizing, his manner of working being more analytical in the classical sense than either Wittgenstein's or the physicalists'. Davidson's views, however, are closer to Wittgenstein's than to those held by most analytical philosophers.

---

* The origin of this paper was a conference in Helsinki on "Psychology in Philosophy", whose topic was philosophers of mind from late scholasticism to the present. I was asked to discuss analytical philosophy of mind from Wittgenstein to Davidson, and in keeping with the conference's historical theme, I dealt with my topic as if it concerned a chapter from the distant past.

9.1 Wittgenstein and the Philosophy of Mind

What themes in Wittgenstein's work in philosophy of mind will be significant in the long term? There are, I suggest, five, which are interconnected in intricate ways.
1. His conception of a philosophical investigation.
2. His rejection of the Cartesian conception of the distinction between the mental and the physical.
3. His reworking of Kant's notion of the inseparability of intuitions and concepts.
4. His conception of action as prior to intellection.
5. His renewal of the notion that the world itself is both evaluatively and motivationally significant.

I want to consider each of these, and first, Wittgenstein's conception of a philosophical investigation – the best account of which is his own *Philosophical Investigations*, especially paragraph 109:

> It was true to say that our considerations could not be scientific ones. It was not of any possible interest to us to find out empirically 'that, contrary to our preconceived ideas, it is possible to think such-and-such' – whatever that may mean ... And we may not advance any kind of theory. There must not be anything hypothetical in our consideration. We must do away with all *explanation*, and description alone must take its place. And this description gets its light, that is to say its purpose, from the philosophical. They are, of course, not empirical problems; they are solved, rather by looking into the workings of our language, and that in such a way as to make us recognize those workings: *in spite of* an urge to misunderstand them. The problems are solved, not by reporting new experience, but by arranging what we have always known. (Wittgenstein 1958a, § 109)

This should be supplemented with paragraph 122, which reads (in part):

> A main source of our failure to understand is that we do not command a *clear view* of the use of our words. Our grammar is lacking in this sort of perspicuity. A perspicuous representation produces just that understanding which consists in 'seeing connections' ... The concept of a perspicuous representation is of fundamental significance for us. It earmarks the form of account we give, the way we look at things. (Wittgenstein 1958a, § 122)

Wittgenstein's conception of philosophy is crucial for understanding his work, and it will be central to any historical account of his philosophical achievement. It also raises more hostility than any other facet of his work, and I want to mention two reasons for this. One is that his conception of philosophy cuts against the grain of the predominance in our culture of a scientific mentality that shows up in the fact, as he himself put it in the *Blue Book*, that "Philosophers constantly see the methods of science before their eyes, and are irresistibly tempted to answer questions in the way science does." (Wittgenstein 1958b, p. 18) I'll give an example of how this works when I come to physicalism. The other is that his view of philosophy is regarded as a 'quietism' that aims at – even announces – the 'end of philosophy', which I think seriously misunderstands his view. Here is a more accurate characterization of it from Marie McGinn:

> The things which we are doomed to misunderstand when we take up a theoretical attitude toward them are, then, just those things "that we know when no one asks, but no longer when we are supposed to give an account of (them)" (Augustine)... What we are concerned with when we ask questions of the form 'What is time?', 'What is meaning?', 'What is thought?' is the nature of the phenomena which constitute our world ... and in asking these questions we express a desire to understand them more clearly. Yet in the very act of framing these questions, we are tempted to adopt an attitude toward these phenomena which, Wittgenstein believes, makes us approach them in the wrong way, in a way which assumes that we have to uncover or explain something ... As soon as we try to catch hold of them in the way our questions seem to require we find that we cannot do it; we find that we "no longer know" ... We think that the fault lies in our explanations and that we need to construct ever more subtle and surprising accounts ... The real fault ... is not in our explanations, but in the very idea that the puzzlement we feel can be removed by means of a discovery. What we really need is to turn our whole inquiry round and concern ourselves, not with explanation or theory construction, but with description ... For our puzzlement concerned the nature or essence of particular phenomena ... and this puzzlement is removed, "not by giving new information, but by arranging what we have always known"... (Our aim should be) a kind of understanding which consists in seeing a pattern or form in what is there before our eyes, but which we had previously neglected or overlooked ... Everything we need to understand is already there and only needs to be arranged correctly. (McGinn 1997, pp. 18, 26)[1]

Let me make two points against the background of this quotation. The first concerns what Wittgenstein *means* in saying that philosophers ought not to construct theories. He does not mean that we should not give arguments or come to conclusions. The constructive task of philosophy is to arrange what we have always known in a perspicuous representation, and that is arduous work and real philosophy. What we have always known is not obvious, and the most significant matters are embedded not in what we believe but in everyday practice and hence have to be made explicit. This requires distinguishing what we have always known from what we *think* we have always known, it requires *articulating* what we have always known, and it requires arranging it *properly*. The latter may require re-arrangement, which must be defended by argument and by

---

[1] This book is an extraordinarily illuminating discussion of central themes in the *Investigation*.

showing *how* it resolves the philosophical problems that give purpose to the inquiry.

The second point concerns Wittgenstein's objections to theory construction, two in particular. One is that philosophers who construct theories invariably play fast and loose with the phenomena they try to explain. They think it is *obvious* what needs to be theoretically explained and hence are content to begin with platitudes, intuitive judgments, folk theories, and the like. They do not take the time to reflect on the phenomena themselves and the role they play in our thought, discourse, and action, and hence what they seek to explain is often the construct of some theory whose credentials are never examined. The other is that philosophical theories simply fail to explain what they claim to explain, the basic reason being that there is nothing to explain in the quasi-scientific sense of explanation that is their model. As philosophers, we must explain in the sense of *elucidate* but – and this is his distinctive claim – if we elucidate free from theoretical preconceptions about what there *must* be and how it *must* work, we will come to see that what theories purport to explain do not stand in need of such explanation.[2]

Wittgenstein's most important substantive contribution to philosophy of mind is his rejection of the Cartesian distinction between the physical and the mental. This distinction conceives of the *physical* as consisting only of what plays an essential role in the new physics, a physics purified of the teleological, intentional, and normative terms of Aristotelean physics. The physical consists, that is, only of what can be specified in *physicalistic* terms that have no motivational or evaluative significance, knowledge of which must be based on observation any person is capable of and which is not interpretive but cumulative – claims can be settled and then added to. The *mental* is everything that takes place within ourselves so that we are immediately aware of it *qua* object of consciousness. It comprises internal states that can be known immediately to (and only to) their possessors through introspection, states which are so independent of behavior that they can be ascribed to immaterial souls (or brains in a vat).

It should be noted that Descartes himself had a third category, namely the mind-body union, which has features that belong neither to the physical nor to the mental, the latter being a distinction reached by *abstraction* from the mind-body union. What I call the Cartesian distinction does not, therefore, work in the same way for Descartes as for the Cartesians. It is the latter that Wittgenstein criticized, a point to which I shall return.

---

[2] For further discussion of this matter, see my "Analytical Philosophy and Metaphysics" (Pihlström 2006).

Wittgenstein's objection to the Cartesians was not that they made a distinction between the physical and the mental. He was not a behaviorist but simply took for granted a distinction between behavior and mental states – between pain behavior and pain, for example. He agreed with the Cartesians that there is an irreducible asymmetry between the ascription of psychological predicates to others and to oneself: I can doubt whether you are in pain (or are just pretending) but cannot doubt whether I am in pain, I can try to find out whether you are really in pain but not whether I am, I can express my pain but cannot express yours, and so forth.

His objection was two-fold. First, that it misconstrued the distinction between the physical and the mental as a distinction between physicalistically described behavior whose features are observable to anyone with working sense organs, and internal states whose features are directly knowable only to their possessors and only by introspection. On this construal, a description of someone as suffering and in agony from pain must be broken into two parts: a description of purely physical happenings observable to anyone, and a description of internal happenings known only introspectively. Wittgenstein thought this was a distorted and obscuring way to describe either behavior or mental states, a form of description we give only because we are captives of a Cartesian theory about how things *must* be. He held that pain behavior is not even observable as such to creatures who have no concept of pain, no sense of what it is to suffer, no instincts to comfort the one afflicted. And he held that pain is not something we recognize in ourselves simply by bare introspection: recognition of it as pain requires that we are competent participants in the language in which pain plays its characteristic role.

Second, he objected to Cartesian attempts to explain *why* we distinguish the physical and the mental as we do – attempts not to *elucidate* the distinction but to *explain* it. Cartesians attempt to explain, for instance, the asymmetry in our ascription of mental states to ourselves and to others by appealing to the doctrine that mental states are internal and known only by introspection. That is supposed to *explain* why I can *doubt* that you are in pain and not doubt that I am, or why I can *express* my pain but not yours. Wittgenstein undertakes to show, in ways too intricate to spell out here, that the explanations are empty: if we work them through in particular cases, they fall apart and are seen, at best, simply to redescribe the phenomena, at worst, to be incoherent.

The failure of such explanation should not disappoint us but help us to see that there is nothing here that needs to be explained in that way. As Marie McGinn puts it, "… This complexity in the grammar of our sensation concepts is not something that needs to be explained … but is something which *in itself* reveals the fundamental distinction between sensations and behavior." (McGinn

1997, p. 123) Philosophical reflection on our sensation concepts no doubt raises problems we find inescapable and difficult, but resolving *those* problems does not call for explanatory theory but for perspicuous representation.

Let me consider one more example of Wittgenstein's objection to the Cartesian distinction, namely, the so-called 'rule-following considerations'. Here the distinctive feature of our practice that the Cartesian aims to explain is that by understanding a word (grasping its meaning), we are able to use it in diverse contexts over time, or (another example of the same phenomenon) by grasping a rule, we are able to continue a series indefinitely or compute any number of sums. Wittgenstein has no objection to what I just said. In understanding the word 'cube', for example, we are able to use it to refer to all sorts of objects that really are cubes, and by understanding the word 'red' we can pick out objects which are red. By grasping the add-two rule, we are able to make the correct move from any natural number to its second successor, and by knowing how to add, we can compute, for instance, the sum of 68 + 57 and come up with the correct answer, namely 125. Wittgenstein was not a skeptic about the meaning of words like 'cube', 'red', 'add', or 'plus' or about our capacity to determine the shapes or colors of objects or the truths of arithmetic. What he was a skeptic about was Cartesian attempts to why our understanding of words and rules determines the ways we use words and apply rules.

These attempts at explanation take at least three forms. One regards understanding as an inner state of grasping a meaning or rule that is at the same time an immediate grasp of all that is required by the meaning or the rule. Another takes understanding to be a mental mechanism that guides us whenever we use a word or apply a rule. A third thinks of understanding in terms of a Platonic vision of logical rails laid out before us: to understand a meaning or rule is to be logically compelled to use a word or follow a rule in the correct way. Wittgenstein argued, again in ways too intricate for discussion here, that if we consider exactly what these attempts at explanation claim about any particular case, we will see that they are empty. Understanding considered as an inner state, a mental mechanism, or a set of logical rails cannot guide us as it is said to do, for we equally need guidance in being guided. This is an intuitive way of putting Kripke's point about 'plus' and 'quus': the grasp we have of 'plus' may require us to go on doing sums *in the same way* but it need not require us to understand 'doing sums in the same way' *in the same way*.[3]

Kripke gave a nice exposition of Wittgenstein's critique of Cartesian explanations of how understanding determines use but in so doing he missed Wittgen-

---

3 Cf. Kripke 1982.

stein's main point. He took Wittgenstein's critique to be a skeptical argument that there is no such thing as a correct use of a word or a correct application of a rule, so that what the Cartesian attempts to explain is an illusion. On Kripke's reading, there is no such thing as understanding the rules of arithmetic and thereby coming up with the correct answer to 68 + 57. All we can say is that in *our community* we *call* 125 the correct answer, for, he argues, Wittgenstein has shown that the idea that 125 *is* the correct answer is empty.

But this is to turn Wittgenstein's skepticism about Cartesian *explanations* of how understanding a word or a rule enables us to apply it correctly into skepticism about whether there is any such thing as correct application, a skepticism Wittgenstein is said to counter by redescribing the phenomena in terms of a new theory, one which holds that assertions about correct application have communal assertability conditions but no *truth* conditions. On this reading, Wittgenstein's reflections on meaning and rule-following begin with a skepticism about their very possibility that is motivated by theoretical considerations and then tries to show that our ordinary practice can be sustained *in spite of* the truth of skepticism, provided we accept an explanation of the practice in terms of a verificationist theory of meaning.

For Wittgenstein, however, our ordinary practice, mathematical or otherwise, needs neither defense nor theoretical explanation, something that would be clear if we had a perspicuous representation of it. We make mistakes within it, but they are correctable from within it. What counts is not what processes go on in our mind or what formulae we grasp as we continue a series or do sums, for nothing can *compel* us to do one thing rather than another. That sense of compulsion is a myth, and hence its rejection does not mean that our application of words or rules is unconstrained by criteria of correctness (which would mean that there is no distinction between correct and incorrect). What counts is that we use words to communicate successfully, and apply rules so as to come up with correct answers, not by sheer luck or accident, of course, but by participation in the practice into which we were inducted as we learned to speak, to count, to add and subtract, to act for reasons, to contradict our peers, to coordinate our actions, and so on. The practice doesn't *make* what we do right nor does our competent participation in it *guarantee* that we will get it right; we nevertheless have the ability to get it right and to know when it is right.

Philosophical problems about our practice will arise as we reflect on it, but they will not be resolved by Cartesian theories about how inner states of understanding or mental mechanisms guide us in our speaking and calculating – nor by theories of any kind. Everything that we need to resolve the problems is already there in front of our eyes in what we have always known but have not been able to arrange perspicuously.

Wittgenstein's conception of philosophy and his rejection of the Cartesian distinction between the physical and the mental are the most significant themes in his philosophy of mind. It is clear that they are not separable: his conception of philosophical inquiry supports his critique of the Cartesian view, and his rejection of that view shows why it is that our practice can be taken for what it is without a theoretical explanation of how it works. The other themes I mentioned can be seen as corollaries of these two and hence I will be brief.

The third theme is Wittgenstein's reworking of the Kantian idea that concepts without intuitions are empty and intuitions without concepts are blind. This is a theme about intentionality about what it is or is not only to *think* or *talk* about anything, rightly or wrongly, but to *respond* to anything as such and such, whether rightly or wrongly. What is decisive is to see that Wittgenstein did not mean it as a philosophical theory, that, contrary to what one might expect, explains how we can think, talk, or respond to the world, other selves, and our own self.[4]

This theme shows up clearly in the so-called private language argument, whose aim is to show that introspection plays no role in defining psychological concepts because the notion of a private ostensive definition is simply an illusion. What a sensation or a feeling is, is to be understood not by looking within ourselves but by examining the roles the phenomena and our concepts of it play in our practice, which is conceptually structured. What this shows is that concepts of sensations or feelings are complex and are intricately related to our behavior – to the behavior that expresses them, that enables us to recognize them in others, that shows our concern, and so on. The point, again, is not to *explain* this complexity – to offer, for example, a theory about why there must be behavioral criteria for sensations or why we must be able to introspect them. It is this very complexity that shows what sensations and feelings are and how they are to be distinguished from behavior. Sensations may be *there* without concepts but without concepts they show us nothing about what they are (we can't recognize them) or what anything else is.

The fourth theme concerns the nature of action and its status as prior to intellection. This is one dimension of his rejection of the Cartesian construal of the mental-physical distinction, a rejection that entails that action is not to be understood as the physical result of internal states or mechanisms, a point that lies back of his critique of understanding as an inner state or mechanism that guides

---

4 John McDowell argues that Kant didn't mean it that way either, that "no one has come closer than Kant to showing us how to find intentionality unproblematic" (except Wittgenstein). (McDowell 1998a, p. 431)

our use of words or our procedures of calculation. The latter cannot be described in physicalistic terms since the notion of using a word or applying a rule has built into it concepts that already belong at the level of understanding and meaning. The same is true of action generally: the behavior that reasons can explain must be already conceptualized in non-physicalistic terms.

This suggests an equally important point about the *status* of action: since it cannot be understood as the physical result of internal states, it is more fundamental than intellection. What is fundamental is not what we think or believe but what we do – the practices in which we participate. This is not unique to Wittgenstein in 20th-century philosophy: it is a motif in philosophers like Heidegger, Merleau-Ponty and John Dewey. Its articulation is, in my view, the most distinctive feature of 20th-century philosophy.

The last theme is Wittgenstein's renewal of the idea that the world is both evaluatively and motivationally significant. This is also a motif in the work of Heidegger, Merleau-Ponty, and Dewey, for it is closely connected with the theme of action as more fundamental than intellection. The rejection of Aristotelean science meant (as Weber put it) the disenchantment of the world, a disenchantment that some philosophers, Descartes and Hume for instance, urge us to live with, and that others – Spinoza and Leibniz are examples – try to overcome by metaphysical theorizing. It is a theme in the background of much analytical philosophy of mind, which has taken for granted, as McDowell puts it, that

> Reason does not find meaning or intelligible order in the world: rather, whatever intelligible order there is in our world picture is a product of the operations of mind, and those operations are themselves just some of what goes on in nature, in itself meaninglessly, as it were. (McDowell 1998b, p. 174)

Wittgenstein neither acquiesces in the disenchantment of the world nor gives us a theory explaining why it is evaluatively and motivationally significant. On his view, what disenchanted the world was not science as such but the position given to science by the Cartesian doctrine that made it the sole arbiter of the external world, with the rest going inside. This intellectualized language and action and robbed the world of its own evaluative and motivational significance. Both value and motivation were regarded as subjective – a result of our desires or other mental states being projected onto the world – not something there is in the world to be discovered. The reason for this is that these things are not manifest to mere physical observation or mental introspection. To understand how they manifest themselves, we need to restore the Kantian theme of the inseparability of concepts and intuitions, not as theory, but as what we have always known, perspicuously arranged.

9.2 Physicalism and the Philosophy of Mind

By 'physicalism' I mean what Fred Dretske calls a 'naturalistic theory of the mind', whose aim Jerry Fodor characterizes as finding a place for the mind "in a physicalistic view of the world" (Fodor 1987, p. 97). But what is a 'physicalistic view of the world'? It can be taken weakly to mean two things: first, that we ought to believe what is entailed by the truths of natural science (physics in particular) and disbelieve what is inconsistent with them and, second, that if you destroy the physical, you destroy everything or, a little less dramatically, any change in the mental entails some change or other in the physical. But that *minimal* physicalism is something just about any philosopher (apart from supenaturalists) would endorse. My topic is *robust* physicalism, according to which as adequate account of the mental must either be, or be vindicated by, an explanatory theory from the natural sciences. On this view, there is a place for the mental in a physicalistic view of the world only if our concepts of the mind and the mental can be shown to function, or made to function, like explanatory concepts of a natural science (physics in particular).

The comings and goings of the diverse accounts of the mental that robust physicalists have proposed constitute a central part of the history of analytical philosophy of mind. The most obvious motivation for these accounts is the unity of science project: to show that any adequate explanation, whether in physics, biology, sociology, history, or everyday life, shares a common form. Carnap's analytical behaviorism was the first memorable such account in analytical philosophy of mind, one based on the *positivist* construal of the unity of science, which assumed a sharp distinction between science as establishing truth and philosophy as analyzing meaning. The unity of science project changed substantially with Quine's attack on the two dogmas of empiricism, which undermined the positivist distinction between science and philosophy and hence Carnap's behaviorist version of physicalism, which was based on an analysis of the meaning of mental statements. The result was that the positivist conception of the unity of science was replaced by a *naturalist* conception that, on the one hand, regarded philosophy and science as continuous and, on the other, regarded science and hence philosophy as essentially theory construction. This paved the way for the robust physicalism that now dominates analytical philosophy – so-called 'analytical metaphysics' whose task is to construct theories like those in the natural sciences and defend them by showing that they are better than alternative theories in explaining the data and in resolving difficulties raised by the theories themselves.[5]

The two best known physicalists of this kind are Paul Churchland and Jerry Fodor, who stand at opposite ends of the physicalist spectrum in that they disagree on the scientific worth of what Churchland calls 'folk psychology' and Fodor 'commonsense psychology'. Churchland thinks that folk psychology is a hopelessly defective theory of our internal processes that is as outmoded as the Ptolemaic theory of the universe or the phlogiston theory of heat.

> ... Folk psychology is a radically inadequate account of our internal activities ... that will simply be replaced by a better theory of those activities ... (It) provides a positively misleading sketch of our internal kinematics and dynamics ... (It) suffers explanatory failures on an epic scale, it has been stagnant for at least twenty-five centuries, and its categories appear (so far) to be incommensurable with or orthogonal to the categories of the (neuro-science) whose long-term claim to explain human behavior seems undeniable. Folk psychology is nothing more and nothing less than a culturally entrenched theory of how we and the higher animals work. It has no ... special status of any kind whatsoever. (Churchland 1981, pp. 72, 74, 76)

Fodor, on the other hand, thinks that commonsense psychology is indispensable and can be given a legitimate scientific vindication.

> Vindicating commonsense psychology means showing how you could have ... a respectable science whose ontology explicitly acknowledges states that exhibit the sorts of properties that common sense attributes to the attitudes ... The main thesis of this book is ... that it is possible to have a scientific psychology that vindicates commonsense belief-desire explanation, (namely) the Representational Theory of Mind ... (Fodor 1987, pp. 3, 10, 16)

This disagreement presupposes agreement on the part of both Churchland and Fodor that commonsense psychology stands or falls with whether it can be scientifically vindicated: that is what makes them robust physicalists in the philos-

---

[5] Quine paved the way for analytical metaphysics but he himself seldom engaged in *philosophical* (as opposed to logical) theory construction. His view of mental concepts was that while they were practically indispensable, there could be no theory of them, scientific or otherwise, for they were a kind of 'dramatic idiom' and "if we are limning the true and ultimate structure of reality, the canonical scheme for us is the austere scheme that knows ... only the physical constitution and behavior of organisms" (Quine 1960, p. 221). The latter makes Quine a kind of eliminativist: for him eliminativism is not a philosophical theory about the mental but the rejection of any such philosophical theory. The aim of *Word and Object* was not to construct an explanatory philosophical theory of language but to show the explanatory emptiness of philosophical notions such as meaning, proposition, property, and the like. Analogous things can be said about Quine's other notable philosophical contributions.

ophy of mind. They also agree on another point, which is more fundamental though often neglected, namely on what commonsense (or folk) psychology is. In the first instance, the term denotes the conceptual features of our everyday practice of understanding, interpreting, justifying, and explaining ourselves and our actions to each other. We ascribe thoughts, desires, hopes, feelings, and sensations to ourselves and others, it is because we have knowledge of such mental states that we can coordinate our activities with each other, these states play an essential role in our responding to situations in the world as reasons for us to act, and so on. These are things no one would dispute; the question is what to make of them. How should we understand them?

Both Fodor and Churchland think this is not a difficult question – not one that calls for serious philosophical reflection. On their view, commonsense psychology is a theory about the internal causes of our behavior: our beliefs and desires (states, "entities, events, whatever", as Fodor puts it) that have content and causal power and whose interactions are instances of general laws connecting actions with states of belief and desire. Here is how Churchland characterizes commonsense psychology:

> Our commonsense conceptual framework for mental phenomena [is] a theory ... Each of us understands others, as well as we do, because we share a tacit command of an integrated body of lore concerning the lawlike relations holding among external circumstances, internal states, and overt behavior ... This body of lore may quite aptly be called "folk psychology"... The recognition that [it] is a theory provides a simple and decisive solution to ... the problem of other minds. [Belief in other minds] is an *explanatory hypothesis* ... that provides explanations/ predictions/ understanding of the individual's continuing behavior. ... The structural features of folk psychology parallel perfectly those of mathematical physics; the only difference lies in the respective domain of abstract entities they exploit – numbers in the case of physics, and propositions in the case of psychology. (Churchland 1981, pp. 68–69, 71)

Fodor characterizes it in this way:

> ... The theory from which we get this extraordinary predictive power is just good old commonsense belief/desire psychology. That's what tells us, for example, how to infer people's intentions from the sounds they make ... and how to infer people's behavior from their intentions ... It takes for granted that overt behavior comes at the end of a causal chain whose links are mental events – hence unobservable – and which may be arbitrarily long ... A psychology is commonsensical about the attitudes ... just in case it postulates states (entities, events, whatever) satisfying the following conditions: 1) They are semantically evaluable. 2) They have causal powers. 3) The implicit generalizations of commonsense belief/desire psychology are true of them ... (Fodor 1987, pp. 10, 16)

Two things about this shared view of commonsense psychology should be noted. The first is that its construal of our everyday practice is badly underargued – indeed, is hasty in the extreme. There are arguments as to why we should call it a theory but they are pursued at a very abstract level, and they simply take it for granted that among the things we have always known are that beliefs and desires are internal states or entities that cause the behavior that is our action. On this view, commonsense psychology is a collection of intuitive judgments, of the things ordinary folk say or would say, of platitudes Granny would deliver – just the sorts of things ordinary language philosophers were criticized for appealing to. No serious attempt is made to comprehend the complexities of our everyday practice and the self-understanding implicit in it, to get some perspicuous overview of it. Real philosophical work, on this view, is not done here but later on.

The second thing to note is that these hasty accounts of our practice are essentially the Cartesian construal of the mental-physical distinction. The physical is regarded as the physicalistic, the mental as internal states and processes that cause behavior physicalistically understood. What is presented as a straight description of phenomena that need scientific vindication and explanation is in fact a theoretically-loaded redescription in Cartesian terms of both the physical and the mental. The physical does not comprise the everyday objects and events we live with, respond to, change and preserve – beautiful and ugly, colored and full of sound – but objects whose properties are definable in physicalistic terms, these other terms applying rather to the internal effects of the physicalistic (which we project back onto the physicalistic). The behavior we observe in each other is physical motion – behavior of organisms at best – but we do not observe people (or animals of any kind) suffering, bored, nervous, angry, satisfied, and so on, for those terms apply not to behavior but to its internal causes.

Commonsense psychology as Fodor and Churchland understand it is, then, a Cartesian theory of the distinction between the physical and the mental, a theory neither challenges but which both take for granted. Where they differ is over what to do at the next stage, where real philosophy, in their view, begins and which involves constructing a theory that will find a place for the mental, understood in the Cartesian way, in a physicalistic view of the world which essentially means to show how we can be Cartesians without being dualists.

This is relatively easy for Churchland because in describing commonsense psychology, he often expresses the Cartesian distinction itself in terms of his own theory. For example, he accepts the Cartesian view that the asymmetry between the first and third person ascription of mental states should be explained by reference to the distinction between the physical as outer and observable, and the mental as inner and introspectable. But he articulates it in terms of a distinction between an 'explanatory hypothesis' in the case of the mental states of others, and "an acquired habit of conceptual response to one's internal states" (Churchland 1981, p. 70) in the case of one's own mental states. Fitting *that* distinction into a physicalistic view of the world is not difficult since what it amounts to is accepting the Cartesian distinction but denying that there are any instances on the mental side. The problem, of course, is that there is no longer any reason to accept Churchland's description of commonsense psychology, but from his point of view that does not matter since it is supposed to be eliminated anyway.

Fodor's task is a little harder, for he wants to give a physicalist explanation of the Cartesian distinction that doesn't simply eliminate the mental half. The idea is to be Cartesian without being dualist by taking the mental to consist of mental states that can be incorporated into a scientific theory in the fullest sense of the term. Fodor uses the computational-functionalist theory, which identifies mental states not with physical states but with computational states, which are internal and whose essential (computational) properties are in cyber space and hence unobservable even in principle. The aim is to make the Cartesian distinction between physical states (hardware) and computational states (software).

Fodor's view cannot fail to impress with its virtuosity and its use of the computer model, which makes it a distinctive 20th-century contribution to philosophy of mind. It remains wedded to the Cartesian distinction, however, and hence is, as Churchland would put it, "a stagnant or degenerating research program" (Churchland 1981, p. 75). I won't criticize it here, however, except to offer an account of why it even appears to have some measure of success as an account of the mind.

This has to do with the three conditions Fodor contends must be met by any adequate physicalistic account of the mind – that it postulate states (entities, events, whatever) which are semantically evaluable, have causal powers, and satisfy the generalizations of commonsense belief-desire psychology. What I want to call attention to is what these conditions do *not* include, namely three features that are implicit in Wittgenstein's critique of the Cartesian distinction and which I regard as essential to any adequate account of commonsense psychology.

The first is the normative dimension of commonsense psychology – the fact that our thought and action are *normatively constituted*.[6] To act for a reason is to take some consideration to be, normatively speaking, a reason for one to act, to

---

6 Fodor's requirement that mental states be "semantically evaluable" has nothing to do with normativity. What he means is that they have truth or reference conditions, neither of which he thinks of as nonnative even in the broadest sense of that term.

believe a claim is to take it to be worthy of belief, and to desire something is to take it to be, in some respect, desirable. The second is the centrality of *persons* (or agents). In commonsense psychology, it is persons who believe, desire, hope, feel, suffer, and so on; these states are not internal states, events, or entities, but states of whole persons. Moreover, to understand why people act as they do, we have to grasp, what, from their point of view, they are doing and what they take to be reasons for them to act, not what internal states or events bring about their acting. The third is the irreducibly *interpretive* character of the descriptions and explanations given and received in commonsense psychology. To grasp what people are doing, we have to grasp the reasons for their action, which requires knowing what those actions are, which requires understanding what they are believing or intending, which presumes we understand their behavior, and so on in the 'hermeneutic circle'. There is no settled starting point for commonsense descriptions and explanations of the actions and mental states of persons: the question of whether someone is in a certain mental state is inseparable from the question of how to describe the state in the first place. There are no standards beyond or beneath these interpretive considerations by which we can judge the interpretive conclusions we reach.

Fodor's construal of commonsense psychology simply omits these essential dimensions, and hence he is not troubled by the fact that they have no place in his scientific explanation of it. The fundamental reason for this omission is that it is intrinsic to the Cartesian distinction itself, even in its dualist version. Normative notions play no constitutive role in the Cartesian account of the mental. Nor do persons as they figure in commonsense psychology play a role, for it is an account of what the mental would be like in isolation from bodily behavior. Finally, neither observation of the physical nor introspection of the mental is interpretive in any significant sense.

The problem with Cartesianism, therefore, is not dualism but the fact that the way it distinguishes the mental from the physical omits these essential features of the mental. Descartes himself did not leave them out in his overall philosophy of mind for they showed up whenever he dealt with the mind-body union. Cartesianism is not Descartes; it is what results when Descartes's dualism is abstracted from his account of the human being as a genuine unity of mind and body. Dropping the dualism from Cartesianism does not change the fundamental point, which is that we have an entirely abstract distinction between the physical and the mental that rules out features that are essential to commonsense psychology.

9.3 Davidson and the Philosophy of Mind

I come now to Davidson, my aim being to show why his philosophy of mind should be seen as with and not against Wittgenstein. This may seem surprising, for Davidson's philosophy of mind is often read as making a significant contribution to robust physicalism. He claims that explanations of intentional actions in terms of reasons must be causal and that causation, whether physical or mental, entails that events have physicalistic descriptions, and he accepts the monistic view that every event (and entity) is physical. On this reading, Davidson is a sophisticated contributor to the physicalistic tradition of Carnap and Quine, who shares the standard analytical attitude toward theories of meaning, the mind-body problem, the explanation of action, and so on.

That is the way Davidson is read not only by physicalists who want to enlist him in their cause but also by many Wittgensteinians, who put him near the top of their enemies list. There is no question that Davidson is a monist but the significance of his view is that it rejects both dualism and robust physicalism. I once said to him that I had wondered if he might be a closet Wittgensteinian; his immediate reply was, "Well, I don't know about the closet." I think he spoke the truth if he meant that his work was significantly influenced by Wittgenstein, and I want to show why he should be read that way. I will focus on his philosophy of action because it is basic to all his work.

(1) The center piece of Davidson's philosophy of action is his account of what it is to act for a reason. As is well-known, he criticized the Wittgensteinian accounts dominant in the 1950s for having no account of the difference between having a reason to act and acting because of a reason. The difference, he claimed, must be causal: reasons which explain our actions cause them. But his account of what this involves has been read in two ways, one of which yields the main-line causalism robust physicalists hold and the other of which yields a much different view that reflects the fact that the most important influence on his philosophy of action was Elizabeth Anscombe, whose *Intention* he regarded as "the most important treatment of action since Aristotle" (Anscombe 2000, cover of book).

The main-line reading of Davidson is as follows. Reasons explanations are causal, and reasons are beliefs and desires that must, therefore, cause the actions they explain. The traditional view of this was the covering law model, which held that beliefs and desires cause actions in virtue of a causal law that connects descriptions of beliefs and desires *as* reasons with descriptions of actions *as* actions – causal laws, that is to say, at the intentional level. On this reading, Davidson showed two things. First, that there are no such causal laws at the intentional level[7] and, second, that there do not *need* to be any because there are causal laws at the physical level that account for the causal power of reasons. Any belief-desire pair that is the reason for which an agent acts is identical with some physical token, and that physical token has a physical description that is related by causal law to a physical description of the action the reason explains. It is the existence of that causal law at the physical level that distinguishes a reason an agent acts because of from one she merely has. Here is a diagram of this reading (Table 9.1).

Table 9.1

Belief-desire pair	→	(causally *explains*)	→	action
(token *identical* with)				(token *identical* with)
Physical event	→	(causally *related to*)	→	physical event

There are very serious problems with such a view[8] that its defenders have tried to deal with by constructing various kinds of theories, but my concern now is whether this is a correct way to read Davidson, which I am convinced that it is not.

Davidson's real view is in his "Actions, Reasons, and Causes" but it is difficult to see there without help from commentators and his later writings. It is this. There is a clear distinction between causal *relations* and causal *explanations*. Causal relations hold only between events, which are entities that can be truly described in any number of ways. They hold no matter how the events are described (sentences ascribing them are *extensional*), but, nevertheless, one event has a causal relation to another only if there is a strict law instantiated by descriptions of the events. This law must be a law of physics (since all strict laws are), and hence any events in causal relations have physical descriptions. It follows that mental events that are causes and effects also have physical descriptions (and are also physical).[9]

---

[7] "We don't know precise laws for explaining and predicting [psychological events]; but unlike the situation in the natural sciences, this isn't because we haven't discovered them yet; it's because there are no such laws." (Stoecker 1993, p. 312)
[8] Cf. Stoutland 1985. I now recognize that I misread Davidson at various points in this paper.
[9] Let me note that does not make Davidson an epiphenomenalist: he does not claim that events are causally related only *in virtue of physical* descriptions or properties. On his view events are not causally related in virtue of anything. Cf. Davidson 1995, pp. 8, 12: "The efficacy of an event cannot depend ono how the event is described, while whether an event can be called mental, or can be said to fall under a law, depends entirely on how the events can be described ... It is ir-

Causal *explanations* must describe causes and effects in explanatorily relevant ways, hence their validity depends on how phenomena are described (so that sentences giving a causal *explanation* are intentional). To be causal, an explanation must meet three conditions.
1. It must explain the occurrence of an *event* (or what entails that occurrence). The cause need not be an event; typically it is a state or condition of some kind. Hence, if 'A causes B' means that A *causally explains* B, then A need not be an event.
2. It must entail the occurrence of some event *associated with* the cause that is *causally related* to the effect. We need not know which event that is, though it must have a physical description that instantiates a strict law.
3. Its validity must depend on generalizations connecting descriptions of the cause and the effect, which are empirical but are *rough* generalizations and *not* strict laws.

Davidson's claim is that rational explanations meet all three of these conditions. It meets the first because an action is an event. The *cause* that explains an action, however, is not an event, because beliefs and desires are not events but *states* ascribed to whole persons. "'Primary reasons', as I have used the phrase", he writes, "are certainly not events ... Beliefs and desire are not changes. They are states, and since I don't think that states are *entities* of any sort, and so are not events, I do not think beliefs and desires are events." (Stoecker 1993, p. 287)

It meets the second because when an agent acts because of a reason, there is an event *associated with* the reason (a belief-desire pair) that is *causally related* to the action. This event might be almost anything: coming to have a belief, changing one's mind, noticing the corner ahead, or change in the brain, etc. This event does not causally *explain* the action (it is not the reason: that is the belief-desire pair) but is a necessary condition for the explanation to be causal. Nor does it *explain why* the agent acted for one reason rather than another; it is rather part what it *means* to say he acted for a given reason. As Davidson puts it, "The explanation provides no reason for saying that one suitable belief-desire pair rather than another (which may also have been present in the agent) did the causing." (Davidson 2004, p. 109)

It meets the third condition because its validity depends on empirical generalizations that are not strict laws. Generalizations are necessary because of the

---

relevant to the causal efficacy of physical events that they can be described in the physical vocabulary. It is *events* that have the power to change things, not our various ways of describing them."

dispositional character of beliefs and desires, but these generalizations hold *only* for the particular agent whose action is being explained.[10] If we try to extend them to agents more generally (by adding *ceteris paribus* clauses), they cease to be empirical and become conceptual or normative principles. This means that the real force of a rational explanation turns on the conceptual and normative principles implicit in our *interpretation* of the actions of rational agents in the light of their reasons. Here is a diagram of how I think Davidson should be read (Table 9.2).[11]

Table 9.2

Belief-desire pair	→	(causally *explains*)	→	action
(*associated* with)				(token *identical* with)
Physical event	→	(causally *related to*)	→	physical event

The decisive differences between this reading of Davidson and the previous one are as follows. First, there is no claim that beliefs and desires are physical because Davidson's argument for the identity of the mental and the physical applies only to events, and beliefs and desires are not events (nor entities of any kind). Second, the events that are causally related to the action are not (except occasionally) *reasons* for the action; they may have a connection with the reasons but they need not, and they do not when we do not know what they are.[12] Third, these causes do not explain why an agent acts for one reason and not another: Davidson does not think there is any such explanation. Finally, what in the end give force to a rational explanation are the normative and con-

---

[10] "The laws implicit in reason explanations are simply the generalizations implied by attributions of dispositions. But then the 'laws' are peculiar to individuals at particular moments." (Davidson 1980, p. 265)

[11] Calling the events 'physical' is redundant since Davidson holds that to be physical is to have a physical description, which every event does; I call them that because of his claim that if they are causally related, they must have physical descriptions that are an instance of a strict law.

[12] "Sometimes the answer [to 'Why did you do it?'] will mention a mental event that does not give a reason: 'Finally I made up my mind.' However, there also seem to be cases of intentional action where we cannot explain at all why we acted when we did. In such cases, explanation in terms of primary reasons parallels the explanation of the collapse of the bridge from a structural defect: we are ignorant of the event or sequence of events that led up to (caused) the collapse, but we are sure that there was such an event or sequence of events." (Davidson 1980, p. 13)

ceptual principles which are used in an overall interpretation of the agent's action in the light of his attitudes, his situation, and his overall behavior.[13]

(2) Given this reading of Davidson's account of rational explanation, we can see the ways in which his point of view in the philosophy of mind is in all major respects *with* Wittgenstein and *against* robust physicalism. The most significant of these is Davidson's clear-headed rejection of the Cartesian distinction between the mental and the physical.

"There are no such things as minds, but people have mental properties, which is to say that certain psychological predicates are true of them." (Guttenplan 1994, p. 232) That is Davidson's account of mental states: they are not material entities – indeed, they are not entities at all – but states of whole persons. To ascribe a belief to a person is to describe *her* in a certain way – to apply a mental predicate to *her* – which is to say that *she* is in a certain mental state. Mental states differ from physical states in that we ascribe them to ourselves without evidence or inference, but this is not because mental states are internal while physical states are external, or because mental states must be introspected by their bearers. It is because to determine the mental states of others, I must interpret actions and speech whereas it makes no sense to speak of interpreting myself.[14]

Interpretation has no significant role to play in physicalist philosophy of mind because it has no significant role to play in the Cartesian distinction between the physical and the mental. It is, however, at the center of Davidson's philosophy of mind. He writes that "What a fully informed interpreter could learn about what a speaker means is all there is to learn; the same goes for what the speaker believes." (Davidson 2001a, p. 148) Intentional states simply are what must be ascribed to an agent to render her behavior (including her speech) intelligible to an interpreter. They cannot, therefore, be *entities* of any kind because, while there are endless truths about entities, intentional states are just what an adequate interpretation takes them to be, and hence there cannot be

---

13 For further discussion and defense of this way of reading Davidson, see my "Intentionalists and Davidson on Rational Explanation" in Meggle 1999.

14 "The existence of first person authority is not an empirical discovery, but rather a criterion, among others, of what a mental state is ... Exceptions do not throw in doubt the presumption that we know our own minds. What accounts for this presumption? ... [The answer is that] we must interpret the thoughts of others on the basis of evidence; interpreting ourselves does not ... make sense ... The difference ... is that when I interpret you, two languages are involved, yours and mine (the same words may mean different things in your language and mine). In the second case, only one language is involved, my own; interpretation is therefore not (exceptional cases aside) in the picture." (Guttenplan 1994)

truths about them only scientific experts (like neuro- or information-scientists) can establish.[15] As we have seen, Davidson elucidates the asymmetry between ascribing mental states to others and to oneself by saying we interpret others but it makes no sense to interpret ourselves. He develops this point further in contending that interpretation is the "source of the ultimate difference" between the mental and the physical, a point he develops in the following striking account of interpretation.

> Success in interpretation is always a matter of degree: the resources of thought or expression available to an interpreter can never perfectly match the resources of the interpreted. We do the best we can ... This is the process of radical interpretation. There is no further court of appeal, no impersonal objective standard against which to measure our own best judgments of the rational and the true.
>
> Here lies the source of the ultimate difference between the concepts we use to describe mental events and the concepts we use to describe physical events, the difference that rules out the existence of strict psychophysical laws. The physical and the numbers we use to calibrate it are common property, the material and abstract objects and events that we agree on and share. But it makes no sense to speak of comparing, or coming to agree on, ultimate common standards of rationality, since it is our own standards in each case to which we must turn in interpreting others. This should not be thought of as a failure of objectivity, but rather as the point at which 'questions come to an end.' Understanding the mental states of others and understanding nature are cases where questions come to an end at different stages. How we measure physical quantities is decided intersubjectively. We cannot in the same way go behind our own ultimate norms of rationality in interpreting others. Priority is not an issue. We would have no full-fledged thoughts if we were not in communication with others, and therefore no thoughts about nature: communication requires that we succeed in finding something like our own patterns of thought in others. (Guttenplan 1994, p. 232)

The two other essential features of commonsense psychology that I noted as absent from the Cartesian distinction are implicit in this notion of interpretation. That the mental is normatively constituted is a prominent theme in Davidson's work, in particular in his arguments that psychology is autonomous and not dependent on the natural sciences. "The study of human action, motives, desires, beliefs, memory, and learning", he writes, "cannot employ the same methods as, or be reduced to, the more precise physical sciences." (Davidson 2001a, p. 240)

---

[15] "If you ask what kind of properties we're attributing when we attribute beliefs, I think a theory about how we tell that belief-attributing sentences are true provides the best answer. This shows what kind of property it is: it's a property which you determine to apply to an individual in the following way ... (and here you describe the method). Is there something more to say about it? I don't see why there has to be." (Stoecker 1993, p. 288)

> The reason mental concepts cannot be reduced to physical concepts is the *normative* character of mental concepts ... The semantic contents of attitudes and beliefs determine their relations to one another and to the world in ways that meet at least. Rough standards of consistency and correctness. Unless such standards are met to an adequate degree, nothing can count as being a belief, a pro-attitude, or an intention. But these standards are norms – *our* norms – there being no others. (Davidson 2004, p. 114)

Davidson also presumes the centrality of persons in commonsense psychology. He regards mental states as states of whole persons, and his way of understanding thought, language and action never loses sight of thinkers, speakers, and agents. He further maintains that to understand mental states, we have to be able to grasp the point of view of their possessors. This is what the principle of charity is all about: understanding another person requires a large enough measure of agreement to ensure that we share a world and a point of view on that world. That does not rule out disagreement; the point is that disagreement presumes a large measure of agreement.

> Some kind of basic agreement, not just in beliefs, but also in values, is essential to understanding ... Understanding another person depends upon finding common grounds not only with respect to beliefs but also with respect to values, right from the start. (Bergström and Føllesdal 1993, p. 220)

Reason-explanations, he writes in another place, "make others intelligible to us only to the extent that we can recognize something like our own reasoning powers at work, (powers which cannot) be reduced to non-normative, perhaps formal, characteristics" (Davidson 2004, p. 115).

Davidson's conception of the mental-physical distinction also rejects the Cartesian conception of the physical as merely physicalistic. What the physical is, is what it presents itself as to ordinary observation, and we can grasp the mental only as we grasp the physical. "Only those who share a common world can communicate; only those who communicate can have the concept of an intersubjective, objective world." (Guttenplan 1994, p. 234) There are non-interpretive truths about the physical world – that is a distinguishing mark of the physical – but only those capable of interpretation can grasp or establish them.

In all these ways, then, Davidson's philosophy of mind is anti-Cartesian, and hence anti-physicalist, its main themes being very much in the spirit of Wittgenstein. The same is true, I would argue, of his conception of philosophy. To many, Davidson's way of working seems opposed to Wittgenstein's because of the extensive use he makes of the notion of theory – a theory of meaning, a theory of interpretation, a theory of the attitudes, and so on. But the fact that a philosopher characterizes his work in terms of 'theory' does not mean he is constructing the kind of theories Wittgenstein urged philosophers to avoid. What Wittgenstein rejected were theories that, on the one hand, obscured or distorted our everyday practice of describing and explaining ourselves and our world and, on the other hand, tried to vindicate and explain that practice by showing why it *must* be so and so or how it can be altered to meet external standards, scientific or otherwise.

Davidson's theories do not do that. His theory of meaning, for example, is a real theory in the technical sense of having axioms and theorems, but it is not *explanatory*. It does not undertake to explain why we speak as we do, why our language must have certain forms, what understanding a language consists in, etc. It *describes* a certain dimension of our linguistic practice in a systematic way that aims at being sensitive to that practice, something that led Davidson to speak in terms of a 'passing theory' that applies only to a particular communicative situation. Such a systematic description of our linguistic practice may be objectionable in a number of ways, but it does not violate the spirit of Wittgenstein's conception of philosophy, or of language as 'woven' into actions. "The concept of meaning", Davidson wrote, "derives all of its content from the case of successful interpretation. That is, cases where a person intends to be interpreted in a certain way and is." (Bergström and Føllesdal 1994, p. 221)

Davidson's use of 'theory' in such contexts as 'theory of interpretation' or 'theory about how we tell that belief-attributing sentences are true' is not a technical use. It simply means an account that is discursive, articulate, systematic, rigorous, and the like, and has nothing to do with scientific theories. Davidson did think it was possible to do philosophy with the same measure of care, explicitness, and argument that characterizes the best kind of scientific work, but that is not to confuse philosophy with scientific theorizing. He showed only a passing interest in the metaphysical theorizing that has taken over analytical philosophy, and even his work on events, identity, and causation was pursued in the context of concrete examples and in relation to problems that arise from the subject matter and not from theories about it. He pursued supervenience only in an informal way and was never tempted by the view that it *explains* anything. His conception of truth avoided the notion that sentences are true *in virtue of* anything, and he offered no theory of truth. "Fact", he wrote, "is for me ... just a general word and you can say there are moral facts just as well as others" (Bergström and Føllesdal 1994, p. 220), and as for properties, they are simply predicates true of something.

Davidson's aim can be characterized as giving a perspicuous representation of what we already know. He often did it in ways Wittgenstein did not, but to learn from someone of Wittgenstein's stature requires not following him slavishly or in a spirit of partisanship. It has been a long struggle to save St. Thomas from the Thomists, Descartes from the Cartesians, Dewey from the Deweyans.

Now the struggle should be to save Wittgenstein from the Wittgensteinians, and there is no better way to engage in that struggle than to learn from Davidson.

10 The Ontology of Social Agency

Philosophers of action have not paid much attention to social agency, that is, to actions performed not by individual persons but by social groups of various kinds. Discussion has centered on what individuals do, believe, or desire, and on the reasons each has for acting, the standard story being that actions consist of bodily movements that are rationalized and caused by the agent's beliefs and desires. Although we often describe an agent's actions in terms of their results rather than in terms of the bodily movements involved, the claim is that *what* we are describing are the agent's bodily movements. Since each of us has a distinct body and moving it is something we do on our own, this view apparently rules out genuinely social agency, that is, agency that is not reducible to the agency of individuals.

Recently, however, there has been increased interest in social agency, which has received careful discussion from a number of philosophers.[1] But most of these discussions, while taking social action seriously, display an individualist, anti-social bias about agents. Many of them focus, for example, on cases like painting a house together or moving a piano, which involve actions people do together but which they could have done separately. Given pianos and our limited strength, most of us could not move a piano alone but it is not incoherent to think of so doing. It is, therefore, not difficult to think of the actions of social groups like these in terms of the actions of each of its members that are coordinated in various ways.

That is not the case for actions like playing a Mozart symphony, passing a law, appointing a president of a university, declaring a stock dividend, or winning the World Series. Those are not actions individuals can perform on their own. Only an orchestra can play a Mozart symphony, only a parliament pass a law, only a university name its president, only a corporation declare a stock dividend, and only a baseball team win the World Series. Only social agents can do or intend to do these things, and while the actions of individual agents are essential to their doing them, it is the groups that act intentionally in these ways.

Philosophers who are biased toward individualism respond to this in different ways. Some take the eliminativist view that there really are no social agents; we may speak in social terms but what we say applies only to the actions, inten-

---

1 See for instance: Bratman 1992, 1993, 1999; Gilbert 1989, 1990; Pettit 2007; Searle 1995; Tuomela 1984, 1991, 2007. For further references, see Baier 1997. Baier's paper was a major source of inspiration for my discussion here, and I am grateful to it for examples and ways of putting things. Her paper documents very well the individualist bias in recent philosophy of action.

tions, beliefs, and reasons of individual agents. Others respond, not by denying that social agents have intentions or beliefs and act for reasons, but by arguing that these are reducible to – definable in terms of – the intentions, beliefs, actions, and reasons of members of the group. Still others reject reductionism, claiming in particular that social intentions and beliefs cannot be defined in terms of individual intentions and beliefs since their content must be mutually referring in distinctive ways. But the anti-social bias remains because the intentions and beliefs themselves are not ascribed to social groups but to their members.

My aim in what follows is to undermine the individualist bias in accounts of the ontological status of social agency by showing, in particular, that social groups – not all of them but many – are not ontologically secondary but have a reality of their own. This involves showing that it is legitimate to ascribe actions, reasons, intentions and beliefs to social groups as such, not only to their individual members. In short, there are, I shall argue, social agents in addition to individual agents.

This is a relatively narrow topic and a uniquely philosophical one, which is only indirectly relevant to claims about the social explanation of behavior, about how individuals are dependent on society, or other claims made by social scientists. The social groups that I am concerned with are not a primary source of the social constraints Durkheim articulated.[2] Orchestras, parliaments, corporations, or baseball teams constrain their members in various ways but that is secondary to their role in making possible a range of actions and attitudes that would not be possible outside the groups. My focus, however, is not on that – on what social groups constitute – but on what constitute groups as social agents and what it is to ascribe to them actions, attitudes, and reasons.

10.1 Social Agents

In our discourse together we constantly speak of the agency not only of individuals but also of social groups. We speak in terms of social agents, of their actions and their reasons for acting, and of their intentions, beliefs and other attitudes. I shall say something about each of these in the course of this paper.

Let us distinguish two kinds of *social agents*. One is *plural* agents, where the agent is referred to as 'they' and agency expressed by 'we': thus they played a Mozart quartet, they played chess, we nailed up that long board, we moved

---

[2] Cf. Aron 1967, p. 72f.

the piano, we took turns, we had a quarrel. The other is *collective* agents, where the agent is not plural but singular, referred to by a name or definite description or as 'it', not as 'they', though typically *expressed* as 'we'. Thus the Senate debated a new tax law but *it* hasn't passed it yet, the Company laid off a lot of employees but *it* will lay off more, and – as an expression of agency – we intend to appoint a new president of the university, and so on.

What I have just said reflects American rather than British English. In the former it is said that the government *is* planning to do such and such, whereas in the latter that in the government *are* planning to so such and such. This shows that the line between these two kinds of agents is not sharp. There are, nevertheless, significant differences. Plural agents come into being just by people coming together and doing things jointly – nailing up a board, playing a string quartet, having a dinner party. Collective agents cannot come to be in that way: they require a history of practice. Even if they are established by fiat – "we formed a new company yesterday" – the fiat is effective only against the background of social groups of that kind that were not established by fiat. The group cannot therefore be transitory or ephemeral: collective agents have a permanence plural agents do not. The senate, the company, or the family outlive particular members or the actions they perform. Plural agents in general do not: the we who nailed up that board does not exist as a we beyond that act.[3]

Another difference is that collective agents typically involve structures that institutionalize authority relations.[4] These enable the decisions of certain members to be decisions of the social group and permit persons to speak on behalf of the group, so that statements they make are statements of the group. When the president of the university speaks, for instance, the university, as a matter of institutional structure, speaks. This is in general not the case for plural agents, which do not institutionalize authority. Individuals may have special authority but it is informal and fluid, based on others letting them have it rather than on their office or status.

Collective agents and plural agents are alike, however, in that neither kind is identical with individual agents. The senate does things individual senators

---

[3] Plural agents can become collective agents. Four musicians who play a quartet together may establish themselves as the Toledo Quartet, which institutionalizes itself and may outlast all the players who began it.

[4] This is not always the case, for example, with families, which are natural rather than instituted social agents. There usually are authority relations in a family, and they may be fairly strict, but they stem neither from the institutional structures typical of collective agents nor from the informal power relations of plural agents. They show another sense in which there is no sharp distinction between the two kinds of social agents.

cannot do, such as pass laws or issue a resolution. The university appoints a new president, which no member of the university can do. The quintet plays Schubert's "Trout", which is something no individual musician can do.[5] This point may be obscured in the case of types of actions that either an individual or a social agent could perform. An example is our holding up a board so we can get it nailed in place, a type of action either of us could (with great difficulty) do alone. This particular act is, nevertheless, the act of a social agent because it is not divisible between the two of us. That entails, I contend, not only that each of us performs the same *type* of action – namely, lifting a board – but that we perform a single act *token*. Lifting a board is something *we* do as a social agent. It is true that in lifting the board, each of us also acts as an individual agent, exercising his own strength and moving in a distinctive way, which makes the social action possible, but these individual acts are not identical with the act performed by the social agent. It was neither you nor I who did so but *we*, that is, the group of which we are members.

10.2 Social Actions

Social agents perform social actions, which are similar to the actions of individual agents in a number of ways. First, there is no acting where there is no *intentional* acting. What distinguishes mere behavior – where things happen but there is no agency – from acting, is that the latter is intentional under at least one description. Acting, that is to say, is *essentially* intentional, and insofar as it falls short of being intentional, it is a diminished form of acting. Second, whenever an agent acts, his so acting is not intentional under other descriptions. Acting always has unintended results, which are diminished forms of acting: in acting intentionally, agents also do things in ignorance, by mistake, accidentally, and so on.

Third, an agent who acts does so, in general, for a reason that yields a description under which her acting is intentional. An agent may act for no reason – whistle idly, for instance – but that is necessarily exceptional and, moreover, an

---

5 Numerous real life instances of social agents are discussed in writings about corporate responsibility and similar topics. A good example is the case of the Ford Motor Company (see French 1984) being sued for murder in the Pinto case, involving a car it produced with a faulty fuel tank. The suit was against the company, not against its officers or employees; the company itself, it was contended, was morally responsible for knowingly killing innocent people. A more recent case is the Minneapolis School Board appointing a company to be superintendent of its schools. The president of the company was interviewed but it was made clear that not he but his company would manage the schools. (This arrangement did not last very long.)

act that could have been done for a reason.[6] It is exceptional because the capacity to act for reasons is essential to agency and hence for the capacity to act intentionally (and hence to act). If one acts for a reason, one acts intentionally (under a description): one cannot have a reason for acting inadvertently or in ignorance because if one did so act for a reason, it would not be acting inadvertently or in ignorance. And if one acts intentionally, one knows what one is doing under a description, which means one knows at least the immediate reason for what one is doing.

These claims, assumed in most conceptions of individual action, apply straightforwardly to social action. The Senate acts only when it acts intentionally under a description, but in so acting it does not act intentionally in all respects. For example, it intentionally passes a budget law, but in so doing, it inadvertently increases unemployment in certain sectors and angers some citizens. Its passing a budget law was intentional because it did so for a reason, namely, because the law was required to bring down the deficit. Its reason for action did not include increasing unemployment or angering citizens, so it was not intentional in those respects. A quartet intentionally plays Beethoven's last quartet because a patron requested it, but unintentionally wakes up a baby or inspires a bad review (which were not requested by a patron). The same analysis, so familiar for the actions of individuals, applies straightforwardly to social action generally.

Many philosophers, however, even among those sympathetic to social action, will reject this account. They may admit that there are social actions in the guise of 'joint actions', which are social in that they are not divisible among the individual agents who make up the group. But they will deny that this indivisibility entails that there is one *token* action the group itself performs.

Take four persons playing a string quartet. If this is a genuine social action, there is, I maintain, one token action that the quartet performs, namely, playing a quartet, which involves a complex pattern of blended sounds. The four players also perform actions of their own, each playing from a score that marks out the notes she will play. But the quartet played consists of the joint sounds that result from the players playing together, which must be heard together to hear the quartet. The harmony, dissonance, tempo, or what have you, that marks a quartet, is played not by individuals but by the quartet: there is numerically one act that it alone performs, namely, producing those sounds that jointly constitute the quartet.

---

[6] "No reason" is a relevant answer to the question why you were whistling, whereas it would not be a relevant answer to the question of why you tripped on the rug.

The reaction to this is sometimes reductionism: there is nothing to a quartet other than four individual players coming together, and the so-called social action of playing a quartet is reducible to the individual actions of four persons performed at the same time, meeting certain conditions of harmony and cooperativeness. Philosophers sympathetic to social action usually reject reductionism, however, on the ground that it fails to admit that there is anything unique about social actions, in particular for failing to take account of their indivisibility. Four persons do not *each* play a quartet, and while it is true that each player plays a distinct part, the joint sounds – the harmonies and dissonances and patterns – are not divisible among them.

But philosophers with an individualist bias deny that there is one *token* action performed by the quartet, claiming rather that the only token actions are those performed by each individual player. What marks out these actions as social is that the action of each individual player is a *type* of action it would not be were it performed in isolation. Reductionism misses this point in claiming that the type of actions players perform when playing on their own is no different from the type of actions they perform when playing a quartet. On the contrary, when playing a quartet, each player must not only play his own part; he must also contribute to the quartet, pay attention to his colleagues, aim at harmony, and the like, all of which involve characteristics his action would not have were he not a member of a group. Social actions are not reducible to individual actions because the former are types of action the latter are not. They can, in other words, be described in ways the actions of isolated individual agents cannot.

On this view, however, social actions still consist of numerically different act tokens performed by distinct individuals: a social action is performed by a social group, not because there is a token action the group itself performs, but because individual persons act in ways they would not act were they not in the group. This individualist bias is more subtle than individualist reductionism in that it recognizes a difference between social and individual actions. But the difference is not between social and individual *agents* – the agents are individuals, each performing a distinct action – but between the kinds of descriptions of the actions performed by individuals.

This individualist view rests on a number of claims, of which I will consider three. First, the attitudes necessarily involved in agency – intentions and beliefs in particular – can be ascribed only to individuals not to social groups, and hence there are no genuinely social agents. Second, action is intentional only if the agent is capable of what Weber called "subjectively understandable action" (Weber 1947, p. 90), but social agents do not have such self-understanding. Third, actions not only always involve bodily movements (if they are not merely mental acts), but actions *consist* of an agent's moving his body in various ways, and since only individual agents have bodies and can directly move only their own, there cannot be genuine social agents. I shall discuss each of these objections in the rest of this paper.

10.3 Social Attitudes

The first objection is the most common, and a great deal of energy and ingenuity has been expended showing how to avoid ascribing intentions, beliefs, and other intentional attitudes to social groups. In my view, this is a mistake: since social actions are not divisible among individual agents, the social attitudes involved are also not divisible among individual agents but are the attitudes of groups as social agents. By social attitudes, then, I do not merely mean intentional attitudes with social *content*. Nor do I mean attitudes directed toward some social rather than individual good, or which involve social rather than individual interests.[7] I mean attitudes whose *subjects* are social agents.

There are numerous examples of such attitudes. A corporation has beliefs and intentions, and while its employees may share the content of some of those attitudes, they are the corporation's attitudes. More typically, its employees will not share its attitudes, and, indeed, there may be attitudes ascribable to the corporation which are not ascribable to any of its members. The corporation may, for example, have set a certain level of sales as its aim for the next fiscal year, even if no member of the corporation shares that aim (perhaps the figure is a compromise, different from the aims of any of the managers or board members).[8] But even if the corporate attitudes are shared by some members, they are *corporate* attitudes, not attitudes of individual agents.

The examples may be extended. Intentions, beliefs, and desires are ascribed to universities, churches, parliaments, charitable organizations, and orchestras, which their members may or may not share, but that in any case are the intentions, beliefs, and desires of the social group. No doubt social agents would not have attitudes if their members did not, and in many cases their attitudes reflect the attitudes of their members. But the converse is also true; individual agents not only reflect the attitudes of the groups to which they belong, but there are

---

[7] This distinction does not line up with the ones I am making here. A social agent, for example, need not act for the social or common good but for its own good or for the good of some individual, just as an individual person may act not for his own good but for the common (or social) good.

[8] If the aim was set by the board, this does not mean a social action has been reduced to individual actions, for the board is itself a social agent.

attitudes they would not have did the group not have them. Expecting to vote in the next election presupposes that the government intends to hold one. Believing that the parliament will raise taxes assumes that it wants to do so. Wanting to cash a check presupposes banks that intend to cash them.

Many philosophers find this objectionable. Reductionists argue that so-called social attitudes are no different from the attitudes of individual agents: they have no distinctive contents that the attitudes of solitary individuals do not have. The beliefs or desires of a church, for example, are just the attitudes of its members, and their contents do not presuppose any social group. To speak of what a church believes is to speak of what is believed by most of its members, beliefs they could in principle have all by themselves.

Individualists who take social action more seriously reject reductionism by maintaining there are attitudes with distinctively social contents that solitary individuals do not have. Consider a social belief, for example, one expressed by a congregation saying, "We believe in God." If that is a genuine social belief, it is, on this view, not simply a case of each member believing in God, for there is nothing social about that. It involves in addition each member believing of the other members that they believe in God, and believing that the other members believe that, and so on, with perhaps other attitudes as well. Attitudes with such mutually referring contents are, it is claimed, distinctive of social beliefs, marking out a type of *contents* individual beliefs do not have. But attitudes with such contents are still not genuinely social if only individuals and not social groups have them,[9] and, indeed, the point of this kind of proposal is precisely to avoid ascribing attitudes to agents other than individuals.

This is, in my view, a mistake: social agency requires not only that attitudes have social content but that they be ascribed to social agents. This is most evident in the case of intentions. The proposal that intentions are social if they have mutually referring contents maintains that to ascribe an intention to a social group is just to ascribe to each member of the group an intention with the *same* mutually referring content. Social intentions, that is to say, are individual intentions with distinctive *common* contents. But there are no such intentions: different agents cannot have intentions whose content is common in the relevant sense.

The reasons for this is that intentions necessarily include reference to the agent who has them. An agent can intend only to do something *herself:* she can-

---

[9] The same is true of Tyler Burge's anti-individualist arguments, which aim to show that the content of attitudes is socially determined, for example, by one's language. Burge assumes that however social the content of attitudes may be, they will be ascribed to individual persons. See, for example, Burge 1979.

not intend anyone else to act, but at best only intend to do something herself that might induce someone else to act. I cannot intend *you* to buy *me* a dinner, but only intend to do something that might have that result. But if the content of an intention always includes an implicit reference to the agent who intends, the intentions of different agents do not have a common content. Art can intend to go to a film and Mary can intend to do the same; but their intentions do not have a common content since Art's intention is *his* going to the film and Mary's is *her* going to the film. This means that the notion of "we intend" cannot be analyzed in terms of the notion of "I intend" since they involve the intentions of different agents. We must either construe social actions in terms of intentions with individual contents or recognize that intentions are social attitudes to be ascribed straightforwardly to social agents.[10]

The first alternative is unacceptable. If an agent can intend only to do something herself, then the only intentions an agent can *fulfill* by her actions are her own. It follows that if a social action fulfills an intention, the intention must be the intention of the agent who performed that action, namely, a social agent. Otherwise the action would be fulfilling the intention of someone other than the agent of the act (an individual agent), which is not coherent since agents can fulfill only their own intentions.

A number of proposals have been made to avoid this objection by arguing that it is, after all, possible to construct a notion of shared intentions with common contents. Here is Michael Bratman's analysis:[11]

> We intend to J if and only if:
> 1. (a) I intend that we J and (b) you intend that we J
> 2. I intend that we J because of 1a and 1b; you intend that we J because of 1a and 1b
> 3. 1 and 2 are common knowledge between us. (Bratman 1993, p. 104)

Bratman takes this analysis to yield an intention with social *contents* that a *social* action can fulfill, thus avoiding the objection that social actions performed by social agents cannot fulfill the intentions of individual agents. Since the contents of "we-intend's" are distinct from the contents of "I-intend's", in that the former are ascribable to individuals only as members of a group, it is not a reductivist proposal. But it does not ascribe intentions to social agents. A shared intention, Bratman notes, is

---

[10] This does not mean that I consider Mary and Art's going to the film to be the action of a social agent. The point of the example is simply to illustrate the point that the only intentions agents, either individual or social, can fulfill are their own.

[11] I have left out some complications which do not concern my discussion.

a state of affairs that consists in attitudes ... of the *participants* and interrelations between those attitudes.... It consists primarily of a web of attitudes of the individual participants [and involves] two main elements: (1) a general treatment of the intentions of *individuals* and (2) an account of the special contents of the intentions of the *individual* participants in a shared intention. (Bratman 1993, pp. 107–108)[12]

Bratman explicitly recognizes the problem I have posed: "What I intend to do is to perform actions of my own; I cannot intend to perform the joint action J. So how will the conception of the joint action get into the intentions of the individuals?" (Bratman 1993, p. 101) To resolve that, Bratman introduces the technical notion of *intention that*, which does not require that what the agent intends be an act of that same agent. I can intend *that* you buy me dinner, and one person can, in general, intend *that* another person do something. If that is so, then an individual can intend *that* a group do something. Since it is just this notion that plays the key role in Bratman's analysis of "we intend ..." – it is given in clause 1 – it is not surprising that we get a notion of shared intention with common content.[13]

There are two objections to this proposal. The first is that Bratman's analysis simply *postulates* a technical notion of intention whose point is just to permit common content, and that begs the question, namely, *whether* the intentions of different agents can have common content. The other is that intentions do not take propositional objects: we may intend to do something or we may act with an intention, but in either case the object of our intending is an activity, not a fact or state of affairs. An agent intends to drive *to* Minneapolis, or is driving *to* Minneapolis with the intention to buy a piano, or intends *to* buy a piano because he intends *to* learn how to play. If these intentions are construed as having propositional objects, they cease to have the distinctive features of intentions and become attitudes of a different kind.[14]

Bratman contends that his notion of *intention that* is not "some new and distinctive attitude [but one] ... already needed in an account of individual intelligent agency. But we are allowing this attitude to include in its content joint ac-

---

12 My emphasis.
13 Wilfred Sellers introduced a notion of "intend that" that is like Bratman's, but he noted that it presupposes the concept of "intend to" and emphasized "the conceptual priority of intentions to do even in the case of intentions that someone do". To intend that such and such be the case, he said, means, roughly that I intend to do that which is necessary to make it the case that such and such. Insofar as there is a non-technical notion of intending that such and such, Sellars' view is surely the correct one. Cf., Sellers 1968, p. 184.
14 For an excellent discussion of intention that is directly relevant to this point, cf. Moran and Stone 2008.

tivity." (Bratman 1993, p. 102) While intentions are indispensable to individual agency, *intention that* is not, because an individual can only intend to do something herself. *Allowing* the attitude to include in its content joint activity is not to *establish* that an agent can intend a joint activity but to construct a new attitude that is essentially different from the intentions we ascribe to individual agents.

An analogous point applies to beliefs. Unlike intentions, beliefs take propositional objects, and their contents may be common to different agents. But the beliefs that play an essential role in explaining an agent's actions as intentional must be beliefs of the agent himself. One may, for instance, act in a certain way because it is necessary for some end, but the necessity of the action will explain one's acting only if one *believes* it is necessary, and that must be the agent's own belief. He may, of course, see that the act is necessary because someone else believes it is and tells him so, but that the act is necessary explains his acting only if he himself comes to believe it is necessary. For a belief to play a role in explaining a social group's action, therefore, it must be a belief of the group itself, not of its members. Its members' beliefs may underlie the beliefs of the group but they play a role in the reasons for which the group acts only by way of beliefs of the group as such.

10.4 Ascribing Attitudes to Social Agents

Not every intentional attitude is ascribable to social agents, any more than every type of action can be performed by a social agent; indeed, those claims are necessarily related. Social agents cannot walk or jump or engage in other bodily actions, and so they cannot intend to do them or believe they are doing them. Since social agents cannot weep or laugh, the range and kind of emotions ascribable to them are also restricted (though perhaps there are metaphorical senses in which social groups weep or laugh). Although more could be said about the kinds of attitudes and emotions that *cannot* be ascribed to social agents, my concern here is to articulate a view that shows why many intentional attitudes *can* be so ascribed.

I want first to consider a primary reason many philosophers refuse to ascribe attitudes of any kind to social agents, namely, a mistaken but entrenched view about the nature and role of the attitudes in explaining action. On this view, the attitudes are causally efficacious events or states internal to an agent's mind/brain, which cause events in his nervous system that in turn cause his bodily movements. They have rational content that are an agent's reason for acting, and if they cause the agent's bodily movements in accord with that content (not accidentally or deviantly), they are intentional under a description and hence are actions of the agent. An agent's action *consists*, then, in his moving his body, and although we describe that in terms of many things, in particular in terms of what the bodily movements cause in the world beyond his body, *what* we are describing are his bodily movements.[15]

This is the so-called 'standard story' of action, which comes in a number of versions that develop in sophisticated ways the simple points set out above. My concern here is with aspects of the story that bear directly on the individualist bias in philosophy of action and thereby rule out an adequate account of social agency. One is its claim that actions consist in bodily movements (which I will discuss in section 11.6), while the others concern the attitudes: that they are events or states internal to an agent's mind/brain, their fundamental explanatory role being the causal production of bodily movements in accordance with their content.

If these claims are accepted, attitudes like intentions, beliefs, and desires cannot be ascribed to social agents because doing so would require that social agents have brains and nervous systems that causally produce their actions. Or it would require that they have superpersonal, collective minds, which might have some metaphorical point but would not fulfill the causal function attitudes have on this view, namely, to be causally productive of an agent's actions. The absurdity of these alternatives is sufficient to account for the individualist refusal to ascribe attitudes to social agents.

But if those claims about the attitudes are rejected, then it is not absurd to ascribe the attitudes to social agents. I think they should be rejected on the ground that they yield an inadequate account even of individual agency. The attitudes are not entities, they are not located in an agent's mind/brain, and their explanatory role is not the causal production of bodily movements (or anything else). Although I cannot adequately defend these counter claims in this paper, I will articulate the conception of the attitudes they presume and show how they apply to social agency.[16]

I have written indifferently of events and states (which is common among defenders of the standard story), but they should be clearly distinguished. Events are particulars in having numerous intrinsic properties (or descriptions), many of which may be undiscovered, and they are causally efficacious in that they are causally related to other events (or things) that they produce. Claims

---

[15] In this paper, I use "bodily movements" both transitively, to mean "moving one's body", and intransitively, to mean "one's body moves", because the distinction is not relevant for my discussion.

[16] The best defense of these claims is Helen Steward (Steward 1997). They are claims Davidson has made. See, for example, Davidson 2003, p. 499 and p. 654, and Davidson 1993b.

about such causal relations are extensional in that they are true under every description of the events; they are not true *in virtue of* some property of the events (and hence false *in virtue of* some other property).

If attitudes were events, they would be causally efficacious, but they are states and not events. Events happen at a time but attitudes do not happen; states, hence attitudes, obtain through time. Nor are attitudes particulars that are located at some time or place or that have undiscovered intrinsic properties. They are property-like and not referred to (as events are) but *predicated* of a subject.[17] It is agents that intend, believe, or desire, and in characterizing an agent as intending to write, believing that it will rain, desiring to own a house, we do not refer to entities in his mind/brain but we characterize *him* as intending to write, and so on. Those are properties of an agent that are individuated by their content – to write, that it will rain, to own a house. We may predicate the very same attitude of different agents, who may have the same belief, the same desire, even (with the important qualifications discussed above) the same intention: each of us may have the intention to write or see a film, although it will be directed in each case to the one who has the intention.

As states, attitudes are not causally efficacious: they are not causally related to – do not produce – bodily movements or other events or things. But they play a role in the explanation of actions (or other attitudes) by being *causally relevant* to actions, other events, states, and so on. A property is causally relevant to an outcome just in case the outcome would have been different had the property been different (or absent). 'Being rotten', for instance, is a causally relevant (but not causally efficacious) property: that the tree was rotten did not cause the tree to fall down; but it was causally relevant because, had the tree not been rotten, it would not have fallen over in the wind. So it is with the attitudes; an agent's beliefs do not causally produce his action, but had he not believed what he did, he would not have (or probably would not have) acted intentionally as he did. There may, of course, be an explanation of why an attitude – intending to build a garage, desiring to own a house – is causally relevant to an action, but causal relevance does not depend on our knowing that explanation, or even on there being one. Many explanations refer to causally relevant states, and their explanatory power does not depend on our knowing why they are causally relevant.[18]

---

17 On this point see Steward 1997, chapter 4. She argues convincingly that the notion of a *token* state (which is to turn a state into a particular) is incoherent.
18 This way of formulating the distinction is from Steward 1997. I developed the distinction, though formulated differently, in Stoutland 2009.

This view of the nature and explanatory role of the attitudes is essentially Davidson's, and I would appeal to his status in the philosophy of action in defense of the view. In any case, it allows the ascription of attitudes, not only to individual agents, but also to social groups of various kinds. We can ascribe to a quartet an intention to play a piece by Mozart, a belief that it should keep a fast tempo, a desire to satisfy its patron's request. It is irrelevant that the quartet has no brain or nervous system or that attitudes directed toward its own actions as a quartet are not causally productive of its actions. The attitudes that we ascribe to the quartet, no more than those we ascribe to individual agents, are not located in a mind/brain; they are properties predicated of the quartet that are causally relevant to its actions as a social agent. Had the quartet not intended to play a piece by Mozart, not believed it should keep a fast tempo, not wanted to please its patron, its actions would have been very different. A complicated story might be constructed about why those attitudes are causally relevant, but we do not know that story, and the explanation does not depend on it.

A similar account can be given of the attitudes of numerous social agents – universities, parliaments, corporations, banks, churches, social agencies, etc. We speak often of their beliefs, intentions, what they want, even what they fear or hope for, and there is no reason to feel uneasy in so doing or to take solace from the philosophical analysis of those committed to individualism. It is true that there would be no social agents without manifold complex relations between individuals more or less like those that philosophers spell out so carefully. But those relations will vary a great deal depending on the social group: they may be cooperative, but they may not; they may not involve mutual knowledge; they may or may not be institutional; there might not be significant intentions shared by members of the group. But what those diverse relations make possible is something new – a social agent to which attitudes are ascribed that are not ascribed to individuals who are members of the group. This is something that need not be resisted given an adequate understanding of the nature and explanatory role of the attitudes.

10.5 Social Agents' Knowledge of What They Are Doing

I want now to consider briefly the claim that action is intentional only if it is what Max Weber called "subjectively understandable" (Weber 1947, p. 90), which in his view is not true of social actions.

Weber defended "methodological individualism", which he defined as the view that "in sociological work collectivities must be treated as solely the resultants and modes of organization of the particular acts of individual persons"

(Weber 1968, p. 13). He argued that only individuals "can be treated as agents in a course of subjectively understandable action" (Weber 1968, p. 13) on the ground that social inquiry is different from that of natural science in that it aims at an interpretive understanding [*verstehen*] of social phenomena. That entails, he held, that intentional action must be the focus of investigation because (as Joseph Heath puts Weber's claim) "Actions can be understood in a way that other phenomena cannot, precisely because they are motivated by intentional states." (Heath 2005). Methodological individualism comes into the picture because Weber also held (in Heath's words) that "only individuals possess intentional states, and so the methodological privileging of actions entails the methodological privileging of individuals" (Heath 2005).[19]

The connection of all this with "subjectively understandable action" (Weber 1947, p. 90) is that investigators aiming at an interpretive understanding of social phenomena must grasp the intentional states that motivate the agent, which means they must grasp the agent's *own (subjective) understanding* of her action: what she intends to be doing, what she believes is necessary to fulfill her intention, how she perceives situations in the world as reasons for her to act, and so on. The agent herself may not have a perfect understanding of such things, but as an agent who acts, she must know what she is doing intentionally, which means she must have a grasp of what she is intending, what she takes to be necessary to achieve her ends, her own reason for initiating action, etc. While investigators must *interpret* an agent to know these things, the agent knows them about herself directly, without interpretation.

Weber is, in my view, right about much of this – about the role of interpretation, about the centrality of intentional action, about the latter being "subjectively understandable" (Weber 1947, p. 90). But he is wrong in maintaining that these claims apply only to individual agents and not to social groups. His claim that only individuals "can be treated as agents in a course of subjectively understandable action" (Weber 1968, p. 13) presumes (if Heath understands him correctly) that only individuals possess intentional states. But this premise, I have argued, is false: we can ascribe attitudes like beliefs and intentions to social agents.

Even if it is granted that social agents can have intentional attitudes, it may be argued that it does not follow that social action is "subjectively understandable" (Weber 1947, p. 90), which I take to mean that social agents do not know what they are doing intentionally and what their intentions, beliefs, or other attitudes are. I think that the relevant sense of 'know' here is, as Anscombe has

---

[19] This is an excellent article though I am not certain that Heath gets Weber exactly right.

argued, "knowledge without observation" (Anscombe 1963, p. 50). If we know what we are doing only by observing our action, then we are not the agents of the action but only observers of it. Similarly, if we need evidence to discover what we intend to do, or what we believe necessary, or what is our own reason for initiating action, then those attitudes are at best remotely connected with our acting intentionally. The issue is whether social agents have such knowledge, at least with respect to more primitive descriptions of their action and their more short-term reasons for acting.[20]

In my view, social agents do have such knowledge. If it were a matter of introspection, if it required that an agent have introspective access to the content of her mind, then such knowledge by a social agent would be unintelligible. But since, in my view, an *individual* agent's knowledge of what she is doing intentionally is not based on introspection, and the attitudes are not items in her mind/brain, there is no reason to think of *social* agents in that way. The knowledge required, I suggest, is what Anscombe called *practical* as opposed to theoretical: agents know what they are doing intentionally not by matching their judgment to their actions but by matching their actions to their intentions. If they are mistaken, the mistake is not in their judgment but in their performance: they fail to do what they intend.

A corporation, for instance, decides to do something, and then its employees are instructed to carry out the decision; if things do not go as decided, the problem is not that the corporation is wrong about how things went but that the decision was not properly executed, that external conditions changed, or that things went wrong in some other way. The mistake with regard to how things went is not in the judgment (the reports) but in the performance. When it is discovered by investigation that things did not go as intended, there is *theoretical* knowledge of the action. But if things did go as decided, the corporation knows what it is doing simply because its decision was carried out as intended: it has *practical* knowledge of its action-knowledge of what is happening by doing it.[21]

---

20 On this point, cf. Anscombe 1957, e.g., # 6 and 28.
21 This is a view articulated by Anscombe (1957), # 33, 34, 45, 46. Since she did not discuss social agency, I do not know if she would agree with my applying her view as I do. She gives an example that does, however, suggest she might agree. It concerns a man "directing a project, like the erection of a building which he cannot see and does not get reports on, purely by giving orders.... He is not like a man merely considering speculatively how a thing might be done.... *His* knowledge of what is done is practical knowledge."

10.6 Bodily Movements and Action

A third objection to the notion of social agents that I shall discuss is that actions *consist* of bodily movements, and since each of us has a distinct body that we move directly only on our own, individuals are the real agents of action. To counter this objection, we should consider carefully how bodily movements actually figure in the actions of individual agents.

Individual agents are, of course, necessary if there are to be social agents. A corporation could not refocus its efforts, declare a dividend, or build a new plant if there were not individual agents at work doing what is relevant to such corporate actions. A quartet could not play Beethoven if each of its members did not play an instrument according to the score. Moreover, the actions of individual agents are, in a sense, sufficient for the actions of a social agent. Once the employees of a corporation have completed their assigned tasks, there is not a *further* action done by the corporation, and once the members of the quartet have played the parts assigned to them, there is no *further* playing on the part of the quartet. The reason these individual actions are 'in a sense' sufficient is that conditions must be right for them so to be. The employees of a corporation must complete their tasks successfully, there must be suitable coordination, their actions must not be countermanded, and so on. Similar things apply to the quartet because what individuals play is not always sufficient for the playing of a quartet.

It is crucial to recognize that analogous points apply to the relation between an individual's bodily movements and his action. An agent acts in the world (and not merely mentally) only if he moves his body, and having moved his body in very complex ways, there is nothing *further* to do in order to act in various ways – provided conditions are right and things work out as he intended. If the world cooperates, then his moving his body is his moving his pen, which is his writing a sentence, which is his writing a letter, which is his pleasing his friend, etc. In moving his body, he may do many things; that is, his acting may have many descriptions that do not mention his moving his body, under some of which his acting is intentional, under many of which it is not.

The standard story of action takes this point to mean that an agent's action *consists* of his moving his body; that is what an action *is*, the rest being descriptions (or properties) of the bodily movements. The descriptions are true of the agent's moving his body because of what those movements result in, but his acting just *is* his moving his body. In Quine's terms, that is the ontology of action and everything else is ideology. Since only individuals move their bodies directly, it follows immediately that the agents of action must be individuals.

In my view, the standard story is mistaken: even if an agent's moving her body is both necessary and, given the right conditions, sufficient for her acting, it does not follow that her acting *consists* of her moving her body. It does not follow, that is, that when we describe the many things an agent is doing, *what* we are describing is her moving her body – that the many descriptions of her acting are only *true of her* moving her body. As Anscombe wrote: "The proper answer to 'What is the action, which has all these descriptions?' is to give one of the descriptions. Anyone, it does not matter which; or perhaps it would be best to offer a choice, saying, 'Take which ever you prefer.'" (Anscombe 1981, p. 209) This is the right answer, although it does not rule out contexts in which one description is more basic than others and hence can, in that sense, be taken as specifying *what* we are describing when we describe an action.

Bodily movement descriptions are rarely basic in that sense because to specify *what* action we are describing, we specify *an* action, that is, something that has a unity as action, and this is rarely a matter of the bodily movements involved. I am, for instance, now writing a paper, which has been my primary task over many days. The ways in which I have moved my body in acting are complex and extremely diverse, and as such they have no unity but are merely a miscellany. My writing a paper, however, is *an* action, one that has a unity so that *it* can be described in many ways. Whatever unity there is to my bodily movements as action derives from my writing a paper and not vice versa, and it, is indeed, more plausible to say that what the bodily movement descriptions are true of is my writing a paper, than to say that what the paper-writing descriptions are true of is my moving my body. Moreover, an explanation of what I am doing that cites my reason for doing it explains my writing a paper, and it is the latter that explains my moving my body as I do.

Given this, it is evident that the actions of individual agents can be both necessary and (given the right conditions) sufficient for the actions of social agents without the latter *consisting* of the actions of individuals or without descriptions of social agents being *true of* individual agents. The members of any social group perform numerous and diverse actions as members of the group. White collar employees of a corporation write letters, hold meetings, offend colleagues, waste time, make decisions, etc., actions that are intentional under a description, but that viewed simply as the actions of individuals are a miscellany with no unity. If we understand, however, that the corporation intends to down-size and focus on one central mission, then we can grasp the unity in those individual actions as directed toward that goal. There is *an* action performed (or intended) by the corporation, an action individual agents cannot perform, and although the individuals' actions are (given the right conditions) sufficient for the corporation's actions, descriptions of the corporation's actions are not true of the individual actions. Moreover, it is not the actions of its employees that explain the corporation's action; on the contrary, the corporation's action explains the actions of its employees. It is because the corporation is down-sizing that its employees have reasons to be active in those diverse ways.

The point is, then, that although bodily movements are necessary and (in a sense) sufficient for individual actions, and although individual actions are necessary and (in a sense) sufficient for social actions, individual actions do not *consist* of bodily movements nor do social actions *consist* of individual actions. Ascribing actions to social agents presumes that we can ascribe attitudes to them that are explanatorily relevant to the actions of the individuals involved, hence causally relevant to the bodily movements of individuals. But it does not presume that social agents have bodies that they are able to move directly.

10.7 Individuating Agents

The underlying issue in this paper can be formulated as how to *individuate* agents and actions. When several descriptions are descriptions of the same thing, then that same thing has been individuated – that is, distinguished from other things – so that different descriptions can be asserted of it. The standard story assumes that there is one right way of individuating agents and actions, namely, in terms of an individual agents' own bodily movements. Philosophers who defend that story disagree on the so-called problem of the individuation of action – whether action should be individuated in a fine-grained or coarse-grained fashion. But these differences are built on agreement that actions consist of an agent's bodily movements, the differences being how finely we should individuate *them*.

There is in current philosophy of action an admirable pluralism about admissible descriptions of intentional action. Most philosophers agree that there are numerous correct ways of describing our action, that most such descriptions are not in terms of bodily movements, that there is no such thing as *the* right way of *describing* what we do. But there is no corresponding pluralism as far as *individuation* is concerned. An action *consists* in an agent's bodily movements, which is *what* we describe in describing action, the reigning view being that no matter how diversely we describe action, we must individuate ultimately in physical terms. Only they identify an action about which we can ask whether *it* is intentional under some description or what an agent's reasons for doing it might be.

What I am urging is that we also be pluralistic about individuation. Just as we do not think it necessary to designate one way of *describing* an agent acting as *the* right way, so we should not think it necessary to designate one way of *individuating* an agent acting as *the* (ultimately) right way. Individualists think there is one right way to individuate, a view assumed by proponents of the standard story who maintain that action consists in the bodily movements of individual agents. The contrary mistake is made by collectivists: they think that *social* individuation is *the* (ultimately) right way to individuate, and that collective agents are therefore more ultimate – more well-founded, more explanatorily or conceptually basic – than individual agents. Pluralism about individuation means the rejection of both: social agency is neither more nor less ultimate, well-founded, or basic than non-social agency.[22]

The ontology of action, therefore, is much broader than is allowed by individualists of various kinds. There are in the world social agents that we describe in various way and to which we ascribe intentional attitudes. That we describe agents and actions in social ways is taken for granted; we ought in the same way to set aside our individualist, anti-social bias and take it for granted that what we are thus describing are genuine social realities.

---

22 Here is another way to put the point. If there is one right way of individuating the world, then the world must consist of a single ultimate domain of individuals, and hence whatever there is must consist ultimately of the same individuals. It may be reasonable to think that those ultimate individuals are physical, which sets the Chinese box analysis going: social action consists of (complex) individual actions, which consist of bodily motions ..., etc., down to physical micro-states which are the ultimate individuals. My claim is that there is no such thing as a single, ultimate domain of individuals. Just as there are alternative ways of describing the world, none of which is ultimate or privileged in a general sense, so there are alternative ways of individuating the world, none of which is ultimate or privileged in a general sense. Social discourse individuates in various ways, depending on the discourse, but we should refuse to admit that this way of individuating lines up with the way of individuating when our concern is with non-social agents or with the explanations of the physical sciences.

11 Searle's Consciousness

John Searle's *The Rediscovery of the Mind* (Searle 1992) is vintage Searle: a good read, memorable examples (the usual Alpine skiing and drinking beer), sweeping claims and criticisms, many arguments – some good, some merely rhetorical – a whole lot of bravado and appeals to what is obvious or "would be clear on a moment's reflection". While little will be surprising to those who have read Searle, it extends and revises earlier work, and only Chapter 9 (which is his 1990 American Philosophical Association Presidential Address) has appeared elsewhere. It is a rich book, with reference to many current discussions, and to read it is to be stimulated to think about some of the most basic issues in philosophy. It is also an infuriating book because Searle oversimplifies the views of others and does not deal seriously with objections to his own. The good news is that it raises the right questions in a way accessible to a lay public; the bad news is that the philosophically unsophisticated may be taken in by claims whose severe difficulties are never confronted.

Its main theme is consciousness, "the essence of the mental" (Searle 1992, p. 11) and hence more fundamental than intentionality: while conscious states may not be intentional – a pain, for instance, is not directed to anything outside itself – intentional states must be accessible to consciousness. A secondary theme is Searle's running battle with cognitive science for positing a computational level neither physical nor conscious. Chapters 4–6 are mainly about consciousness, while Chapters 7, 9, and 10 criticize cognitive science. Chapter 8 is a restatement of his views about "the Background" required for intentional states.

Because of space limitations, I will not discuss Searle's views on computational psychology but will focus entirely on consciousness. Although his basic aim is admirable – a conception of the mental which is neither dualist nor materialist – he fails to achieve that aim. But his views are worth serious attention, not only because of the importance and difficulty of the subject but because Searle turns his first rate philosophical intelligence to views many philosophers hold but whose consequences they fail to see or repress.

First, a few words about Chapters 1–3 (left out of my summary above) which reject both dualism and materialism. Chapter 1 lists "six unlikely theories of mind" (Searle 1992, p. 5) (all are versions of eliminativism), and seven "foundations of modern materialism" (Searle 1992, p. 10) (functionalist materialists would in general accept them; Searle thinks they are "profoundly unscientific ... and incoherent" (p. 12)), gives an impressionistic survey of the (mainly Cartesian) "historical origins of the foundations" (Searle 1992, p. 12), and concludes with seven counter claims, which I list here:

1. "Consciousness does matter." (Searle 1992, p. 18).
2. "Not all of reality is objective; some of it is subjective." (Searle 1992, p. 19).
3. "It is a mistake to suppose that the methodology of a science of the mind must concern itself only with objectively observable behaviour." (Searle 1992, p. 20).
4. "It is a mistake to suppose that we know of the existence of mental phenomena in others only by observing their behaviour." (Searle 1992, p. 21).
5. "Behaviour or causal relations to behaviour are not essential to the existence of mental phenomena." (Searle 1992, p. 23).
6. "It is inconsistent with what we in fact know about the universe and our place in it to suppose that everything is knowable by us." (Searle 1992, p. 23).
7. "The Cartesian conception of the physical as *res extensa*, is simply not adequate to describe the facts that correspond to statements about physical reality." (Searle 1992, p. 25).

Chapter 2 gives a history of materialist theories from behaviorism (which for Searle is ancient philosophy) to the present, its theme being the impossibility of satisfying the materialist urge "to give an account of reality that leaves out any reference to the special features of the mental, such as consciousness and subjectivity, while at the same time account for our 'intuitions' about the mind" (Searle 1992, p. 52). While the critique – partly technical, partly intuitive – is sprightly and often insightful, it conveys no sense of why these theories flourished. Chapter 3 is a series of thought experiments supposed to show that "ontologically speaking, behaviour, functional role, and mental relations are irrelevant to the existence of conscious mental phenomena" (Searle 1992, p. 69). The experiments involve silicon replacements of parts of the brain and invite imagination of such things as "that your external behaviour remains the same, but that your internal conscious thought processes gradually shrink to zero" (Searle 1992, p. 67). I was not able consistently to imagine this and I cannot imagine any but dualists or the unwary will be convinced. Where, it may be asked, is the critique of dualism? Searle claims that since materialism is "that form of dualism that begins by accepting the Cartesian categories ... of mental and physical" (Searle 1992, p. 26), a critique of one will do for both. That would be true if there were a genuine critique of the Cartesian categories, but there is none, and the same categories come back renamed as 'subjective' and 'objective'. Moreover, many of Searle's criticisms of materialism, such as the thought experiments, assume a point of view only dualists will find congenial.

Consciousness, however, is the main theme here, and to that I want to turn. Conscious states, Searle writes, are "inner, subjective, qualitative, first person mental states" as opposed to "publicly observable third-person phenomena"

(Searle 1992, p. 7). These states form a unified domain with an essence, namely, subjectivity, which Searle intends in roughly Nagel's sense, and of which he gives two accounts.

On the first, subjectivity is "first person existence", which involves a "subjective ontology", rather than the objective ontology of "third person existence". That "is just a fancy way of saying that every mental state has to be somebody's mental state" (Searle 1992, p. 70), but since that is as true of a leg as of a pain, more has to be said: "Leg transplants are possible; in that sense, pain transplants are not" (Searle 1992, p. 94) – conscious states as conceptually non-transferable. That tricky idea is immediately dropped, however, in favor of the idea that anyone can be directly aware of my leg whereas only I can be directly aware of my pain, and Searle settles on that: a conscious state is one directly accessible only to the person who has it. What distinguishes subjective from objective existence is the epistemic mode of access to the entities involved.

While Searle insists that his conception of subjectivity is ontological and not epistemic, by 'epistemic' he means 'observer-relative', which he takes to mean existing only "relative: to users and observers" (Searle 1992, p. 211). Since he thinks mental phenomena are not relative to anybody's attitudes or stances (he thinks that amounts to saying they don't exist) but are rather intrinsic, they cannot be epistemic in the sense of being observer-relative. But they are epistemic in the perfectly ordinary sense of being defined in terms of epistemic mode of access. What makes his account also an ontological one is his assumption that what we have first person access to must have a special kind of reality: we cannot have first and third person access to the same kind of reality. That implies that what is subjective cannot also tie objective, and hence that the subjective is ontologically irreducible to the objective. (First person access is often called 'privileged access' which Searle rejects (Searle 1992, p. 98). But his argument is that privileged access involves a spatial metaphor of entering a private space; to reject that metaphor is to reject one form of privileged access, not the general doctrine, to which Searle is committed.)

Searle's other account of subjectivity is also epistemic but it defines it not in terms of what we have first person access to but in terms of the nature of that access (or awareness) itself. In ordinary observation, we distinguish between the act of observing and what is observed, but when it comes to the act of observing itself, we cannot make that distinction. For we cannot observe other persons' acts of observing at all but only their behavior, and in the case of my own act of observing, there is no distinction between my act and my observing it because "any introspection I have of my own conscious state is itself that conscious state" (Searle 1992, p. 97). There is "no way for us to picture subjectivity as part of our world view because, so to speak, the subjectivity in question is the picturing" (Searle 1992, p. 98).

The difference between these two accounts is that the first characterizes subjectivity in terms of the special kind of reality – a special kind of objects of awareness – defined in terms of the kind of access we have to them. The second characterizes subjectivity in terms of the access or awareness itself, where the awareness is defined precisely by saying that it cannot be an object of awareness. Searle thinks these are two ways of making the same point: a subjective state just is a state where there is no distinction between the object we are aware of and our awareness. I will argue below that this is a confusion.

Searle denies that this conscription of consciousness as subjectivity is dualist because in his view, not only objective states but also subjective states are physical.

> The brain causes ... conscious mental states, and these conscious states are simply higher-level features of the brain. Consciousness is a higher-level or emergent property of the brain in the [sense] in which solidity is a higherlevel emergent property of H_2O molecules when they are in a lattice structure (ice)... Consciousness is a mental, and therefore physical property of the brain ... (Searle 1992, p. 14)

Like solidity, consciousness can be accounted for causally at the lower level, in terms of neurophysiological processes in the brain, and like it, it is spatial: "We are not aware in conscious experience of either the spatial location or the dimensions of our conscious experience, but why should we be?" (Searle 1992, p. 105) Common sense thinks that pains are in various parts of our bodies (a "spectacular example" of how wrong it can be) but we now know they are all "literally in the physical space of the brain". Indeed, "All my mental life is lodged in the brain." (Searle 1992, pp. 62–63)

This is pretty simple-minded stuff. All pains, thoughts or feelings are located in the brain, emergent features of neurophysiological processes. Searle thinks these claims need no clarification or defense other than that they are required by our scientific world picture, which

> ... provides a rather simple account of the mode of existence of consciousness. According to the atomic theory, the world is made up of particles. These particles are organized into systems. Some of these systems are living ... Among these, some have evolved brains that are capable of causing and sustaining consciousness. Consciousness is, *thus* [my emphasis] a biological feature of certain organisms in exactly the same sense of 'biological' in which photosynthesis, mitosis, digestion, and reproduction are biological features of organisms. (Searle 1992, p. 93)

Few accept this view of consciousness, yet Searle can write that "anyone who has had even a modicum of 'scientific' education after about 1920 should find nothing at all contentious or controversial in what I have just said" (Searle 1992, p. 93). This is surely scientism at its worst – the kind of view which usually leads to the crude materialism of, say, Lenin (who got it before 1920).

But Searle rejects materialism because its assumption that what is mental cannot also be physical leads it to eliminate consciousness, either outright or by reducing it to something else. In rejecting that assumption, which he claims is essentially dualist ("as a consistent dualist, you will eventually be forced to materialism" (Searle 1992, p. 26)), Searle argues that he can hold that consciousness is a physical feature of the brain but irreducibly subjective.

That consciousness is irreducible cannot mean that it is irreducible to the physical, for Searle says that it is "therefore physical" (Searle 1992, p. 14). His view is that subjective existence is irreducible to objective existence, which amounts to the claim that conscious states are irreducible to neurophysical states. Consciousness can be causally reduced: the "existence and a fortiori the causal powers" of consciousness are "entirely explainable in terms of the causal powers" of neurophysiological processes (Searle 1992, p. 114). Causal reduction normally leads to ontological reduction: color has been reduced to light reflectances, sound to air waves, etc. This is riot the case for consciousness since "a perfect science of the brain would still not lead to an ontological reduction of consciousness" (Searle 1992, p. 116). We cannot say that pain, for example, is nothing but patterns of neuron firings, for then "the essential features of pain would be left out", namely, "unpleasant conscious sensations (which) you are experiencing ... from your subjective, first-person point of view" (Searle 1992, p. 117). Searle appeals to Nagel, Jackson, and Kripke for the argument, which is "ludicrously simple and quite decisive".

This looks like property dualism: conscious states are states of something physical but are not themselves physical. Searle's short reply is that property dualism assumes that what is physical cannot also be mental, which he rejects. Conscious states are both physical and mental, so there is no property dualism.

But that is a dodge. The issue is not whether both conscious states, which are subjective, and neurophysiological states, which are objective, are physical, but whether the same state can be both subjective and objective, and ontological irreducibility implies that they cannot, which is just property dualism under a new name. The same point can be made using the old names. Since both conscious and neurophysiological states are physical, the irreducibility of the first to the second means that some physical states are irreducible to others: those physical states which are also mental are irreducible to those which are not also mental.

One might ask what the point of such a concept of the physical is. Searle wants it to cover not only points of mass/energy, particles, waves, etc., but also things which have no place in modern physics, like points scored in football games, interest rates, and governments (Searle 1992, p. 26) – plus consciousness. One can stipulate that the physical is to cover just about anything (except things like God or an immaterial soul (Searle 1992, p. 90)) but as a way beyond dualism and materialism that has, as Russell put it, the advantage of theft over honest toil. Honest toil requires saying what all these things have in common which makes it important to call them 'physical', which Searle doesn't do.

Searle would no doubt reply that this omits an essential part of his discussion of irreducibility. When we reduce heat to molecular motion or color to light reflectances, we simply "redefine heat and colour in terms of the underlying causes of ... the subjective experiences" (Searle 1992, p. 119). We could do that for pains, redefining them as "patterns of neuronal activity that cause subjective sensations of pain" (Searle 1992, p. 121), but we don't because what interest us about pains are the subjective experiences themselves, whereas what interests us about heat are the underlying physical causes of the subjective experiences. This means that

> the irreducibility of consciousness is a trivial consequence of the pragmatics of our definitional practices. A trivial result such as this has only trivial consequences. It has no deep metaphysical consequences for the unity of our overall scientific world view. (Searle 1992, p. 122)

Searle's point is that there is no metaphysical difference between pains or other sensations and experienced heat, light or color. But that means not that he has a new conception of pain and other sensations or of heat, light and color, but that he is an ordinary dualist about all of them. He thinks that experienced heat, light or color are "subjective experiences" which exist in the mind-brain just as much as pains do, a view serious anti-dualists ought to reject but which Searle takes for granted. Extending the term 'physical' to cover both subjective experiences and their objective causes does nothing toward overcoming an ontological dualism between the subjective and the objective, which are just new names for the old Cartesian bifurcation between the internal and the external world, names to which no dualist should object.

Although Searle claims to be neither a dualist nor a materialist, he is a dualist on some issues, a materialist on others. He is a dualist on the nature of the mental: mental phenomena form a unified domain of conscious states whose essence is subjectivity. Subjective states are directly accessible only to those who have them, and no state which is subjective can also be objective. They are inner states, causally dependent on brain states, conceptually independent of behavior (conceivably, anything could be conscious) but causally productive of it. They are the only source of normativity (Searle 1992, p. 51) and the constitutive cause of intentional behavior. Like objective states, they are ontologically determinate (there is a fact-of-the-matter for whether any predicate applies to them – cf. Searle 1992, pp. 79–81) and independent of any social context. They can be directed to objects even if nothing other than the states themselves exist. (The non-intentional 'background' capacities prerequisite for such directness do not affect this point since they are also in the head. (cf. Searle 1992, p. 188)) All of these claims are distinctive of Cartesian dualism's conception of consciousness and mentality.

Searle is a materialist about the subject of conscious states: what has conscious states is the brain, which is definable in terms of physics. This explains how Searle can claim both that the world "consists entirely of physical particles in fields of force" (Searle 1992, p. xii) and that consciousness is irreducible to such things. To say the world consists entirely of what physics specifies means that physics individuates the world in the correct way – that the individuals of physics are the ultimate individuals – which is materialism about the subject of conscious states. But those individuals can have features of which physics knows nothing, which is dualism about the conscious states themselves.

This combination of dualism and materialism is not novel, and it is not obviously incoherent. But it is not an alternative to dualism and materialism; on the contrary, it means being in the grip of both, unable to shake their common assumptions. This surely is the case for Searle, whose dualism shows no trace of Wittgenstein and whose materialism is no model of subtlety.

In spite of his mixed views, only dualists will welcome Searle as an ally partly because Searle criticizes materialism from a dualist point of view. That would be enough for the mainstream of contemporary philosophy to reject his views, but categorizing is not criticizing, and Searle's account of consciousness merits criticism better than the standard textbook 'refutations' of dualism. His account goes wrong in at least three ways.

First, there is no pre-philosophical notion of consciousness which is reasonably enough in order to be used for philosophical purposes. Much of what Searle takes to be obvious originates in philosophical views whose historical roots can be traced (some no further than 19th-century Britain). 'Consciousness' denotes not a natural kind with an essence, but a diverse domain unified at best by family resemblances. Some are normative, some descriptive, some a matter of what merely seems to be the case, others of what must be the case, some are cognitive, some are not. To find it obvious that these have in common something deep or important is to beg the crucial philosophical questions. This does not mean that we should disregard prephilosophical concepts of the mental; on the contrary, only by attending to them can we check philosophers' pretensions to go beyond what they support.

Second, Searle gives two accounts of subjectivity, which he does not distinguish. The first characterizes it in terms of a special kind of objects of awareness, the second in terms of the awareness itself defined precisely as what cannot itself be an object of awareness. Searle, like many dualists, shifts back and forth between thinking of subjectivity (i.e., consciousness) as a domain of objects and thinking of it as awareness. If awareness itself is not an object, we can say little about it. We can say a lot about what we are aware of, but most is not relevant to subjectivity since what we are aware of are sticks and stones and our own bodies, which have nothing special to do with subjectivity. Only by shifting back and forth between subjectivity as a set of objects and as awareness of objects can we appear to say anything special about subjectivity. Searle's second account of subjectivity is more promising: awareness that cannot be an object of awareness, picturing that cannot be pictured. But that means subjectivity is not conscious states or properties, which are objects we can be aware of or picture. Searle is right not to "develop a special mode of picturing, a kind of super-introspection", but he is only stamping his foot in urging that we "just acknowledge the facts ... that biological processes produce conscious mental phenomena and these are irreducibly subjective" (Searle 1992, p. 98).

Third, dualism and materialism both assume that the mental is a domain of objects (states, properties, events) which is determinate: there is a fact-of-the-matter for any assertions made about the domain. This means, not that we have evidence sufficient to determine which assertions are correct, but that in principle there is evidence that would determine it. Having assumed that assertions about a domain of objects are correct or incorrect only if what is asserted is made true or false by those objects, it is concluded there will always be sufficient evidence – though we may not find it – for determining if they are correct, dualists think these objects are non-physical, materialists think they are physical or, failing that, do not exist. They agree that the mental is determinate – agree on what is nowadays called 'intentional realism'.

The alternative here is that the mental is often indeterminate. Thus Wittgenstein: "We don't need the concept 'mental' (etc.) to justify that some of our conclusions are undetermined, etc. Rather this indeterminacy, etc., explains the use of the word 'mental' to us" (Wittgenstein 1993, p. 63). Quine holds that the mental is an "essentially dramatic idiom" (Quine 1960, p. 219) whose claims are not determinate ("there is nothing approaching a fixed standard" (Quine 1960, p. 218)), which is why they are not reducible to the physical. For Davidson "the distinguishing feature of the mental is not that it is private, subjective, or immaterial but that it exhibits what Brentano called intentionality" – hence the indeterminacy of interpretation (Davidson 2001a, p. 211). The correctness of assertions about the mental may not even in principle be determined by evidence, but may be inescapably interpretive, involving trade-offs between one set of interlocked assertions and another, trade-offs on which evidence has no bearing. Examples are Quine's 'gavagai', Davidson on the inseparability of belief and meaning, the so-called 'hermeneutic circle'. These involve assertions which evidence cannot single out as uniquely correct, and the claim is that this indeterminacy distinguishes the mental from the physical (or the subjective from the objective, in one legitimate sense of those protean terms).

Searle makes consciousness more basic than intentionality because of his fervor to reject the indeterminacy of the mental, a fervor due to his identifying the indeterminate with the observer-relative and the determinate with the intrinsic. What are observer-relative exist only "relative to observers and users", whereas to call things intrinsic "just means they are the real thing" (Searle 1992, p. 80). Since there really are mental things – subjective features – they must be intrinsic and not observer-relative, which Searle takes to mean that assertions about them (as well as about objective features) must be determinate.

(Searle has a third category, namely, 'derived', supposed to be correlative with the other two. But this is confused: 'derived' contrasts with 'intrinsic' not as meaning the real thing but as meaning 'non-relational'. Sentences and pictures, unlike mental states, have derived intentionality but they have the real thing; the difference is that mental states have intentionality in themselves, whereas sentences or pictures have it only in virtue of their relation to mental states.)

Searle's contrast between intrinsic and observer-relative (which he says is obvious) presumes a whole metaphysics. Pains are intrinsic, though their existence is inseparable from consciousness, whereas bathtubs and chairs are observer-relative, because "if there had never been any users or observers, there would be no such features ... as being a chair or a bathtub" (Searle 1992, p. 211). What Searle has in mind is not whether the existence of an entity is relative to observers but whether its features are. So, a pain may exist only if someone is aware of it but awareness does not make it painful; a bathtub may exist even if no one is aware of or uses it, but only observers or users make the physical stuff to be a bathtub. The contrast is between features which are there to make what is asserted true or false, so there is always a fact-of-the-matter about the assertions – that is the domain of reality – and features which are merely projections of what we assert or think ("they do not exist except in the eye of the beholder" (Searle 1992, p. 215)) – that is the domain of appearance.

Reality comprises the features of the world we think about; appearance comprises the features of our thinking about it.

To think of indeterminacy in terms of this contrast gets it all wrong. Those who defend the indeterminacy of the mental reject that kind of contrast between appearance and reality and the associated contrast between being made true by the world and being made true by thought or language. They would drop the notion of making true or false to which Searle appeals (Searle 1992, pp. 25, 159–161, for example) except as a way of affirming the equivalence between utterances of 'p' and of 'p' is true'. Some of our assertions we know to be correct, whole others are such that evidence cannot determine their correctness because they are radically indeterminate or interpretive. But that does not mean they are about different domains, about our thought rather than about the world, or that they are made true in different ways. That is the modern equivalent of Plato's doctrine that the objects of knowledge must be different from the objects of belief – unacceptable doctrine in spite of its illustrious ancestry. The natives' claims about gavagai are indeterminate but they are about rabbits or rabbit stages, not about the natives. Our assertions about indirect quotation are indeterminate but they are not about us. Normative judgments are interpretive but they are about art, language, reasons for action, wildernesses, and so on, not about interpreters.

It is true that Quine denies – for reasons of indeterminacy – that the mental exists: "If we are limning the true and ultimate structure of reality, the canonical scheme for us ... is only the physical constitution and behaviour of organisms." (Quine 1960, p. 221) Davidson rejects that kind of eliminativist materialism; it is required neither by indeterminacy nor by the sort of minimal physicalism to which Quine commits himself explicitly: "Nothing happens in the world, not the flutter of an eyelid, not the flicker of a thought, without some redistribution of microphysical states." (Quine 1981, p. 98) Both determinate and indeterminate (interpretive) discourse can be about the same domain, which is in some sense physical. That does not mean they are about the same objects: if we reject physicalism about individuation, then different discourses may individuate differently, and if they do, they are about different objects. That is a doctrine Searle ought to admit, for while he rightly says that type identity with the entities of physics is not required for the existence of points in football games, interest rates, or governments, to believe consistently in the real existence of those things, one must also deny token identity since the objects of athletic, economic or political discourse are incommensurable with the objects of physics.

To take indeterminateness as a mark of the mental is not, therefore, to make the mental observer-relative but precisely to reject the contrast between the observer-relative and the intrinsic. That is a contrast dualists and materialists standardly assume, and it is only by rejecting it that we can avoid commitment to either one. That is why philosophers like Wittgenstein, Quine, or Davidson are so significant for philosophy of mind. Searle is wrong in thinking they deny the obvious in favor of the obscure or the false; undermining entrenched distinctions can be tortuous, even if he final aim is to stale what is pretty obvious. But the obvious is what we aim at in philosophy; it cannot be what we start with – certainly not in the case of the mess philosophers call consciousness.

12 Self and Society in the Claims of Individualism

Individualism is an old and powerful tradition in American life. Its political form is articulated in the familiar words of the Declaration of Independence: "We hold these truths to be self-evident, that all men are created equal, that they are endowed by their Creator with certain unalienable rights." It is a central theme in such 19th-century writers as Thoreau, Emerson, Melville, and Twain, who portray the struggle to maintain individuality over against social conformity. It is expressed in the solitary life of American folk heroes – the cowboy, the prospector, the lonely entrepreneur. It is inescapable in the experience of immigrants, who, although usually belonging to ethnic communities, had separated from their social roots and often came alone. Observers often note the individualism of American religion, from the idea that a religious community is a voluntary association to the creation of new religions by single individuals. Individualism, wrote Herbert Hoover in *American Individualism*, "is the most precious possession of American civilization" (Hoover 1922, p. 70).

Individualism has never been without its critics. Tocqueville, writing in 1835, saw it as central to the American character and, although grudgingly recognizing its virtues, regarded it as a grave danger to the new republic in that "in the long run, it attacks and destroys all [virtues] and is eventually absorbed into pure egoism" (Lukes 1978, p. 13). Hegel and Marx were implacable critics, and their ideas found their way into a number of strands of American intellectual life, the pragmatism of Dewey and Mead, for example, and the sociological tradition. Many American theologians have been critical of the individualistic understanding of both religion and society, and social critics have persistently regarded individualism as a major factor in the social malaise of American life.

The criticisms of individualism have increased markedly in recent years. Social philosophers have mounted increasingly influential attacks on individualist conceptions of moral and political life (e.g. MacIntyre 1981, Sandel 1982, Walzer 1983, Taylor 1985). In philosophy of mind, of language, and of action anti-individualism is a strong theme, and there is renewed interests in such anti-individualist thinkers as Dewey, Heidegger, and Wittgenstein. Recent feminist thought (Grimshaw 1986) has attacked individualist understandings of persons and society, and observers of the 'third world' often argue that individualist preconceptions are an impediment to perceiving its reality. Literary critics have argued that 19th-century American literature appears to be dominated by individualism only because the literary canon was defined by white, male critics who were blind to strong communitarian strands in the tradition.

The best-known of the recent criticism of individualism is *Habits of the Heart* (Bellah et al. 1985), sub-titled, "Individualism and Commitment in American Life", its central argument is that individualism is now the "first language" of American discourse about "moral, social, and political matters" (Bellah et al. 1985, p. 334) and that is something that should concern us deeply. Individualism, it contends, makes it difficult "to preserve or create a morally coherent life" (Bellah et al. 1985, p. vi), and while the lives of Americans are not yet completely under its spell, it is the only language in which most Americans are able to articulate their vision of what makes their lives worthwhile. There is therefore a "tension between how we live and what our culture allows us to say" (Bellah et al. 1985, p. vii), which may lead to domination by individualist values to the exclusion of those communitarian ideals necessary for any decent life. What is now the "second language" of the American people, namely the communitarian language of the Biblical and civic republican traditions, ought to be restored to primacy.

It is clear that there is not just one issue involved here, and one of the merits of *Habits of the Heart* is its recognition that individualism is not a single conception of how to understand the self and society. It is a complex phenomenon, not something that can simply be accepted or rejected. Some individualists are egoists, but many are not. Some seek solitude, others fear it. Those who emphasize individual rights often stress that only in society can such rights be preserved or exercised. Individualists value individuality highly, but some hold that it means rejecting society, others that it requires it. There is no such thing as being a critic of individualism; one can only be a critic of one *or* another individualist claim about the self and society.

At the same time, there are affinities, often very interesting ones, between the claims of individualism, and it would be a mistake to assume that the term is simply ambiguous. To assess individualism it is necessary to distinguish among its claims, while being alert to their important affinities. *Habits of the Heart* does this, but I think it can be done better, and my aim in this paper is to sort out the various claims of individualism about the self and society in the interests of a balanced assessment.

Individualism, I shall argue, should be understood in terms of five core claims. 1) *Philosophical individualism* is a *theory*, which holds that individuals are distinct from society in their reality, in their capacity for knowledge, and in the ways in which their thought and behavior must be explained. 2) *The dignity of the individual* is a *moral* claim about the status of human individuals. 3) *The ideal of individuality* is a *value* claim about diversity in life and society. 4) *Moral individualism* is a comprehensive, individualistic moral *theory* about how people should live their lives and relate to society; to deny it is to hold what I shall call a communitarian view of morality. 5) *Liberalism as a political conception* is a morally based theory about the justice of social, political and economic institutions.[1]

While these claims are logically independent of each other, they have other sorts of relationships, and versions of individualism often combine them. Since, as I see it, some of these claims are well-grounded and some are not, assessing versions of individualism which combine them requires sorting out what is well-grounded and what is not in a complex position. Claim 1) is crucial because it is at the root of the doctrines most critics of individualism, including myself, find objectionable. It is also the most difficult to criticize since it is deeply entrenched in modern consciousness. It should be noted that 2) is a *moral* claim and 3) a *value* claim, but that neither are individualist *theories*. Both 4) and 5) have been called 'liberalism'; I shall argue for rejecting liberalism as a comprehensive moral theory (claim 4) but for keeping it as a political conception, that is, as a conception of social justice (claim 5).

12.1 Philosophical Individualism

By 'philosophical individualism' I mean a three-fold doctrine. a) *Ontological individualism* claims that the reality of the self is independent of the reality of society. A society is a collection of individuals whose essential nature is given apart from society. It does not constitute individuals; its nature is rather entirely determined by the nature of the individuals which belong to it. The denial of this claim I shall call "social realism". b) *Epistemological individualism* claims that the capacity for knowledge is not socially constituted; that is, it is one individual knowers have even apart from any social context. Empiricism is a paradigm of this view; it holds that all knowledge is based on sense awareness, which is possible for anyone whose senses are normal, no matter what their social context,

---

[1] *Habits of the Heart* distinguishes three senses of individualism: a) belief in the inherent dignity of the human person – my second claim; b) 'expressive individualism' – a version of my third claim; and c) 'utilitarian individualism' – an egoist version of my fourth claim. Lukes (1978) distinguishes eleven claims of individualism: 1) The dignity of man. 2) Autonomy. 3) Privacy. 4) Self-development. 5) The abstract individual. 6) Political individualism. 7) Economic individualism. 8) Religious individualism. 9) Ethical individualism. 10) Epistemological individualism. 11) Methodological individualism. Lukes argues that the two "core values", liberty and equality, underneath these claims should be defended, while most of the other claims, depending in some way on what I call 'philosophical individualism', should be rejected. I agree with the general thrust of Lukes' argument but I characterize the claims of individualism in a rather different way.

past or present. c) *Methodological individualism* claims that all social facts are reducible to facts about individuals and that all acceptable explanations of social behavior must refer only to facts about individuals.

These are highly theoretical claims, whose connections with the moral and political issues at the center of public debate about individualism are not immediately apparent. The connections are there, nevertheless, and they are important, for these claims lie at the heart of the individualist doctrines which recent critics find most objectionable. Some individualist claims, like the belief in human dignity, have been almost universally defended in modern times. But when such defensible claims get embedded in philosophical individualism, objections arise, and this tempts critics to reject individualist claims they would and should otherwise accept. This temptation results from failure to distinguish such claims from the philosophical individualism in which they are embedded, hence the importance of clarity about what that doctrine is.

This clarity is difficult to attain, for these claims are so entrenched in modern consciousness that they seem self-evident or go unnoticed and unarticulated. While there are a number of reasons for this,[2] the most illuminating involves the scientific revolution of the 16th century, so crucial for modern consciousness. As a result of that revolution, natural science acquired a distinctive form, taking mechanistic explanation as its ideal, which involved conceiving of nature as atoms in motion to which only concepts like space, time, mass, and energy were applicable. It differed from ancient and medieval natural science in rejecting teleological explanations of nature, and this meant that concepts applicable to physical phenomena had no application to social phenomena, since social phenomena require teleological explanations, the result being a sharp divide between the physical world and the social, human world.

The philosophy that accompanied the rise of modern natural science was Cartesian dualism, which makes a sharp distinction between the physical, which is in the domain of the natural sciences, and the mental, which comprises the phenomena of consciousness. Cartesian dualism involves a particular way of understanding how the world of the natural sciences is related to the human world, that is, to the world of meaning, thought, feeling, and whatever is distinctively human. It puts the human world in individual consciousness, leaving the rest of reality, stripped of its meaning and significance, to the natural sciences. To do this is to conceive of the human world as a collection of individual minds and their experiences, and thus to force a conception of social reality as only a

---

2 Marx, for example, thought philosophical individualism was a by-product of capitalist modes of production. There may be something to this, but I find other explanations more compelling.

collection of individual minds. No room is left for a genuinely social conception of the social world.³

Although Cartesian dualism is no longer in favor, the philosophical individualism which is spawned remains entrenched. To get clear about philosophical individualism, we must try to articulate its claims and envisage an alternative to it. I shall focus on ontological individualism, whose central claim is that the distinctive characteristics and capacities of human beings do not depend on any social context for their nature or reality. While the basic needs and interests of individuals, and their emotional and intellectual capacities, may be influenced by their social setting, their basic nature and existence do not depend on it. They depend on the interaction of biologically fixed features of human nature with variable and non-social factors like physical environment and heredity. Society may play an indispensable role in serving the needs and interests of individuals, but, on this view, to play such a role these needs and interests must already exist, independently of any social context, for society to serve them.

Society, therefore, consists of individuals whose distinctively human characteristics and capacities do not depend on this society or any other. Hence to get at what human individuals are in their essential nature, we must *abstract* from the particular characteristics their participation in a society has produced in order to get at the universal characteristics and capacities they share with every human being in every society. Individuals are essentially (to use the language of its critics) *abstract individuals*.⁴

---

3 This may account for philosophical individualism and the doctrines on the self and society which depend on it, not being prevalent in the pre-modern world. The concepts of modern natural science do not apply to the human and social world, something to which Cartesian dualism responded with an individualistic understanding of the human and social world. But in the pre-modern world, there was no sharp distinction between the natural world and the human and social world, because the same sorts of concepts applied to both, and hence there was no motivation either for Cartesian dualism or for the individualism it involves. At the same time, since we cannot return to a pre-modern conception of natural science, we cannot return, in any immediate way, to pre-modern conceptions of the self and society. An adequate response to philosophical individualism must respect the fact that there is a clear distinction between the concepts in terms of which we understand nature and those in terms of which we understand the human and social world, but it must not articulate this distinction in terms of physical-mental dualism.
4 Lukes characterizes the doctrine of the "abstract individual" as follows: "Individuals are pictured abstractly as given, with given interests, wants, purposes, needs, etc.; while society and the state are pictured as sets of actual or possible social arrangements which respond ... to those individuals' requirements. This givenness of fixed and invariant human psychological features leads to an *abstract conception* of the individual who is seen as merely the bearer of those features, which determine his behavior, and specify his interests, needs and rights." (Lukes 1978,

Another way of putting this is to say that ontological individualists hold that individuals are not *socially constituted*. This is not a *causal* claim about society and its effects on individuals, not a claim that human beings could survive or mature in isolation from each other, or that their needs and desires could be met if they were hermits. It need not deny the necessity of community for any decent human life, but may hold – as did Hobbes, the paradigm of a philosophical individualist – that a life apart from society is nasty, brutish and short. Such claims can as well be made by individualists as by social realists.

What distinguishes ontological individualism is a *constitutive* claim about the role of society in what it is to *be* an individual human self. It holds that the concept of a human individual is intelligible without reference to society, and that a society is made up of persons whose reality is intelligible apart from it. Social realists claim, on the contrary, that the very concept of an individual independent of society is unintelligible, for society constitutes the human individual. Ontological individualists deny, while social realists affirm, that the concept of an individual human being is a *socially constitutive concept*.

Here is an example of a socially constitutive concept. Individuals can write checks, even if they are all alone, but checks cannot be written unless there is a monetary system, banks to honor them, people or firms to write them to, and so on. This is not just causally impossible, in the way it would be impossible to write a check without a writing instrument or a check blank, or if one's arms were tied up. It is unintelligible to think a person might write a check apart from any social context. We might draw up a check blank, sign our name to it, etc., but it wouldn't be a check for all that, unless the proper social institutions were in place.

There are numerous other examples of socially constitutive concepts. An individual can vote, but only if there is an election and a host of other institutions inconceivable apart from a society. Only in a social context can there be laws, and hence obedience or disobedience to law, treaties, contracts to be made or broken, property on theft, occupations, wages or salaries. Social realists affirm that the concept of an individual human self is like these in being socially constitutive. This does not mean that human bodies are socially constituted; as merely material things, they are not.[5] It means that the characteristics and capacities which mark out a distinctively human self are socially constituted – unintelligible apart from a social context, in the way the concept of a check is unintelligible

---

p. 73) P. H. Bradley criticized the idea as follows: "The 'individual' apart from the community is an abstraction ... [Man] is a social being; he is real only because he is social." (Lukes 1978, p. 78)

5 "We can think that the individual is what he is in abstraction from his community only of we are thinking of him *qua* organism." (Taylor 1975, p. 102)

apart from a social context. Human needs or interests, our emotional and intellectual capacities, require a social context; apart from that they are inchoate urges or mere instinctual behavior. Even our capacity to think is unintelligible apart from a social context, for thought depends on language, and language makes no sense apart from a linguistic community. Nor do our perceptual capacities, for human perception is conceptual, and concepts require a language.[6]

The dispute whether the individual self is socially constituted is also a dispute about how to understand society. Ontological individualists think of a society as analogous to a voluntary association, which persons join to satisfy their interests, needs, or desires. They hold, that is to say, an individualist conception of society. This does not rule out their valuing social relations and various forms of community life; what it rules out is that a society is *constitutive*, something it makes no sense to think a person might join, since there would be no persons able to join it if the society had not already constituted those persons. Social realists hold that society is constitutive, they hold, as Charles Taylor (1985, p. 192) writes, that "what man derives from society is not some aid in realizing his good, but the very possibility of being an agent seeking that good".

The dispute between ontological individualism and social realism raises philosophical issues of the deepest sort – issues where differences are so wide that it is difficult to find common ground on which to base arguments. In such a situation, critical discussion must take a different route than the usual sorts of arguments. One way of criticizing ontological individualism, for example, is to consider why it is so deeply entrenched in modern consciousness. The analysis I gave, in terms of how dualism accompanied the rise of modern science, is not an argument against it. But it shows that ontological individualism arose as a result of specific historical circumstances, and this undermines its apparent selfevidence and the tendency to take it for granted.

---

6 Cf. Marx: "Man is in the most literal sense of the world a *zoon politikon*, not only a social animal, but an animal which can develop into an individual only in society. Production by isolated individuals outside of society – something which might happen as an exception to a civilized man who by accident got into the wilderness and already dynamically possessed within himself the forces of society – is as great an absurdity as the idea of the development of language without individuals living together and talking to one another." (Lukes 1978, p. 76) On the point about perception, cf. Giddens, who argues that although sensation can be understood in individualist terms, perception cannot, for it is conceptual, and concepts "are always common to a plurality of men. They are formed by means of words, and neither the vocabulary nor the grammar of a language is the product of one particular person. They are rather the result of a collective elaboration, and they express the anonymous collectivity that employs them." (Giddens 1972, p. 267)

Another way to criticize it is to note that it is often without plausible rivals simply because its entrenchment makes it very difficult to avoid individualistic language in the very expression of an alternative. Thus social realists have sometimes spoken of society as if it were an individual over and above people, and individualists have rightly protested that this amounts to believing in "invisible powers and dominions", conceived as "impersonal entities at once patterns and realities, in terms of [which] ... men and institutions ... must behave as they do" (Berlin, 1969, p. 76). But social realists need not think of society as a super-individual, or even as an individual of any kind; to do so is to hold that only individuals can be real, which is itself a central claim of ontological individualism.

A third way to criticize it is to recognize that major support for ontological individualism has come from epistemological and methodological individualism but that these doctrines no longer appear as plausible as they once did. If the capacity for knowledge is not socially constituted, there is every reason to think that individuals are not socially constituted. If adequate explanations of social behavior must ultimately refer only to facts about individuals, then it is natural to hold that the reality of individuals is essentially independent of society. But both of these doctrines have been effectively attacked in recent years. Empiricism is the most prominent version of epistemological individualism, and it is in full scale retreat because of influential critics ranging from Wittgenstein to Quine to Kuhn. Methodological individualism, in spite of its revival by many cognitive scientists, has also been effectively attacked, and irreducibly social explanations are widely used with no sense of unease.

Finally, there are a number of developments in various academic disciplines which support social realism. Sociologists, with some prominent exceptions, Weber, for example, have always supported it, rejecting "the naive assumption that individuals are somehow more real and therefore more important in the explanatory scheme of things than the society to which men owe their existence and from which they derive their particular natures" (Campbell 1981, p. 11). Historians more and more turned to the social matrix of the actions of individuals. Philosophers of language have developed powerful arguments that language is not the expression of thoughts of which solitary individuals are capable, but a way of using words that is possible only in a community, and they have argued that thought itself requires a social context.[7]

---

[7] Wittgenstein (1953) and Quine (1960) are prominent defenders of this point of view, and there have been explicit attacks in recent years on individualist conceptions of thought and language in such philosophers as Putnam (1975) and Burge (1986).

These considerations do not show that philosophical individualism is false, only that there are no compelling reasons to accept it. This is important, however, for if the doctrine has what appear to be pernicious consequences for social and political morality, we are free to reject it without being accused of rejecting obvious truths simply because they conflict with our moral or political convictions. Our task then is to develop conceptions of social and political morality which do not depend on philosophical individualism but which preserve the moral and political insight in other individualist claims. In what follows, I shall explore some ways of doing this, ways in which the defensible claims of individualism can be separated from the dubious claims of philosophical individualism.

12.2 The Dignity of the Individual

The second individualist claim I shall discuss is belief in the dignity of the individual.[8] Dignity implies *respect* and *equality*. All human beings are worthy of respect; they are, to use Kant's language, to be treated as ends in themselves and never merely as means to ends. To treat them merely as means, even if the ends are as worthy as the good of a whole society, is to fail to respect their dignity as human beings. This does not rule out evaluating people for what they contribute to society; it rules out treating them *merely* in terms of their contribution. The dignity of individuals must be respected no matter what their talents, no matter what they have done to frustrate the common good, no matter how bad they are thought to be.

Dignity also implies equality – some cannot have more of it than others hence respect must be understood in terms of equality. In respecting persons as ends in themselves, we respect them equally; human beings are, I shall say, *morally equal*. That does not mean they are equally good or alike in their talents or achievements; it means they should be respected equally in spite of such differences. Nor does it mean that all persons should receive equal treatment, for treating individuals with equal respect may require unequal treatment. To treat the handicapped with equal respect, for example, may require that special pro-

---

[8] This is one of the ways *Habits of the Heart* uses 'individualism': "A belief in the inherent dignity and, indeed, sacredness of the human person." The authors hold that "in this sense, individualism is part of all four of the American traditions we have described in this book" (Bellah et al. 1985, p. 334).

visions be made for them, in such matters as education or transportation, that are not made for others.⁹

To speak of *moral* equality implies two things. First, that it is not simply desirable to treat all persons with equal respect but a moral duty. Second, that the belief in dignity must have consequences for the way people are treated in human society. The idea that all persons are children of God may, for example, underlie the belief in moral equality, but if it simply means that persons should be treated equally in some other life, regardless of how they are treated in this life, then it is not an idea of *moral* equality.

The concept of dignity has been rejected by few modern thinkers, and it is accepted in most of the modern world, at least in the sense that few defend their conduct with no regard for whether it respects the dignity of individuals. There are, of course, examples of practices – torture, genocide, racism, sexism – which are inconsistent with belief in the dignity of the individual, but even their perpetrators try to show that the practices do not violate human dignity, by claiming that their victims brought it on themselves, or that they are not fully human, or that the practices are not what they seem to be, and so on. To deny the claim in the modern world is to join the ranks of the wicked, to be a Nazi or a Stalinist.¹⁰

But the belief is not universal in human history. Lukes, for example, argues that it was absent from earlier Judaism, which made "the nation of Israel, not the individual human being the concern of God" (Lukes 1978, p. 45) and that, although present in the New Testament, it was de-emphasized in the Middle Ages with its idea of the "corporational structure" of society. He argues that it was rearticulated only in renaissance humanism. Peter Berger argues that dignity is a modern concept, which should be contrasted with the more ancient concept of honor. While both rest on the moral claim that human beings have an "intrinsic humanity" that must not be violated, "the concept of honor implies that identity is essentially ... linked to institutional roles, [whereas] the modern

---

9 In a society which has systematically failed to treat blacks or females with equal respect, it may be that equal respect will itself require, at least for a time, that the conditions of their life and work be given special consideration. What equal respect requires is a complex issue with which theories of social and political morality are designed to deal. An excellent discussion is Dworkin (1977).

10 Robert Jay Lifton (1986, p. 460), speaks of the Nazi conception of the doctor as the ultimate biological warrior who was healing and purifying the German *Volk* by eliminating those "unworthy of life". Here the individual is totally subordinated to the group, but even so there is the suggestion that the extermination of individuals was justified not simply for the good of the *Volk* but also because they were not fully human.

concept of dignity ... implies that identity is essentially independent of institutional roles" (Berger 1970, pp. 153–154). The essential difference concerns moral equality. The concept of honor implies that not all persons are entitled to equal respect; respect depends on one's institutional roles, which are almost invariably hierarchical. The concept of dignity implies that persons are entitled to equal respect, for it "pertains to the self as such, to the individual regardless of his position in society" (Berger, Berger, and Kellner 1974, p. 83).

The point of the contrasts made by Lukes and Berger (assuming they are right that the concept of dignity was not prevalent in the pre-modern world) is that to deny the dignity of the individual in the pre-modern world was not to deny the moral worth of human beings. Human beings were to be valued above all other creatures, but that did not mean they were to be respected equally; some were worthy of more respect than others because of their status in society. What is distinctive about the modern concept of the dignity of the individual, and what makes it an individualist claim, is that it implies that all individuals are worthy of equal respect, regardless of their status or role in any society or community. It lies behind the belief that there are human rights all individuals have, which are inalienable in that no society is morally permitted to over-ride them.

This individualist claim about dignity must, however, be distinguished from *theories* about it. Such theories often presuppose philosophical individualism; they attempt to ground the individualist claim about the dignity of the individual in an individualist conception of what it is to be a human being, arguing that individuals have rights regardless of their social status only because the reality of individuals is independent of society (this is the doctrine of the 'abstract individual'). These theories are controversial, however, while the belief in human dignity is not, or at least ought not to be. Controversy over it is usually due to confusing the underlying moral claim with theories about it.

The distinction between belief in the dignity of the individual and theories about it is not an easy one to draw, especially when it comes to defending the belief, for defenders traditionally appeal to some theory. I think it is possible to defend it without appeal to a *theory* of dignity (though perhaps not without appeal to theories on other matters) but making the case would take me too far afield. Even if defense requires a theory, the distinction between the universality of the belief and the diversity of theories about it remains, and this allows the individualist claim about dignity to be disentangled from more dubious individualist claims. I return to this important matter below, in suggesting a communitarian basis for the belief in human dignity.

12.3 The Ideal of Individuality

The 'ideal of individuality' refers to the claim that it is desirable that individuals be unique or distinctive in some sense and that they become so by developing their own distinctive capacities. This is often called the ideal of 'self-development', involving, as Karl Weintraub puts it, "the belief that, whatever else he is, [a person] is a unique individuality, whose life task is to be true to his very own personality" (Weintraub 1975, p. 835). It is the core idea of what *Habits of the Heart* calls "expressive individualism": "each person has a unique core of feeling and intuition that should unfold or be expressed" (Bellah et al. 1985, p. 334).

Like the belief in dignity, this is not a theory but a *claim* underlying various theories. It is one I am prepared to defend, provided it is not embedded in philosophical individualism, but only if it is taken to be (unlike the belief in dignity, which is a moral claim) a *value* claim about what it is desirable or good to do or be. Individuality is desirable, but to take it as a moral obligation is inconsistent with the belief in human dignity (a matter discussed in section 12.4), which requires that all persons have an equal right to pursue their own conception of the good, including the kind of life which does not prize individuality.

It is clearly an individualist claim; indeed, when people think of individualism, they often think first of individuality. It means being unique or singular, sometimes to the point of eccentricity, sometimes simply being who one is, whether or not one is different from others. Rousseau put it in its extreme form at the beginning of his *Confessions:* "I am made unlike anyone I have ever met; I will even venture to say that I am like no one in the world. I may be no better, but at least I am different." (Lukes 1978, p. 66) Kierkegaard affirmed it in speaking of that 'singular individual': It was a central concern of such 19th-century American writers as Thoreau, Emerson, Melville, and Twain, who belong to the standard canon, as well as of female and black writers who do not, but who themselves struggled, and who portrayed characters who struggled, with a society which stifled individuality and self-expression.

Like all the claims of individualism, the ideal of individuality is modern, and this in two senses: it is not found in traditional societies, and it plays no important historical role in ancient or medieval times. The first sense was emphasized by Durkheim, who took *it* to be a mark of a traditional society that it lacked any strong sense of individuality. Durkheim thought that the unity of a traditional society "is to be found in the fact that there exists a strongly defined set of values and beliefs which ensures that the actions of all individuals conform to common norms" (Giddens 1972, p. 6). In such a society there is "a low level of individuation: since every individual is a microcosm of the collective type, only restricted opportunity is offered for each member of the society to develop specific and particular personality characteristics" (Giddens 1972, p. 6). As traditional values dissolve, members of a society acquire more and more freedom to act and develop in their own ways, and the ideal of individuality replaces the ideal of conformity to consensual norms covering *the* full range of life. This does not mean, Durkheim argued, that collective values disappear, for the ideal of individuality is itself "the result of the collectivity". It means rather that what is collectively valued is diversity and self-expression rather than conformity to traditional norms governing the behavior of all members of the society.

The ideal of individuality is also modern in the sense that ancient and medieval people did not, for the most part, prize individuality. In thinking about the good life, for example, they proposed a model of excellence valid for everyone. In contrast, writes Karl Weintraub, the ideal of individuality

> is characterized by its very rejection of a valid model for the individual ... The subtle set of differences whereby any individual is distinguished from every other individual is now not perceived as an 'accidental' variation from the norm ... but as a matter of great importance. It then appears to be a precious aspect of the human existence that each and every individual is individually distinctive, that every person is unique ... Each life, as a one-time only actualization of the potential, is marked by an irreplaceable value. (Weintraub 1975, p. 838)

This way of valuing the unique and the distinctive over the general and the universal, of paying attention to what distinguishes individuals from each other, is a peculiarly modern idea.

The articulation of individuality as an ideal is usually traced to Rousseau and Goethe, who differed from Rousseau in thinking that individuality did not require the rejection of society. The romantics made it central, and it was eloquently defended by Novalis, Schlegel, Schleiermacher, von Humboldt, and Byron. Kant, in spite of his emphasis on its universal moral law, prized it highly, as did Hegel, and Marx equaled the romantics in the eloquence of his defense of it. Chapter 3 of Mill's *On Liberty* is entitled: "Of Individuality, as one of the Elements of Well-being", and we have noted its significance in 19th-century American literature. There are few writers and thinkers since the 18th century for whom the ideal of individuality has not figured as an important motif,[11] and it is not surprising that people think of it first when they think of individualism.

---

[11] For some excellent citations see Lukes 1978, chapter 10. Here is one from von Humboldt: "That towards which every human being must ceaselessly direct his efforts, and on which especially those who design to influence their fellow men must ever keep their eyes, is the *Individuality of Power and Development.*" (Lukes 1978, p. 69)

Its links with other individualist claims are complex. It has, for example, functioned as an ideal as much for societies and cultures as for individuals. The romantics, for example, stressed the uniqueness and diversity of societies and cultures and held that each should develop its own distinctive 'genius'. For some, the emphasis shifted totally from the individual person to the society or culture, and there grew up a conception of society as an organism in which individual identity was submerged (fascism is an extreme example), so that individuality applied more to society than to individuals. Here the claim about individuality seems opposed to other individualist claims.

Normally, however, the ideal of individuality for societies or cultures joined with the ideal of individuality for persons, and as such it has been very influential.[12] It marks out an approach to the study of history, culture and society, which is now dominant, and which holds that since each historical period, culture, or society is unique, it can be understood only in its own terms. This historicist approach to the study of history and society sometimes leads to relativism of various kinds, for example, that it is impossible to understand a culture other than one's own, or that what one culture takes to be good and right must be good and right for that culture. Relativism is in dispute, but the influence of individuality is not, and the historicist approach to history and society is now widely assumed.

The ideal of individuality also links up with the concept of liberalism, understood (pending further discussion in the next section) as the claim that a just society ought to embody the principle of equal liberty – the principle that individuals should have maximum equal liberty to live out their own conceptions of the good. One link between individuality and liberalism is that a society committed to liberalism seems necessary for individuality to flourish. Thus Weintraub suggests that "the cultivation of individuality is possible only in a society permitting the individual full freedom for self-definition, a society committed to individualism" (Weintraub 1975, p. 839).[13] Weintraub also notes that individualism is not

---

[12] Lukes nicely summarizes the situation as follows: Individuality "specifies an ideal for the lives of individuals ... It is either anti-social, with the individual set apart from and hostile to society (as among some of the early romantics), or extra-social, when the individual pursues his own path, free of social pressures (as with Mill), or highly social, where the individual's self-development is achieved through community with others." (Lukes 1978, p. 71)

[13] This may oversimplify the situation. Individuality has been present in aristocratic groups even in societies in which ordinary citizens have little liberty. Whole societies need not be individualistic for individuality to exist in groups in the society. Moreover, while it seems unlikely that individuality could have attained its widespread appeal without societies committed to individualism, once the ideal caught on, it has been able to flourish even in societies severely restrictive of the liberties of its members.

sufficient, for even under conditions of maximum liberty, persons may choose to live in a conformist way.

The obverse of this is that the ideal of individuality has been a powerful motivating force for the development of liberal societies – societies which seek to embody the principle of equal liberty. Taking individuality as an ideal suggests that conceptions of the good should vary widely, because it is desirable that persons work out their own distinctive conception of what they want their lives to be. This often gives rise to relativism about the good: what is a good life is relative to each individual, there being no universal standards to which a good life must conform. This implies that persons ought to have maximum liberty to pursue their own conceptions of the good: if individual conceptions of the good are highly valued, or are purely relative, a society ought not to favor any conceptions of the good over others. I do not think, as I argue in section 12.5, that liberalism requires either individuality or relativism, but these have been historically important in its development.

Finally, there is one individualist claim enthusiasts for individuality have often resisted, namely, philosophical individualism's doctrine of the abstract individual and its rejection of the social constitution of the self. Liberalism, I argue below, does not have to be based on this conception of the self – it can be disentangled from philosophical individualism – but it often is, and it is individualism in this sense, and in particular, societies where the conception of the self as an abstract individual dominates the culture, to which many who value individuality have objected. For abstract individuals are like all other individuals in what makes them human, which means that individuality has no vital link with what is distinctively human.

This is ironic, for individualism is supposed to value the individual, but the abstract individual has no individuality. Indeed, the irony may run deeper, for Durkheim contends that the doctrine of the abstract individual has more than an accidental connection with belief in the value of individuality. In a traditional society, what is valued is not individuality but what one shares with the social group to which one belongs. Consciousness of what one shares with one's own social group also involves, however, in traditional societies where the social world outside one's own community is alien, lack of consciousness of what one shares with human beings at large. As the sense of individuality develops, individuals value less what they share with other members of their own social group and become correspondingly more aware of what they share with the rest of humanity. They become, as Giddens phrases Durkheim's point, "more conscious of their generic characteristics as human beings to the degree to which they become more aware of themselves as separate and distinct personalities" (Giddens 1972, pp. 9–10). This leads to the view that these generic characteristics are not constituted by any kind of social participation and that they constitute our essential humanity, which is the doctrine of the abstract individual.

That the ideal of individuality and the doctrine of the abstract individual may develop together helps explain the intensity of the criticism enthusiasts for individuality have directed against the abstract individual. Critics contend that the cultural expression of the abstract individual is mass society, society as a collection of anonymous persons, who do what everyone else does, read what everyone else reads, feel and think as everyone else feels and thinks. Kierkegaard thought this was corrosive of the inner life, of subjectivity, and hence of what made it worthwhile to be human. Wordsworth and Thoreau thought it deadened our sensibilities and produced lives of quiet desperation. Nietzsche thought it brought everyone down to the lowest common denominator and undermined the culture which made humans more than dumb animals. Recent partisans of what *Habits of the Heart* calls "the culture of therapy" make similar criticisms, affirming the value of feelings because they instance the particularity and uniqueness of individuality.

The ideal of individuality is, then, one of the most powerful and protean of individualist ideas. Self-development and self-expression, diversity in thought and sensibility, are things the modern world has made possible and which many of us value highly. But they are not moral imperatives: a society in which individuality does not play a central role need not be unjust, and, indeed, the ideal of individuality itself implies that communities should be left to resist the ideal if they so desire. One of the most intriguing aspects of individuality is its complex relation to liberalism, due as much as anything to complexity in the concept of liberalism itself, a topic to which I now turn.

12.4 Moral Individualism

The rest of this paper is essentially a discussion of *liberalism*, something no discussion of individualism can avoid, for it has been extraordinarily important in the theory and practice of the western world for a long time, and it is increasingly significant for the rest of the world as well. Almost as protean as individualism itself, it involves a variety of claims, some defensible and some not.

What links these claims as varieties of liberalism is that they are all based on a particular way of construing the individualist belief in the dignity of the individual. Liberalism (which, of course, derives from 'liberty') construes the belief in dignity, that is, in the moral equality of human beings, as belief in their *equal liberty*. Human beings are, it holds, distinctive in their capacity for liberty, which they share equally, however much they differ in other respects. It is because of this capacity that they have dignity and merit equal respect. Liberalism, that is to say, construes belief in moral equality as belief in equal liberty, so that to respect individuals equally is to respect them as equal in their liberty.

I can do no more than suggest the main lines of what liberalism means by liberty. The essential idea is that our lives as human beings do not merely conform to pre-determined patterns innate to the species nor are they simply governed by instinct. Unlike the other animals, we have a capacity for liberty, or choice, with respect to the patterns of our lives, to the ends we pursue, and to the kinds of activities in which we take satisfaction. We are, that is to say, capable of having and acting on a conception of the good: our larger aims in life, the long-term ends we seek to realize, are aims and ends we pursue not because they are part of our nature but because we in some sense believe them to be worthwhile. While many of us may not in fact choose our larger aims or long-term ends, but just find ourselves pursuing them, we nevertheless have the capacity to choose or alter them, for they are not necessitated by our nature.

The ability to exercise this capacity for liberty may, of course, vary over time – as children we are less able to exercise it than as adults – or from one individual to another – depending, for example, on one's rational powers. It may also be conceptualized in various ways. Some, for example, base it on the doctrine of the abstract individual and think of it as a capacity human beings possess apart from society; others think of it as a socially constituted capacity, one unintelligible outside a social context. But despite these variations in our ability to exercise it or in the way it is conceptualized, the capacity for liberty, liberalism contends, is shared equally by all human beings and accounts for their dignity. Human beings are morally equal and deserving of equal respect, because they have a capacity for liberty in the conceptions of the good they seek to realize.[14]

---

14 For a helpful discussion of this, cf. Morris (1976), Morris takes liberty to be the capacity for choice and then argues that "We treat a human being as a person provided, first we permit the person to make the choices that will determine what happens to him and, second, when our responses to the person are responses respecting the person's choice." (Morris 1976, p. 839) To treat human beings as persons is to respect their moral equality. Morris points out that we cannot always respect individual's choices – if they are insane or children, for example but in such cases we do not, justifiably, treat human beings as persons. This raises hard issues but they do not affect the basic point. John Rawls also has an excellent discussion of this sense of liberty: "The basic intuitive idea is that in virtue of what we may call their moral powers, and the powers of reason, thought and judgment connected with those powers, we say that persons are free. And in virtue of their having these powers to the requisite degree to be fully cooperating members of society, we say that persons are equal ... The two [essential] moral powers are a capacity for a sense of justice ... and a capacity for a conception of the good: the capacity to form, to revise,

This yields the central moral claim of liberalism, namely, the principle of equal liberty: respect for the dignity of human beings requires that their liberty to pursue their own conceptions of the good must not be restricted except to insure the equal right of others to do the same. While versions of liberalism differ on their interpretation of this principle, they all hold that persons ought to have maximum liberty to pursue what they regard as most valuable in life, what they think gives it meaning or purpose, provided everyone else has equal liberty to do the same. For restricting a person's liberty to pursue a conception of the good on grounds other than the equal liberty of all to do the same, would be to favor some conceptions of the good over others, and that would be to fail to show equal respect to every human being.

I take liberalism's construal of dignity and moral equality in terms of equal liberty to be an individualist claim which ought to be accepted, for I think liberalism's construal of the concept of dignity is the best one we have. I shall not attempt to defend it, however, but consider rather some of the ways in which the claim has been developed. For liberalism comes in different versions, some more acceptable than others.

The versions of liberalism take one or another of two forms. On the one hand, liberalism takes the form of a comprehensive, individualistic moral theory about the good and about our rights and duties. This form is the concern of this section; I shall call it *moral individualism*. It is opposed to communitarian conceptions of morality defended in diverse ways by thinkers from Plato and Aristotle to Hegel and Marx to Alasdair MacIntyre and recent feminists. *Habits of the Heart* takes one version of moral individualism – 'utilitarian individualism' – as its main critical target, contending that it undermines the conditions necessary "to preserve or create a morally coherent life" (Bellah et al. 1985, p. vi). It is what most people have in mind when they speak about the dangers of individualism and urge a communitarian point of view to counteract individualism prevalent in American society.

On the other hand, liberalism may take the form of a theory about what it is for a society's main institutions to meet the demands of justice. This form of liberalism is the concern of the next section; I shall call it *liberalism as a political conception*. It is a morally based theory of how social justice requires the embodiment of the principle of equal liberty, not a comprehensive moral theory about how people should live their lives. Indeed, its fundamental claim is that a society

---

and rationally to pursue a conception of one's rational advantage or good ..., which must not be understood narrowly, but rather as a conception of what is valuable in human life." (Rawls 1985, p. 233) The rest of my paper has been much influenced by this paper, as well as by his (1971) *A Theory of Justice*.

is just only if its basic institutions are structured so that persons have maximum equal liberty to live whatever kinds of live they choose. It ought not be tightly linked to *any* comprehensive moral theory, therefore, for if it is, one conception of the good life will be privileged over others.

I come then to liberalism as moral individualism, which, as a comprehensive moral theory, includes a theory both of the good and of our rights and duties, and I shall sketch out the main lines of each. My primary concern *is* not with the content of moral individualism but with what makes it an individualistic, rather than a communitarian, theory.

Moral individualism understands the good to be whatever satisfies an individual's desires, interests, values, preferences, and so on.[15] It also holds that only individuals have preferences, and hence that all goods are individual goods, that is, goods for, and assignable to, particular individuals, it being in principle always possible to specify which individual a good is a good for. A society has no preferences over and above those of its members; there are no social goods not reducible to individual goods, a social good being something that satisfies the preferences of many or most individuals in a society. To promote the common good means to promote the good for many or most individuals in a society. To subordinate one's private interests to the public interest means to subordinate one's own private interests to the private interests of many other individuals. To serve the public welfare means to serve the personal welfare of many individuals – to help many persons satisfy their individual preferences.

For moral individualists, the good life is a life in which such desires, interests, values, and preferences are maximally realized. Many hold that what motivates us to satisfy our preferences is the happiness (sometimes pleasure) that brings, which yields the individualist notion of the happy life as one in which one's preferences are more often (perhaps much more often) satisfied than frustrated. This is a conception of happiness and the good life which fits well with the ideal of individuality, for preferences usually vary widely from individual to individual (and if they do not, moral individualists characteristically argue that they should), and hence the form that happiness or the good life takes will vary widely. Moral individualists have a model of the good life in a sense – it is one which maximally satisfies individual preferences – but it does not specify any one ideal for what the shape or content of a good life ought to be.

---

15 In what follows I shall often use the term 'preferences' to cover all of these. It is the term favored by economists for the good reason that the interests, desires, or values of persons normally manifest themselves in their behavior in the form of preferences.

On this view, no one is in any better position than anyone else to know what is good, since individuals can know for certain only what their own preferences are. There are, therefore, no experts about the good. It is true that some may know more than others about the good life, since that requires figuring out which preferences can be satisfied together and which not, something one does not know simply by knowing one's own preferences. Nevertheless, in the final analysis, we are all our own authorities on whether we have achieved the kind of life which we find satisfying and therefore good.

In holding that social goods are reducible to individual goods, moral individualists need not deny the importance of society for realizing those goods. Many preferences may not be satisfiable in solitude, and the support of a community may be indispensable for realizing a conception of the good life. What is distinctive about moral individualism is not that it thinks people can or should get along without society but that it regards society as wholly instrumental to satisfying the individual preferences of its members. This means that interests, desires, values, and preferences are not socially constituted but are formed independently of participation in society, a view moral individualists must hold, for if a society is good only insofar as it satisfies the preferences of its members, those preferences must already be there to be satisfied.

It is clear that moral individualism is simply the development of the moral side of philosophical individualism. Ontological individualism underlies the claims that goods must be goods for particular individuals and that preferences are not socially constituted. Epistemological individualism plays an important role, especially in its empiricist form, which believes that all knowledge is based on sense awareness. If we have knowledge of the good, therefore, it must be known through sense awareness, and since, argue empiricists, we know our own preferences through inner awareness of them, it is plausible to identify the good with what satisfies our own preferences. Inner awareness, moreover, is something one can have only of oneself, and hence the view that we are all own authorities on what is good.[16]

The alternative to moral individualism is *communitarianism*. Just as moral individualism is the moral side of philosophical individualism, so communitarianism is the moral side of social realism. Its main claim about the good is that not all goods are individual goods but that many are irreducibly social. This means, on the one hand, that many goods are not goods for, or assignable, to particular

---

[16] A variant of this is that there is no such thing as moral knowledge at all, that judgments about the good are simply expressions of feelings for which there can be no criteria of truth or falsity. MacIntyre calls this the "emotivist self" (MacIntyre 1981, p. 30) and interestingly connects it with other facets of individualism.

individuals, and on the other, that many goods are inconceivable apart from a social context. They are, that is to say, socially constituted: society is necessary, not only instrumentally for their realization, but for their very possibility. All goods connected with the socially constituted characteristics of individuals are of this nature.

This can be illustrated in the case of a family. A family is an instance of a social good. To be good, it must normally be good for its members. But to propose, for instance, that the institution of the family be abolished in favor of an alternative which might do more good for its members (which for individualism means satisfy more of their preferences) is, on the communitarian view, absurd because the family is so constitutive of individuals that without it, there would be no fully human individuals to do good for (and no preferences other than inchoate urges). A good family is, moreover, an example of an irreducibly social good: its good cannot be understood as the sum of the goods individual members gain from it, since the idea of allocating its good to each member is not intelligible. The good of a family is not the sum of individual preferences it satisfies.

Many goods which are not goods for particular individuals involve what Alasdair MacIntyre calls "internal" as opposed to "external" goods. He makes this distinction in connection with the concept of a practice, which is

> any coherent and complex form of socially established cooperative human activity through which goods internal to that form of activity are realized in the course of trying to achieve those standards of excellence which are appropriate to, and partly definitive of, that form of activity ... (MacIntyre 1981, p. 175)

Examples are games, the arts and sciences, various skilled occupations, and, in general, any social activity with standards of excellence which define what it is to be a competent participant and which require effort to master. Goods are *external* to a practice if they could be achieved in some other way than by engaging in the practice; they are external rewards of various kinds like wealth, social position, or fame. Goods are *internal* if they can be achieved only by engaging in the practice and, therefore, only by submitting oneself to the discipline of a practice in order to master its standards of excellence. They are called 'internal' because they cannot be understood except in terms of the practice itself and its standards of excellence; apart from the practice, they can be neither specified nor recognized. If one plays chess, for example, simply to realize the good that comes from measuring up to the standards of a good chess player, then one is playing it to realize internal goods; if one plays chess for money or fame, then one is playing it to realize external goods.

It is characteristic of external goods "that when achieved they are always some individual's property and possession"; they are, that is to say, goods assignable to a particular individual. Moreover, external goods, like money or fame, are "such that the more someone has of them, the less there is for other people ... [They are] characteristically objects of competition in which there must be losers as well as winners." As for internal goods, on the other hand, while they are "the outcome of competition to excel, ... it is characteristic of them that their achievement is a good for the whole community who participate in the practice" (MacIntyre 1981, p. 178).[17] Internal goods are, then, irreducibly social; they are socially constituted and they are not assignable to particular individuals. Their status is not that of being goods for particular individuals.

This is not to say that such social goods do not benefit particular people; it is to say that their doing so by meeting the preferences of individuals is not what makes them good. Individuals may draw on them, as it were, but they are there whether or not anyone draws on them. Moreover, some persons will be in a better position than others to determine what are goods, for "those who lack the relevant experience are incompetent thereby as judges of internal goods" (MacIntyre 1981, p. 176). Communitarians will regard the most important goods as social goods in this sense.

While my main concern is not to criticize moral individualism but to clarify its claims and contrast it with communitarianism, I do want to discuss briefly some possible criticisms. It is often criticized for being egoist, that is, for holding that the good life involves maximally satisfying one's own *selfish* preferences, and it is the egoist form of moral individualism which has rightly inspired the most sustained criticism. It inevitably involves privatism and undermines a sense of public spirit; it leads to the fragmentation of society and a loss of any social solidarity; it produces loneliness, detachment and narcissism. It is what *Habits of the Heart* criticizes as "utilitarian individualism", so-called because its devotees see everything in terms of its *utility* for satisfying their own selfish preferences.[18] They may not neglect society or communities, but the latter are seen only in relation to their own ego.

It is important to note, however, that egoism is not the only form of moral individualism. Egoism does not follow from the individualist claim that if some-

---

17 Cf. Grimshaw "Human needs and interests arise in a context of relationships with other people, and human needs *for* relationships with other people cannot be understood as merely instrumental to isolable individual ends." (Grimshaw 1986, p. 175)

18 What *Habits of the Heart* calls "expressive individualism" it usually characterizes as egoist as well, the difference being that expressive individualists worry more about what their *real* interests, desires and preferences are.

thing is good, there must be a particular individual whose preferences it satisfies. To think that it does is to assume that the preferences *of* individuals must be preferences *for* themselves or preferences for their own well-being. The preferences *of* a self, however, need not be preferences *for* that self; they may be self-sacrificing preferences for other persons or things. I may, for example, have a strong preference that someone else be happy; it is *my* preference but it is not a preference for my own happiness but for someone else's. It is not necessary that one's own preferences have oneself as their object, that is, be selfish preferences.

This is important because it means that it is a mistake to assume that to criticize egoism is to undermine all forms of moral individualism, for there are forms which are not egoist but which are equally opposed to a communitarian conception of the good life.[19] This is true of the altruistic form, which shares the view that the only good is what satisfies the preferences of individuals, but which holds that many preferences are altruistic, that is, take as their object the well-being of other persons through the fulfillment of *their* preferences. Altruistic individualism emphasizes not selfishness but benevolence, compassion or sympathy. Unlike egoism, it thinks a good society should primarily fulfill altruistic preferences, but like moral individualism generally, it views society not as constituting these but as instrumental to their satisfaction.

Altruism is morally preferable to selfishness, but altruistic individualism shares too many things with egoism to be satisfactory. In particular, it shares the view that preferences must be either selfish or altruistic, that is, be directed either to one's own well-being or to the well-being of others. Most people most of the time, however, are not directly concerned either with their own well-being or with the well-being of others. Their concern is with such things as work, family,

---

19 Durkheim makes this point very forcefully: "The condemnation of individualism has been facilitated by its confusion with the narrow utilitarianism and utilitarian egoism of Spencer and the economists. But this is very facile. It is not hard to denounce as a shallow ideal that narrow commercialism which reduces society to nothing more than a vast apparatus of production and exchange ... There exists another individualism over which it is less easy to triumph. It has been upheld for a century by the great majority of thinkers: it is the individualism of Kant and Rousseau and the spiritualists ... It is so far from making personal interest the aim of human conduct that it sees personal motives as the very source of evil ... Duty consists in turning our attention from that which concerns us personally, from all that relates to our empirical individuality, so as to pursue solely that which is demanded by our human condition, that which we hold in common with all our fellow men." (Giddens 1972, pp. 147 ff.) Durkheim also emphasizes in his penetrating discussion that individualism is itself a social phenomenon, a value system which is as much a product of the *conscience collective* as the value systems of traditional societies; the difference is that the value system of individualism is diffuse and does not require the same degree of conformity of action to common norms.

various kinds of causes, the communities in which they live. Much of what we do, perhaps the most important part, is directed not to satisfying either selfish or altruistic preferences but to carrying out various tasks which themselves determine, apart from anybody's preferences, what we have to do.

Among these various tasks are what MacIntyre calls practices, and the criticism I am making of both egoistic and altruistic individualists is that in thinking of goods solely in terms of what satisfies individual preferences, they rule out the role of practices in human life. The reason for this is that individual preferences are essentially connected with external rather than internal goods. Internal goods are not matters of individual preference, for they are necessarily linked with standards of excellence one has to master, and they are not assignable to particular individuals. One may engage in a particular practice in the first place as a matter of preference for some external good, but once engaged, the goods that predominate are internal to the practice, and hence are not (merely) matters of individual preference. If practices are central to an adequate conception of the good life, then a theory, like moral individualism, which has an inadequate account of internal goods has an inadequate conception of the good life.

Insofar as individualism has no conception of social goods as anything other than the sum of individual goods, it will, even when it is not egoist, tend towards the ills for which egoism is criticized – towards privatism and a loss of public spirit, toward social fragmentation and the dissolution of social bonds. For it will undervalue the structures and institutions of society, in particular, the institutions whose role is to sustain practices,[20] and it will lend support to the view that the only way to reform a society is to transform its members, overlooking that it may be society itself and its institutions that need transforming. Even while valuing community, moral individualists overlook the importance of society in constituting preferences, so that transforming the structures of society may be the only way in which individuals can be transformed. Institutions can be even more oppressive and corrupt than individuals, and moral individualism ob-

---

[20] The role of institutions in sustaining practices is an extremely important topic I cannot develop here. The hard issue is that institutions, by their nature, cannot escape encouraging desirable behavior by distributing such external goods as salary and promotion. The problem is whether they can do this and also sustain activities where internal goods are primary, i.e., sustain practices. The issue is prominent in education, for education itself is a practice, but one which cannot exist without educational institutions. The latter cannot escape external goods – salaries, etc., for teachers, and the external rewards of education for students – but they ought to deal with them in such a way as not to undermine the goods internal to the practice of education.

scures that, even while it may lend support to institutions which, in fitting the individualistic ideal, are peculiarly oppressive.

Let's now consider moral individualism about rights and duties. Our main concern will be the way moral individualists develop the principle of equal liberty that individuals should have maximum liberty to pursue their own conception of the good, provided this is consistent with the right of everyone else to do the same. Liberalism understands social justice as requiring that a society embody this principle, and it takes the right to equal liberty to be our basic right. That in turn grounds our basic moral duty: we must not do anything which violates the right to equal liberty, and we must further what is required to safeguard it for all.

What is distinctive about moral individualism is that it develops the principle of equal liberty in terms of a conception of rights and duties based on two corollaries of philosophical individualism. The first is that individuals are the only irreducible subjects of rights and duties. To say a society has rights or duties means that its members do. To say we have duties to a society means we have duties toward its members; to say we have rights over against a society means that we have rights over against its members. The second is that basic rights and duties belong to individuals as 'abstract individuals', independent of membership in any social groups. Basic rights must be universally respected just because individuals have them apart from any social groups. They are rights individuals bring to society and which every society must respect.[21]

With this as background, let us consider some of the theories moral individualists have developed to explain the role the principle of equal liberty should play in a just society. Three have been prominent: *Classical utilitarianism*, *Libertarianism*, and *Social contract individualism*. *Classical utilitarianism*[22] conceives equal liberty as requiring that no individual's preferences should count more than anyone else's, and this it construes as meaning that it must not matter *whose* preferences are at stake. If the fact that it is *my* preferences is given any positive weight, then I am being treated as morally superior to others, and that violates the principle of equal liberty. What should count is only 'the great-

---

21 This conception of rights is clearly just the moral side of the doctrine of the abstract individual. Cf. Turgot: "The citizens have rights, rights that are sacred for the very body of society; the citizens exist independently of society; they form its necessary elements; and they only enter it in order to put themselves, with all their rights, under the protection of those very laws to which they sacrifice their liberty." (Lukes 1978, p. 77)

22 This is rather different from what *Habits of the Heart* calls "utilitarian individualism", which sees society in terms of its utility for egoistic individuals. Classical utilitarianism is quite the opposite of egoism.

est good for the greatest number', so that if satisfying my preferences frustrates other preferences and results in fewer preferences being satisfied overall, then my preferences should be over-ridden, and I should not be allowed to satisfy them.

Utilitarianism is clearly not egoist because if I am an egoist, what matters is my own preferences for my own well-being, whereas on this view the fact that it is my preferences must not matter at all. Indeed, utilitarianism implies that my preferences should not be satisfied if that will increase the overall satisfaction of preferences in a society. In this sense, it has a very strong notion of the common good, for a society is to be judged only in terms of the common pool of satisfied preferences, regardless of whose they are. It has been argued, therefore, that utilitarianism makes room for a notion of the common good often lacking in individualist theories.

However, many criticize the utilitarian notion of a common good because it requires an individual's preferences to be over-ridden, even if they touch on matters of the greatest importance, if doing so will further the common good. Even curtailing the liberty of some individuals or doing evil of other kinds may be justified on these grounds. These critics hold that the utilitarian understanding of equal liberty is defective, for to disregard preferences of the greatest importance to some individuals in the interests of the common good, that is, in the interests of maximizing the satisfaction of the many, is to treat some individuals merely as means to the common good, which violates their dignity as individuals.

Utilitarianism's understanding of the common good is individualistic, for the common good is just the sum of individual goods. But this criticism implies that its conception of rights violates a basic individualist claim, namely, liberalism's construal of dignity and moral equality as equal liberty. For its contention that what the majority perceives as the common good may over-ride the right to liberty of the minority is inconsistent with the right of all persons to equal liberty to realize their own conception of the good.

The other two prominent theories developed by moral individualists attempt to avoid this criticism. *Libertarianism* is the view that the only legitimate role of a society is to ensure that all its members have liberty to pursue their preferences no matter what they are, subject to the right of everyone else to the same liberty. While this may seem merely an affirmation of liberalism, libertarians in fact construe liberalism in a very special way in that they abstract completely from differences in the abilities of individuals to satisfy their preferences. Some persons are better able than others to get what they want, because they are stronger, brighter, richer, or have a more privileged social position. Libertarians argue that such differences do not affect the equal liberty of individuals to *pursue* their conceptions of the good, and while they may affect their chances of actually *satisfying* them, that, they argue, is irrelevant, for equal liberty does not require any kind of equality of satisfaction. On this view, society should be a kind of referee, ensuring that individuals do not interfere with the liberty of other individuals to pursue their preferences. If society does more, if it tries to ensure that there is some kind of genuine equality of opportunity for individuals to satisfy their preferences, then it inevitably restricts liberty unequally.

Libertarianism is a radically individualistic theory of society, the kind sometimes called 'rugged individualism', which is especially wary of social interference with economic liberties. It is consistent with egoism, for egoists have as much right to pursue their preferences as anyone else, but it is also consistent with altruism about the good. It holds that rights belong solely to individuals and it pushes to the extreme the doctrine that they belong to them in abstraction from any social context. The fact that some individuals are in a better position to satisfy their preferences because they inherited wealth, social privilege, or socially approved talents is to be disregarded, for it means taking into account the social context in which individuals exercise their capacities and satisfy their preferences. All that is to count is that individuals not be hindered in exercising the right to liberty they have just as human beings, regardless of what liberty amounts to in an actual social context. For libertarians, it is the abstract individual alone which matters.

By *social contract individualism*, I mean a theory which thinks of our relation to society as analogous to a contract made among individuals for their mutual benefit. All individuals have the right to maximum liberty in pursuing their preferences, but because of differences in the ability of individuals to realize them, differences which are not their responsibility but due to accidents of birth, social position, or fate, some individuals are able to satisfy many preferences, others few. If this is not taken account of, those favored by the accidents of birth, social position, or fate will have much at the expense of those not so favored. There will be, moreover, uncontrollable and unforeseeable shifts in who are favored and who are not. It is, therefore, to everyone's long-term benefit no matter what their preferences – to contract with other individuals to form a society and give up to it certain rights in the interests of a more secure life.

The contract need not be actual; society can be thought of *as if* it were the result of a contract made among its members for their mutual benefit. In order to insure a fair contract, one to which all members of a society may be understood to have agreed, its terms must have been drawn up fairly. Individuals must be understood to have agreed to it when they were equal in power and liberty, and they must not favor such things as their own gender, race, or social position and, especially, their own conception of the good. These conditions for fair agreement insure that the contract will be fair to all individuals, regardless of their gender, race, social position or conception of the good, thus insuring that a society based on it embodies the principle of equal liberty.

Social contract individualism holds that a society based upon such a hypothetical contract will ensure not only the equal right of all individuals to pursue their preferences, but will also ensure that persons have genuine equality of opportunity to realize them, no matter what their natural abilities, their social position, or other factors for which they are not responsible. It will differ from libertarianism, therefore, in granting to society the right to arrange things so that those less fortunate are given resources others are not in order to insure genuinely equal opportunity for all to satisfy their preferences. Were those more fortunate to have a greater chance to realize their conceptions of the good than those less fortunate, the society would be unjust in not adequately embodying the principle of equal liberty.

Social contract individualism is a version of moral individualism because the parties to the contract are individuals concerned to protect and further only their own individual preferences. Moreover, these preferences must be intelligible independent of any society because the idea is to form a society which will do a better job at furthering everyone's preferences than any alternative, which implies that the preferences are there to be tested in terms of alternative forms of society. The preferences need not be egoist, however, nor need they be preferences for a life apart from community. The parties to the contract may be concerned to protect their preferences for such things as a self-sacrificing life devoted to religious principles or a thoroughly communal life. The idea of social contract individualism is that a just society should allow equal opportunity to satisfy *any* conception of the good life.

Although social contract individualism seems to me more acceptable than either utilitarianism or libertarianism, there remain valid communitarian objections to the version I have sketched.[23] Communitarians will object to its assumption that the parties to the contract must have their basic preferences prior to their participation in society. This is the notion of the abstract individual again, the individual whose interests, desires, values, and preferences are independent of any society and hence are not socially constituted. Even if individuals contract to protect their preference for a communal life, this is not a community in the constitutive sense; it is a community one joins to further preferences one already has. The theory is not, therefore, genuinely neutral with respect to con-

---

[23] It may be that a social contract theory does not have to take this individualistic form. Rawls thinks his does not, though it's not clear whether he thinks he can avoid the individualistic assumptions and still have social contract theory as a comprehensive moral theory, as opposed to a political conception such as I sketch in the next section. Cf. Rawls 1985, pp. 238 ff.

ceptions of the good, for in spite of the diversity of conceptions of the good allowed, they are all individualistic conceptions. The theory is strongly biased against communitarian conceptions of the good.

In my view, all three of these theories of society developed by moral individualists who face a serious difficulty. They are correct in their commitment to the individualist belief in human dignity and to liberalism's construal of this as requiring that a just society embody the principle of equal liberty for realizing conceptions of the good. The difficulty is that none of them takes adequate account of conceptions of the good which are not individualistic: they do not, in spite of their intentions, carry through adequately on the principle of equal liberty because they are so strongly wedded to individualist conceptions of the good. A society whose culture embodies them will be more and more strongly dominated by individualistic conceptions of the good, and communitarian conceptions will have only a marginal place. There may be equal liberty for diverse individualistic conceptions of the good, but there will not be equal liberty for communitarian conceptions, and the result will be the social malaise critics trace to the malevolent influence of individualism.

This has led some to argue that we should give up liberalism and not require that a society embody the principle of equal liberty for conceptions of the good. MacIntyre for example, suggests that we return to pre-modern conceptions of the political community, which regard it as "one of the tasks of government to make its citizens virtuous, just as it is one of the tasks of parental authority to make children grow up so as to be virtuous adults" (MacIntyre 1981, p. 182).[24] Such a view would embed one conception of the good in the culture and institutions of a society, with other conceptions being officially excluded or systematically discouraged. It would abandon the liberal claim that dignity requires that individuals have equal liberty to pursue their own conceptions of the good life.

Such a view strikes me as simply nostalgic; it fails to recognize the diversity of conceptions of the good which is such a striking fact of the modern world. The western world has had, at least since the Reformation, a range of religious, moral and philosophical beliefs and commitments, which are deeply held and which affect many areas of people's lives; to think in terms of a dominant conception of the good life would require ignoring or suppressing such important differences in belief and commitment. Modern societies are marked as well by the coming together of peoples from diverse cultures. This is especially striking in the United States, most of whose citizens are immigrants or descendants of

---

[24] At the same time, he holds that "The modern state is indeed totally unfitted to act as moral educator of any community."

immigrants from widely differing backgrounds and who bring often strikingly different conceptions of how to live their lives. While the United States may be becoming less pluralistic in this sense, this is something to be regretted rather than applauded (if for no other reason than by appeal of individuality). The idea of a society built around a dominant conception of the good may seem more feasible for societies less pluralistic than the United States, but most such societies have minorities who do not share the dominant culture, and the burden borne by minorities in these homogeneous societies is very high.

To give up liberalism's central claim about equal liberty is to give up too much. Fortunately, such a desperate move is not necessary; liberalism can be defended as a political conception without commitment to moral individualism.

12.5 Liberalism as a Political Conception

Liberalism as a political conception – sometimes 'political liberalism'[25] – is a conception of what is required if a society is to be a reasonably just society. It holds that a society meets the demands of justice only if its main social, economic, and political institutions conform to the principle of equal liberty. It is a morally based conception in that it rests on belief in human dignity and liberalism's construal of this as equal liberty. But it is not a comprehensive moral theory. It is concerned with the institutional structure of a just society, not with what is required to live a happy, meaningful, or worthwhile life. For its fundamental claim is that the main institutions of a just society must be such that all individuals have equal liberty to live out their own concept of the good life.

It is left an open question whether any society which does not embody the principle of equal liberty could be a just society. What is claimed is that in a modern society, where conflicting and competing conceptions of the good life are the rule and not the exception, a just society must embody the principle. Where diverse conceptions of the good are deeply held, a society which favors some conceptions over others fails to respect equally the dignity of all its members. It is also left an open question whether diversity in conceptions of the good is desirable. Political liberalism does not rest on the ideal of individuality, nor does it rule out the belief that there is one and only one adequate or best conception of the good life. It does not, therefore, assume relativism about the good or skep-

---

[25] I realize the danger of such a term in the American political context, where the term 'liberal' often means something quite different. My use of the term is historically justified, and I do not know of a better one. For a good discussion of the term, cf. Dworkin 1977.

ticism about the good life. What it assumes is simply that individuals do in fact have diverse conceptions of the good and the good life. Conceptions of the good are to be respected not because they are right, or because no one knows whether they are right, or because it is unimportant whether they are right, but because the principle of equal liberty implies that it is morally wrong not to respect them all equally, whether they are right or wrong.

Political liberalism also recognizes, whether or not it regrets, the presence of other kinds of diversity in the modern world. In particular, it recognizes that there are in philosophy, in theology, in the intellectual and cultural world in general, differing views about the moral life, the nature of the self, the relation of the self to society, and so on. It admits that these differences are unlikely to disappear by themselves, and it regards them as too important to be settled by any merely political resolution, so that a workable political conception of society has to take them for granted. Nor can it wait for some other kind of resolution, for a morally acceptable resolution would be possible only in a society which already embodied the principle of equal liberty.

This means that an adequate conception of social justice should be compatible with differing views about such matters as the moral life, the nature of the self, or the structure of society. It should not require adherence to some specific view about these disputed matters. Political liberalism claims to be such a conception, for it claims to be consistent with a wide variety of such views. The principle that there should be equal liberty for diverse views not only requires equal liberty for the adherents of such views, it is itself a principle that adherents of diverse views can support.[26]

Although I contend that political liberalism can be affirmed from within many points of view, I shall defend this contention only for moral individualism and for the sort of communitarianism sketched in section 12.4. That it holds for moral individualism is clear, for that point of view explicitly affirms political liberalism. While I have argued that moral individualists, because of their exclusive concern with individualistic conceptions of the good, do not give an adequate role to the principle of equal liberty in their conceptions of society, that does not mean that they do not affirm political liberalism. They do affirm it, and that affirmation remains even if the critics are right that their theories of society do not do justice to the principle of equal liberty.

---

[26] Cf. Rawls: "We conjecture that these ideas [about justice in political liberalism] are likely to be affirmed by each of the opposing comprehensive moral doctrines influential in a reasonably just democratic society. Each comprehensive doctrine, from within its own point of view, is led to accept the public reasons of justice specified by justice as fairness." (Rawls 1985, p. 246)

As to communitarianism, there are two issues. The first is whether the communitarian conception of the good is opposed to political liberalism. Communitarians see the good as rooted in the structures of society and not (only) in the preferences of individuals. Some have argued, therefore, that a society ought to favor those conceptions of the good (perhaps only one) whose embodiment in the culture of the society seems necessary for its long term stability and excellence. Others have argued that in a society based on the principle of equal liberty, the conception of the good favored by, or in the interests of, those most powerful will become more and more dominant. Since, it is argued, individualistic conceptions of the good are favored by, because they are in the interests of, the most powerful, adherence to the principle of equal liberty would necessarily marginalize all communitarian conceptions of the good.[27]

These points show that communitarians may have reasons to oppose political liberalism that moral individualists do not; they do not show that communitarians ought to oppose it. From a theoretical point of view, communitarians can surely affirm political liberalism even if their view does not entail the principle of equal liberty. All that is required is that the two be consistent, which they are. For although communitarianism entails that communitarian conceptions of the good must not be disadvantaged, it does not entail that individuals should not have equal liberty to pursue their own conceptions of the good life. While it is true that many of the prominent theories of how society should embody the principle of equal liberty rest on individualistic theories of the good, this need not be the case: a properly conceived political conception of liberalism need not rest on *any* conception of the good, individualistic or communitarian.

From a practical point of view, the diversity in modern societies of conceptions of the good and of views about the self and society leaves, I have argued, no alternative to political liberalism. The important thing is that political liberalism must also be practiced in a society, that is, that its institutional structures do not in practice favor some conceptions of the good over others. Many so-called liberal societies have been dominated by individualistic conceptions of the good, and they have not, therefore, always been fair in practice to communitarian conceptions. They have, for example, often been elitist: those who govern the society have tried to impose their own 'advanced' ideals – ideals of individuality, for example – on traditional communities or on marginalized groups, in misdirected efforts to 'modernize' a society. But that does not undermine the claim that lib-

---

[27] The objection which appeals to the long-term stability of society is made by conservatives, the objection which appeals to the interests of the powerful is made by Marxists. Both think that communitarian conceptions of the good rule out political liberalism.

eral societies cannot be fair to communitarian conceptions. Indeed, the principle of equal liberty itself may require that communitarian conceptions receive special attention and concern in societies dominated by individualism.

It may be true that power determines which conceptions of the good are dominant, and that individualistic conceptions of the good are favored by those in power in liberal societies because such conceptions are in the interests of the powerful. Marxists who oppose political liberalism argue that this is true for all liberal societies, which they think are and must be capitalist societies, whose ruling classes benefit from individualistic conceptions of the good. But political liberalism does not require capitalism. Moreover, to the extent to which this point about power is true, it will be equally true for societies which do not embody political liberalism, and a liberal society has the incomparable advantage that its members have the right to alter its structures in order to put into practice the principle of equal liberty for all conceptions of the good.

The second issue about communitarianism concerns its conception of rights and duties, and I can only make some suggestions about this very complex issue. Two approaches suggest themselves. One is to argue that a communitarian conception of the good is compatible with an individualist theory of rights and duties. The latter makes (as we saw in section 12.4) two claims. First, that social rights and duties are reducible to the rights and duties of individuals. Second, that the basic rights and duties which individuals have, they have *as* human beings (as abstract individuals), not *as* members of any society; basic rights and duties are not socially constituted.

The advantage of such a view is that the right to have one's conception of the good respected equally holds for all societies, since one had the right just *as* a human being. Since its status is independent of whatever society one belongs to, no society is morally permitted to violate it. The problem with such a mixed view, however, is that it would require that goods, but not the right to equal liberty, be socially constituted, and the coherence of such a view is problematic.

The other approach involves a conception of rights and duties which is itself communitarian and rooted in a social realist understanding of individuals and society. A communitarian conception of the right to equal liberty would hold, on the one hand, that individuals have the right regardless of their status in any particular society and, on the other hand, that the capacity for liberty on which it is based is socially constituted. The former calls for a notion of a right human beings have regardless of the particular society to which they belong; the latter requires that the right be based on a capacity which is constituted only by participation in some particular society. The basic problem is to bring together the *universality* implicit in the idea that human beings have the right in all societies with the *particularity* implicit in the idea that only individuals constituted by their participation in a particular society have the capacity for liberty which underlies the right. There are a couple of ways in which this problem, one in need of considerably more work, might be approached.

The first is to argue that there are ways of treating individuals which every society, as a matter of fact, regards as unjust and that all these modes of unjust treatment exemplify in their own distinctive way a disregard for equal liberty. The right to equal liberty is a universal right, then, simply because it is in fact respected in every particular society, with each society respecting it in its own way and for its own reasons, no general account being possible as to why the right is respected in every society.

The difficulty with this way of socially grounding the right to equal liberty is that there is no recourse against a corrupt society which did not respect it, even though it was respected everywhere else. The fact that one society did not respect it would, on this view, be sufficient to show that it is not a universal human right. To argue that it is irrelevant that a corrupt society does not recognize a right would, of course, simply be to give up this view, since if its corruption consists in its not recognizing a right, we are no longer conceiving the notion of human rights simply as rights recognized in all societies.[28]

Another way is to argue that the capacity for liberty which underlies the right to equal liberty is a capacity necessary for *membership* in any society capable of constituting individuals as human individuals. This capacity is universal in the sense that it is required for participation in *any* human society; but it is a capacity which can be developed only in a particular society and hence the form it takes will vary from society to society. Individuals are entitled to respect insofar as they have this capacity: they have the right in any society to what is required for the nurturing of the capacity for liberty without which they cannot participate in any society. The capacity is social both in that it is a capacity for social participation and in that only social participation can develop it. Working

---

28 There is more to be said for this view, but it would take me too far afield to deal with it further. Peter Berger (1977) takes this view in an interesting paper, which distinguishes between rights recognized only in the modern west and those recognized everywhere. In the former are "civil liberties and civil rights"; in the latter are protection against genocide, deliberate starvation, desecration of religious symbols, the destruction of institutions which embody ethnic identity. Berger suggests that the latter are necessarily a diverse lot not reducible to some basic right. At the same time, he speaks with approval of the "fundamental equality of all human beings", and I would argue that this basic right underlies his diverse list.

12.5 Liberalism as a Political Conception — 275

this out would give us a communitarian conception of the right to liberty which was based on a social realist account of individuals.[29]

One way of working this out would be to emphasize that individuals belong to communities which do not encompass the whole of a society. It is in such communities that their capacity for liberty (and all that goes with that) is nurtured, so that their basic rights stem from participation in such communities, not from their abstract essence as human. The whole society, and especially its political institutions, i.e., the apparatus of the state, would not only be morally forbidden to undermine these communities but would be obliged to foster them and to allow individuals liberty to participate in them. These communities would be a buffer between the individual and the state. At the same time, the state would ensure that the communities do not abuse their position by oppressive behavior toward their members. But, again, the appeal would not be any concept of the abstract human individual; it would rather be to the idea that it is not necessary that individuals be members of any *particular* community, and therefore, not necessary that they be subject to the sanctions of any particular community, something which the state would insure. On this view, all rights are socially based, but they are not anchored exclusively in any particular community but in what is required for participation in some community or other.[30]

This is sketchy, but fortunately a defense of political liberalism does not require working it out. All that is required is that political liberalism be consistent with a communitarian conception of rights and duties, and this sketch is sufficient to show that it is. Political liberalism does not depend on resolving such difficult and controversial issues since it is designed precisely for societies in which such controversies exist. We can, therefore, affirm the principle of equal liberty without commitment to the more dubious claims of individualism, for

---

[29] Cf. Taylor: "Social views see some form of society as essentially bound up with human dignity, since outside of society the very potentiality to realize that wherein this dignity consists is undermined ... For the social view, there is a parallel to the notion of inalienable rights: types of relationships that men should be able to enter into and remain in, and which cannot be normatively over-ridden by other considerations." (Taylor 1985, pp. 292 and 296) Also Rawls: "To view citizens as free and equal persons ... is to regard them as having the requisite powers of moral personality that enables them to participate in society viewed as a system of fair cooperation for mutual advantage." (Rawls 1985, p. 277) Individuals who do not have the capacity for liberty because of severe mental handicaps would not thereby be devoid of rights; but they would not have the right to equal liberty which is the possession only of those capable of full participation in society.

[30] Durkheim suggests a view like this with the role he assigns to 'corporations' or occupational associations as mediating between the state and the individual. Cf. Giddens 1972, pp. 16 ff. Walzer's (1983) *Spheres of Justice* is also analogous.

a conception of society can be based on the principle without commitment either to moral or philosophical individualism. That each individual's conception of the good should be respected equally does not require a society committed to individualistic conceptions of the good. Indeed, the principle of equal liberty itself may require that a society show special concern for communitarian conceptions of the good and devote unequal resources to developing institutions which sustain them.

Many societies which have come to embed, to one degree or another, the principle of equal liberty in their social, economic, or political institutions have done so as the result of the influence of moral individualism. This had led to the development of institutional structures which favor individualistic conceptions of the good over communitarian ones. Such is the case with American society, which is biased in favor of individualistic conceptions of the good. In such a context the principle of equal liberty requires that communitarian conceptions receive special attention.[31]

That I take to be the central moral task that the authors of *Habits of the Heart* set for themselves, and the favorable reception of the book can be explained by a wide-spread feeling that this is a necessary task. Its concern is for "those cultural traditions and practices that, without destroying individuality, serve to limit and restrain the destructive side of individualism and provide alternative models for how Americans might live" (Bellah et al. 1985, p. vi). This should not be taken to mean that we must give up political liberalism, but rather that we should restore the conditions of equal liberty for communitarian conceptions of the good. If it is individualistic conceptions of the good that make this restoration necessary, it is only a society committed to individualist claims about human dignity and equal liberty and the political conception of liberalism which is its social expression that can make it possible.

---

31 Charles Taylor (1985, p. 316) writes that the real nature of the critique leveled by both Left and Right against our present society concerns as much if not more its failure to embody or allow for certain excellences of the good life, as it does for its alleged unfairness. I would argue that this is a failure of equal liberty with regard to certain important conceptions of the good life, which is a profound form of unfairness.

13 Interpreting Davidson's Philosophy of Action

Davidson's early papers on philosophy of action were immensely influential and no doubt largely responsible for there being a 'standard story': actions are those bodily movements caused and rationalized by beliefs and desires. It is not false to say that Davidson asserted that claim, but proponents of the standard story understand it somewhat differently than he did. His writings, I shall argue, spawned a widely accepted view that differs from his own in a number of respects.[1]

Wittgensteinian critics of the standard story generally assume that Davidson accepted it, as do its defenders, who invariably cite him as their inspiration and often credit him for rooting the story in physicalism. Jaegwon Kim, for instance, writes that Davidson's "main task has been that of finding for mind a place in an essentially physical world ... [in which] we find nothing but bits of matter and increasingly complex aggregates made up of bits of matter" (Kim 2003, p. 113).

But both critics and defenders overlook the substantial influence of Elizabeth Anscombe's work on Davidson – Anscombe's *Intention* being characterized by Davidson as "the most important treatment of action since Aristotle" (Anscombe 2000, cover).[2] Although usually viewed as having replaced an account like Anscombe's with the standard story, Davidson rather thought that such an account was consistent with a causal account of action. He also thought that the latter was consistent with significant claims of other philosophers influenced by Wittgenstein – von Wright, for example, or Kenny, Melden, and Hampshire – whom he read and learned from, as he did from Wittgenstein himself, noting "those long hours I spent years ago admiring and puzzling over the *Investigations*" (Davidson 1999, p. 268). He was critical of their work, and in the last analysis his view was quite distinct from theirs, but an adequate interpretation of his philosophy of action must nevertheless see it against the background of all these philosophers.

The most consequential misunderstanding of Davidson's account of action rests on missing the import of his distinction between causal *relations* and causal *explanations*. His well-known claim that to differentiate an agent's acting *because* of a reason from her merely *having* a reason requires a causal 'because', is often misunderstood since merely asserting that reasons cause actions blurs that distinction. Causal relations hold *only* between *events* (hence Davidson

---

[1] For the 'standard story', see Smith 2004, p. 165. I long regarded Davidson as holding a version of the standard story, a mistake I want to correct here.
[2] From the cover of the 2000 Harvard edition of her *Intention* (Anscombe 2000). My citations refer to the original edition (Anscombe 1957).

called this "event causation"), and they obtain no matter how the events are described, so that sentences ascribing them are *extensional*. Ascriptions of causal relations need not, therefore, *explain* phenomena: saying truly that what Karl referred to last night was the event-cause of what happened to Linda a year ago does not explain the phenomena.

Although event causation holds only between particulars, Davidson thought it involves generality, hence his thesis of the "Nomological Character of Causality": if events are causally related, there must be a *strict law* instantiated by true descriptions of the events.[3] We need not know those descriptions, but since laws are strict only if the events described belong to a *closed system* (one such that whatever can affect the system is part of the system being described), and since, Davidson held, only physics describes a closed system, all strict laws belong to (a completed) physics.[4] Because Davidson held that events are physical if they have a physical description, he also held that all causally related events are physical.

It does not follow that event causation does not involve mental events: since events are mental if they have a mental description, and since events are causally related no matter how described, mental events can be causally related to either physical or to mental events.[5] What does follow is that *reasons* are not causally related to actions since the beliefs and desires Davidson took to be reasons are not events. "'Primary reasons' ... are certainly not events ... Beliefs and desires are not changes. They are states, and since I don't think that states are *entities* of any sort, and so are not events, I do not think beliefs and desires are events." (Davidson 1993b, p. 287)

When Davidson asserted that reasons cause actions, he meant they causally *explain* actions: his view was that *rational explanation is a kind of causal explanation*. An explanation does not relate events but sentences (propositions, facts) since to explain phenomena is always to explain them *as* such and such, that is,

---

[3] "Where there is causality, there must be a law: events related as cause and effect fall under strict deterministic laws." (Davidson 2001a, p. 208)

[4] A strict law is "something one [can] at best hope to find in a developed physics: a generalization that [is] not only 'law-like' and true, but [is] as deterministic as nature can be found to be, [is] free from caveats and *ceteris paribus* clauses; that [can], therefore, be viewed as treating the universe as a closed system" (Davidson 2005a, p. 190).

[5] Cf. Davidson 2005a, p. 191: "The efficacy of an event cannot depend on how the event is described, while whether an event can be called mental, or can be said to fall under a law, depends entirely on how the event can be described." The main source for this is Davidson's "Mental Events", in Davidson, *Essays on Actions and Events* (2001a), pp. 207–224. An extremely helpful supplement is the piece he wrote about his own work (Davidson 1994c).

under a description (so that explanation sentences are *intensional*).[6] The point of an explanation is to render phenomena intelligible, and what does so under one description of the phenomena may not do so under another. Moreover, the same phenomenon may have different kinds of explanation, each explaining it under a different description.[7]

Not all explanation is causal; to be *causal* an explanation should, according to Davidson, meet three conditions.[8] First, its *explanandum* should describe either an event or a state whose existence entails an event. if the *explanandum* is that the bridge is slippery (a state), it follows that it became slippery, which is an event.

Second, its *explanans* should either describe an event *causally related* to the *explanandum* or entail that there is an *associated* event[9] so causally related. That is, if A causally explains B, A either describes an event causally related to B or has associated with it an event that is so causally related. What 'associated with' denotes will vary. The description of A may entail a description of the associated event: for example, if the car skids because the road is icy (a state), the associated event is the car's contacting the ice. Or there may be a generalization connecting A with the associated event: if the slippery road explains the car accident, the associated event is the car's skidding. Or the associated event may occur without anyone knowing what it is.

Third, the explanation depends on an empirical generalization that connects a description of the cause with a description of the effect but which is a rough generalization and not a strict law. Davidson held that causal explanations must involve generality but do not cite strict laws since their point is to explain phenomena when we do not know, or because there cannot be, strict laws covering the phenomena. Since Davidson often called these strict laws "causal laws", he said that the causal *concepts* involved in a causal explanation do not figure in causal *laws*. "It is causal *relations*, not [causal] concepts that imply the existence of [strict] laws ... Causal *concepts* don't sit well with strict causal laws because

---

[6] "Explanation, like giving reasons, is geared to sentences or propositions rather than directly to what sentences are about." (Davidson 2001a, p. 171)
[7] Strawson has an excellent discussion of this point, writing, for instance: "Causality is a natural relation that holds in the world between particular events or circumstances, just as the relation of temporal succession does or that of spatial proximity ... But if causality is a relation which holds in the natural world, explanation is a different matter ... It is an intellectual or rational or intensional relation and does not hold between things in the natural world ... [but] between facts or truths." (Strawson 1985)
[8] Although Davidson does not put it in this way, what follows is an accurate summary of his view. I discuss this matter in more detail in Stoutland 1999b.
[9] The term is Davidson's; cf., Davidson 2001a, p. 12.

they enable us to evade providing strict laws." (Davidson 1993a, p. 312) While physics has lots of causal *laws*, "it is a sign of progress in a science that it rids itself of causal concepts" (Davidson 2004, p. 96).

Davidson held that *rational* explanations meet these conditions. They meet the first because their *explananda* describe actions, which are events. They meet the second because, although an agent's reasons for action are states and not events, the *explanans* of a rational explanation (like that of causal explanations generally) entails that there is an event *associated with* the reason that is causally *related* to the action. Sometimes the reason *entails* the associated event: if Mark bought a book because he believed it important for his work, the associated event is his coming to believe that. Sometimes the context determines the event: if I wave to you because you are my neighbor, the event is my recognizing you across the street. Or we may not know what the event is but there is, nevertheless, an event that causes the action at a particular time and place.

They meet the third condition because desires are dispositional states, and hence ascribing a desire to an agent entails a rough generalization connecting the desire with a description of her action.

> A want is, or entails, a certain disposition to act to obtain what one wants. That someone has a certain disposition may be expressed as a generalization or law governing the behavior of that person ... [It means] we can say of someone who has a desire or end that he will tend to behave in certain ways under specified circumstances. (Davidson 2001a, p. 263)[10]

These generalizations are law-like because they support claims about what someone *would* do *were* he to have those desires, but they are not strict laws since they require *ceteris paribus* conditions.

They are empirical but in the special sense of being implicit in the concept of desire: to know someone's desire is *thereby* to know a rough generalization about what she would tend to do given certain conditions. What is empirical is whether someone has a certain desire; if she does, her action will necessarily (*ceteris paribus*) exemplify a rough generalization.[11] The latter is very low level,

---

10 See also Davidson 2004, p. 108: "If a person is constituted in such a way that, if he believes that by acting in a certain way he will crush a snail then he has a tendency to act in that way, then in this respect he differs from most other people, and this difference will help explain why he acts as he does. The special fact about how he is constituted is one of his causal powers, a disposition to act under specified conditions in specific ways. Such a disposition is what I mean by a pro-attitude."

11 This is like Anscombe's point that "The primitive sign of wanting [rather than wishing or hoping] is trying to get." (Anscombe 1957, p. 68)

however, since what someone with a given desire would tend to do depends on her belief about how to fulfill it, and the generalization applies only to someone who has the relevant belief. "The laws implicit in reason explanations are simply the generalizations implied by attributions of dispositions. But then the 'laws' are peculiar to individuals at particular moments." (Davidson 2001a, p. 265)[12]

Although such low-grade generalizations yield little explanatory force, Davidson insisted that "the main *empirical* thrust of ... a reason explanation [comes from] the attributions of desires, preferences, or beliefs" (Davidson 2001a, p. 265), and he refused to give these generalizations a more significant role by extending their scope to what *all* agents would do under certain conditions. Any list of such conditions that made a generalization about what all agents would do plausible, would also make the generalization non-empirical. It cannot be empirical, for example, that *anyone* who has a desire for fresh air and believes opening the window will provide it, opens the window, provided he meets a list of conditions. If someone appeared to have the desire and belief and to meet the conditions but had no tendency to open the window, we would conclude, not that the generalization was false, but that we were mistaken about his attitudes, about our list, or about whether he met the conditions. We must not look to empirical generalizations to understand the force of rational explanations.

If we take seriously the distinction between causal relations and causal explanations, Davidson's claim that reasons cause actions looks different than often supposed. It does not mean that reasons are event-causes, but that they are states whose contents causally *explain* actions, a claim Davidson defended against two criticisms. The first appealed to Hume's thesis that causal explanations require general laws, the criticism being that since there are no general laws covering reasons and actions (no laws connecting content descriptions of reasons with descriptions of actions as intentional), reasons cannot causally explain actions. Von Wright accepted that criticism because he accepted Hume's thesis, but since Davidson rejected the thesis, he could claim that rational explanations are causal (in a non-Humean sense) even if there are no general laws connecting reasons and actions. Davidson and von Wright agreed, therefore, that rational explanations required no covering laws, but disagreed on what it is for an explanation to be causal.[13]

---

12 See also p. 274: "The laws that are implicit in reason explanation seem to me to concern only individuals – they are the generalizations embedded in attributions of attitudes, beliefs and traits."
13 Von Wright also thought that rational explanations were causal in some non-Humean sense: "Those who think that actions have causes often use 'cause' in a much broader sense than I do

The second criticism (also credited to Hume, who asserted that cause and effect are distinct existences) was that conceptual connections exclude causal connections, and hence the conceptual connections between reasons and actions entail that reasons do not causally explain actions. Davidson recognized such connections, but rejected the criticism by appealing to the distinction between causal relations and causal explanations. The claim that cause and effect are distinct existences applies only to *events* and hence only to causal *relations* between events. *Conceptual* connections hold, not between events, but between sentences (propositions) or descriptions and hence are relevant only to causal *explanations*. The claim that causes and effects cannot be conceptually connected is, therefore, either nonsense or false. It is nonsense to speak of *events* as conceptually connected, while it is false to claim that *descriptions* of events (even if causes and effects) cannot be conceptually connected. It is a conceptual truth, for instance, that the cause of E causes E, but the connection between the *descriptions* 'the cause of E' and 'E' is distinct from the causal relation between the *events* described. Whether descriptions are conceptually connected is independent of whether the events described are causally related.

Davidson saw conceptual connections between reasons and actions as crucial to rational explanation. He wrote, for instance, that "There is a conceptual connection between pro attitudes and actions ... When we explain an action, by giving the reason, we do redescribe the action; redescribing the action gives the action a place in a pattern, and in this way the action is explained." (Davidson 2001a, p. 10) Indeed, he held that there is no principled distinction between what *constitutes* action and what *explains* it.

> Explanation is built into the concepts of action, belief, and desire ... We already know, from the description of the action, that it must have been caused by such a belief-desire pair, and we know that such an action is just what such a belief-desire pair is suited to cause ... Beliefs and desires explain actions only when they are described in such a way as to reveal their suitability for causing the action ... [They] explain an action only if [their] contents ... entail that there is something desirable about the action, given the description under which the action is being explained. (Davidson 2004, pp. 108, 115)[14]

---

when I deny this. Or they may understand 'action' differently. It may very well be, then, that 'actions' in their sense have 'causes' in theirs." (von Wright 1971, p. viii)

14 This view is superficially similar to Anscombe's claim that "What distinguishes actions which are intentional from those which are not ... is that they are actions to which a certain sense of the question 'why?' is given application; the sense is of course that in which the answer, if positive gives a reason for action." (Anscombe 1957, p. 9) The difference is that whereas Davidson defined an intentional action as one explained in terms of the agent's reason for acting, Anscombe did not require that the action be explained but only that the question 'why?' applies – is appropriate.

Why did Davidson hold that such explanation is *causal?* After all, explanation always aims at understanding phenomena – at rendering them intelligible – which can be achieved in different ways. One might re-describe the phenomena, specify their parts, spell out their function in a system, articulate the role they play in a narrative – or construct a causal explanation of them. Why count explanations that meet Davidson's three conditions as *causal?*

John McDowell claims that an explanation is causal "if the understanding it supplies is causal understanding", which rational explanations provide because they involve "responsiveness to reason [which] makes a difference to what happens – a causal difference" (McDowell 2006, pp. 139, 67). An explanation yields causal understanding if it describes the *explanans* in a way that makes it intelligible why the *explanandum* – as described – came, ceased, or continued to be. This allows for different kinds of causal explanation. On Davidson's view, rational explanations provide causal understanding in that they describe, redescribe, or interpret an agent's acting, not instead of, but as a way of explaining *why* she acted intentionally as she did. They specify the reasons that made a difference in what she did and as a result in what happened. They are, therefore, *causal* even though they cite no exceptionless general laws or identify a reason with the event that causes the action.

Davidson's account of rational explanation includes a condition central to the standard story that Wittgensteinian accounts omit, namely, that as causal it involves a causal *relation.* Although reasons are states and not events, Davidson thinks they explain actions only if there are associated events that cause the actions.

Most defenders of the standard story find no difficulty in this condition. They think the distinction between causal relations and explanations is irrelevant since beliefs and desires are easily construed as events, either by turning the nouns – 'beliefs' and 'desires' – into verbs – 'believing' and 'desiring' – or by speaking of *coming* to believe or desire, which are changes and hence events. In my view, both moves are objectionable.

The former changes labels but does not alter the status of beliefs and desires, which Davidson insisted are states and not events. It is, in any case, the *contents* of the attitudes that play the crucial role as reasons for action, and they are not event-causes.

Davidson himself suggested the latter move, but it is problematic. Whether a reason explains an action is independent of its coming to be. Furthermore, even if my coming to have a belief or desire is an event associated with my reason, it is seldom the reason for which I act. If I buy a book because it is important for my work, my reason for buying it is not my coming to believe that but the content of the belief I have come to have. In any case, Davidson did not require that the associated event be conceptually connected with the reason. For instance, the event-cause of an agent's waving at someone may be his recognizing her across the street, but his reason for waving is his desire to be friendly to his neighbor. Besides, since the event-cause of an action may, Davidson held, be unknown to the agent, it is evident that such an event does not increase the force of an explanatory reason.

Davidson insisted, nevertheless, that although reasons are not event-causes of actions,[15] there must be event-causes associated with explanatory reasons. He had, apparently, three reasons for this, which I, however, do not find persuasive.

The first is that a rational explanation should account for an agent's acting at a time and place, and hence there must be an event causing the action to occur at that time and place. This strikes me as weak: even if there is such an event, it is irrelevant to the many explanations that do not account for an agent acting at a particular time and place. Buying a book because I needed it for my work does not explain why I bought it when or where I did (for which there may be no *rational* explanation). If time and place *are* significant, they will be integral to the reason for the action: if I bought the book at Border's before 10 because of their short-term sale, then the time and place of my action is explained by my wanting to save money, not by an event that caused the action then and there.

The second is that Davidson thought the difference between an agent merely *having* a reason and her acting *because* of it is not in the content of the reason but is additional. My reason to buy a book is that I need it for my work. If I do not buy the book, I merely have that reason, but if I buy it because of it, then there is an associated event that causes my buying the book. The reason is the same in both cases, but in the second there is an event-cause in addition to the content.

Davidson, unlike defenders of the standard story, did not think this account *explains why* an agent acted because of some reason. Any explanation of that is not part of a rational explanation since the latter "provides no reason for saying that one suitable belief-desire pair rather than another (which may also have been present in the agent) did the causing" (Davidson 2004, p. 109), that is, was associated with an event that caused the action. Davidson elucidated

---

[15] Cf. Davidson 1993b p. 288: "Beliefs and desires are not changes. They are states, and since I don't think that states are *entities* of any sort, and so are not *events*, I do not think that beliefs and desires are events ... [There is] a broad popular use and a rather more limited use of the notion of cause ... The more limited use allows only events to be causes [and in this sense] *reasons are not causes.*"

what we *mean* by the assertion, "She acted because of reason R", but he gave no account of why she acted because of reason R rather than another reason.[16]

Davidson did not hold that *verifying* that an agent acted because of a certain reason requires verifying that an associated event caused the action (or that the associated event and the action have descriptions instantiated by a strict law). His view that what an agent did and her reason for doing it are conceptually connected means they cannot be verified independently. This sets up an interpretive circle, and there is no appeal except to interpretation in order to verify whether an agent acted *because* of a reason.[17] Having established a plausible interpretation of an agent's reasons and actions, we do not establish *in addition* that there was an associated event that caused her action, since (Davidson claimed) the interpretive conclusion that she acted because of a certain reason *entails* that there was an event associated with that reason that caused the action.

This meets one objection to Davidson's account but strengthens another since it implies that knowing there is an associated event comes *after* having established an explanation of the agent's action, which means the associated event is irrelevant to the force of the explanation. To claim that such an event is entailed is unobjectionable simply because "associated event" is so broad there can hardly fail to be one. If we are more specific, however, the idea looks implausible. Consider actions like driving to Chicago or writing a paper, each of which is *an* action done for a reason. We can speak here of *an* action only if we count a complex and disorderly cluster of events as *an* event that is an action, whose event-cause must also consist of such a cluster. We could get the appropriate cause and effect only by implausibly cutting and stretching the notion of event. To respond that this is a mere consequence of the requirement that there be such causes and effects simply undermines the requirement.

Davidson's third reason for his claim about associated events is that it yields a plausible account of the relation between rational and nomological explanation. Given that if an agent acts for a reason, there is an event that causes her action, and given Davidson's view of the nomological character of causality, it follows that there are physical descriptions of the event and of her action that instantiate a law of physics. This shows that rational explanations not only do not conflict with the laws of physics but are linked with them.

---

16 This is contrary to Mele, who offers this as the causal theory's view: "In virtue of what is it true that he mowed his lawn for this reason and not the other, if not that the reason (or his having it) and not the other, played a suitable causal role in his mowing his lawn." (Mele 2003b, p. 70)

17 Davidson did not hold that in order to know an agent's reasons and actions we must interpret or verify them. We may, for instance, know such things simply by observing an agent.

This is often construed as physicalism because it is thought that Davidson took events to be causes *in virtue of* having physical descriptions and hence concluded that all events that are causes or effects are physical rather than mental. Kim, for instance, argued that Davidson held that mental events as such are causally impotent since they have causal force only because they have physical descriptions, which "renders mental properties and kinds causally irrelevant ... [They are] causal idlers with no work to do" (Kim 1996, p. 138), which is epiphenomenalism about the mental. This assumes, however, that events are causes *because* they have physical descriptions that instantiate the laws of physics, a claim that Davidson rejected along with all its variants – that events are causes *in virtue of* their physical properties, *because* they fall under physical kinds, or *qua* being physical – as inconsistent with events being causes no matter how described, the latter entailing that "it makes no literal sense" (Davidson 2005a, p. 196) to speak of events as causing things because of, or in virtue of, anything.[18]

By the nomological character of causality, Davidson meant that A's causing B *entails* that there are physical descriptions of A and B that instantiate a law of physics. His defense of this was that events require *real* changes, which are not relative to how a situation is described, a point he illustrated by Goodman's discussion of predicates like green, grue, blue, and bleen. An object may 'change' from being grue to being bleen but that is not a real change, for the real color of the object stays the same. Descriptions of real changes involve projectible, lawlike predicates, and since causal relations obtain only between real changes, there are causal relations only where there are laws, which shows that "singular causal statements ... entail the existence of strict laws [of physics]" (Davidson 2005a, p. 219).

---

18 The misunderstanding is partly due to some ways Davidson formulated his Principle, for example, that "all causally related events instantiate the laws of physics" (Davidson 2005a, p. 194) or "If a singular causal claim is true, there is a law that backs it ..." (Davidson 2005a, p. 202). But he states his view clearly in this passage: "The efficacy of an event cannot depend on how the event is described, while whether an event can be called mental, or can be said to fall under a law, depends entirely on how the event can be described ... It is irrelevant to the causal efficacy of physical events that they can be described in the physical vocabulary. It is *events* that have the power to change things, not our various ways of describing them." (Davidson 1995, pp. 8, 12) Kim's response to this is to insist that if the causal relation obtains between pairs of events, it *must* be "because they are events of certain kinds, or have certain properties" (Kim 1993b, p. 22). But that makes Davidson an epiphenomenalist only if he first accepts Kim's (metaphysical) principle that causal relations must be explained by reference to properties of the events, which Davidson rejects.

That summary does not do justice to his paper,[19] which defended a subtle Kantian view, but I'm not persuaded that a causal relation between events entails a law of *physics* covering the events. He wrote that "The ground floor connection of causality with regularity is not made by experience, but is built into the idea of objects whose changes are causally tied to other changes ... Events are as much caught up in this highly general net of concepts as objects." (Vermazen and Hintikka 1985, p. 227) Accepting that obscure claim does not imply that whatever regularity causality involves entails laws of *physics* and hence physicalistic (not merely physical) predicates.[20]

In any case, arguing that there are causal relations only where there are strict laws, is quite different from *grounding* rational explanations in the laws of physics, and Davidson rejected the latter in denying that events are causes *because of* physical laws. His account of the role of event causation in rational explanation was not intended to develop or defend physicalism. It is, moreover, different from the standard story because the latter makes event causation central to explanation of action, whereas in Davidson's account it is, as I have argued, peripheral to causal explanation. I would disregard it,[21] which brings his account closer to Wittgensteinian ones, but even if it is kept, Davidson's view lends no support to claims like Hartrey Field's "that there is an important sense in which all facts depend on physical facts and all good causal explanations depend on good physical explanations" (Field 1992, p. 271).[22]

Unlike most defenders of the standard story, Davidson held that "there is an irreducible difference between psychological explanations that involve the propositional attitudes and explanations in sciences like physics and physiology" (Davidson 2004, p. 101). He accepted Collingwood's view that "the methodology of history (or, for that matter, any of the social sciences that treat individual human behavior) differs markedly from the methodology of the natural sciences" (Davidson 2005a, p. 282). The former belongs, as Sellers put it, to the logical

---

19 For an excellent discussion of the paper and wider issues, see Hahn 1999, pp. 601–618.
20 Davidson wrote (quoted in Hahn 1999, p. 610) that "Our concept of a *physical* object is the concept of an object whose changes are governed by law" (emphasis added).
21 John McDowell makes a similar criticism of Davidson, urging that we "drop the idea that for intentional items to belong to any causal nexus at all is for them to belong to 'the causal nexus that natural science investigates,' in a way that would need to be spelled out be redescribing them in non-intentional terms". McDowell also thinks that dropping this idea would undercut Davidson's monism because what underlies it is "the naturalistic picture of *the* causal nexus" (McDowell 2006, p. 69). My view is that while it does undercut physicalism, it does not undercut Davidson's weak monism, which is based on supervenience. I discuss this below.
22 Field simply assumes this as "beyond serious doubt".

space of reasons, the latter to the logical space of laws. Davidson noted three significant differences between these two kinds of explanation.

The fundamental one is the *normativity* of rational explanations, which has two dimensions.[23] One is that ascriptions to an agent of beliefs, desires, intentions, intentional actions and the like, must preserve the rationality (or intelligibility) of the agent and hence meet standards of consistency and correctness: there cannot *be* attitudes or intentional actions that do not meet such norms. The other is that rational explanations appeal to reasons for action, which are considerations that bear normatively on an agent's acting by showing it to be good in some sense. Both are lacking in the physical sciences, which "treat the world as mindless" (Davidson 2001b, p. 71), making it irrelevant whether the subject matter investigated meets normative standards. Phenomena treated as mindless do not occur because it would be good (or apparently good) if they did.

The second is that rational explanations can be verified only by *interpretive* inquiry that resembles interpreting a text. We want to understand a text in its own terms but we do not know what those terms are unless we already understand the text (the 'hermeneutical circle'). So with action: we want to explain an agent's actions in terms of her own standards of rationality or intelligibility – in terms of what she takes to be sufficient reasons to act – but we do not know what those standards are unless we already know what she is doing intentionally and hence her reasons for so acting. Assuming we *share* standards of rationality would be idle, for that simply assumes we already know what her standards are. Nor can we appeal to the standards of others to show that our standards are correct, because we must assume that our own are correct in order to determine the standards of others.

> The interpreter has ... no other standards of rationality to fall back on than his own ... There is no going outside this standard to check whether we have things right, any more than we can check whether the platinum-iridium standard kept at the International Bureau or Weights and Standards in Sevres, France weighs a kilogram. (Davidson 2001b, pp. 215, 217)

The physical sciences are different, for "when we try to understand the world as physicists ... we do not aim to discover rationality in the phenomena" (Davidson 2001b, p. 217), and hence we use standards that we share with other investigators and that must be agreed on before using them.

---

[23] I use 'norms' and 'normative' to refer not only to normative *requirements* but to evaluative standards generally. The notion of a reason showing an action to be good is in this sense a normative notion.

> The physical world and the numbers we use to calibrate it are common property, the material and abstract objects and events that we can agree on and share. But it makes no sense to speak of comparing, or coming to agree on, ultimate common standards of rationality, since it is our own standards to which we must turn in interpreting others. This should not be thought of as a failure of objectivity but as the point at which questions come to an end. Understanding the mental states of others and understanding nature are cases where the questions come to an end at different stages. How we measure physical quantities is decided intersubjectively. We cannot in the same way go behind our own ultimate norms of rationality in interpreting others. (Davidson 1994c, p. 232)

The third difference is that rational explanations are *first-person:* they appeal to, and hence require that we identify, what the agent took herself to have done and to be her reason for doing it. They are first-person because the normative significance of states of affairs – their practical significance as reasons for an agent's action – is manifest only when viewed from that agent's point of view. Understanding why someone takes a Stockhausen concert to be a reason to go to Chicago requires understanding what it is about that concert that appeals to him – requires grasping, without necessarily accepting, that person's point of view. The physical sciences, by contrast, aim at a kind of understanding and explanation that does not depend on understanding the agent's own point of view. Neuroscientific explanations, for instance, cite brains states, cellular structures, computational mechanisms, and the like that experts in the field understand but that may be unintelligible to agents whose behavior is being explained.

That rational explanations are first-person is consistent with their being interpretive because the aim of the interpreter in using his own standards is to interpret other agents' understanding of their own actions. It is also consistent with *radical* interpretation, which is a third-person point of view but a feature not of rational explanation but of Davidson's approach to mental phenomena. Its purpose is to show that meaning, thought, and action are socially grounded and hence publicly accessible: "What a fully informed interpreter could learn about what a speaker means is all there is to learn; the same goes for what the speaker believes." (Davidson 2001b, p. 148) What a fully informed interpreter could learn is precisely the features of meaning, thought, and action that are first-person, and hence Davidson denied that first person phenomena are private, internal, or known only to introspection. The third person point of view does not exclude the first but is a philosophically perspicuous way of understanding it:

> The point of the study of radical interpretation is to grasp how it is possible for one person to come to understand the speech and thoughts of another, for this ability is basic to our sense of a world independent of ourselves, and hence to the possibility of thought itself. (Davidson 2004, p. 143)

These considerations show that Davidson rejected physicalistic reductions of rational explanations and did not attempt to ground them in the laws of physics. But it is widely thought that he embraced non-reductive physicalism as a consequence of his commitment to supervenience, and he has undoubtedly motivated many philosophers to accept such a view. I think, nevertheless, that the monism entailed by Davidson's conception of supervenience is not physicalism even of the non-reductive kind.

Davidson characterized physicalism as an anti-realism that "tries to trim reality down to fit within its epistemology" (Davidson 2001b, p. 69), writing that

> I have resisted calling my position either materialism or physicalism because, unlike most materialists or physicalists, I do not think mental properties (or predicates) are reducible to physical properties (or predicates), nor that we could, conceptually or otherwise, get along without mental concepts ... Being mental is not an eliminable or derivative property. (Vermazen and Hintikka 1985, p. 244)

He rejected both physicalism and dualism – physicalism because entities can have both mental and physical predicates, dualism because there is but one kind of entity. Showing how to reject both was one of his most significant achievements.

Davidson first formulated supervenience as follows:

> Mental characteristics are in some sense dependent, or supervenient, on physical characteristics. Such supervenience might be taken to mean that there cannot be two events alike in all physical respects but differing in some mental respect, or that an object cannot alter in some mental respect without altering in some physical respect. (Davidson 2001a, p. 214)

This implies that "a change in mental properties is always accompanied by a change in physical properties, but it does not imply that the same physical properties change with the same mental properties" (Davidson 2005a, p. 189).[24] He later wrote that his first formulation is "easily misunderstood" in using "dependent on" as equivalent to "supervenient on", which suggests that an object's physical predicates *explain* its mental predicates (Davidson 2005a, p. 187). But he denied that supervenience is explanatory, agreeing with Kim that "Supervenience itself is not an explanatory relation ... It is a 'surface' relation that reports a pattern of property covariation." (Kim 1993b, p. 167)[25]

But Davidson did not agree with Kim's further claim that supervenience suggests "the presence of an interesting dependency relation that might explain it".

---

24 Davidson 2005a, p. 189.
25 Cf. Horgan 2002, p. 151.

He gave as a "noncontroversial example of an interesting case" the supervenience of semantic on syntactical predicates:

> A truth predicate for a language cannot distinguish any sentences not distinguishable in purely syntactical terms, but for most languages truth is not definable in such terms ... [This] gives one possible meaning to the idea that truths expressible by the subvenient predicates "determine" the extension of the supervenient predicate, or that the extension of the supervenient predicate "depends" on the extensions of the subvenient predicates. (Davidson 2005a, p. 187)

The scare quotes are Davidson's, for he did not mean 'depend' or 'determine' to be explanatory: the supervenience of semantic on syntactic predicates suggests no underlying explanation, nor does the supervenience of the mental on the physical. The latter holds simply because a change in mental predicates *accompanies* some change in physical predicates, but not vice versa, which, as Davidson noted, is a very weak relation.

Davidson did hold that "supervenience in any form implies monism" (Davidson 2005a, p. 187) because, if entities having distinct mental predicates also have distinct physical predicates sufficient to distinguish the former, then all entities have physical predicates. Davidson said this meant the *identity* of mental events with physical events, but this is identity of tokens not of types; his conception of supervenience rules out the latter because the same mental predicates may be accompanied by different physical predicates. Moreover, if a mental event is identical with a physical event, the latter is also identical with the former (identity being symmetrical). The only physical events not identical with mental events are events without mental descriptions,[26] but the latter are not mental and hence are not events physical events *could* be identical with.

Davidson's monism would be a version of physicalism only if physical predicates were more *basic* overall than mental ones. They are more basic in that every entity has a physical predicate but may not have a mental one, which implies that if you destroy everything physical, you thereby destroy everything mental but not vice versa. They are also more basic in that physical predicates are supervenient on mental predicates but not vice versa, but that has no consequences for explanation: explanations (and causal relations) can run from the

---

[26] Davidson once noted (Davidson 2001a, p. 212) that mental descriptions can easily be constructed that apply to *every* entity so that every entity would be both physical and mental. He also noted that this since this "failed to capture the intuitive concept of the mental" perhaps not all entities have mental descriptions. Even if they did, it would not make him a dualist. My own view, it should be said, is that *token* identity should also be rejected because physical and mental events (including intentional actions) are *individuated* differently.

physical to the mental and from the mental to the physical, and whether a physical or mental explanation (or cause) is more basic depends on the context. In an overall sense, physical predicates are not more basic than mental ones, which means that Davidson's conception of supervenience allows for monism without commitment to physicalism of any kind.[27]

Davidson understood the assertion, "Actions are those bodily movements caused and rationalized by beliefs and desires", differently from the way most proponents of the standard story do. Having considered how he understood "caused and rationalized by", I want now to consider his understanding of "actions are bodily movements".

He wrote in a well-known passage that "Our primitive actions, the ones we do not by doing something else, mere movements of the body – these are all the actions there are. We never do more than move our bodies: the rest it up to nature." (Davidson 2001a, p. 59) Proponents of the standard story often see this as central to Davidson's supposed project of finding for mind a place in a physicalistic world with (in Kim's words) "nothing but bits of matter and increasingly complex aggregates made up of bits of matter" (Kim 2003, p. 113). They think Davidson claimed that actions *consist of* the bodily movements of neuro-physiology and hence are nothing but complex aggregates of bits of matter. While actions are *described* in other ways, *what* are described are mere bodily movements. In Quine's terms, the *ontology* of action is physicalistic, while everything else is *ideology*.

On this reading, mere bodily movements count as actions only if they are also caused (in the right way) by an agent's (coming to have) beliefs, desires, or intentions. Thus Mele:

> A necessary condition of an overt action's being intentional is that (the acquisition of) a pertinent intention 'proximately cause the physiological chain' that begins concurrently with, and partially constitutes, the action ... The causal route from intention acquisition to overt bodily movements in beings like us involves a causal chain initiated in the brain ... (Mele 1992, p. 201)[28]

---

27 In his later work Davidson seems to have endorsed Spinoza's view that explanation in physical terms cannot *explain* the mental and vice versa, but that would only reinforce my claim that Davidson did not make physical explanations more basic overall than mental ones – see Davidson 2005a, p. 308. For further discussion of this point, see Chapter 15 in this volume, "The Problem of Congruence".

28 See Fodor, who says that "Commonsense belief/desire psychology ... takes for granted that overt behavior comes at the end of a causal chain whose links are mental events – hence unobservable – and which may be arbitrarily long." (Fodor 1987, p. 16)

This involves 'mental causation' – neural events cause beliefs, desires, or intentions that cause the physiological chain that causes bodily movements – and hence raises the classical problem of how mental-physical causation is possible, which many defenders of the standard story would resolve by appeal to non-reductive physicalism. Thus Mele again: "Causalism is typically embedded as part of a naturalistic stand on agency according to which mental items that play causal/explanatory roles in action are in some way dependent upon or realized in physical states and events." (Mele 1997, p. 3)

In brief, defenders of the standard story typically attribute to Davidson the view that action consists of mere (physicalistic) bodily movements caused (in the right way) by mental events. Although they may not regard his ontology of mental events as physicalistic, they think his ontology of *action* surely is.

There are numerous reasons for rejecting this as Davidson's view. As I have argued, he was not a non-reductive physicalist and he did not think action explanation is dependent on physical explanation or that causal relations are fixed by anything. He denied that mental causation is a problem, writing that "the mental is not an ontological but a conceptual category" (Davidson 2004, p. 114), that is, a matter of how events are described. Since event causation is not dependent on how events are described, whether an event is mental or physical does not affect its causal relations to other events.

Moreover, he regarded beliefs, desires, and intentions not only as states rather than events but as states of persons not of brains (or minds): "Beliefs, desires and intentions belong to no ontology ... When we ascribe attitudes we are using the mental vocabulary to describe people. Beliefs and intentions are not ... little entities lodged in the brain."[29] (Davidson 1999, p. 654) Since changes in attitudes are events, they can figure in event causality, but

> Since beliefs, desires, and intentions are not entities, it is a metaphor to speak of them as changing, and hence an extension of the metaphor to speak of them as causes and effects. What happens is that the descriptions of the agent changes over time. The relevant entity that changes is the person ... The only thing that changes when our attitudes change is us. (Davidson 1999, pp. 654–655)

Such changes no doubt have causes and effects, but to think that the former are neural events in the brain or that the latter are physiological changes that produce bodily movements, is vastly oversimplified, if not far-fetched.

---

29 Nor are they neural processes in the brain that either are or realize functionally defined beliefs, desires, and intentions (or our acquiring them).

For Davidson, the role of beliefs, desires, and intentions is to rationally *explain* actions and hence also the bodily movements essentially involved in them (as *bodily* actions). This is fundamentally not a matter of event causation, but of causal *explanation* in the logical space of reasons,[30] and it is in the light of this that we should consider Davidson's claim that "our primitive actions ... mere movements of the body ... are all the actions there are" (Davidson 2001a, p. 59).

A primitive act is one *not* done by doing some other act, hence one we must do whenever we act, on pain of a vicious regress of being unable to act until we have already acted. This formulation is misleading, however, because Davidson's view (which he ascribed to Anscombe) was that an agent whose act has many results acts only once, although her acting has as many descriptions as it has results. A primitive act is, therefore, not numerically distinct from the acts done by performing it: whether an act is primitive depends on how it is described, so the notion is *intensional*. If I illuminate the room by pulling on the light cord by moving my arm, I act only once but my acting has three descriptions: the first two describe what I did *by* (because caused by) moving my arm, but the first does not describe anything I did by which I moved my arm – does not describe my arm's moving as the result of anything I did – and hence, unlike the other descriptions, it is primitive.[31]

Described as primitive, my act may have a rational explanation (I moved my arm because of my desire to illuminate the room), but while it has many results, it is (as primitive) not described in terms of any of them. Nor is it (as primitive) described in terms of its cause, although as intentional it had a cause: "If my arm going up is an action, then there must also be an intention. But in my view, the intention is not part of the action, but a cause of it." (Davidson 2004, p. 105) By "cause" here, Davidson surely meant "causally explain" since intentions are states and not events and since, if the intention were only an event-cause of the movements, it would cause them no matter how they were described, in

---

[30] Davidson would reject Fodor's claim (for example, Fodor 1987, pp. 16–17) that causation is physicalistic (syntactic) and hence that content (semantic) is causally impotent. Davidson's view is that event causation is independent of ontological categories, while rational explanation is a matter of contents that are themselves *causally* explanatory.

[31] Defenders of the standard story often think this view of the individuation of action is something one may take or leave. But Davidson (and Anscombe) thought it absurd to say that when I illuminate the room by pulling the cord by moving my arm, I am acting three times. What is optional is a metaphysical theory about how many actions there really are somehow underneath my one acting. But that is metaphysical speculation of the kind Davidson thought pointless and not explanatory.

which case it would not account for their being intentional under some descriptions but unintentional under others.

Actions described as primitive therefore, are intentional under *some* description, and if primitive actions *are* bodily movements, the latter are also intentional under some description. Davidson held that whether we use "bodily movement" transitively – 'S moved his body' – or intransitively – 'S's body moved' – we describe the same event (Davidson 2004, p. 105),[32] and hence if moving my body at *t* is intentional, so is my body's moving at *t:* it is an intentional bodily movement.

When Davidson wrote that "our primitive actions ... mere movements of the body ... are all the actions there are [and] the rest is up to nature", he did not, therefore, mean by "*mere* movements of the body" the non-intentional bodily movements of neuro-physiology. He meant that actions are primitive if *merely* described as movements of the body, which must, since they are the movements of an agent who moves her body intentionally, be intentional under some description. And when he said that such bodily movements are all the actions there are, the rest being up to nature, he did not mean that we only move our bodies. He meant that we illuminate rooms, destroy buildings, start wars, make revolutions, etc. *by* moving our bodies, but that whether we succeed is up to nature because it is not up to us whether moving our bodies will actually result in rooms being illuminated, wars beginning, and so on. It is when such things do result from intentionally moving *our* bodies that they are actions *we* perform, and it is because intentionally moving our bodies is not the result of any act of ours that 'moving our bodies' is a primitive description.[33]

This, then, is my reading of Davidson's claim that all actions are primitive and hence *merely* movements of the body. We can put that as the claim that actions *consist of* bodily movements only if we recognize that he meant "bodily movements *intentional* under a description". Bodily movements are, of course, non-intentional under many descriptions, but since, in his view, all actions are intentional under some description, the bodily movements of which they consist are also intentional under a description. They are movements of our limbs – our arms, legs, fingers, and so on – which if we are not disabled, we move intentionally, something we cannot do with our fingernails, kidneys, or hearts, which are not limbs since it is not their nature to move or be moved intentionally.

It follows that Davidson is not committed to a physicalist ontology of action because on his view whatever is intentional under a description has a mental

---

[32] See also Davidson 2004, pp. 102–103.
[33] I think there are consequential confusions in Davidson's account of primitive actions, but I do not have the space here to discuss them.

predicate. Physicalists may think that is *ideology* not *ontology*, the latter concerning *what* is described, namely the bodily movements of neuro-physiology. But this ignores Davidson's view that although events occur under any description, whether they are mental or physical depends on how they are described. Bodily movements described as intentional are mental, described as neuro-physiological they are physical. It may be responded that nothing has yet been said about *what* is described, to which Davidson might respond with Anscombe: "The proper answer to 'What is the action, which has all these descriptions?' is to give one of the descriptions, any one, it does not matter which; or perhaps it would be better to offer a choice, saying 'Take which ever you prefer'." (Anscombe 1981, p. 209) The claim that *what* has all these descriptions is just the movements of neuro-physiology can only mean that descriptions in those terms are *basic* – that they yield the essential nature of bodily movements – whereas descriptions under which bodily movements are intentional are not basic. But Davidson did not take the logical space of laws to be more basic overall than the logical space of reasons; indeed, the latter is the basic level for understanding action since there is no action where there is no intention. It is essential to having limbs that one can move them intentionally: they are limbs only in name if one cannot do that.

Davidson's ontology of action (like Aristotle's and Spinoza's) is

> ontological monism accompanied by an uneliminable dualism of conceptual apparatus ... There is only one [kind of] substance [but] the mental and the physical are irreducibly different modes of apprehending, describing, and explaining what happens in nature. (Davidson 2005a, p. 290)

There are no non-physical entities – none that cannot be described as physical – but this is not physicalism because all actions are intentional under some description and hence are (also) mental.

There are two objections to Davidson's account of action I want to discuss, one by defenders of the standard story, one by its critics. The first concerns the problem of *deviant causal chains*, which is taken to arise because an agent's beliefs and desires can cause his bodily movements without their being actions. An example is Davidson's climber, who

> might want to rid himself of the weight and danger of holding another man on a rope, and he might know that by loosening his hold on the rope he could rid himself of the weight and danger. This belief and want might so unnerve him as to cause him to loosen his hold, and yet it might be that he ... [did not do] it intentionally. (Davidson 2001a, p. 79)

The problem is that the climber's movements are not caused in "the right way", which calls for a specification of conditions necessary and sufficient for a causal chain to constitute the agent's bodily movements as action, hence intentional under a description. Davidson contended that we cannot give conditions "that are not only necessary, but also sufficient, for an action to be intentional, using only such concepts as those of belief, desire, and cause" (Davidson 2001a, p. 232). Many have attempted, nevertheless, to specify these conditions, sometimes by appeal to scientific investigation.

His position on this issue is complex.[34] Were we to take him to mean by 'cause' *event causation*, then we surely could not give the conditions necessary and sufficient for a bodily movement to be intentional using only concepts of belief, desire, and cause. Since event causation obtains between events no matter how described, an event-cause, however complex, cannot constitute an event as an intentional action, because an action is not intentional no matter how described, but intentional under some descriptions and unintentional under others. No event-cause can account for the latter, regardless of what conditions are put on it.

Davidson takes 'cause' here to mean *causally explain*, and hence the problem arises because of his contention that in order for an agent's belief and desire to causally explain his action, not only must their contents be his reasons for acting but they must be associated with an event that causes the bodily movements that are intentional under a description yielded by his belief and desire. Thus, if the climber's belief and desire causally explain his intentionally letting go of the rope, their contents must not only be his reason for letting go but must be associated with an event that causes the bodily movements intentional as "letting go". In the deviant case, the agent's bodily movement are caused by his becoming nervous (associated with his belief and desire), and they are not, therefore, intentional under the description "letting go". The difficulty is that the bodily movements for which his belief and desire are a reason are not the same bodily movements caused by the event associated with his belief and desire. That requires that the bodily movements are caused in the right way, that is, that their cause is *appropriately associated* with his reason for acting. Davidson despaired of specifying the conditions for such an appropriate association and, indeed, given his overall view, he could not specify them because that would re-

---

[34] Thanks to John Bishop for pushing me on this issue – I doubt that he is still satisfied yet.

quire the kind of lawful connections his view ruled out. It was not a problem that could be solved and hence not worth pursuing.[35]

There is another way of viewing Davidson's discussion of the climber that I find more interesting. The climber has a belief and desire whose content he takes to be sufficient reason for him to act and that causes his body to move, but is not a reason *because of* which he acts. The problem is whether we can fill in the gap between taking the content of a belief and desire to be sufficient reason to act and really acting because of that reason. If we do act because of it, then we may rightly claim that the reason causally explained our action, but we have adequate grounds for that only *after* we have acted. Before we act there is no assurance that what we take to be the strongest reason to act will actually explain our action, whereas after we act we can make that claim, at least about ourselves, and normally be right.

Davidson considered filling the gap with additional factors that would link reasons to act with acting for those reasons but concluded that "it is largely because we cannot see how to complete the statement of the causal conditions of intentional action that we cannot tell whether, if we got them right, the result would be a piece of analysis or an empirical law for predicting behavior" (Davidson 2001a, p. 80). An *empirical* law would require stating "the antecedent conditions in physical, or at least behavioristic terms" (Davidson 2001a, p. 81), which presumes psycho-physical laws of the kind Davidson rejected and would rule out explanation in mental terms. An *analysis* would let "the terms of the antecedent conditions remain mentalistic, [but] the law would continue to seem analytic or constitutive" and hence not explanatory.

If we were able to fill in this gap, we would eliminate the "need to depend on the open appeal to causal relations. We would simply say, given these (specified) conditions, there always is an intentional action of a specified type." (Davidson 2001a, p. 80) The scientist in us may regret that gap, but as autonomous agents we should, in my view, prize it. It enables an explanation to be both causal and normative since the open-ended nature of causal claims permits the adjustments in our ascriptions of attitudes and actions that may be necessary to preserve an agent's rationality. Moreover, it rules out causal laws connecting an agent's beliefs and desires with his action, thereby meeting one condition for agent autonomy.

The other objection comes from critics of the standard story, who think Davidson's view cannot accommodate the knowledge of an agent's own actions that Anscombe called "practical" in contrast with "theoretical" or "speculative"

---

[35] This problem would not even arise if we rejected Davidson's claim that causal explanation requires an event causally related to the action.

knowledge. I contend that this criticism misses the mark (though I agree with critics that practical knowledge should play a more central role in an account of action than it does in Davidson' account).

Anscombe's "certain sense of the question 'why?' [that] is given application" to events that are intentional actions is "refused application by the answer: 'I was not aware I was doing that.'" (Anscombe 1957, p. 11) Although we act in many ways of which we are not aware, we act *intentionally* only if we are aware of our acting in that way. Anscombe claimed such knowledge is not based on observation – either perceptual or introspective – for then it would be theoretical, which would make it mysterious since it is not confined to knowing our own beliefs, desires, or intentions, but includes some knowledge of what we are doing in the world, hence what happens (under a description). Knowledge by observation of what happens is theoretical, but what is essential to intentional action is *practical* knowledge – knowledge of what happens because we *do* what happens.

Rosalind Hursthouse nicely put Anscombe's account this way:

> Practical knowledge is "the cause of what it understands".... The intentional action must match the knowledge in order to be that action. Suppose I am intentionally painting the wall yellow. Then my knowledge of what I am doing makes it to be the case that it is so. I am so doing because (in virtue of the fact that) I know it ... When I am in error, the mistake lies in the performance, not in a judgment about what I am doing ... [The agent's knowledge] is conceptually guaranteed by the nature of intentional action itself. An intentional action essentially is that which is determined by the agent's knowledge. (Hursthouse 2000, p. 103)

That is to say, what makes it the case that I am intentionally painting the wall yellow is that I know I am doing it under that description: it would not *be* that intentional act if I did not know (without observation) in doing it, what I am doing.

Hursthouse thinks no causal account of action (one that *defines* an intentional act as one with the right kind of cause) can allow for practical knowledge making it the case that the agent is acting intentionally: "Since agent's knowledge could not make it the case that the action had certain causes, the intentional action could not essentially be an action with this further feature." (Hursthouse 2000, p. 103) Nor can it allow for expressions of intention, for example, my expressing my intention to paint the wall yellow next week, which is not a prediction because if I fail to paint the wall yellow, I make an error not in judgment but in performance (or I may change my mind). But "on the causalist view, an agent's knowledge-of-his-present-or-future-intentional-action *must* be speculative knowledge of action-caused-by-certain-mental-items" (Hurthouse 2000, p. 104).

This objection applies to the standard story but not to Davidson's account, for two reasons. First, Hursthouse thinks of causal accounts in terms of causal relations, not causal explanations. Her objection that an agent's knowledge "could not make it the case that the action had certain causes" (Hursthouse 2000, p. 103) is surely true if it means that prior causes of the action could not be determined by the agent's knowledge in acting. That, however, misses Davidson's view that causal *explanation* is basic to action, since reasons explain actions only under descriptions, whereas causal relations are indifferent to descriptions. While Davidson thought that there must be an event associated with an explanatory reason, the agent need not know that event, which, therefore, plays no role in his knowledge of what he is doing or in determining the description under which his acting is intentional.

Second, Davidson held, as noted above, that there is a conceptual connection between the reason that explains an agent's acting and the description under which he acts intentionally, and hence the reason determines what the action it explains *is* (*qua* intentional) just *because* the action is causally explained by the reason. Hence to know the reason for which one is acting *is* (except in unusual cases) to know what one is doing intentionally.

This is not theoretical knowledge because agents know the reasons for which they are acting not by observation but simply by taking considerations to be reasons for acting (on Davidson's view, by having beliefs and desires). This is not a matter of agents noticing the reasons for which they act, but of their acting for those reasons. Nor is knowledge of the intention with which one acts theoretical: if what one does is not what one intends to be doing, then the error is in what does: one is wrong about what one is accomplishing, not because one has an erroneous belief but because what one did was not what one intended.

My aim here has been to pry Davidson's account of action apart from the standard story and shield it from criticisms aimed at it that too often do not apply to his account but to the standard story. I do not think his account in unflawed; indeed, I think that in the end both the deep assumptions that underlie it and the belief-desire model of reasons for action that it incorporates should be rejected. But it is much better than most of its critics think – an extraordinary philosophical achievement that escapes facile objections, is philosophically penetrating and instructive, and one that no adequate account of action can ignore. He should be recognized, even by philosophers in a broadly Wittgensteinian tradition, as a collaborator in resisting physicalism and other extravagant metaphysical theories while insisting on careful distinctions, argumentative precision, and a larger vision of the aim of philosophy.

14 The Problem of Congruence

Von Wright discussed the problem of congruence a number of times, always dealing with it in similar ways but always feeling a certain unease about his approach to what he called "perhaps the deepest problem in action theory" (von Wright 1989, p. 807). The notion of *congruence* refers to the fact that when an agent behaves intentionally – when he pulls on a bell to alert the gatekeeper, or walks across the room to fetch a book – various movements of his body and limbs occur that enable him to act in those ways and that are legitimate targets for neuroscientific explanation. There is, that is to say, congruence between what an agent does because of a reason and the ways in which his body and limbs move because of neural processes.

That my action exhibits congruence does not entail that the factors cannot fall apart: my body and limbs could move the way they would were I acting intentionally even if I am not and I may set out to act, to pull on the bell, for instance, but the movements of my body sufficient for me to act in that way may fail to occur. But if this sort of thing happened too often, there would be no congruence and hence I would be unable to pull on a bell (or act in other ways), since what I set out to do and the ways my body moved would have fallen apart. As von Wright put it:

> If the behavior required for a certain act would occur frequently without being 'embedded' in that action, then we should perhaps give up a claim that we can perform the action in question. And the same might happen, if our limbs and other bodily parts often fail to function, when we intend to perform the action for which they are required. It is a basic fact about man, about his 'natural history', that *he* can *act*, do various things, and therefore can be confident that his muscular activity, on the whole, 'obeys his will' and does not go on strike or work at odd hours. (von Wright 1989, p. 809)

Congruence, then, is necessary for our being able to act intentionally; the *problem* of congruence by contrast arises only if we attempt to give a *substantive* explanation[1] of this congruence. The attempt to do that is a primary motivation for philosophers who aim to unify rational explanation and neuro-scientific explanation of behavior, either by reducing reasons to neural states or by showing that the explanatory force of a rational explanation requires that it supervene

---

[1] The attempt to give a *substantive* explanation of congruence is to be distinguished from explaining it in the sense of elucidating the concept – getting clear about what it involves. The latter, of course, is precisely what I am doing in this essay. To avoid confusion, I shall use the expression "explaining congruence" to mean explaining it substantively.

on a neural explanation of the movements of the body. Von Wright's basic objection to such theories is not that they fail to explain why congruence obtains but that they take for granted that there is something that could and should be explained. He argues that if we get clear about what a substantive explanation of congruence could be, we will see that it has no clear sense. The way to deal with the problem, he writes, "is to try to formulate it clearly – and then see that there is no question at all to be answered" (von Wright 1998, p. 3).

I believe that von Wright's approach to congruence is correct and in what follows I shall articulate his view, defending it in terms that he himself might not have used but that bring it into more explicit contact with current work in the philosophy of action. I shall begin by discussing what I take to be a misleading way to state the problem and then lay the groundwork for a more adequate statement by developing the distinction between rational and neuro-scientific explanation. I will then lay out what I take to be the right way to state the problem and show how it dissolves if we think through what it would amount to in ex post facto explanations of an agent's behavior. I will conclude with some reflection on explanation that is not ex post facto and on the sense in which rational explanation is prior to neuro-scientific.

It is often regarded as a basic task of philosophy of action to explain why congruence obtains between an intentional action done because of a reason and the bodily movements involved in the action that occur because of neural processes.[2] The characteristic way philosophers pursue the task is to construct a theory of action whereby the reasons for which the agent acts intentionally are in some manner *joined* to the neural processes that cause the bodily movements involved in the action. On such a theory, reasons for acting are beliefs and desires (or other psychological states) that also figure in the neural explanation of bodily movements, either by being identical with neural states, by supervening on them, or by being realized by them.

Jaegwon Kim expresses such a theory in claiming that "somehow your beliefs and desires must cause your limbs to move in appropriate ways …" (Kim 1996, p. 127), using that claim to motivate his reductive physicalism about action. Alfred Mele contends that "unless desires, intentions, or their physical realizers play a causal role in the production of a person's bodily motion … there is the threat … that the person is not acting at all" (Mele 2003a, p. 6). And Fred Dretske takes the following as the central theme of his philosophy of action:

---

[2] By 'bodily movements' I mean, unless indicated otherwise, what Jennifer Hornsby (1980, p. 2) calls "bodily movements", where the subscript stands for "intransitive". I do not mean a case of an agent's moving his leg or arm but a case where her leg or arm moves; only the latter could (normally) be explained by neural processes.

> I go to the kitchen because I want a drink and think I can get one there. If I didn't have those reasons, I wouldn't move ... My lips, fingers, arms and legs, those parts of my body that must move in precisely coordinated ways for me to do what I do, know nothing of such reasons. They, and the muscles controlling them, are listening to a different drummer. They are responding to a volley of electrical impulses emanating from the central nervous system [and will occur] ... whatever reasons might be moving me toward the kitchen. If, then, my body and I are not to march off in different directions, we must suppose that my reason for going into the kitchen – to get a drink – is, or is intimately related to, those events in my central nervous system that cause my limbs to move so as to bring me into the kitchen. My reasons, my beliefs, desires, purposes, and intentions, *are* – indeed they must be – the cause of my body's movements.
> What appeared to be two drummers must really be a single drummer. (Dretske 1988, p. ix)

In working this out, Dretske constructs an intricate theory that identifies beliefs and desires with those neural states of an agent that have acquired the functional role of representing certain states of affairs; according to the theory, which bodily movements neural states cause is determined by which states of affairs they represent (that is their role as reasons), while the way they cause those bodily movements is a matter of neuroscience. Neural states are thereby taken to have the dual role of causing the bodily movements sufficient for an action and, in virtue of what they represent, also being reasons that explain the agent's action. The intent is to explain congruence by the fact that neural states have this dual role.

My aim here is not to criticize these theories per se (though I do not think they can survive criticism), but to consider the assumption that the fact of congruence can and should be given a substantive explanation. What these philosophers do, in effect, is give content to that assumption by characterizing congruence in terms of the same theories that make it appear necessary to explain it, theories that they then defend on the ground that they succeed in explaining it. On my view, however, the claim that these theories succeed in explaining congruence counts against rather than for them, since an adequate account of congruence would show that there is no clear sense to explaining it. Defending the latter is the main aim of this paper, but we must first give some care to the distinction between rational and neuro-scientific explanations.

Von Wright maintained that the fundamental way to distinguish between intentional action done for reasons and movements of the body and limbs that occur because of neural processes was to distinguish between "the behavior which can be explained teleologically as action" and the behavior which can "be explained causally as movement", a distinction that is grounded in "two ways of conceptualizing behavior" – either "as action or as mere movement" (von Wright 1989, p. 808)[3] I take this to be the right thing to say, although it needs to be spelled out carefully if the point is to be correctly grasped.

It should be noted that by "explained causally" von Wright meant, "explained in terms of laws" in the sense in which laws figure in the physical sciences. Whenever he used the term 'cause', he meant what he called a 'Humean cause', which is defined by its law-like character. In denying that explanations of behavior as intentional are causal, therefore, he was denying that they are nomological, which does not rule out their being causal in some other sense that does not depend on nomological connections at any level and that clearly distinguishes them from explanations in the physical sciences.

By speaking of the "behavior which we explain teleologically as action", von Wright meant behavior whose explanation appeals to what the agent intended it to be. Consider Alice, who got out of her chair, walked across the room to the book case, and reached up for a book. The point of what she did, what she intended her behavior to be, was to fetch a book from the shelf. Her walking across the room might have been a means toward that end, but it might have simply been what her walking across the room and reaching out to the book case *was*. "To explain behavior teleologically as action" does not require explaining it as a means to an end but only explaining it in terms of what the agent intended it to be. If she succeeded in her intention, that is what it *was*, whereas if she failed, it was what she *tried* to do.

This is a teleology of reasons in a strong sense. Alice not only acted in order to get a book, but she took that to be a reason for her acting: she responded to her need for a book *as* a reason for her to act. Brute animals, by contrast, eat in response to a reason for their eating (their need for nourishment) but they do not respond to that need *as* a reason; they do not *take* it to be a reason for them to eat. Because human agents act for what they take to be reasons for them to act, there is an essentially normative (or evaluative) dimension to their acting, in two senses. Consider Alice again. First, in taking her need for a book to be a reason

---

[3] I use the term 'behavior' in a non-technical way to denote the observable and external ways in which an agent's body, limbs, or other parts of her body move, perhaps because she moved them (in which case her moving them is also behavior), perhaps because of other factors. This is a way of using 'behavior' that is neutral between its use in intentional psychology and its use in neuro-science. I do not think of this use as something fundamental, however, as, for instance, denoting a *constituent* (or common factor) of what is denoted by its intentional and neuro-scientific uses. Behavior figures *in* explanation (as I shall argue) only as described either in commonsense psychology or in neuro-science, but there is no answer to the question of what is described in these two ways (except by giving further descriptions). Similar remarks apply to my use of the term 'bodily movements'.

for her to get out of her chair, she (implicitly) made an evaluative judgment that would have been mistaken if the book was useless and hence no (normative) reason for her action. Second, what she intended to do by her behavior set a standard for her success that she might have failed to meet: she walked across the room to get a book but would have failed if the book was not there.[4]

To explain behavior teleologically as action, therefore, is to put it in the context of the reasons for which agents act, that is to say, in the context of a rational *explanation*. Such explanation, like explanation generally, explains why phenomena occur by rendering their occurrence intelligible; what makes it distinctive is the kind of intelligibility to which it appeals, namely one that depends on specifying what the agent takes to be a reason for her behaving. To use Sellars' terms, rational explanations put behavior in the *logical space of reasons*, where items are related to each other by normative standards such as correct, appropriate, favoring, justified, obligatory, or permissible.[5]

Sellars contrasted the logical space of reasons with the logical space of causes but, given von Wright's use of 'cause', the better contrast is with the *logical space of laws*, which is the logical space in which the physical sciences function.[6] To put behavior in the logical space of laws is required to give it a nomological explanation, which, unlike rational explanation, is not normative. Scientific *explaining* is, of course, normative – it can be correct, appropriate, justified, and so on – but that is because it is itself a mode of intentional action. There is no normativity, however, in the nomological explanations themselves: they render phenomena intelligible by placing them in the context of laws that are not normative or evaluative. This is the case even when we use the term 'reason', for instance, in claiming that one reason car radiators break is that water expands when it freezes. We use 'reason' here because the explanation functions to make something intelligible: if the reason the radiator broke was that the water in it froze and hence expanded, then it is intelligible to us how and why it happened. This is an intelligibility of laws, however, and the notion of reason in this context has no normative dimension: it is not intelligible to ask whether freezing temperatures favor water expanding, or whether it is appropriate that radiators break given that water expands when it freezes, or whether it is correct or justified for a radiator to break because the temperature goes below freezing.

---

[4] The claim that rational explanation is normative does not mean that to explain an agent's action, we must evaluate the action (or the agent). It means that we must use normative terms in our explanation and hence that the action (or the agent) *could* be evaluated in relevant ways.
[5] I use 'normative' in a broad sense also to include the evaluative.
[6] John McDowell helpfully discusses this point (1996, p. xiv). Having borrowed these terms from Sellars by way of McDowell, it may be that my use of them is different, but that does not worry me.

A similar point applies to what an agent took to be a reason for him to act. Since taking something to be a reason may become determinate only in the course of his acting, others may know better than the agent himself what he took to be a reason to act. That does not conflict with the claim that reason explanations are agent-centered, for such knowledge requires identifying the point of view from which the agent himself apprehended a situation as a reason for him to act in a certain way.

The deeper point here is that the normative significance of states of affairs – their practical significance as reasons for action – manifests itself only to persons able to view them from a certain point of view.[7] If there is such a thing as a "view from nowhere", it is not a point of view that would enable the agent to respond to reasons for him to act. To understand what an agent responds to as a reason, we need not agree with his point of view, but we must be able to grasp how the world presents itself from that point of view. That is the connection between rational explanations having a normative dimension and their being agent-centered: to identify the reason for which an agent acts, we must identify at least one consideration he takes to be, normatively speaking, a reason for him to act in that way, and that requires understanding the point of view from which a state of affairs presents itself to him as such a reason.

Moreover, rational explanations are *interpretive*. What is crucial to interpret in a discourse is that there are no criteria external to the discourse that determines how properly to interpret it. The classic application of this is to texts: the criteria for the correct interpretation of a text are part of what must be found out by interpreting the text itself. While there are general criteria for interpreting texts, these are formal and abstract, and their application to a particular text cannot be determined independently of understanding – hence having interpreted – the text.

Rational explanations resemble texts in that our criteria for establishing what an agent did is not independent of establishing the reason for which she did it, and neither is independent of what she took to be a reason for her to do it, which may require establishing what she believed or desired, which may require finding out what she did, and so on. We cannot, therefore, simply use our own concepts and distinctions in describing and explaining an agent's action but must seek to understand how she understands what she did and the reason for which she did it. To get that understanding may be difficult, for it requires understanding what she took to be a reason, which may be remote from what we would take to be a reason for such an action. But that is the

---

[7] For further discussion see McDowell 1998a, especially chapters 6 and 10.

way rational explanations work: they explain why people acted as they did, not in addition to but in and through interpreting them and their actions, an activity that is fundamentally like interpreting texts.

Neuro-scientific explanations are neither agent-centered nor interpretive. They are not agent-centered in that, while they are intelligible to anyone versed in neuro-science, the agent herself may know nothing of them. They are not interpretive because rendering an agent's behavior intelligible from a neuro-scientific point of view does not require making intelligible the agent's own understanding of her behavior. They may be holistic in the Duhemian sense of involving complex trade-offs between theory and observation in the explanatory process itself, but they are not holistic in having to take account of the complex trade-offs in *what* is being explained, where any account of the agent's action can be validated only by showing that it contributes to making maximum overall sense of numerous claims about the agent and her behavior. That open-ended process is necessary for confirming an explanation in the logical space of reasons, and it often involves indeterminacy in our conclusions. There is nothing like it in the logical space of laws, which, presumably, is a reason many philosophers think nomological explanations are superior to rational explanations. If, however, we see them as serving different functions, then we should expect different criteria for when they succeed.

Given this distinction between rational and neuro-scientific explanation of behavior, let us consider what leads philosophers to characterize congruence so as to make it seem imperative to explain why it obtains. In my view, the basic reason is the assumption that we can straightaway investigate bodily movement, intentional action, reasons, psychological states, causation, and so on without adequate attention to the fact that our investigation depends on the way we understand, describe, and explain them. It is taken for granted that various events, processes, and states are there to be investigated and that our primary philosophical task is to construct a theory about their nature and relationships. But this neglects the vital task of considering how we understand them as we do, why we describe them in various ways, and whether there are different kinds of explanations of the phenomena so understood and described.

On the assumption I am criticizing, congruence is presented as holding between bodily movements caused by neural processes and actions caused by beliefs and desires, which immediately raises the problem of how to explain why two distinct causal processes should be congruent. Unless we are willing to accept some version of dualist interactionism or pre-established harmony, the only explanation that appears plausible is that the causal processes are, after all, not distinct. Actions are identical with bodily movements, and beliefs and desires, insofar as they are genuine explanatory factors, are identical with neural processes, or at least supervene on or are realized by them. The presumption is that there is only one kind of adequate explanation for what appear to be two kinds of causal processes, and since the problem is set up on that basis, it must also be solved in those terms. Hence the claim that either the two causal processes are only one or that the acting-for-reasons process supervenes on the neural-scientific process.

This way of thinking neglects the central role of descriptions in an adequate account either of action or of explanation. It is essential to an account of action that an agent's behavior be intentional under some descriptions but not under others. Consider Lars who pulled on the bell rope in order to alert the gate-keeper. He acted intentionally under the description 'pulling on the bell' and 'alerting the gate keeper' but he also frightened the birds and cracked the bell, though his action was not intentional as described in those ways. He did those several actions (and many more), but his behavior in doing them was not multiple: in acting once, he accomplished many things, most of which were not intentional. To make this point, we need the notion of under a description.[8]

This is also true for *explanations* of behavior as intentional, which put the behavior in the logical space of reasons. There was no reason for which Lars frightened the birds or cracked the bell because his behavior was not intentional under those descriptions. Because his action has been put in the space of reasons, however, a kind of rational explanation of his behavior is forthcoming: it was by mistake that he frightened the birds, and his cracking the bell was an accident. We do not characterize behavior described as mere bodily movements in such normatively related ways but we do so characterize behavior described as action since only behavior intentional under some description can be mistaken or accidental under others.

It is often overlooked that the notion of description plays an essential role in explanations generally and hence in nomological and, a fortiori, in neuro-scientific explanations. The notion of explain is *intentional:* from the fact that E explains x and that x=y, it does not follow that E explains y. The fact that water expands when it freezes explains why the radiator in Tom's car broke last night but does not explain why the component in his car he replaced a week ago broke the night he slept on the couch. The referent is the same but an explanation is of a referent only insofar as it renders it intelligible as *described* in the explanation.

A neuro-scientific explanation may explain the same behavior that a rational explanation does, but whereas a rational explanation explains behavior (only)

---

[8] Or its equivalent; I do not mean to be defending this particular piece of terminology.

as having a description under which it is intentional, an explanation from neuroscience explains it (only) as neuro-scientifically described movements of the body, muscles, and limbs. From this point of view, congruence is not a matter of the relation to each other of two kinds of causal processes but rather of the relation to each other of two different kinds of description of the same behavior and two different kinds of explanation of that behavior as thus described, one of which belongs to the logical space of laws and the other to the logical space of reasons.

Let me make three further points of clarification about this distinction. The first is that it is often formulated in terms of the one and the many. An intentional action of one type can involve different bodily movements – my pulling on a bell can involve my right arm or my left, different motions of my body, etc. – and bodily movements of one type can be involved in many different intentional actions – my arm rising might be involved in my pulling on a bell, exercising, asking a question, starting a race, etc. There is no denying that this difference implies that explanations of behavior as action differ from explanations of behavior as bodily movements. Jerry Fodor, for instance, uses the point to argue against the eliminativist claim that "commonsense psychology" can be dropped in favor of neuro-science. The former, Fodor argues, allow us to formulate useful generalizations that can be made "scientifically respectable" but that cannot be formulated in neuro-scientific terms. (Fodor 1987, ch. 1)

Fodor's claim shows, however, that the one-many distinction is not fundamental, for as he formulates it, it is entirely within the logical space of laws, thus yielding not two distinct kinds of explanation but nomological explanations that involve two kinds of classification. It is true that we classify people's actions differently from the way we classify movements of their bodies and limbs, and this is true even if the behavior we describe as action is the same behavior we describe as bodily movements. But the fundamental difference is not that we classify actions and movements differently but that we explain the former by placing them in the logical space of reasons, the latter by placing them in the logical space of laws.

The second point is that rational explanations, unlike neuro-scientific ones, are *constitutive:* a human agent capable of acting intentionally must also be capable of giving and receiving reasons for the actions of herself and others. Being able to place behavior in the logical space of reasons is not a specialized capacity for experts. It is the ground of a human life where one takes responsibility for what one does intentionally but not for (most) other things one does, where one can distinguish things that just happen from mistakes one makes or erroneous conclusions one draws, where one knows the difference between remorse and regret. Even more basically, it is what enables us to respond to the world as an arena of reasons for doing some things and refusing to do others. While neuro-scientific explanations may be indispensable for describing and explaining many dimensions of human behavior, especially for rendering intelligible various incapacities, their mastery is not necessary for acting intentionally or for giving and receiving reasons for what is done.

The third point is that explanations of behavior may be neither rational nor neuroscientific. The behavior of brute animals is often explicable only by reference to their goals and needs – to find food, shelter, a mate, and so on – explanations that resemble rational explanations more than neuro-scientific ones. We rightly speak of a cat as stalking a bird that it intends to catch, of its mistaking a decoy for a bird, of its accidentally breaking a dish in stalking the bird, of the bird's movements as a reason for the cat's crafty behavior. But these are not rational (or teleological) explanations in the strong sense sketched out above because brute animals do not have the concept of a reason for their acting. The cat does not *take* catching a bird as a reason for its stalking: it perceives the bird whose presence is a reason for (that favors) its stalking but the cat does not apprehend the bird to be a reason for its stalking. Such behavior cannot, therefore, be made intelligible by explanations either from the logical space of reasons (as I have construed it) or the logical space of laws, so that our overall scheme should have another kind of explanation.

It may be that an adequate account of rational explanation will incorporate an account of the behavior of brute animals. The view would be that the capacity to act for what one takes to be a reason presupposes the capacity to behave in the entirely natural way animals do – behavior that can be very skilled, flexible, and responsive to the animal's environment but in which powers of judgment and conceptualization play no role. On this view, the capacity for behavior that can be explained in the logical space of reasons presumes the capacity to behave like a skilled animal, the latter capacity having been conceptualized as a result of the agent's growing up in a human community and acquiring the training and education that involves. This conceptualization is not an addendum to animal behavior but what such behavior has become for human beings who have, through education and training, acquired a second nature.[9]

Whether this is correct does not affect my aim in this paper, which is to clarify the relation of neuro-scientific to rational explanation. Introducing a third kind of explanation does not clarify the relation because the relation of neuroscientific explanation to this third kind raises the same kind of issues as its relation to rational explanation. A sense of congruence can be characterized for

---

9 For a view like this see McDowell 1996, pp. 114–123.

the relation between neuro-scientifically described bodily movements and goal-directed animal behavior that is parallel to the congruence between the former and human behavior done for reasons, and there are analogous issues about whether there is any clear sense in explaining congruence of either kind.

If I have correctly portrayed the distinction between rational and neuro-scientific explanation, there is no hope either for reducing rational explanation to neuro-scientific or for any interesting sense in which the former supervenes on the latter. The two kinds of explanation and their associated descriptions are too diverse for reducing one to the other, and while changes in rational descriptions may entail changes in neuro-scientific descriptions, this must be at the *global* level, since the former depend on factors external to the agent and cannot be supervenient only on changes in the agent's own neural processes.[10]

This accounts for why philosophers who propose reduction or supervenience generally presume that the two kinds of explanation are much more alike than I have argued – indeed, so alike that rational explanations are a species of nomic explanation. The strategy back of this is to assimilate descriptions of behavior as intentional with neural descriptions of it by reconstruing each kind of description. A typical procedure is to hold, on the one hand, that what is distinctive to an intentional description is that it involves intentionality in the Brentano sense ('aboutness'), which is only minimally normative and is neither agent-centered nor interpretive.[11] It is held, on the other hand, that neural descriptions also have a minimal normativity: an example is Dretske's view that neural states function as representations, which require the possibility of misrepresentations and hence a kind of normativity.[12] The aim is to emasculate intentional descriptions and enrich neural descriptions in order to show that the explanation s of behavior associated with each kind of description are in the logical space of laws.

The strategy of assimilating intentional and neural descriptions as a prelude to putting all explanation in the logical space of laws *is* question-begging since the assimilation is not a prelude to reduction or strong supervenience but the

---

10 I have argued for this point in Stoutland 1998.
11 A related strategy is Fodor's claim (noted above) that rational descriptions differ from movement descriptions simply in the way they classify.
12 This is a minimal normativity because if a neural state misrepresented what its function is to indicate, it would not follow that the neural state behaved in an inappropriate, unjustified, or impermissible way. We could make such a normative judgment only if we had defined what it would be for a component of a system to behave normally, as we have done, for example, with hearts or kidneys. That notion of normativity cannot, however, be characterized in the logical space of laws since it requires irreducible teleological notions. For an illuminating discussion of this point, see Needham 2003, chapter 6.

heart of the matter (although that point usually goes unnoticed). The price of so doing is the loss of any substantive explanation of behavior in the logical space of reasons, which is an extravagant and unacceptable reconstruction of our understanding of ourselves as agents who give and receive reasons. Rational explanations and neuro-scientific explanations play distinct roles in our lives, and we cannot have what we need by putting behavior exclusively in the logical space of reasons or exclusively in the logical space of laws. The former is essential not only to our self-understanding as agents but to there being neuroscientific explanations of any kind. The act of giving a nomological explanation belongs to the logical space of reasons, and the identification of behavior as apt for neuro-scientific explanation presupposes that we can individuate an agent's behavior in intentional terms. In that sense, neuro-scientific explanation presupposes rational, although the former is, nevertheless, essential to our understanding the neural mechanisms that enable us to act for reasons and that explain why agents are or become incapable of acting in various ways.

The best way to clarify the issue of congruence is to consider ex post facto explanations of behavior. To do that we begin with a case where we are presented with an agent's behavior and consider, on the one hand, whether we can correctly describe the behavior as his having acted and give a rational explanation of it in the logical space of reasons and, on the other hand, whether we can also describe the behavior as movements of his body and limbs[13] and give a neuro-scientific explanation of it in the logical space of laws. The question is what congruence between what is described and explained in these two *ways* amounts to and whether there is sense to the notion of giving a substantive explanation of the congruence.

Consider Lars' behavior in having intentionally pulled on a bell. A rational explanation of his behavior would specify the description under which he acted and the reason for his having so acted, namely, to alert the gate-keeper. A neuro-scientific description of the behavior would describe it as certain movements of Lars' body and limbs – those movements that brought about the ringing of the bell – thus putting his behavior in the logical space of laws by describing it in terms that are irrelevant to what the agent took to be reasons favoring or disfavoring his action. Any behavior can, in principle, be described in the latter way although it is not easily done. We ordinarily observe agents intentionally doing things and do not take note of the particular ways their limbs and bodies move. Behavior typically presents itself to us as having the *form* of intentional

---

[13] Recall that I am using 'movements of the body' intransitivity, hence not as referring to an agent's moving her body, which is a transitive description.

action.¹⁴ This is especially true of complex actions, extended ones, for example we describe a person who went shopping as having performed a single action for which we cite one reason (he needed groceries), but fail to notice his particular bodily movements, whose description would be very complicated.

Whether behavior so described can always be explained in neuro-scientific terms is another question. The descriptions might be so complex that explanation is beyond our power, or there might be so many external factors affecting the behavior that the idea of a neuro-scientific explanation loses its point.¹⁵ The situation is different for rational explanation because, although agents can behave intentionally for no reason (for example, whistling or humming idly), intentional behavior is characteristically identified by the reason for which the agent acted, and hence there is a conceptual link between behavior being intentional under a description and its having (under that description) a rational explanation. Someone whose behavior could rarely be given a rational explanation would not be an agent since acting intentionally for no reason must be an exception against a background where intentional actions are characteristically performed for reasons. There are, therefore, conceptual grounds for thinking that behavior described as intentional action has a rational explanation but not for thinking that behavior described as bodily movements has a neuro-scientific explanation.

Given that the same behavior could be described both as action that is intentional and as mere movements of the agent's body and limbs, could it also have both a rational and a neuro-scientific explanation? Jaegwon Kim maintains that this is not possible:

> A 'purposive' explanation of human action in terms of the agent's 'reasons' and a 'mechanistic' (e.g. neurobiological) explanation of it in terms of physiological mechanism must be regarded as incompatible and mutually exclusionary – unless we accept an appropriate reductive relationship between intentional states and underlying biological processes. (Kim 1993a, p. xiii)

His argument for this appeals to the 'principle of explanatory exclusion': "There can be no more than one 'complete' and 'independent' explanation for any single explanandum." (Kim 1993a, p. xiii)

On my view, Kim is mistaken in holding that the two kinds of explanation are incompatible. Let us assume that they are independent in that intentional

---

14 Cf. Anscombe 1957, p. 87.
15 Experimental set-ups that severely restrict the conditions under which behavior occurs are designed to deal with the latter difficulty, but they leave open the question of whether or how their results can be generalized and applied.

states cannot be reduced to underlying biological processes. Let us further assume that both kinds of explanation are complete in that each would, if adequate, answer the question, 'why?' by making it intelligible why, in the one case, the agent acted intentionally as he did and, in the other, why his (mere) bodily movements occurred as they did.

In defending the compatibility of the two kinds of explanation, I do not appeal to the notion that rational explanations are *merely* interpretive (or 'hermeneutic') – that they render an action intelligible by interpretively tracing out its conceptual links with an agent's reasons, her psychological states, other actions of hers, etc. but are essentially impotent as far as explaining the behavior we thus interpret. A rational explanation explains behavior as intentional action, and a neuro-scientific explanation explains that same behavior as (mere) bodily movements, but, I contend, both explain why the behavior, as understood, took place. To think otherwise overlooks the fact that *any* explanation that aims to show why phenomena occurred does so by rendering their occurrence intelligible. Rational explanations are distinctive not in explaining why agents acted by rendering their action intelligible but in the kind of intelligibility to which they appeal, namely one that places their action in the logical space of reasons. Doing so requires interpretive procedures but what is interpreted are not inert structures but agents behaving actively in the world, whose behavior is explained in term of their reasons for so acting.[16]

Von Wright's way of putting this matter can be misleading. In "Action", for example, he writes that an action has two aspects,

> an outer or performative one and an inner or intentional one ... The outer aspect ... is physical, a sequence of changes in the physical world, the inner aspect is something mental ... [which] does not mean that it is what we ordinarily call a 'mental state' or 'mental process'. [It is rather] the intentionality of the change(s) or not-change(s) which constitute its outer aspect. (von Wright 2003, p. 157)

He goes on to suggest that the inner aspect of action is the concern of rational explanation while the outer or performative aspect is the concern of neuro-scientific explanation. On this reading, while rational explanation concerns the structure of intentionality, explanation of what goes on in the world – actions

---

[16] Whether this requires that such explanation must be causal is another issue that depends, as noted above, on how one understands 'causal'. It may be misleading not to call such an explanation 'causal', but if 'causal' is taken to mean 'nomological explanation' (as von Wright assumes), calling it 'causal' is equally misleading. I have come to think that it is, on the whole, better to extend 'causal' to cover all explanations of why something occurred, including those outside the logical space of laws.

and their results – is to be traced to neuro-science. Rational explanations explain the sense in which behavior is intentional, while neuro-scientific explanations explain why the behavior occurs.

This is a misreading, however, for it is clear that von Wright's view is that we have two kinds of explanation of the agent's behavior as bringing about various changes in the world. But to have two kinds of explanation, the agent's behavior must be described (or understood) in two kinds of ways – as bodily movements or as intentional action. The behavior is observable as described in either way and in *that* sense what is described in *both* ways is the *outer* aspect of behavior. But the intentionality of behavior – its being described as intentional action – is inner in the sense that it must be understood from the point of view of the agent (and is known by the agent without observation), whereas the behavior as bodily movement requires no such point of view and is, by contrast, outer (and cannot be known without observation). Moreover, behavior understood as intentional is often characterized as 'mental', and understood as movement it is characterized as 'physical', though this is acceptable only if 'mental' denotes the rational (or intentional) and 'physical' the nomological (which is how Davidson, for instance, typically construes these terms).

Von Wright's view is, then, that the same behavior can be explained by either a rational or by a neuro-scientific explanation. This does not violate Kim's 'principle of explanatory exclusion' – "there can be no more than one 'complete' and 'independent' explanation for any single *explanandum*" (Kim 1993a, p. xiii) – since, although we have two complete and independent explanations for the same behavior, the explanations are not of the same kind nor is there a single explanandum because what is explained is (as with explanation generally) the behavior *as* described, and it is described either in terms of the logical space of reasons and given a rational explanation or in terms of the logical space of laws and given a nomological explanation. Each kind of explanation may be complete in its own terms,[17] but there is no incompatibility between them.

Let us assume that Lars' behavior has both a rational explanation and a neuro-scientific one. Since what he did was not merely a matter or luck but done intentionally, his action exhibited his *capacity* so to act and, therefore, exhibited congruence between his intentional actions and mere movements of his body and limbs. Not only had his body and limbs moved in the way sufficient for

---

[17] There are other senses in which neither kind of explanation is complete. Knowing that the reason Lars pulled on the bell was to alert the gate-keeper, we may want to know why he took that to be a reason for him to act, or why he thought pulling on the bell was the way to do that. Knowing the neural explanation of his movements, we may want a further account of the events that led up to the processes in his brain. But these senses of complete are not relevant here.

him to have pulled on that bell, but movements of that kind have not, in general, occurred unless he acted. Moreover, when he has on other occasions set out to pull on the bell or act in similar ways, the movements of his body and limbs sufficient for him to act in that way have almost always taken place.

There is, I maintain, no clear sense to giving a substantive explanation of why this congruence obtained. To see that this is so, consider that in giving a rational explanation of Lars' having pulled on the bell we take it for granted that he had also moved his arm in pulling on the bell. We thereby put his having moved his arm in the logical space of reasons: it was done for a reason (to pull on the bell) and its description has evaluative, agent-centered, and interpretive dimensions. But a description of Lars' behavior as his having moved his arm for a reason entails that his arm had moved – that his moving it had caused it to move.[18] It does not entail that his arm had moved in a particular way but only in some way or other that made it true that he had moved it. This kind of description of his arm having moved puts that movement in the logical space of reasons: it also has (perhaps minimally) evaluative, agent-centered, and interpretive dimensions in that his arm movement was correct, appropriate (or the contrary), it was intelligible to the agent herself, and there is no external criterion for what movement counted as an *arm* movement.

A neuro-scientific account of Lars' behavior does not describe it in such a way but (in Hull's famous phrase) as "colorless movements" (Hull 1943, p. 25) devoid of normative significance, nor does it describe it in terms of such effects as a belt-ringing or a gate-keeper, waking up. The primary descriptions are of the movements of Lars' body and limbs, centrally of the movement of his arms (secondarily of his muscle contractions). They are detailed and precise descriptions of the particular movements made by Lars' arms (not merely generic descriptions of whatever movements are sufficient conditions for *moving* his arm). Our example has assumed that there is also a neuro-scientific *explanation* of why these

---

18 'Caused' is not, of course, used here in the nomological (Humean) sense but in a sense that belongs to the logical space of reasons. Anscombe (1981, p. 137) suggests a defense of this use in her inaugural lecture: "… In learning to speak we learned the linguistic representation and application of a host of causal concepts. Very many of them were represented by transitive and other verbs of action used in reporting what is observed … The word 'cause' can be *added* to a language in which are already represented many causal-concepts. A small selection: *scrape, push, wet, carry, eat, burn, knock over, keep off, squash, make* (e.g., noises, paper boats), *hurt*. But if we care to imagine languages in which no special causal concepts are represented, then no description of the use of a word in such languages will be able to present it as meaning *cause*." I am not at all certain, however, that 'caused' in *any* sense denotes the relation between moving an arm and an arm moving; it remains an open question for me how to elucidate the truism that if an agent moved her arm, her arm moved.

movements occurred, and this obviously will be acceptable only if it yields those movements – the ones that occurred when Lars acted.

Given this clarification of what our example involves, it is evident that if there were a substantive explanation of why congruence obtained in this case, it would have to explain why the movements of Lars' arm sufficient for his intentionally moving it are congruent with the movements of his arm as described in neuro-science. But there is no clear sense in giving an explanation of *that* because those are the same movements differently described, one in the logical space of reasons, the other in the logical space of laws. If Lars intentionally moved his arm in order to pull on the bell, then a correct neuroscientific explanation of his arm movements *cannot* fail to be an explanation of the movements sufficient for his having moved his arm in that way because the arm movements explained (in the logical space of reasons) by his moving his arm are the movements explained (in the logical space of laws) neuro-scientifically. The movements are, of course, described differently, but what neuro-science describes *are* the movements sufficient for Lars to move his arm in order to ring the bell.

This does not mean that what we take to be an agent's intentional action and the movements of his body cannot fall apart. If Lars had set out to ring the bell but he had (unknowingly) become paralyzed, he would have been unable to perform the movements required to pull on the bell. The question of congruence, however, would be moot because his behavior could not be described as his intentional pulling on the bell or even intentionally moving his arms, and could not be put in the logical space of reasons. The question of congruence between the two kinds of explanation could not arise since his behavior, in these circumstances, although it presented itself as having the form of action could be explained only as bodily movement in the logical space of laws.

A related example is the case of reflex action, for example, the movement of Lars' leg caused by the doctor's using a hammer to tap on his knee in order to test his reflexes. If this really is reflex action, then (necessarily) it is not intentional, and hence has no rational explanation, and the question of congruence does not arise. But note that we call the behavior caused by the doctor's hammer reflex *action* because it has the same *form* as an intentional leg movement. There are numerous reflexes in the human body, but this one, having the form of an action, can be individuated like an action, so that the doctor knows exactly what to expect from his tapping on the knee. He also knows that the leg movement has no rational explanation precisely because it occurs only because he tapped on Lars' knee: although Lars presumably has the capacity to move his leg in the normal way, he did not move it for a reason, and given that it was tapped on, he could not have stopped it. Nevertheless, had he moved it intentionally, congruence would have obtained in the way indicated above.

Finally, consider Lars as not wholly paralyzed but unable, because of some neural defect, to move his arms, in which case he would have been unable to pull on the bell with either arm. He could have used his teeth, however, and then the rational explanation of the movements that caused the bell to ring would be his having clenched his teeth on the bell rope and pulled it by moving his head. Those movements could also have been described in neuro-scientific terms and a neuro-scientific explanation of them proposed; the explanation would be acceptable, however, only if it in fact explained the occurrence of the movements on this occasion of Lars' acting. Lars managed to pull on the bell rope in spite of the fact that he could not move his arms, which means congruence obtained between his intentionally pulling on the bell and the movement of his limbs because both the rational explanation and the neuro-scientific explanation have now to explain, each in its own way, the same movements, not of Lars' arms, but of his teeth and head – and that is not a substantive explanation of congruence.

In explaining an agent's behavior, therefore, congruence of the relevant kind obtains *necessarily* if the agent's behavior can be given a rational explanation. If she failed to act intentionally as expected because she could not move her limbs in the way required for *that* action but was able to act in *another* way by making different movements, then the movements that resulted from her intentionally moving her body and limbs would also be different. But so would the neuro-scientific descriptions of her behavior since they describe those same movements (though in neuro-scientific terms), and their neuro scientific explanation would be adequate only if it yielded the movements as thus described. It is, that is to say, conceptually impossible for an agent to have acted unless her body and limbs had moved in whatever way was sufficient for her acting as she did.

Those who object to this account of congruence are apt to do so because they think it is a mere artifact of ex post fact explanation. They may argue as follows. The account assumes that the agent's behavior is on hand and hence that explanation is not of why the behavior occurred but of how to describe it and relate descriptions of it as intentional to descriptions of it as neuro-scientific. The really hard problem, therefore, is ignored, namely, how to explain the occurrence of the behavior in the first place. This is surely a matter of nomic explanations, which, therefore, are basic.

My strategy, it is argued, is essentially to take rational explanations as basic and require that neuro-scientific explanations conform to them: if an agent has acted intentionally, then there is a rational explanation of movements of his body thus described, and a neuro-scientific explanation must yield descriptions of an agent's behavior that are congruent with them. But that is to give rational explanations priority over neuroscientific explanations, which is unacceptable to anyone sympathetic to the achievements and status of modern physics.

My response to this is, first, to reiterate the point that explanation in general, whether rational or nomic, renders the occurrence of some phenomenon intelligible, the phenomenon in this case being human behavior. A nomic explanation does so by showing that behavior is describable so as to be, in some sense, an instance of a law of nature, while a rational explanation shows that the behavior can be described as intentional action and explained by the agent's reason for acting. Both are genuine explanations of why the behavior, thus described, occurred, the difference being that one aims to make its occurrence intelligible in the logical space of laws, the other in the logical space of reasons.

I would argue, next, that such explanation is always ex post facto because we do not explain the occurrence of what has not yet happened. We may, of course, explain why something will happen; but that is to construe explanation as prediction. Nomic explanation often allows for prediction, the paradigm being astronomy and its stunning ability to predict the tides, the revolution of the earth on its axis, eclipses, the path of the planets around the sun, etc. But prediction of that kind does not extend very far even in the logical space of laws, not only because we do not know the various contextual factors which affect the application of laws but because of other factors that undermine the very project of prediction.[19]

It is often argued that the main function of rational explanation is to enable us to predict what others will do and hence respond to them intelligently. While such prediction is important, the predictions we make are vague, they always come with sweeping *ceteris paribus* clauses, and they are often wrong – something that does not motivate us to find something better than rational explanations. The main function of rational explanations is to enable us to make sense of the people we encounter so that we can respond to each other as how we are, how we feel, and the ways our lives are shaped. This is an explanatory function in which prediction plays a role, but to regard it as having a major role would be to assimilate rational explanation to the kind of nomic explanations of Newtonian physics.[20]

---

[19] Cf. Anscombe (1981, p. 143): "The high success of Newton's astronomy was in one way an intellectual disaster: it produced an illusion from which we tend still to suffer. This illusion was created by the circumstance that Newton's mechanics *had a good model in the solar system.* For this gave the impression that we had here an ideal of scientific explanation; whereas the truth was, it was mere obligingness on the part of the solar system, by having had so peaceful a history in recorded time, to provide such a model."

[20] Eliminativists often indict rational explanations for failing to explain phenomena that it is clearly not their function to explain. Paul Churchland (1981, p. 73), for example, complains

A related point is that a neuro-scientific explanation of behavior aspires to render the behavior intelligible not only by citing the factors nomically connected with its description as movements of the body and limbs but also by specifying the underlying explanatory mechanism that brought about the movements. A rational explanation, on my view, does not aspire to specify any underlying mechanisms that explain the agent's behavior, which means that a philosophical account of rational explanation will not attempt to specify any explanatory mechanisms. It will attempt to describe such matters as the way in which an agent has taken some consideration to be a reason for her to act, how that leads to her intending to act for that reason, which then becomes the intention with which she acts, and hence the reason because of which she acted as she did. But these are descriptions of processes that are accessible to an agent's reflection, not specifications of underlying explanatory mechanisms that are in the domain of experts.

When we act intentionally, such explanatory processes surely go on, but they vary enormously from case to case and knowledge of them sheds no light on the role of rational explanations in our life, on their internal structure, or the way they work. It does not follow that rational explanations merely interpret what an agent did: to insist that genuine explanations require an underlying mechanism (even a mental one) is to assimilate explanation in the logical space of reasons to explanation in the logical space of laws.

This point is an application of Wittgenstein's discussion of rule-following in the *Philosophical Investigations* where he argues that it is hopeless to expect that a philosophical elucidation of, for instance, the notion of understanding would specify the underlying processes that explain why someone understands a rule or a sentence. The task is rather to describe what it is to understand and what conditions characterize successful understanding. What processes go on underneath that might explain such success is a different matter that is not the concern of philosophy. Von Wright makes a parallel point in these perceptive comments on his own work.

> From the beginning my concern was with explanation. Given the action, we 'look back' on the grounds and reasons which make it intelligible. Had I realized how different the two

---

that what he calls "folk psychology" has utterly failed in accounting for "the nature and dynamics of mental illness, the faculty of creative imagination ... the nature and psychological functions of sleep ... the internal construction of a 3-D visual image ... the rich variety of perceptual illusions ... the miracle of memory ... the nature of the learning process itself ..." If by "folk psychology" he means what I call "rational explanation", then failure to explain such phenomena is irrelevant since they call for explanation in the logical space of laws.

attitudes or perspectives are [back-ward looking as opposed to forward-looking], I should have separated them and made it clear that the relation whose nature I was anxious to clarify was, in the first place, the relation between the action as a fa.it accompli and its motivational background. Many confusions of which I have been guilty might have been avoided, and certain misunderstandings of my aims and intentions would perhaps never have arisen. (von Wright 1989, p. 804)

Those who object to my account of congruence are right that I think rational descriptions and explanations of human behavior take priority over neuro-scientific ones. This is not always the case, for there are conditions under which neuro-scientific descriptions and explanations are prior. There might, for example, be doubt about whether an agent's behavior was intentional, even doubts the agent himself might have come to share as he reflected on his behavior. We might discover that he could not have done what he thought he did because he had suffered neurological damage that made it impossible to have moved his limbs in the way required for his action. Or investigators might show that although his limbs moved as they would have had he acted intentionally in a certain way, he suffered from a condition that made it extremely unlikely he had the ability to do such action intentionally, in which case we would withdraw the rational explanation in favor of a nomological one. But these are highly unusual, and in the typical case it is a kind of datum that an agent has acted intentionally – something we have observed directly or that we take for granted – and hence any neuro-scientific explanation of his behavior will have to yield the movements of his body and limbs required for him to act intentionally as he did – will have, that is to say, to yield congruence.

The main sense in which nomic explanation is prior to rational is the one we have just illustrated with our example of agents who are incapable of certain actions. Rational explanation cannot explain such incapacities because explanation of an agent's behavior as intentional action presupposes that the agent is *capable* of acting and hence that she is normal, that is, not subject to various kinds of abnormalities. There are ways in which an agent cannot act that can be explained by a rational explanation,[21] but the incongruence that consists in being incapable of moving one's body and limbs in the way required for specific actions is not one: incongruence is an abnormality that requires a nomic explanation.

---

[21] A rational explanation might explain an agent's inability to act because he is, for instance, tied up or because someone has removed the opportunity for his acting. It can also indirectly explain other kinds of incapacity by arguing, for example, that someone deliberately injured a person's limbs or neural system.

To the extent that an agent is normal, however, rational explanation takes priority, which means that there will necessarily be congruence between her behavior as intentional action and as movements of her body and limbs. But explanation of that congruence makes no clear sense because, as we may now put it, abnormality can be given a substantive explanation but normality cannot. It does not follow that there cannot be an explanation of why beings with the potential to become normal agents have come to exist. Given our post-Darwinian science, explaining why there are such beings is a task, not of rational explanation, but of evolutionary considerations that are in the logical space of laws: there are clear survival benefits to beings capable of behavior that can (often) be given a rational explanation.

Of course, such beings might never have come to exist, in which case there would have been no behavior that could be explained in the logical space of reasons. Neural systems might exist in such a world, but there would be no neuroscientific *explanation* since that requires explainers, who must be normal agents. Such an impoverished world illustrates an indirect sense in which neuro-scientific explanations are basic, namely, what would have been explained had there been explainers can exist without normal agents, but not vice versa. That is one way of expressing global supervenience of the intentional on the physical: destroy the physicalistic and you destroy everything else, though the contrary is not true. I accept that, but it has no consequences for the nature and function of rational explanation.

We can explain further how particular human beings become normal agents by appeal to their slow maturation and to their being trained and educated in and by the human community to act for reasons. We can explain how the capacity to act for reasons is developed and sustained by appeal to the way reasons for acting under diverse circumstances are embedded in various practices and the way our participation in such practices can affect the structure of the brain and nervous system. But what we explain in these ways is the development and sustenance of the capacities of agents for behavior that can be explained both in the logical space of reasons and in the logical space of laws. We must not attempt a substantive explanation of why these two ways of explaining behavior are congruent since there is no such thing – no such thing as a substantive explanation of why my body and I do not march off in different directions.

15 Analytic Philosophy and Metaphysics

In an essay on metaphysics, P. F. Strawson writes:

> Over much of the philosophical world in this century the doctrine of the impossibility of metaphysics became almost an orthodoxy, and the adjective 'metaphysical' a pejorative word. Some of the reasons for this devaluation should now be clear. The conceptual distortions and final incoherence of systems, the abstract myths parading as Reality, the grandiose claims and the conflicting results – these seemed to many the essence of the metaphysical enterprise and sufficient reason for condemning it; and the extravagances of metaphysics were by some of them contrasted with the sobrieties of a method of philosophical analysis which aims to make clear the actual functioning of our concepts in use. (Strawson 1960, pp. 259 – 260)[1]

Anyone who knows anything about 20th-century philosophy will recognize Strawson's description as an integral part of the self-understanding of the analytic philosophy that dominated large parts of the philosophical world in the century just ended. The main lines of the story of its rejection of metaphysics are also familiar. It began with two paradigms of analytic philosophy, Moore and Russell, who rejected the metaphysics of idealism (developed by such philosophers as Bradley, Joachim, and A. E. Taylor), which dominated their philosophical world at the turn of the 20th century. It continued with Wittgenstein, who wrote in the *Tractatus* that the "right method of philosophy" would be to demonstrate to anyone who "wished to say something metaphysical ... that he had given no meaning to certain signs in his propositions" (Wittgenstein 1922, § 6.53). Carnap interpreted this as a doctrine which showed that metaphysics involved a violation of the rules of the logical syntax of language:

> [It involved] pseudo-statements [which] consist of meaningful words, but the words are put together in such a way that nevertheless no meaning results. The syntax of a language specifies which combination of words are admissible and which are inadmissible. The grammatical syntax of natural languages, however, does not fulfill the task of elimination of senseless combinations of words in all cases. (Carnap 1959, p. 67)

For that task we need 'logical syntax' whose rules eliminate metaphysics once and for all. Others associated with the Vienna Circle argued that metaphysics consists of sentences which are neither empirically verifiable nor analytic, and hence violate the criterion of 'cognitive meaning' and are neither true nor

---

[1] The article (like all the others) is unsigned, though obviously written by Strawson, who is included in the list of contributors.

false. While ordinary language philosophers shunned the Vienna Circle, they also ruled out metaphysics on the ground that it attempted to establish claims which were inconsistent with the truth of what ordinary persons would say in their everyday discourse.

Now, however, more than forty years after Strawson's essay, the situation is quite different. Metaphysics is flourishing among analytic philosophers – a metaphysics which, while called 'analytic', is just the kind whose rejection had been taken as a distinctive mark of analytic philosophy. That it is a favored methodology in many areas is shown by examples like these:

- A metaphysics of possible worlds, inspired by modal logic, which envisages this world as only one of countless other existing worlds, in many of which we exist and in many of which we do not exist.
- A metaphysical view of persons which claims that there is no such thing as personal identity.
- Physicalist metaphysicians who deny that there are beliefs, desires or other attitudes.
- Philosophers of mind who posit an innate language of thought, hard-wired in the brain, which means that each of us learns our mother tongue as a second language.

Metaphysicians of this type differ from the metaphysical idealists Moore and Russell sought to refute in only one essential respect: they are physicalists rather than idealists. Like the idealists, they construct intricate theories, which float free of everyday discourse and practice, and which are defended on the ground that they are more coherent than their rivals, or better balance complexity of entities with simplicity of structure, or leave fewer theoretical problems unsolved, and so on.

Again, like the idealist foes of Russell and Moore, these metaphysicians do not shrink from denying what Moore called "the Commonsense view of the World" (Moore 1993, p. 118). Unlike the idealists, they do not deny either the reality of material objects or of space or time but rather the reality of beliefs and other attitudes, of persons who endure through time, of the capacity to mean plus by 'plus', of the ability to learn a language without already knowing one. G. H. von Wright was surely correct in asserting that "the philosophy which had set itself the task of a 'Überwindung der Metaphysik durch logische Analyse der Sprache' has become, in some of its latest branchings, the perhaps most metaphysically loaded and speculative of all contemporary brands of philosophy worth being taken seriously" (von Wright 1993, p. 44).

Why is it that metaphysics is flourishing in a philosophical tradition typically characterized in terms of its opposition to metaphysics? There are several reasons, some external to philosophy itself (for example, its professionalization in universities organized around the production and testing of scientific theories), some internal (like the influence of Quine's 'naturalism'), but the main one is that analytic philosophy has always been dominated by the metaphysical spirit. While there are significant exceptions, most of its practitioners, major and minor, have done philosophy in a metaphysical way, and even their attempts, especially their attempts I would say, to show the impossibility of metaphysics have manifested the metaphysical spirit. The current flourishing of metaphysics is not a re-birth of something that died out but a re-surfacing of something always there.

This is evident in the case of Moore and Russell, whose target was not metaphysics in general but the metaphysics of idealism. Moore engaged in metaphysical activity reluctantly and cautiously (with his theories of facts and propositions, for example), but Russell did so enthusiastically throughout his long career, from his theory of descriptions through logical atomism to various attempts at constructing a 'scientific philosophy'. The case of the *Tractatus* is more complex, depending on whether one reads it in the standard way as itself putting forward a metaphysics of facts, simple objects, complex states of affairs, and so on, or whether one reads it 'resolutely' as a radical rejection of all such metaphysical constructions. In the former case, it is explicitly metaphysical; but in the latter case, it is metaphysical underneath, given (as Wittgenstein came to see) that the view of language which was supposed to ground strict limits on what could be said was itself metaphysical.[2]

Carnap's notion of logical syntax is metaphysical in that it involves a construction of the rules which are supposed to make a language possible, which is metaphysical in two senses: it is not based on an investigation of how language actually works, and it results in constraints on how language *must* work. Something very similar is true of the positivist criterion of cognitive meaninglessness. Since it was neither empirically verifiable nor analytic and was, therefore, by the standard of the criterion itself, cognitively meaningless, it was taken as a proposal about how to define 'meaningless', a proposal which was constantly modified to fit antecedent understandings of what *must* transcend empirical verification, all of which shows how strongly attracted to metaphysics the positivists were. The metaphysical spirit was less prevalent among ordinary language philosophers but not wholly absent, showing itself, for instance, in the way appeals to the 'paradigm case' were used as a general require-

---

[2] The second ('resolute') reading has been persuasively argued in Diamond 1991 and Conant 2002.

ment which *must* be met by various kinds of claims, regardless of the context in which they were made.

These remarks suggest what I take to be true, namely that it is extremely difficult to avoid metaphysics and the metaphysical way of doing philosophy. Indeed, if the task is to rule out metaphysics once and for all, it is impossible: any attempt to show that metaphysics can be avoided in principle will entangle one in metaphysics. Recent analytic philosophy may have taken that to heart by giving up the attempt to eliminate metaphysics once and for all and embracing it as enthusiastically as any philosophers at the end of the 19th century.

Now this claim takes for granted the terms 'metaphysics' and 'metaphysical way', but they very much need clarification, and that is the task to which I now turn. I have surely given away my own attitude, which is that the kind of metaphysics which has dominated analytic philosophy is a way of doing philosophy which ought to be resisted; it is at best an unproductive diversion, and at worst dialectical illusion, which only appears to make truth-evaluable claims. It is important to note that this pejorative use of the term is not the only legitimate one: there are conceptions of metaphysics which are not objectionable and which deserve more discussion and commendation than I can give them here. My aim in this paper is to articulate a sense of the term in which it *is* objectionable, something we ought to resist. One philosopher who always used the term in this way was Wittgenstein, who thought of metaphysics, as von Wright puts it, as a "jungle" in which philosophy "loses itself" – as something to "fight against" (von Wright 1993, p. 99).[3] It is this sense of metaphysics that I want to characterize, making it explicit just what this way of doing philosophy is and why it should be fought.

A characterization of metaphysics in this pejorative sense should meet certain conditions. It should, for example, show why it is unproductive or its claims illusory, but it should also characterize a way of doing philosophy whose practice is not confined to second rate thinkers but is engaged in by even the most competent philosophers. Metaphysical activity often involves creative intelligence of the highest order, and it is not typically the result of inattentive or superficial thinking. Wittgenstein took it to be a temptation which any serious philosopher would face and succumb to more or less often, his attitude reflecting what Kant said about dialectical illusion:

---

[3] Von Wright continues: "It is ironic that the metaphysics which Wittgenstein was fighting was exactly the one in the cobwebs of which the logical positivists and a good many of their followers among analytic philosophers according to him had been caught." (von Wright 1993, p. 99)

> There is a natural and unavoidable dialectic of pure reason, not one in which a bungler might be entangled through lack of acquaintance, or one that some sophist has artfully invented in order to confuse rational people, but one that irremediably attaches to human reason, so that even after we have exposed the mirage it will still not cease to lead our reason on with false hopes, continually propelling it into momentary aberrations that always need to be removed. (Kant 1998, A 298/B 354)

We need next a characterization of metaphysics such that the claim that a certain discourse is metaphysical is not itself a metaphysical claim. This means that metaphysics cannot be characterized as something which can be overcome or eliminated in principle once and for all, since such a claim would itself be metaphysical and hence self-defeating. Finally, an adequate characterization of metaphysics should allow that a sentence might be metaphysical as used in one way and not as used in another, or that a certain discourse might be metaphysical in one cultural or historical context and not in another. A hylomorphic account of intentionality developed by contemporary philosophers would, for example, very likely be metaphysical in the pejorative sense, whereas similar accounts from the 13th century would not be, the reason being that in the 13th century hylomorphism was part of a comprehensive physical theory which figured in the scientific practice of the time, whereas today hylomorphism has no role to play in scientific practice but turns up only in philosophical speculation. The same is true of cosmological or teleological arguments for the existence of God, which were integral to 13th-century physics but now play no significant role either in physical science or in religious discourse.

A characterization meeting these conditions cannot construe metaphysics in terms of subject matter because there is nothing objectionable about metaphysics if it is characterized simply as investigating topics like reality, appearance, substance, goodness, truth, God, the mind, and so on. These topics belong to metaphysics in a traditional and unproblematic sense: they are part of metaphysics rather than, say, epistemology, ethics or aesthetics. But these metaphysical topics – along with topics from epistemology, ethics, or aesthetics – can be pursued metaphysically or non-metaphysically; if the former, then they fall under metaphysics in the pejorative sense, even if the topics are not metaphysical in the unproblematic sense of the term.

Nor is metaphysics objectionable if understood as investigating "powerful, deep, crucial assumptions about the world" (Dupré 1993, pp. 1–2), assumptions which may or may not be distinctive to a given culture or historical epoch but which nevertheless play a crucial role in a particular culture or society. Such investigation may be metaphysical in the pejorative sense, but it need not be. Indeed, there is an activity continuous with what many who call themselves metaphysicians have engaged in which Wittgenstein himself thought central to philosophy, namely, the attempt to give a "perspicuous representation [which] produces just that understanding which consists in 'seeing connections'". Wittgenstein took this to be "of fundamental importance for us. It earmarks the form of account we give, the way we look at things." (Wittgenstein 1958a, § 122) This, I take it, is what Strawson was aiming at with his notion of 'descriptive' metaphysics.[4]

One other point: a characterization of metaphysics as pejorative should not be epistemic, for example, as consisting of "speculative conclusions unjustified, and probably unjustifiable, by any known facts" (Lyons 2001, p. 256) or, as Carnap once put it, "The field of alleged knowledge of the essence of things which transcends the realm of empirically founded, inductive science." (Friedman 2000, p. 13) Metaphysics, to the extent that it makes intelligible claims, often fits these characterizations, but it need not: metaphysicians may appeal to claims which do not transcend the known facts or the realm of science but use them in the service of metaphysical activity. On the other hand, there are claims which transcend known science and the facts, which are not metaphysical but simply highly speculative. Or they may be what Wittgenstein called "certainties", propositions which "stand fast for us", but which should not be thought of as claims to knowledge. The fundamental objection to metaphysics is not that it transcends what we can know.[5]

What we need is an account of metaphysics in terms of a characteristic pattern in the way philosophical problems are dealt with where, as Wittgenstein puts it, "a philosophical problem has the form: 'I do not know my way about'." (Wittgenstein 1958a, § 123) This way of dealing with philosophical problems, I contend, is objectionable but it is also very tempting and extremely difficult to avoid – there is no set of rules for avoiding it. Let me prepare the ground for characterizing this metaphysical procedure with some quotations from Wittgenstein. First, from the *Tractatus*:

> The right method of philosophy would be this: To say nothing except what can be said, ... i.e., something that has nothing to do with philosophy: and then when someone else wished to say something metaphysical, to demonstrate to him that he had given no meaning to

---

[4] Cf. his "Individuals: An Essay in Descriptive Metaphysics" (Strawson 1959).

[5] Kant once characterized metaphysics as "a wholly isolated speculative cognition of reason that elevates itself entirely above all instruction from experience and that through mere concepts (not, like mathematics, through the application of concepts to intuition) where reason thus is supposed to be its own pupil" (Kant 1998, B xiv). That is an epistemic characterization in one sense, but Kant's basic point was not that we could not know whether such concepts applied but that such concepts were, as used by human subjects, mere forms which lacked any intelligible content.

certain signs in his propositions. This method would be unsatisfying to the other – he would not have the feeling that we were teaching him philosophy – but it would be the only strictly correct method. (Wittgenstein 1922, § 6.53)

In order to recognize the symbol in the sign we must consider the context of significant use. (Wittgenstein 1922, § 3.326)

Frege says: Every legitimately constructed proposition must have a sense; and I say: every possible proposition is legitimately constructed, and if it has no sense this can only be because we have given no *meaning* to some of its constituent parts. (Even if we believe that we have done so.) (Wittgenstein 1922, § 5.4733)

What these passages show (in the context of the work as a whole) is that in the *Tractatus* Wittgenstein thought of metaphysics as the result of philosophers' failing to give meaning to certain signs in their propositions, so that they fail to say anything intelligible. This failure is not due to a proposition being unverifiable or defective in its logical syntax – propositions as such are neither metaphysical nor non-metaphysical – but to the philosopher's abstracting the proposition from its 'context of significant use' and failing to see that the meaning it has in one context is not carried over to a different context. Wittgenstein (in a part of 5.4733 not quoted above) gives this example:

... 'Socrates is identical' says nothing, because we have given *no* meaning to the word 'identical' as *adjective*. For when it occurs as the sign of equality it symbolizes in an entirely different way – the symbolizing relation is another – therefore the symbol is in the two cases entirely different; the two symbols have the sign in common with one another only by accident. (Wittgenstein 1922, § 5.4733)

If, that is to say, we had a notation (a 'Begriffsschrift') in which different symbols were always expressed by different signs, it would be as obvious that 'Socrates is identical' says nothing as that 'Socrates the give' says nothing.

Wittgenstein later altered this rather austere characterization of metaphysics because it rested on a view of language which was, at a deeper level, itself metaphysical (in that it imposed on a language the requirement that whatever is said must be expressible in a Begriffsschrift). But he did not alter it because it was a self-defeating attempt to rule out metaphysics on principle. It was not that because, already in the *Tractatus*, Wittgenstein saw that whether a proposition (a sentence) is metaphysical depends on the use we try to put it to, not on what it is in itself – apart from any consideration of "the context of significant use" (Wittgenstein 1922, § 3.326) – so that any proposition we attempt to use metaphysically could be used in another way – used to say something meaningful.

Now consider these passages from Part I of the *Philosophical Investigations*:

> For philosophical problems arise when language *goes on holiday*. (Wittgenstein 1958a, § 38)
>
> We are under the illusion that what is peculiar, profound, essential, in our investigation, resides in its trying to grasp the incomparable essence of language. That is, the order existing between the concepts of proposition, word, proof, truth, experience, and so on. This order is a *super*-order between – so to speak – *super*-concepts. Whereas, of course, if the words 'language', 'experience', 'world', have a use it must be as humble a one as that of the words 'table', 'lamp', 'door'. (Wittgenstein 1958a, § 97)
>
> It was true to say that our considerations could not be scientific ones ... And we may not advance any kind of theory. There must not be anything hypothetical in our considerations. We must also do away with all *explanation*, and description alone must take its place. And this description gets its light, that is to say its purpose, from the philosophical problems; they are solved, rather, by looking into the workings of our language, and that in such a way as to make us recognize those workings: *in spite of* an urge to misunderstand them. The problems are solved, not by giving new information, but by arranging what we have always known. Philosophy is a battle against the bewitchment of our intelligence by means of language. (Wittgenstein 1958a, § 109)
>
> When philosophers use a word – 'knowledge', 'being', 'object', 'I', 'proposition', 'name' – and try to grasp the *essence* of the thing, one must always ask oneself: is the word ever actually used in this way in the language-game which is its original home? – What we do is to bring words back from their metaphysical to their everyday use. (Wittgenstein 1958a, § 116)
>
> Philosophy simply puts everything before us, and neither explains nor deduces anything. – Since everything lies open to view there is nothing to explain. For what is hidden, for example, is of no interest to us.
> One might also give the name 'philosophy' to what is possible *before* all new discoveries and inventions. (Wittgenstein 1958a, § 126)
>
> Such a reform [of language] for particular purposes, an improvement in our terminology designed to prevent misunderstandings in practice, is perfectly possible. But these are not the cases we have to do with. The confusions which occupy us arise when language is like an engine idling, not when it is doing work. (Wittgenstein 1958a, § 132)

I will come back to these passages, now familiar to (if not understood by) most philosophers, but I want first to consider whether there is a unifying point which underlies them and which yields a characterization of the metaphysical way of doing philosophy.

Cora Diamond has argued persuasively that these passages are linked together in urging us to cease laying down, for ourselves and others, external requirements which *must* be met by any philosophical investigation which is serious and deep rather than frivolous or superficial. "I understand by metaphysics", she writes in *The Realistic Spirit*, "the laying down of metaphysical requirements, whether in the form of views about what there is ... or in the rather different form exhibited by the *Tractatus* ..." (Diamond 1991, p. 20) The phrase, "views about what there is" refers to various 'isms' – empiricism, idealism, physicalism, scientific realism, etc. – which lay down metaphysical requirements for anything to be real (or true). The reference to the *Tractatus* is to its failing to be consistently non-metaphysical. It is anti-metaphysical in trying to show that there is no "genuine philosophical question whether there are or are not metaphysical features of reality underlying structural or logical characteristics of language ...", but it is metaphysical in laying down "requirements which are internal to the character of language as language, in there being a general form of sentence, in all sentences having this form ... [The metaphysics is in] the 'metaphysical must' ... the 'must' of logical analysis, of total determinacy of sense." (Diamond 1991, pp. 18–19) In Diamond's view, "the characteristic activity of the metaphysical spirit" is not the taste for speculation, the search for the transcendent, the quest for system but "the laying down of philosophical requirements [which is to] be contrasted with looking at the use, looking at what we do" (Diamond 1991, p. 21).

Consider two other passages in which Diamond expands on the idea of metaphysical requirements as something we must resist. The first clarifies the sense in which Wittgenstein's notion of metaphysics as nonsense differs from that of Carnap and the positivists in not taking propositions to be nonsensical in themselves and in principle.

> The *Tractatus* and the *Investigations* have this in common: they do not invite us to give up the making of philosophical propositions *because* such propositions are nonsensical ... They both treat philosophical propositions as constructions we make on the basis of linguistic analogies, patterns, or images in our language. We may come to see that we do not want to go on doing anything with these linguistic constructions; the satisfaction of our needs does not lie that way. We abandon them; we leave them unused; we say 'These we *do not* want.' To call them nonsensical is to exclude them in that way from the commerce of our lives. (Diamond 1991, p. 35)

Although I would narrow the target here by speaking of metaphysical (rather than philosophical) propositions, the claim being made is a very good one. Its point is not that we should turn our backs on what metaphysical philosophers are doing and cease to take any interest in what interests them, but that we should not rule out metaphysics on the basis of some (metaphysical) doctrine about the nature of nonsense and, in particular, about what *makes* propositions nonsensical. To call metaphysical propositions nonsensical is simply to say that the use philosophers (try to) make of them is not relevant to the philosophical problems which motivate our investigations, and that is not something we can say prior to our own trying to deal with those problems.

The second relates the rejection of external requirements to the idea that philosophy leaves everything as it is:

> The sense in which philosophy leaves everything as it is is this: philosophy does not put us in a position to justify or to criticize what we do by showing that it meets or fails to meet requirements we lay down in our philosophizing. If there are language-games we engage in because we think that playing them ... will enable some philosophical requirement to be met, we shall indeed no longer want to play such games ... – the interest of doing so will be gone ... Leaving everything as it is is consistent with showing that the interest of a game rests on mythology or fantasy or a failure of understanding of what it is for our own real needs to be met. (Diamond 1991, p. 22)

This notion of being committed to external requirements which *must* be met by philosophical work in metaphysics, epistemology, ethics, or what have you, which *must* be met if concepts like truth, fact, value, mind, understanding, meaning, and knowledge are to be rendered intelligible, seems to me an illuminating way of characterizing the metaphysical way of doing philosophy. It links together a number of the themes found in the passages from Wittgenstein quoted above, themes which can be seen as connected in a significant way with the role of external requirements in the metaphysical way of dealing with philosophical problems. I want to consider three of these themes here.

The first is expressed in Wittgenstein's remark that "It was true to say that our considerations could not be scientific ones." (Wittgenstein 1958a, § 109) Wittgenstein was trained as an engineer and knew well what science was and what it had achieved, but a sharp distinction between science and philosophy was a motif in all his work. In rejecting scientific inquiry as a model for philosophy, he was rejecting an external requirement: the imposition of scientific method on an activity whose aim is quite different. Hence his contention that the "the real source of metaphysics" is the tendency of philosophers "to answer questions the way science does", a point von Wright sets in a wider context:

> The thinking Wittgenstein calls metaphysical is stamped by the linguistic patterns and thought habits of a predominantly scientific civilization. The metaphysics [he] is fighting is thus not one rooted in theology but one rooted in science. He is fighting the obscuring influence on thinking, not of the relics of a dead but of the habits of a living culture. Of this he gives clear warning in the *Blue Book* where he wrote: "Philosophers constantly see the methods of science before their eyes, and are irresistibly tempted to answer questions in the way science does. This tendency is the real source of metaphysics, and leads the philosopher into complete darkness." He immediately give examples: The craving for general theories, what he calls 'the contemptuous attitude to the particular case'; the tendency to explain the concept of number, to reduce the infinite to the finite, mathematics to logic, intentional behavior to bodily movement. The most vulgar examples of these tendencies we find, it seems to me, in contemporary philosophy of mind ... Farther into the jungle

of metaphysics, as Wittgenstein saw it, philosophy can hardly lose itself than in these latter day phenomena of a philosophic culture gone 'scientist'. (von Wright 1993, pp. 99–100)[6]

The second theme is Wittgenstein's wariness about generality, which also turns on the rejection of external requirements. It is important to note that he did not deny philosophy's legitimate interest in giving a general account of concepts central to our life and thought; his criticism was of the wrong kind of generality, one which involved the external requirement that a concept must be constituted by what it is that all its instances have in common.[7] To be governed by that notion of a concept in giving a general account is to follow an *abstractive* procedure, which requires *dropping* features instances do not have in common and hence to eliminate features integral to the way the concept functions in what Wittgenstein calls "the language-game which is its original home" (Wittgenstein 1958a, § 116), which is where our investigations must be anchored. "One cannot guess how a word functions. One has to *look at* its use and learn from that." (Wittgenstein 1958a, § 340)[8] When philosophers do not look, their procedure is governed by external requirements, and as a result it deals with problems which do not arise from reflection on the workings of our concepts but are created by the metaphysical procedure itself. Many of the thought experiments so popular in analytic metaphysics are clear cases of this abstractive procedure, particularly when the experiments appeal to invented outré examples, which are (by design) far removed from the everyday contexts of the concepts involved – so far removed that it is dubious that the words that figure in the thought experiments express the same concepts as the ones being investigated.[9]

The third theme is Wittgenstein's insistence that philosophers should not construct explanatory theories.

---

6 The Wittgenstein quotation is from Wittgenstein 1958b, p. 18.
7 Philosophers (especially those influenced by Rush Rhees) who take Wittgenstein's point to be that we should not attempt any kind of general account of concepts like truth, reality, understanding, language jump too quickly from eschewing the wrong kind of generality to eschewing generality completely. Moore's notes on Wittgenstein's lectures record him as having said that "what he was doing resembled traditional philosophy in that 1) it was very general; 2) it was fundamental both to ordinary life and to the sciences; 3) it was independent of any special results of the sciences" (Wittgenstein 1993, p. 113). That was true for all of Wittgenstein's career.
8 The passage continues: "But the difficulty is to remove the prejudice which stands in the way of doing this. It is not a *stupid* prejudice." (Wittgenstein 1958a, § 340)
9 Wittgenstein invented language games in order to investigate the workings of our language but they were entirely different from the outré thought experiments of analytic metaphysics.

We may not advance any kind of theory. There must not be anything hypothetical in our considerations. We must also do away with all *explanation*, and description alone must take its place. And this description gets its light, that is to say its purpose, from the philosophical problems; they are solved, rather, by looking into the workings of our language, and that in such a way as to make us recognize those workings: *in spite of* an urge to misunderstand them. The problems are solved, not by giving new information, but by arranging what we have always known. (Wittgenstein 1958a, § 109)

The crux of this passage is the rejection of *explanation* in anything like the sense in which it is sought in the sciences. The search for explanation in that sense results from our laying down requirements instead of looking at and reflecting on the workings of our language. We assume that if philosophical problems arise through reflection on phenomena which are deeply significant and thoroughly puzzling, then there *must* be something which demands something like a scientific explanation, which demands *that* kind of clarification; to assume otherwise is philosophically superficial and intellectually frivolous. But, Wittgenstein insists, to undertake that search is to give in to our urge to misunderstand the problems, which are solved not by constructing explanatory theories but by "arranging what we have always known" (Wittgensten 1958a, § 109).[10]

This does not mean the rejection of explanation in every sense of the term. What Frege called 'elucidation' is a kind of explanation, and that is an activity which is crucial to the *Tractatus* and which Wittgenstein always took to be central to philosophy, although his conception of what it was underwent major changes. In writing that "Since everything lies open to view there is nothing to explain" (Wittgenstein 1958a, § 126), he did not mean that achieving the kind of clarity which enables us to resolve philosophical problems is easy. To explain things in the sense of articulating, rendering intelligible, distinguishing, illustrating, putting in context, and so on, is central to philosophy.

Wittgenstein followed his remark that "We may not advance any kind of theory" with the remark that "There must not be anything hypothetical in our considerations"[11] (Wittgenstein 1958a, § 109), which shows that what was foremost in his mind was scientific theories: systems of explanatory hypotheses. His rejection of explanatory theories is not a rejection of theory in all senses

---

10 Cf. Wittgenstein: "Thought can as it were fly, it doesn't have to walk. You do not understand your own transactions, that is to say you do not have a synoptic view of them, and you as it were project your lack of understanding into the idea of a medium in which the most astounding things are possible." (Wittgenstein 1967, #273)

11 Cf. Kant: "In this kind of inquiry it is in no way allowed to hold opinion, and ... anything that even looks like a hypothesis is a forbidden commodity, which should not be put up for sale even at the lowest price but must be confiscated as soon as it is discovered." (Kant 1998, A xv)

of the term. Some philosophers who characterize their work as 'theory' or 'theoretical' simply mean that they are engaged in reflection rather than political activity or consciousness-raising, or that they intend to be rigorous or methodical, and Wittgenstein himself was theoretical in those senses. Davidson articulated a famous 'theory of meaning' on the basis of Tarski's theory of truth, and although many analytic philosophers have interpreted both Davidson and Tarski in a metaphysical way, I would argue that neither of them constructed theories which fall under Wittgenstein's strictures. Tarski's is not a philosophical theory but a logical theory, and Davidson's theory of meaning is not a metaphysical theory in the pejorative sense, for it was not meant to *explain* anything in the sense Wittgenstein objected to. It is an attempt to give a systematic *description* of the truth conditions of the sentences of a given language, and it is explanatory only in the sense that it aims to illuminate or elucidate the structure of a language. It does not aim to explain why a language works as it does, nor explain how it is possible for us to learn or be competent in a language, and it is certainly not meant to be a theory about mental or cognitive processes. There are no doubt objections to it from a Wittgensteinian point of view, but the mere fact that it is a theory should not be one.[12]

Wittgenstein's rejection of explanation must not be identified with the 'quietism' often ascribed to him, the idea that he simply refuses, for one reason or another, to pursue the explanation of various puzzling phenomena, particularly if that seems to require an explanatory theory. Wittgenstein's stance is rather that distinctively philosophical problems never turn on phenomena which *need* an explanation in the sense he rejects or about which one *could* have an explanatory theory. The fundamental reason for the failure of the explanations metaphysicians propose is not that they are obscure, extravagant, or question-begging, but that they are directed at phenomena which theoretical explanation does not help us understand and whose puzzling features it does not clarify. Marie McGinn has given a very illuminating account of the kind of phenomena these are:

> The things which we are doomed to misunderstand when we take up a theoretical attitude toward them are, then, just those things 'that we know when no one asks, but no longer know when we are supposed to give an account of [them]'[13]... What we are concerned

---

[12] In my view, Davidson is much less metaphysical than most analytic philosophers, and I think that Wittgensteinians who take him as a primary target of their criticism ought to see him rather as an ally, even if not an entirely trustworthy one.

[13] The quote is from Augustine's remark in his *Confessions* about the question "What, then, is time?", which Wittgenstein discusses in the *Philosophical Investigations*, § 89.

> with when we ask questions of the form 'What is time?', 'What is meaning?', 'What is thought?' is the nature of the phenomena which constitute our world ... and in asking these questions we express a desire to understand them more clearly. Yet in the very act of framing these questions, we are tempted to adopt an attitude toward these phenomena which, Wittgenstein believes, makes us approach them in the wrong way, in a way which assumes that we have to uncover or explain something ... As soon as we try to catch hold of them in the way our questions seem to require, we find that we cannot do it; we find that we 'no longer know'... We think that the fault lies in our explanations and that we need to construct ever more subtle and surprising accounts ... The real fault ... is not in our explanations, but in the very idea that the puzzlement we feel can be removed by means of a discovery. What we really need is to turn our whole inquiry round and concern ourselves, not with explanation or theory construction, but with description ... For our puzzlement concerned the nature or essence of particular phenomena ... and this puzzlement is removed. 'not by giving new information, but by arranging what we have always known'. [*Philosophical Investigations*, § 109] ... [Our aim should be] a kind of understanding which consists in seeing a pattern or form in what is there before our eyes, but which we had previously neglected or overlooked ... Everything we need to understand is already there and only needs to be arranged correctly. (McGinn 1997, pp. 18–19, 26–27)

That such puzzling phenomena cannot be clarified by quasi-scientific explanation is not *obvious*. The philosophical problems may arise precisely because the phenomena appear to stand in need of explanation, and that they do not so stand has to be *shown*, something that requires hard philosophical work.[14] Indeed, it might turn out that explanation *is* relevant to understanding certain puzzling phenomena, although that is likely to mean that the problems are not philosophical and should be dealt with as scientific. Consider again the *Philosophical Investigations*,§ 126: "Since everything lies open to view there is nothing to explain. For what is hidden, for example, is of no interest to us. One might also give the name 'philosophy' to what is possible *before* all new discoveries and inventions." (Wittgenstein 1958a, § 126) This doesn't say that it is *obvious* what does or does not lie open to view or that thinking there is something to explain in a philosophically perplexing situation is somehow deviant. There might be something hidden in the situation but *that* would be something "of no interest to us" as philosophers, though it might be interesting to those who can make "new discoveries and inventions".

On this view, then, metaphysics is not objectionable because it is speculative, because it longs for the transcendent, or because it attempts to give a general account of concepts like reality, truth, knowledge, nature, or goodness. Nor

---

[14] "How does it come about that philosophy is so complicated a structure? ... Philosophy unties knots in our thinking; hence its result must be simple, but philosophizing has to be as complicated as the knots it unties." (Wittgenstein 1967, #452)

is it objectionable on the ground that it fails to make intelligible claims and descends into nonsense. Metaphysical activity *may* result in sentences which are unintelligible in the *Tractatus* sense – which are used in such a way that we cannot both give them a determinate sense and interpret them as the metaphysician would like. The more typical case in analytic philosophy, however, is that metaphysical activity results in intellectual constructions which are objectionable because their intricacy and ingenuity give the illusion of resolving philosophical problems, when in fact the real problems have been replaced by puzzles generated by the metaphysical activity itself.[15] The philosopher is no longer *looking* at the way concepts work in our life and thought; she is considering how they *must* work in the context of a metaphysical construction of her own creation. The result is what von Wright calls

> the 'free-wheeling' of language which occurs when words get detached from their actual use in the language-games of communicative discourse and are being used for constructing what Wittgenstein calls *Luftgebäude* (translated 'houses of cards') in the linguistic isolation of the philosopher's mind. (von Wright 1993, p. 99)

We may admire those ingenious linguistic constructions in various ways but we may also, as Diamond puts it in a passage I discussed above,

> come to see that we do not want to go on doing anything with [them]; the satisfaction of our needs does not lie that way. We abandon them; we leave them unused; we say 'These we *do not* want.' To call them nonsensical is to exclude them in that way from the commerce of our lives. (Diamond 1991, p. 35)

This characterization of metaphysics has been abstract, and I want to make it more concrete by discussing a particular example of analytic metaphysics to show how it involves a pattern of activity which is objectionable in the sense just characterized. I will use as my example a book by Marian David called *Correspondence and Disquotation*, which is a defense of the correspondence theory of truth over against so-called "disquotational" (or minimalist) theories. David's book is a very good book of its kind, admirably clear and skillfully argued, and my criticism is not directed against the competence of the book or its author. My criticism is that, however competent, it is a paradigm of the kind of metaphysical way of doing things which should be resisted as an unproductive diversion from what philosophical activity can and should achieve. It sheds little light on how

---

[15] John Dewey calls such constructions "dialectical constructions"; he uses "dialectical" in much the same pejorative (and Kantian) sense in which I use "metaphysical".

the concept of truth functions when it is doing work in the thought and discourse of human life, but offers instead an account of how the concept fits into a world constructed to meet requirements derived from antecedent views about what language, thought and reality must be. I begin by quoting a number of passages from David's book as a basis for my critical discussion.

> 'Truth is a relation to reality; therefore, truth has to be explained in terms of a relation to reality.' That is the fundamental intuition underlying [the correspondence theory of truth]... Its central claim is the thesis that something is true just in case it corresponds to a fact, and false just in case it does not correspond to a fact ... The thesis is motivated by intuitively plausible judgments of the following kind: The sentence 'Bats are mammals' is true because it corresponds to the fact that bats are mammals; the sentence 'Snow is white' is true because it corresponds to the fact that snow is white ... The central definition of the [theory] ... is a straightforward generalization of such examples:
> (C) x is a true sentence $=_{df}$ x is a sentence, and there is some fact y such that x corresponds to y.
> [At this point David links this definition to the conceptions of truth of Aquinas, Moore, and Russell. He claims that the definition entails a *generalization:*] a sentence is true just in case it corresponds to a fact. The generalization has modal force, namely the force of a metaphysical necessity, which probably comes out better if it is read like this: For a sentence to be true *is* for it to correspond to a fact ...
> [There are two tasks for defenders of the correspondence theory.] The ontological task will be to account for the notion of facts ... The ideological task will be to account for the correspondence relation ... This double task for a full-fledged correspondence theory is most naturally approached by construing correspondence as 'congruence'. The basic idea behind this account is that sentences and facts are both complex structured entities ... The account then proceeds by showing how sentence-to-fact correspondence can be constructed from further correspondence relations that obtain between the constituents of sentences and the constituents of facts ... [This] will, eventually, lead into a *semantic* theory that explains how names, predicates and logical particles can *refer* to things, properties, relations, sets, and functions ... (David 1994, pp. 17–21)
>
> [Perhaps we should give up theorizing and recognize] that the notion of fact [and correspondence] is a rather, ordinary, nontechnical notion ... [But] this skirts all the important issues: funny facts, identity criteria for facts, and the question of which sentences correspond to which facts. These are precisely the issues that indicate that our ordinary intuitions, untutored, are not good enough for the correspondence definition. Our ordinary intuitions on these issues are so obscure and confused that one seems forced to admit that the terms 'fact' and 'correspondence' – as they appear in the definition – really invoke technical notions that overlap only partially with our ordinary notions ... (David 1994, p. 23)
>
> [The kind of theory needed is as follows]... It is natural to hold that what is distinctive about sentences that are true or false is that they *represent* reality as being a certain way. True ones represent it as it actually is, while false ones represent it as it is not. The ways reality can be represented as being are often called *states of affairs*, which are entities that are typically denoted by that-clauses. A state of affairs ... can *obtain* or fail to obtain. For example, the state of affairs that snow is white obtains, while the state of affairs that snow is green

does not obtain. If a sentence represents a state of affairs that obtains, then it is true in virtue of representing that state of affairs and in virtue of that state's obtaining. [Hence this refined definition:]
(R) x is a true sentence = $_{Df}$ x is a sentence, and there is a state of affairs y such that x represents y and y obtains ...
I shall call (R) – or rather, the kind of theory in which (R) is the central definition, the *representation theory of truth*. It is rather popular among philosophers nowadays ... (David 1994, p. 31)

I shall not develop a specific version of the representation theory in any detail, nor shall I give anything like a complete catalogue of all the options available to a representation theorist. Instead, I want to indicate some areas in which representationalists are likely to encounter difficulties ... [These difficulties show] the rather daunting task that is involved in working out a full-fledged representation theory of truth ... The attempt to develop a satisfying representation theory of sentence-truth will face a number of intricate questions about the nature of representation – questions which anything worth of the name 'theory' will have to address. (David 1994, pp. 34, 40, 45)

These passages illustrate with unusual clarity and specificity a pattern of activity which is exemplified, explicitly or implicitly, by most analytic metaphysics. In the next section I will show where, in my view, activity of this kind goes wrong. But I first want to give a sympathetic, rational reconstruction of the main steps in the pattern and then sketch out the kind of defense typically given for proceeding in this way. Here, then, are the main steps:

1. Cite what are taken to be "intuitively plausible judgments", for example, "... the sentence 'Snow is white' is true because it corresponds to the fact that snow is white" (David 1994, p. 17) or "'Bats are mammals' is true because it corresponds to the fact that bats are mammals."
2. Generalize these initial judgments to yield a thesis which is supposed to be equally plausible, for example, "Something is true just in case it corresponds to a fact." (David 1994, p. 17).
3. Reformulate the thesis in philosophically acceptable language ("philosophers' English"): x is a true sentence =$_{Df}$ x is a sentence and there is some fact y such that x corresponds to y. David calls this "The central definition of the classical correspondence theory of truth" (David 1994, p. 31) and holds that it "is a straightforward generalization" of the judgments referred to in step 1.
4. Formulate a simple theory, in this case the thesis that "a sentence[16] is true just in case it corresponds to a fact" (David 1994, p. 17). The *words* here

---

[16] I shall speak in terms of 'sentence' throughout, even though I recognize (as does David, though for different reasons) that the term is by no means unproblematic in this context.

are the same as in step 2, but because of step 3, with '$=_{Df}$' doing the work, what they now express is 'has the force of a metaphysical necessity' and hence is better formulated as, 'For a sentence to be true is for it to correspond to a fact.'

5. Link the simple theory to accounts of truth from the history of philosophy (Aquinas, Russell, and Moore), whose additional claims are used to enrich the simple theory.
6. Formulate problems with which the enriched theory will have to deal. These may be problems familiar from earlier accounts of truth or new ones suggested by the enriched theory or by theories about truth-related topics. David classifies the problems as ontological or ideological. The former arise from inquiry into what it is *to be a fact*, which raises such issues as whether there can be logical, ethical, or modal facts, whether facts can be disjunctive, conditional, or negative, whether such facts can be reduced to less problematic ones. The latter arise from the question of what it is for a sentence to *correspond* to a fact, and their resolution requires 'a semantic account of word-to-world relations', and hence further theory construction.
7. Solve these problems by refining and elaborating the theory, typically by formulating alternatives as *options* for choice. David claims that this task "is most naturally approached by construing correspondence as 'congruence'" (David 1994, p. 21), which introduces the notion that sentences are structures of names, predicates, and logical particles, which are correlated with facts as structures of things, properties, relations, sets, and functions. The task is "to explain how the simple constituents of facts combine into complex wholes, and ... to identify the 'glue' that keeps the constituents together". This ought to yield "identity criteria for facts" and "an answer to the question of which sentences correspond to which facts" (David 1994, p. 21).
8. Develop arguments to show that which of the options which have been formulated is superior. The arguments appeal to virtues of the truth theory (consistency, simplicity, coherence), its success in dealing with counter-examples (typically outré examples which constitute thought experiments), its wide acceptance by the philosophical community, the plausibility of contiguous theories, and so on.

What motivates this pattern of activity is a line of thought which goes more or less as follows. Philosophical inquiry should begin with intuitively plausible judgments people take for granted. These are the untutored beliefs which constitute folk psychology, folk physics, folk ontology, or what have you – a miscellany of intuitive judgments which provide the data for philosophical inquiry. While reflection convinces some metaphysicians ('eliminativists' or 'error theorists') that these beliefs are, on the whole, simply false, most metaphysicians conclude that they are not outright false but rather obscure, confused, and often inconsistent. Reformulating them in a philosophically acceptable way (preferably in terms of a respected philosophical theory) resolves some of these difficulties, but further reflection shows that there are deeper problems hidden beneath the surface, whose resolution requires constructing a theory which formulates theoretical claims about the nature and structure of the (presumed) objects of these intuitive judgments.

If this procedure is challenged, it will be defended in various ways. Some will defend it on the ground that the exact sciences proceed in this way, their success being sufficient reason to commend the method to philosophers. Others who are less question-begging about the relation of philosophy to the sciences will argue that the construction of theories is simply a rigorous and systematic way of pursuing the kind of explanation which should be the goal of any intellectually serious philosophy. The only alternative, it is claimed, would be to acquiesce in the everyday beliefs and loose speech of philosophically untutored folk, to refrain from asking why things are as they are, and to think that philosophical problems never touch on things that require a substantive explanation.

This is, in my view, to be held captive by a *picture* about how philosophy *must* proceed, which involves taking Wittgenstein's assertion that we must do away with all explanation as a rejection of serious philosophical work. What Wittgenstein proposes, they think, is intellectually frivolous: it substitutes aphorism for argument, arresting examples for complex explanations, and well-turned phrases for worked out theories.

While Wittgensteinians have no doubt produced at least their share of intellectually frivolous work, those held captive by this picture miss Wittgenstein's claim that there is another kind of inquiry, which is also critical and probing, equally rigorous and intellectually serious, but not metaphysical. Philosophical inquiry can be critical by bringing "words back from their metaphysical to their everyday use" rather than by rejecting our everyday judgments, and it can be probing even if it "simply puts everything before us and neither explains nor deduces anything". Doing this well is extremely demanding and rigorous, and it is anything but frivolous, for the problems dealt with "have the character of depth; they are deep disquietudes ..." (Wittgenstein 1958a, § 111).

To spell out further what this way of doing philosophy without metaphysics involves, let us take a critical look at the example of metaphysical construction whose eight step pattern I sketched out above. From the point of view of metaphysicians, the first three steps are not part of the real philosophical work but non-controversial preliminaries to it. The first step cites "intuitively plausible judgments", the second expresses what is supposed to be merely a summary generalization of those judgments, and the third reformulates the generalization in a "philosophically acceptable" way. While the movement here is intended to advance clarity, it is not regarded as altering the content of the judgments in step one because those are data – the uncontroversial starting point.

From the point of view of someone who thinks the metaphysical way should be avoided, however, these three steps are not uncontroversial. "The decisive movement in the conjuring trick has been made, and it was the very one that we thought quite innocent." (Wittgenstein 1958a, § 308) What the metaphysician takes as innocent preliminaries to real philosophical work are precisely where the rigorous work needs to be done. What were chosen as uncontroversial examples of "intuitively plausible judgments" – for instance, 'Snow is white' is true because it corresponds to the fact that snow is white – might be fair starting points if the philosophical use made of them was attentive to their role in the everyday contexts from which judgments taken to be data must be drawn. But these judgments are considered in abstraction from any such role and thereby become mere platitudes – metaphysical platitudes, if you will – whose only role is in (mostly idle) talk *about* the concept of truth. What many philosophers call 'intuitions' (as in "what my intuition tells me") often have this same status: they are thoughts *about* truth rather than examples of judgments in which the concept is actually put to use.

This becomes evident in step 3, which gives a definition of truth in terms of fact. On one level, the definition is quite innocent because 'true' and 'fact' are interchangeable in ordinary contexts, but if that is all that is involved, the definition would not yield a substantive thesis about truth and related notions. The definition, however, is not used innocently, but is taken to imply the existence of facts as *entities*, correspondence to which *explains* why sentences are true (or false),[17] which is a substantive thesis not supported by the judgments specified in step one, and certainly not by those judgments when seen in contexts in which they are doing real work.

Indeed, such judgments are already superseded by step two. The claim there that sentences are true because they correspond to *a* fact (not to a particular fact) is not what the intuitive judgments say; they say that 'p' is true because it corresponds to *the fact that p*. Moreover, David's choice of examples shows that his data consist of specially chosen "intuitively plausible judgments". Consider some examples he did *not* choose:

---

17 "If one accepts the definition and maintains that there are true sentences, one has thereby committed oneself (ontologically) to the existence of facts; and by accepting the definition alone, one has already committed oneself (ideologically) to invoke the notion ... of correspondence as an explanatory resource of one's theory." (David 1994, p. 20)

'Snow is not white' is true just in case it corresponds to the fact that snow is not white.

'He would not have been injured had he jumped' is true just in case it corresponds to the fact that he would not have been injured had he jumped.

These are just as intuitively plausible as the ones David cites, but he did not cite them because he regards them as in need of radical reformulation, since (taken in the way he takes the examples he did cite) the first implies the existence of negative facts, the second the existence of counterfactual facts, and the existence of such facts (which David calls "funny facts") conflicts with requirements which he is convinced *must* be met by an adequate account of facts.[18] Already by step two, that is to say, David is not only appealing to platitudes but he has made a choice about which platitudes to appeal to, a choice justified by requirements external to the judgments in which the concept of truth does its work.

To abandon a procedure of this kind is not to acquiesce in the confusions, obscurities, and silliness people come up with when they talk about truth or other concepts which concern philosophers. This procedure is not flawed because it tries to correct the shortcomings of platitudes about truth which are bandied about; it is flawed because it doesn't distinguish between platitudes and the judgments which play a working role in the life, thought, and (non-metaphysical) discourse of human beings. The result is that it deals in a hurried and careless way with those ordinary judgments with which most philosophers, even most metaphysicians, think philosophical investigation must begin. It makes no attempt to trace out the intricate ways in which concepts like truth, falsity, fact, reality, correspond, and so on, are used in contexts outside metaphysical theorizing, and there is no attentive inquiry into how these terms interact in that everyday discourse which is supposed to be the basis of theory construction. It might be said with considerable justification that it is the metaphysicians themselves who, acquiescing in everyday platitudes, take ordinary language for granted by failing to reflect on it with any seriousness.

What a serious philosophical investigation of concepts like truth in contexts where they are not idling would look like is something I will not discuss, if for no other reason than that there are no procedures for carrying it out which could be usefully described apart from considering at length some concrete examples. There is no method for getting clear about how such concepts function in the complex and varied activities of everyday human life: in ordinary conversation,

---

18 Facts of this kind are, David writes (1994, p. 22), "funny" facts which a theory ought to show can be "reduced" to other, more "serious" facts. The same point holds of moral or mathematical facts.

in moral and religious reflection, in scientific experiment and theory, in the discourse of economists, political theorists, or military strategists, in literature or criticism of the arts, in the discourse of the courageous or the penitent.

Nor is there a method for dealing with the puzzlement which inevitably arises in the course of philosophical reflection of any kind. Concepts like truth function in extremely complex ways, and to get an overall picture of how they function is difficult. Even the most careful reflection – *especially* the most careful reflection – will involve misunderstanding, will turn up apparent inconsistencies and incoherencies, will pose philosophical problems of various kinds. Indeed, as Wittgenstein wrote, this kind of investigation "gets its light, that is to say its purpose, from the philosophical problems" (Wittgenstein 1958a, § 109).

What we must *not* do, however, in dealing with these problems, is follow the remaining steps of the pattern I sketched out by building a more and more intricate metaphysical structure, which is more and more removed from the contexts in which concepts like truth do their real work. The crucial move in David's construction is made in step four, where the platitude of step two ("Something is true just in case it corresponds to a fact") is transformed by a sleight of hand into a thesis which "has modal force, namely the force of a metaphysical necessity, which probably comes out better if it is read like this: For a statement to be true *is* for it to correspond to a fact." (David 1994, p. 19) At this point David cuts loose from any intuitive judgments, commenting that the "definition" in step three should not, after all, be taken as specifying "what we mean when we apply the word 'true' to sentences" (David 1994, p. 19). From now on we have pure theory construction, whose aim is not to clarify the concept of truth as it works in ordinary contexts nor to resolve problems that arise in those contexts (since there has been no serious investigation of how the concept works in those contexts) but to resolve problems whose point depends on the theory being constructed.

David is explicit about the latter point. Were we to deal with notions like fact or correspondence as they occur in ordinary discourse, we would, he writes, "skirt all the important issues: funny facts, identity criteria for facts, and the question of which sentences correspond to which facts" (David 1994, p. 22). These are issues that arise only in the context of the theory, a fact which, far from troubling David, indicates to him the superiority of theory over "our ordinary intuitions" (David 1994, p. 23).

I do not want my critique of the metaphysical way of doing philosophy to be taken as suggesting that in an ideal world metaphysics would be banned or that in the real world there is not a great deal to be learned from the work of metaphysicians. I am not unique in believing that I often learn more from working through the works of philosophers who do not try to avoid the metaphysical way than from those who do. There are two main reasons for this. One is that those who think of themselves as followers of Wittgenstein too often fail to avoid the ways of metaphysics because they put external 'Wittgensteinian' constraints on philosophical activity, which are more restrictive than any put on it by those committed to metaphysics. This leads to an unfortunate dogmatism, which may be shown in the failure to expose one's view to the critical scrutiny of those who do not share them, or in the way philosophical views are criticized, namely by dealing with them in the most generalized way, ignoring the particulars of a given view. Sometimes it is shown in a refusal to take seriously the work of any but a few select philosophers, which means careless reading and criticism of those not among the select, and sometimes even a refusal to consider their work.

The other reason is that trying to avoid the metaphysical way too often means trying to avoid argument. This may be because it is thought that Wittgenstein's claim that "description alone" must take the place of explanation means that argument is out of place, but that is surely wrong, both as an interpretation of Wittgenstein and as a principle of philosophy. It is very difficult "to bring words back from their metaphysical to their everyday use" (Wittgenstein 1958a, § 116), and it cannot be done just by saying "that is not using ordinary language" or "we wouldn't say that". Arguments are needed at this point also – especially at this point – and that is a demanding task for which we need all the help we can get, not least from metaphysicians.

These comments reflect the context of my own personal encounters with philosophers, but there is a further reason not to ignore the work of metaphysicians, which is that the line between philosophical work which is metaphysical and work which is not is neither sharp nor clear. The first task of one who would avoid metaphysics is to take to heart Wittgenstein's remark that "The problems are solved, not by giving new information, but by arranging what we have always known" (Wittgenstein 1958a, § 109). But if to arrange what we already know means to put it in some order – to arrange it properly, even correctly – then the line between arranging what we already know and constructing a theory of the phenomena may not be sharp and may not even be clear. The difference is largely a matter of intention – of what we aim to achieve in our philosophical work – which *is* a significant difference but not one which requires a consistently negative attitude toward metaphysical construction. For we can often construe the latter not as construction or as revisionary proposals about our concepts, but as attempts to arrange what we already know by ordering it in a more intelligible way. From that point of view, we can see metaphysicians as not only constructing theories but as correcting our misconceptions of what we already know and suggesting difficulties in the way we have arranged what we (think we) already know.

The failure of the metaphysical way must not be taken for granted. There is no guarantee, *a priori* or otherwise, that theory construction may not be required to resolve certain problems which arise even from philosophical reflection that is attentive to the way our concepts function in everyday life. Perhaps Wittgenstein was convinced that there were no such problems, that all philosophical problems are solved "by looking into the workings of our language, and that in such a way as to make us recognize those workings: *in spite of* an urge to misunderstand them" (Wittgenstein 1958a, § 109). There are good reasons for this conviction but they are not sufficient to *establish* his view about all philosophical problems. The only thing that could establish that would actually be to resolve all the problems, all the "deep disquietudes" (Wittgenstein 1958a, § 111), to attain that "*complete* clarity" we are aiming at, something which, or so it seems to me, we are now no closer to attaining than we were at the bright dawn of analytic philosophy a hundred years ago.[19]

---

19 This paper has gotten a lot of discussion and criticism, and the fact that I do not know how to deal with much of it does not lessen my appreciation to those who reacted to it. Its inspiration was a conference at the Finnish Institute in Paris to honor G. H. von Wright, and versions of it have also been read in Trondheim, Uppsala, Umeå, Chicago, and at Saint Olaf College; in all these places I got pertinent and useful comments. Special thanks to: Lilli Alanen, Zed Adams, Lisa van Alstyne, Arthur Collins, James Conant, Alberto Emiliani, Martin Gunderson, John Haugeland, Sara Heinämaa, Ingvar Johannson, Sten Lindström, Georg Meggle, Anthony Rudd, Sören Stenlund, Jan Osterberg.

Bibliography

American Heritage Dictionary (1982). 2nd ed. Boston: Houghton Mifflin.
Anscombe, G. E. M. (1957). *Intention*. Oxford: Basil Blackwell.
Anscombe, G. E. M. (1963). *Intention*. 2nd ed. Oxford: Basil Blackwell.
Anscombe, G. E. M. (1981). *Metaphysics and Philosophy of Mind: Collected Papers, Vol. 2*. Minneapolis: University of Minnesota Press.
Anscombe, G. E. M. (2000). *Intention*. Cambridge: Harvard University Press.
Aron, R. (1967). *Main Currents in Sociological Thought*, Vol. 2. London: Penguin.
Baier, A. (1997). Doing Things with Others: The Mental Commons. In: L. Alanen, S. Heinamaa and T. Wallgren, eds., *Commonality and Particularity in Ethics*. New York: St. Martin's Press, pp. 15–44.
Barwise, J. and Perry, J. (1983). *Situations and Attitudes*. London: MIT Press.
Bellah, R., Madsen, R., Sullivan, W., Swindler, A. and Tipton, S. (1985). *Habits of the Heart*. Berkeley: University of California Press.
Berger, P. (1970). On the Obsolescence of the Concept of Honor. *European Journal of Sociology* 11(2), pp. 339–347.
Berger, P., Berger, B. and Kellner, H. (1974). *The Homeless Mind*. New York: Vintage.
Bergström, L. and Føllesdal, D. (1994). Interview with Donald Davidson in November 1993. *Theoria* 60(3), pp. 207–225.
Berlin, I. (1969). Historical Inevitability. In *Four Essays on Liberty*, Oxford: Oxford University Press, pp. 41–117.
Brandom, R. (1994). *Making It Explicit: Reasoning, Representing and Discursive Commitment*. Cambridge: Harvard University Press.
Bratman, M. (1992). Shared Cooperative Activity. *Philosophical Review* 101, pp. 327–341.
Bratman, M. (1993). Shared Intention. *Ethics* 104(1), pp. 97–113.
Bratman, M. (1999). *Faces of Intention*. Cambridge: Cambridge University Press.
Burge, T. (1979). Individualism and the Mental. *Midwest Studies in Philosophy* 4, pp. 73–122.
Campbell, K. (1981). The Metaphysics of Abstract Particulars. *Midwest Studies in Philosophy* 6, pp. 477–488.
Campbell, T. (1981). *Seven Theories of Human Society*. Oxford: Clarendon Press.
Carnap, R. (1959). The Elimination of Metaphysics Through the Logical Analysis of Language. In: A. J. Ayer, ed., *Logical Positivism*, 1st ed. New York: The Free Press, pp. 60–81.
Cartwright, N. (2002). The Dappled World. *Philosophical Books* 43(4), pp. 241–278.
Church, A. (1943). Review of Rudolf Carnap, Introduction to Semantics. *The Philosophical Review* 52(3), pp. 298–304.
Church, A. (1956). *Introduction to Mathematical Logic*. Princeton: Princeton University Press.
Churchland, P. M. (1981). Eliminative Materialism and the Propositional Attitudes. *The Journal of Philosophy* 78(2), pp. 67–90.
Conant, J. (1998). Wittgenstein on Meaning and Use. *Philosophical Investigations* 21(3), pp. 222–250.
Conant, J. (2002). The Method of the Tractatus. In: E. H. Reck, ed., *From Frege to Wittgenstein: Perspectives on Early Analytic Philosophy*. Oxford: Oxford University Press, pp. 374–462.
Dancy, J. (2000). *Practical Reality*. New York: Oxford University Press.

David, M. (1994). *Correspondence and Disquotation: An Essay on the Nature of Truth.* New York: Oxford University Press.
Davidson, D. (1963). Actions, Reasons, and Causes. *Journal of Philosophy* 60(23), pp. 685–700.
Davidson, D. (1986). A Coherence Theory of Truth and Knowledge. In: E. Lepore, ed., *Truth and Interpretation: Perspectives on the Philosophy of Donald Davidson.* Oxford: Basil Blackwell, pp. 307–319
Davidson, D. (1990). The Structure and Content of Truth. *The Journal of Philosophy* 87(6), pp. 279–328.
Davidson, D. (1993a). Reply to Peter Bieri. In: R. Stoecker, ed., *Reflecting Davidson: Donald Davidson Responding to an International Forum of Philosophers*, 1st ed. Berlin: De Gruyter, pp. 311–313.
Davidson, D. (1993b). Reply to Ralf Stoecker. In: R. Stoecker, ed., *Reflecting Davidson: Donald Davidson Responding to an International Forum of Philosophers*, 1st ed. Berlin: De Gruyter, pp. 287–290.
Davidson, D. (1994a). Radical Interpretation Interpreted. *Philosophical Perspectives* 8, pp. 121–128.
Davidson, D. (1994b). The Social Aspect of Language. In: B. McGuinness and G. Oliveri, eds., *The Philosophy of Michael Dummett*, 1st ed. Dordrecht: Kluwer, pp. 1–16.
Davidson, D. (1994c). Donald Davidson. In: S. Guttenplan, ed., *A Companion to the Philosophy of Mind*, 1st ed. Oxford: Basil Blackwell, pp. 231–236.
Davidson, D. (1995). Thinking Causes. In: J. Heil and A. Mele, eds., *Mental Causation*, 1st ed. Oxford: Clarendon Press, pp. 3–17.
Davidson, D. (1999a). Reply to James Hopkins. In: L. E. Hahn, ed., *The Philosophy of Donald Davidson* (The Library of Living Philosophers, vol. 27), 1st ed. Chicago: Open Court, pp. 286–288.
Davidson, D. (1999a). Reply to Edna Ullmann-Margalit. In: L. E. Hahn, ed., *The Philosophy of Donald Davidson* (The Library of Living Philosophers, vol. 27), 1st ed. Chicago: Open Court, pp. 497–500.
Davidson, D. (1999a). Reply to Bruce Vermazen. In: L. E. Hahn, ed., *The Philosophy of Donald Davidson* (The Library of Living Philosophers, vol. 27), 1st ed. Chicago: Open Court, pp. 653–656.
Davidson, D. (2001a). *Essays on Actions and Events: Philosophical Essays Volume I.* 2nd ed. Oxford: Clarendon Press.
Davidson, D. (2001b). *Inquiries into Truth and Interpretation: Philosophical Essays Volume II.* Oxford: Clarendon Press.
Davidson, D. (2001c). *Subjective, Intersubjective, Objective: Philosophical Essays Volume III.* Oxford: Clarendon Press.
Davidson, D. (2004). *Problems of Rationality.* Oxford: Clarendon Press.
Davidson, D. (2005a). *Truth, Language and History.* Oxford: Clarendon Press.
Davidson, D. (2005b). *Truth and Predication.* Cambridge: Harvard University Press.
Dennett, D. (1969). *Content and Consciousness.* London: Routledge and Kegan Paul.
Dewey, J. (1916). *Essays in Experimental Logic.* Chicago: University of Chicago Press.
Dewey, J. (1925). *Experience and Nature.* Chicago: Open Court.
Dewey, J. (1938). *Logic: The Theory of Inquiry.* Chicago: Holt.
Dewey, J. (1958). *Experience and Nature.* New York: Dover.

Dewey, J. (1980). *The Middle Works of John Dewey.* Vol. 10: *1916–1917: Journal Articles, Essays, and Miscellany.* Carbondale: Southern Illinois University Press.
Diamond, C. (1991). *The Realistic Spirit: Wittgenstein, Philosophy, and the Mind.* Cambridge: MIT Press.
Donellan, K. (1966). Reference and Definite Descriptions. *The Philosophical Review* 75, pp. 281–302.
Dretske, F. (1988). *Explaining Behavior: Reasons in a World of Causes.* Cambridge: MIT Press.
Dummett, M. (1964). Truth. In: G. Pitcher, ed., *Truth*, 1st ed. Upper Saddle River: Prentice-Hall, pp. 93–111.
Dummett, M. (1991). *The Logical Basis of Metaphysics.* Cambridge: Harvard University Press.
Dupré, J. (1993). *The Disorder of Things: Metaphysical Foundations of the Disunity of Science.* Cambridge: Harvard University Press.
Dworkin, R. (1977). *Taking Rights Seriously.* London: Duckworth.
Earman, J. (1992). *Inference, Explanation, and Other Frustrations.* Berkeley: University of California Press.
Feigl, H. and Sellars W. (1949). *Readings in Philosophical Analysis.* New York: Appleton-Century-Crofts.
Field, H. (1972). Tarski's Theory of Truth. *The Journal of Philosophy* 69(13), pp. 347–375.
Field, H. (1992). Physicalism. In: J. Earman, ed., *Inference, Explanation, and Other Frustrations*, 1st ed. Berkeley: University of California Press, pp. 271–292.
Fodor, J. (1987). *Psychosemantics: The Problem of Meaning in the Philosophy of Mind.* Cambridge: MIT Press.
Føllesdal, D. (1969). Quine on Modality. In: D. Davidson and J. Hintikka, eds., *Words and Objections.* Dordrecht: Reidel, pp. 175–185.
French, P. (1984). *Collective and Corporate Responsibility.* New York: Columbia University Press.
Friedman, M. (2000). *A Parting of the Ways.* Chicago: Open Court.
Giddens, A. (1972). *Emile Durkheim: Selected Writings.* Cambridge: Cambridge University Press.
Gilbert, M. (1989). *On Social Facts.* London: Routledge.
Gilbert, M. (1990). Walking Together: A Paradigmatic Social Phenomenon. *Midwest Studies in Philosophy* 15, pp. 1–14.
Gillett, C. and Loewer, B. (2009). *Physicalism and Its Discontents.* Cambridge: Cambridge University Press.
Gödel, K. (1944). Russell's Mathematical Logic. In: P. Schilpp, ed., *The Philosophy of Bertrand Russell* (Library of Living Philosophers), 1st ed. Chicago: Open Court, pp. 123–153.
Grimshaw, J. (1986). *Philosophy and Feminist Thinking.* Minneapolis: University of Minnesota Press.
Grover, D. L., Camp J. L. and Belnap, N. D. (1975). A Prosentential Theory of Truth. *Philosophical Studies: An International Journal for Philosophy in the Analytic Tradition* 27(2), pp. 73–125.
Grover, D. L. (1992). *A Prosentential Theory of Truth.* New Jersey: Princeton University Press.
Gustafsson, M. and Hertzberg, L. (2002). *The Practice of Language.* Dordrecht: Kluwer.
Guttenplan, S. (1994). *A Companion to the Philosophy of Mind.* Oxford: Basil Blackwell.
Hahn, L. (1999). *The Philosophy of Donald Davidson* (The Library of Living Philosophers, vol. 27). Chicago: Open Court.

Hastings, J. (1913). *Encyclopedia of Religions and Ethics.* New York: Charles Scribner's Sons.
Heath, J. (2015) Methodological Individualism. In *Stanford Encyclopedia of Philosophy* (Spring 2015 Edition), Edward N. Zalta (ed.), URL https://plato.stanford.edu/archives/spr2015/entries/methodological-individualism.
Hertzberg, L. (2001). The Sense Is Where You Find It. In: T. G. McCarthy and S. C. Stidd, eds., *Wittgenstein in America*, 1st ed. Oxford: Clarendon Press, pp. 90–102.
Hoover, H. (1922). *American Individualism.* New York: Doubleday, Page.
Horgan, T. (2002). From Supervenience to Superdupervenience: Meeting the Demands of a Material World. In: D. J. Chalmers, ed., *Philosophy of Mind*, 1st ed. New York: Oxford University Press, pp. 150–162.
Hornsby, J. (1980). *Actions.* London: Routledge and Kegan Paul.
Hull, C. (1943). *Principles of Behavior.* New York: Appleton-Century-Crofts.
Hursthouse, R. (2000). Intention. In: R. Teichman, ed., *Logic, Cause, and Action: Essays in Honour of Elizabeth Anscombe*, 1st ed. Cambridge: Cambridge University Press, pp. 83–106.
Hurthouse, R., Lawrence, G. and Quinn, W. (1995). *Values and Reasons.* Oxford: Oxford University Press.
Kant, I. (1998). *Critique of Pure Reason.* Translated by P. Guyer and A. W. Wood. Cambridge: Cambridge University Press.
Kim, J. (1993a). *Supervenience and Mind.* Cambridge: Cambridge University Press.
Kim, J. (1993b). Can Supervenience Save Anomalous Monism? In: J. Heil and A. Mele, eds., *Mental Causation*, 1st ed. Oxford: Clarendon Press, pp. 19–26.
Kim, J. (1996). *The Philosophy of Mind.* Boulder: Westview.
Kim, J. (2003). Philosophy of Mind and Psychology. In: K. Ludwig, ed., *Donald Davidson*, 1st ed. Cambridge: Cambridge University Press, pp. 113–136.
Kober, M. (1996). Certainties of a World-Picture: The Epistemological Investigations of *On Certainty.* In: H. Sluga and D. Stern, eds. *The Cambridge Companion to Wittgenstein.* Cambridge: Cambridge University Press, pp. 411–441.
Kripke, S. (1982). *Wittgenstein on Rules and Private Language.* Oxford: Basil Blackwell.
Lepore, E. and Ludwig, K. (2005). *Donald Davidson: Meaning, Truth, Language, and Reality.* Oxford: Oxford University Press.
Lepore, E. and Ludwig, K. (2007). Radical Misinterpretation: A Reply to Stoutland. *International Journal of Philosophical Studies* 15(4), pp. 557–585.
Lepore, E. and McLaughlin, B. (1985). *Actions and Events: Perspectives on the Philosophy of Donald Davidson.* Oxford: Basil Blackwell.
Lifton, R. (1986). *The Nazi Doctors: Medical Killing and the Psychology of Genocide.* New York: Basic Books.
Lukes, S. (1978). *Individualism: Key Concepts in Social Science.* Oxford: Basil Blackwell.
Lyons, W. (2001). *Matters of the Mind.* London: Routledge.
MacIntyre, A. (1981). *After Virtue.* Notre Dame: University of Notre Dame Press.
Malcom, N. (1986). *Nothing Is Hidden: Wittgenstein's Criticism of his Early Thought.* Oxford: Basil Blackwell.
McDowell, J. (1996). *Mind and World.* 2nd ed. Cambridge: Harvard University Press.
McDowell, J. (1998a). *Mind, Value, and Reality.* Cambridge: Harvard University Press.
McDowell, J. (1998b). The Woodbridge Lectures. *The Journal of Philosophy* 95(9), pp. 431–491.

McDowell, J. (2006a). Reponse to Bilgrami. In: C. Macdonald and G. Macdonald, eds., *McDowell and His Critics*, 1st ed. Oxford: Basil Blackwell, pp. 66–72.
McDowell, J. (2006b). Response to Dancy. In: C. Macdonald and G. Macdonald, eds., *McDowell and His Critics*, 1st ed. Oxford: Basil Blackwell, pp. 134–141.
McDowell, J. (2009). *The Engaged Intellect: Philosophical Essays*. Harvard: Harvard University Press.
McGinn, M. (1997). *Wittgenstein and the Philosophical Investigations*. London: Routledge.
McGuinness, B. and Oliveri, G. (1994). *The Philosophy of Michael Dummett*. Dordrecht: Kluwer.
Meggle, G. (1999). *Actions, Norms and Values: Discussions with Georg Henrik von Wright*. Berlin: De Gruyter.
Mele, A. (1992). *Springs of Action: Understanding Intentional Behavior*. Oxford: Oxford University Press.
Mele, A. (1997). *The Philosophy of Action*. Oxford: Oxford University Press.
Mele, A. (2003a). *Motivation and Agency*. Oxford: Oxford University Press.
Mele, A. (2003b). Philosophy of Action. In: K. Ludwig, ed., *Donald Davidson*, 1st ed. Cambridge: Cambridge University Press, pp. 64–84.
Moore, G. E. (1993). A Defence of Common Sense. In: G. E. Moore, *Selected Writings*. Edited by T. Baldwin. London: Routledge, pp. 106–133.
Moran, R. and Stone, M. (2008). Anscombe on Expression of Intention. In: C. Sandis, ed., *New Essays on the Explanation of Action*. London: Palgrave Macmillan, pp. 132–168.
Morris, H. (1976). *On Guilt and Innocence: Essays in Legal Philosophy and Moral Psychology*. Berkeley: University of California Press.
Nagel, T. (1986). *The View From Nowhere*. Oxford: Oxford University Press.
Neale, S. (1995). The Philosophical Significance of Gödel's Slingshot. *Mind* 104(416), pp. 761–825.
Neale, S. and Dever, J. (1997). Slingshots and Boomerangs. *Mind* 106(421), pp. 143–168.
Needham, P. (2005). *Law and Order*. Stockholm: Stockholm University Department of Philosophy.
Needham, P. (2006). Substance and Modality. *Philosophy of Science* 73, pp. 829–840.
Niiniluto, I. (1999). Tarskian Truth as Correspondence–Replies to Some Objections. In *Truth and Its Nature (if Any)*. Dordrecht: Kluwer, pp. 91–104.
Papineau, D. (2002). *Thinking About Consciousness*. Oxford: Clarendon Press.
Peregrin, J. (1999). *Truth and Its Nature (if Any)*. Dordrecht: Kluwer.
Pettit, P. (2007). Responsibility Incorporated. *Ethics* 117, pp. 171–201.
Pihlström, S. (2006). *Wittgenstein and the Method of Philosophy*. Helsinki: Acta Philosophica Fennica.
Pitcher, G. (1964). Introduction. In: G. Pitcher, ed., *Truth*. Englewood Cliffs: Prentice-Hall, pp. 1–15.
Prior, A. (1967). The Correspondence Theory of Truth. In: P. Edwards, ed., *The Encyclopedia of Philosophy*, Vol. 2. London: Macmillan, pp. 223–232.
Putnam, H. (1975a). *Mathematics, Matter, and Method: Philosophical Papers, Vol. 1*. 2nd ed. Cambridge: Cambridge University Press.
Putnam, H. (1975b). *Mind, Language, and Reality: Philosophical Papers, Vol. 2*. Cambridge: Cambridge University Press.
Putnam, H. (1978). *Meaning and the Moral Sciences*. London: Routledge and Kegan Paul.

Putnam, H. (1981). *Reason, Truth, and History*. Cambridge: Cambridge University Press.
Putnam, H. (1983). *Realism and Reason: Philosophical Papers, Vol. 3*. Cambridge: Cambridge University Press.
Putnam, H. (1987). *The Many Faces of Realism*. LaSalle: Open Court.
Putnam, H. (1988). *Representation and Reality*. Cambridge: MIT Press.
Putnam, H. (1990). *Realism with a Human Face*. Cambridge: Harvard University Press.
Putnam, H. (1992a). *Renewing Philosophy*. Cambridge: Harvard University Press.
Putnam, H. (1992b). Truth, Activation Vectors, and Possession Conditions for Concepts. *Philosophy and Phenomenological Research* 52(2), pp. 431–447.
Putnam, H. (1994a). *Words and Life*. Cambridge: Harvard University Press.
Putnam, H. (1994b). Sense, Nonsense, and the Senses: An Inquiry into the Powers of the Human Mind [Dewey Lectures]. *The Journal of Philosophy* 91(9), pp. 445–517.
Quine, W. V. O. (1960). *Word and Object*. Cambridge: MIT Press.
Quine, W. V. O. (1981). *Theories and Things*. Cambridge: Harvard University Press.
Quine, W. V. O. (1995). *From Stimulus to Science*. Cambridge: Harvard University Press.
Ramsey, F. P. (1990). *Philosophical Papers*. Cambridge: Cambridge University Press.
Rawls, J. (1985). Justice as Fairness: Political Not Metaphysical. *Philosophy and Public Affairs* 14(3), pp. 223–251.
Russell, B. (1912). *Problems of Philosophy*. Oxford: Oxford University Press.
Russell, B. (1956). The Philosophy of Logical Atomism. In: R. C. Marsh, ed., *Logic and Knowledge*, 1st ed. London: Allen & Unwin, pp. 177–281.
Sandel, M. (1982). *Liberalism and the Limits of Justice*. Cambridge: Cambridge University Press.
Searle, J. (1983). *Intentionality: An Essay in the Philosophy*. Cambridge: Cambridge University Press.
Searle, J. (1992). *The Rediscovery of the Mind*. Cambridge: MIT Press.
Searle, J. (1995). *The Construction of Social Reality*. London: Allen Lane: The Penguin Press.
Sehon, S. (2000). An Argument against the Causal Theory of Action Explanation. *Philosophy and Phenomenological Research* 60(1), pp. 67–85.
Sehon, S. (2005). *Teleological Realism: Mind, Agency and Explanation*. Cambridge: MIT Press.
Sellers, W. (1968). *Science and Metaphysics*. London: Routledge and Kegan Paul.
Sluga, H. (1980). *Gottlob Frege: The Arguments of the Philosophers*. London: Routledge and Kegan Paul.
Sluga, H. and Stern, D. (1996). *The Cambridge Companion to Wittgenstein*. Cambridge: Cambridge University Press.
Smith, M. (2004). The Structure of Orthonomy. In: J. Hyman and H. Steward, eds., *Agency and Action*. Cambridge: Cambridge University Press, pp. 165–93.
Smith, N. (2002). *Reading McDowell: On Mind and World*. London: Routledge.
Steward, H. (1997). *The Ontology of Mind*. Oxford: Oxford University Press.
Stoecker, R. (1993). *Reflecting Davidson: Donald Davidson Responding to an International Forum of Philosopher*. Berlin: De Grutyer.
Stoutland, F. (1969). Basic Actions and Causality. *Journal of Philosophy* 65, pp. 467–475.
Stoutland, F. (1982a). On Realism and Anti-Realism in Davidson's Philosophy of Language I. *Crítica – Revista Hispano-Americana de Filosofia* 14(41), pp. 13–53.
Stoutland, F. (1982b). On Realism and Anti-Realism in Davidson's Philosophy of Language II. *Crítica – Revista Hispano-Americana de Filosofia* 14(42), pp. 19–48.

Stoutland, F. (1985). Davidson on Intentional Behavior. In: E. Lepore and B. McLaughlin, eds., *Actions and Events. Perspectives on the Philosophy of Donald Davidson*. Oxford: Basil Blackwell, pp. 44–59.

Stoutland, F. (1998). Review of William Child, Causality, Interpretation and the Mind. *Philosophy and Phenomenological Research* 58(3), pp. 711–715.

Stoutland, F. (1999a). Do We Need Correspondence Truth? In: J. Peregrin, ed., *Truth and Its Nature (if Any)*. Dordrecht: Kluwer, pp. 81–90.

Stoutland, F. (1999b). Intentionalists and Davidson on Rational Explanations. In: G. Meggle, ed., *Actions, Norms and Values: Discussions with Georg Henrik von Wright*. De Gruyter, pp. 191–208.

Stoutland, F. (2001). Responsive Action and the Belief-Desire Model. *Grazer Philosophische Studien* 61, pp. 83–106.

Stoutland, F. (2009). Determinism, Intentional Action, and Bodily Movements. In: C. Sandis, ed., *New Essays on the Explanation of Action*. London: Palgrave Macmillan, pp. 313–337.

Strawson, P. F. (1959). *Individuals: An Essay in Descriptive Metaphysics*. London: Methuen.

Strawson, P. F. (1960). Metaphysics. In: J. O. Urmson, ed., *The Concise Encyclopedia of Western Philosophy and Philosophers*, 1st ed. New York: Hawthorne Books, pp. 256–262.

Strawson, P. F. (1985). Causation and Explanation. In: B. Vermazen and M. B. Hintikka, eds., *Essays on Davidson: Actions and Events*, 1st ed. Oxford: Clarendon Press, pp. 115–137.

Tarski, A. (1956). The Concept of Truth in Formalized Languages. In: A. Tarski, *Logic, Semantics, Metamathematics*. New York: Oxford University Press, pp. 152–278.

Taylor, B. (1985). *Modes of Occurrence: Verbs, Adverbs, and Events*. Oxford: Basil Blackwell.

Taylor, C. (1975). *Hegel*. Cambridge: Cambridge University Press.

Taylor, C. (1985). *Philosophy and the Human Sciences: Philosophical Papers 2*. Cambridge: Cambridge University Press.

Thompson, M. (1995). The Representation of Life. In: R. Hursthouse, G. Lawrence and W. Quinn, eds., *Values and Reasons*. Oxford: Oxford University Press, pp. 247–296.

Travis, C. (1989). *The Uses of Sense: Wittgenstein's Philosophy of Language*. Oxford: Clarendon Press.

Tuomela, R. (1984). *A Theory of Social Action*. Dordrecht: Reidel.

Tuomela, R. (1991). Intentional Single and Joint Action. *Philosophical Studies* 62, pp. 235–262.

Tuomela, R. (2007). *The Philosophy of Sociality: The Shared Point of View*. Oxford: Oxford University Press.

Tye, M. (1998). Adverbial Theory of Mental States. In: E. Craig, ed., *Routledge Encyclopedia of Philosophy*, 1st ed. London: Routledge, pp. 314–317.

Urmson, J. O. (1960). Metaphysics. In J. O. Urmson, ed., *The Concise Encyclopedia of Western Philosophers*, 1st ed. London: Hutchinson, pp. 259–264.

Vermazen, B. and Hintikka, M. B. (1985). *Essays on Davidson*. Oxford: Clarendon Press.

Von Wright, G. H. (1971). *Explanation and Understanding*. London: Routledge and Kegan Paul.

Von Wright, G. H. (1974). *Causality and Determinism*. New York: Columbia University Press.

Von Wright, G. H. (1989). Action, Intentionality, and Practical Reason. In: P. A. Schilpp and L. E. Hahn, eds., *The Philosophy of Georg Henrik von Wright*. LaSalle: Open Court, pp. 804–826.

Von Wright, G. H. (1993). *The Tree of Knowledge and Other Essays*. Leiden: Brill.

Von Wright, G. H. (1998). *In the Shadow of Descartes: Essays in the Philosophy of Mind*. Dordrecht: Kluwer.

Von Wright, G. H. (2003). Action. In: K. Segerberg and R. Śliwiński, eds., *A Philosophical Smorgasbord: Essays on Action, Truth and Other Things in Honour of Frederick Stoutland*. Uppsala: Uppsala University Department of Philosophy, pp. 157–166.

Walzer, M. (1983). *Spheres of Justice*. New York: Basic Books Inc.

Weber, M. (1947). *The Theory of Social and Economic Organization*. Translated by A. M. Henderson and T. Parsons. New York: Oxford University Press.

Weber, M. (1968). Basic Sociological Terms. In: G. Roth and C. Wittich, eds., *Economy and Society*, 1st ed. Berkeley: University of California Press, pp. 3–62.

Weintraub, K. (1975). Autobiography and Historical Consciousness. *Critical Inquiry* 1(4), pp. 821–848.

Williams, B. (1978). *Descartes: The Project of Pure Inquiry*. New York: Penguin.

Winch, P. (1988). True or False? *Inquiry* 31(3), pp. 265–276.

Winch, P. (1998). Judgement: Propositions and Practices. *Philosophical Investigations* 21(3), pp. 189–202.

Wittgenstein, L. (1922). *Tractatus Logico-Philosophicus*. Translated by C. K. Ogden. London: Routledge and Kegan Paul.

Wittgenstein, L. (1953). *Philosophical Investigations*. Translated by G. E. M. Anscombe. Oxford: Basil Blackwell.

Wittgenstein, L. (1958a). *Philosophical Investigations*. Translated by G. E. M. Anscombe, 2nd ed. Oxford: Basil Blackwell.

Wittgenstein, L. (1958b). *The Blue and Brown Books*. 1st ed. Edited by R. Rhees. Oxford: Basil Blackwell.

Wittgenstein, L. (1960). *The Blue and Brown Books*. 2nd ed. Oxford: Basil Blackwell.

Wittgenstein, L. (1967). *Zettel*. Translated by G. E. M. Anscombe and G. H. von Wright. Oxford: Basil Blackwell.

Wittgenstein, L. (1969). *On Certainty*. Translated by G. E. M. Anscombe and D. Paul. Oxford: Basil Blackwell.

Wittgenstein, L. (1977). *Remarks on Colour*. Berkeley: University of California Press.

Wittgenstein, L. (1992). *Last Writings on the Philosophy of Psychology: The Inner and the Outer, 1949–1951, Vol. 2*. 1st ed. Edited by H. Nyman and G. H. Von Wright. Hoboken: Wiley-Blackwell.

Wittgenstein, L. (1993). *Philosophical Occasions: 1912–1951*. 1st ed. Edited by J. Klagge and A. Nordmann. Indianapolis: Hackett Publishing Company.

Index of Names

Alanen, Lilli   24, 51, 139
Anscombe, G. E. M   49, 165, 168, 201, 224f., 227, 277, 280, 282, 294, 296, 298f., 313, 316, 319
Aquinas, Thomas   16, 18

Baier, Annette   210
Barwise, Jon   1, 19
Belnap, Nuel   89
Berger, Peter   250f., 274
Bishop, John   297
Bradley, F. H.   1, 246
Brandom, Robert   38, 41, 77, 98
Bratman, Michael   210, 218–220
Burge, Tyler   217, 248
Byron, Lord   253

Carnap, Rudolf   1, 3, 6, 9, 11, 142, 195, 201
Church, Alonso   11f.
Churchland, Paul   196–199, 319
Collingwood, R.G.   287

David, Marian   1, 15–18, 20–22, 170
Davidson, Donald   2, 8–15, 17–19, 21f., 26, 29–32, 76f., 91, 94, 106–108, 110, 112–143, 149–156, 160, 163, 166, 168f., 179f., 185f., 201–209, 221, 223, 277–300, 315
Descartes, René   141, 148, 189, 194, 200, 208
Dewey, John   15, 53, 73f., 140–149, 154–157, 194, 208, 241
Diamond, Cora   3, 8–10, 15
Donellan, Keith   9f.
Dretske, Fred   195, 302f., 311
Dummett, Michael   38, 43, 55–57, 68, 72f., 94, 96, 115, 129
Durkheim, Émile   211, 252f., 255, 263, 275

Emerson, Ralph Waldo   241, 252

Feigl, Herbert   128
Field, Hartrey   92, 98, 174–178, 180, 287

Fodor, Jerry   113, 119, 128f., 134, 138, 195–200, 292, 294, 309, 311
Frege, Gottlob   1f., 6f., 12f., 21, 67, 102, 138, 142, 185f.

Gadamer, Hans-Georg   154
Giddens, Anthony   247, 252f., 255, 263, 275
Gödel, Kurt   1f., 19–22, 24, 27–31
Goethe, J.W. von   253
Grice, H.P.   129
Grover, Dorothy   89
Gustafsson, Martin   78f., 82

Heath, Joseph   224
Hegel, G.W.F.   85f., 241, 253, 258
Heidegger, Martin   194, 241
Hobbes, Thomas   246
Hornsby, Jennifer   302
Humboldt, Wilhelm von   253
Hume, David   194, 281f.
Hursthouse, Rosalind   299f.

Jackson, Frank   5
Joachim, H.H.   1

Kant, Immanuel   4–6, 12, 62f., 89, 129, 133, 142, 168, 187, 193, 249, 253, 263
Kenny, Anthony   277
Kierkegaard, Sören   252, 256
Kim, Jaegwon   172f., 277, 286, 290, 292, 302, 313, 315
Kripke, Saul   5, 43, 135, 191f.
Kuhn, T.S.   248
Kuusela, Antti   139

Leibniz, G.W.   62, 194
Lenin, V.I.   5
Lepore, Ernest   112–125, 127–138
Lifton, Robert Jay   250
Ludwig, Kirk   112–125, 127–138, 186
Lukes, Steven   241, 243, 245–247, 250–254, 265

Index of Names

MacIntyre, Alasdair   241, 258, 260–262, 264, 269
Malcolm, Norman   35
Malpas, Jeff   139
Marx, Karl   241, 244, 247, 253, 258
McDowell, John   63, 77, 142, 154, 193f., 283, 287, 305f., 310
McGinn, Marie   13f., 188, 190
Mead, G.H.   241
Melden, A.I.   277
Mele, Alfred   285, 292f., 302
Melville, Herman   241, 252
Merleau-Ponty, Maurice   194
Mill, J.S.   253f.
Moore, G.E.   1–3, 11, 16, 18, 36, 94, 138, 186
Morris, Herbert   257

Nagel, Thomas   3, 5, 93
Neale, Stephen   2, 15f., 20–22, 27–29, 31, 33
Needham, Paul   2, 15, 139, 175, 311
Nietzsche, Friedrich   256
Novalis   253

Peirce, Charles Sanders   80, 94, 98
Perry, John   1, 19
Pitcher, George   31
Prior, A. N.   55, 102
Putnam, Hilary   33, 46, 52–80, 82–86, 248

Quine, W.V.O.   3, 8–12, 65f., 70, 85, 92, 117, 129, 142, 195f., 201, 226, 248, 292

Ramsey, Frank   82
Rawls, John   257f., 268, 271, 275
Rhees, Rush   11
Rorty, Richard   77, 140, 142

Rousseau, J.J.   252f., 263
Royce, Josiah   79
Russell, Bertrand   1–3, 6, 11, 14, 16, 18, 20, 25–27, 45, 94, 96, 101, 138, 186

Schlegel, K.W.F.   253
Schleiermacher, Friedrich   253
Searle, John R.   1–11, 13, 19–21, 28, 63f., 74, 100f., 106, 108–110, 128, 138, 210
Sehon, Scott   158–167, 169f., 172–174, 177, 180–182, 184f.
Sellars, Wilfrid   94, 128, 219, 305
Sluga, Hans   102
Spinoza, Baruch   194, 292, 296
Strawson, P.F.   1f., 6, 129, 279
Svensson, Frans   139

Tarski, Alfred   13f., 54, 91f., 103f., 107, 113, 155, 184
Taylor, A.E.   246
Taylor, Barry   1, 18–20
Taylor, Charles   246, 275–276
Thoreau, Henry David   241, 252, 256
Tocqueville, Alexis de   241
Travis, Charles   46, 78
Twain, Mark   241, 252
Tye, Michael   100f., 106

Weber, Max   194, 215, 223f., 248
Weintraub, Karl   252–254
Williams, Bernard   63
Winch, Peter   35, 37, 40, 47f., 51
Wittgenstein, Ludwig   1, 3–15, 19f., 22–24, 35–52, 73–75, 77f., 81, 85–87, 94, 101, 155, 168, 186–194, 199, 201, 205, 207–209, 241, 248, 277, 320
Wordsworth, William   256

Index of Subjects

absolute conception of the world 63
abstract individual 243, 245, 251, 255–257, 265, 267f., 273
abstraction 20, 63, 79, 131, 145, 148, 153, 156, 181, 189, 246, 267
abstract objects 32, 62, 170, 206, 289
action 33, 37, 48, 70, 85, 106, 137, 140–146, 149, 152, 154–157, 160–169, 172f., 175–179, 182–185, 187, 189, 192–194, 197–208, 210–229, 241, 248, 252, 263, 277f., 280–285, 287–289, 291–309, 312–322
adverbial theory 100, 105f.
agency 146, 158, 160, 210–215, 219, 293
agreement 41f., 48, 103, 146, 196, 207, 228, 267
altruism 263f., 267
American 1, 165, 212, 241f., 249, 252f., 258, 270, 276
American character 241
American life 241f.
analogy 123-124
analytical metaphysics 195f.
analytic philosophy 1–4, 15, 24, 88, 94, 100, 128, 138f., 186, 189, 194f., 208
analytic-synthetic distinction 57, 118, 128, 135, 140
anaphoric sentence 89
animal 142, 144–146, 149, 152, 157, 160, 174, 181, 196, 198, 247, 256f., 304, 310f.
anomalous monism 153, 290-297
anti-individualism 217, 241
a posteriori 118f., 128, 134f.
a priori 24, 59, 63, 118f., 121f., 128, 134f.
argument from analogy 123f.
Aristotelean physics 189
Aristotelian science 140f.
assertibility 69, 73, 76
assertibility conditions 43f., 57, 69, 77f., 84
assertion 8–10, 19, 24, 30, 41–43, 56, 58, 60, 66, 68, 71, 73, 76, 78–83, 88, 91, 94–96, 98, 100, 113, 115f., 126, 172, 192, 285, 292
assertoric utterance 38
attributive use 9–11, 24, 27, 29, 33
authority relation 212
axiom 21, 107, 114–116, 131f., 208

bedeuten 1
Bedeutung 1, 75
Begriffsschrift 7
behavior 3, 7, 10, 37, 58, 94, 114, 117f., 121, 123f., 126f., 136f., 146, 155, 158–161, 165–167, 169–173, 175–179, 181f., 189f., 193f., 196–198, 200, 205, 211, 213, 242, 244f., 247f., 253, 259, 264, 275, 280, 287, 289, 292, 298, 301–305, 307–322
behavioral evidence 120, 124f., 164
behaviorism 2, 195
belief 2, 5, 9f., 18f., 41f., 57–59, 61, 71, 76, 79–81, 83, 91, 93–100, 116–122, 125–128, 133, 135, 137, 140f., 145f., 149–152, 154, 156, 162, 164, 168f., 172, 180, 185, 196–201, 203–208, 210f., 215–217, 220–224, 243f., 249–252, 255–257, 269f., 277f., 281–284, 288, 292–294, 296–300, 302f., 307
belief context 5
belief-desire model 162, 300
belief-desire pair 202–204, 282, 284
biconditional 17, 103–105
biology 164, 195
bodily movement 10, 141, 146, 152–154, 173, 177f., 210, 215, 220–222, 226–229, 277, 292–297, 302–304, 307–309, 311, 313–315, 317
brain 2, 4f., 7, 60, 116, 125, 151, 167, 172, 182, 189, 203, 220–223, 225, 292f., 315, 322
brain state 7, 166, 169, 289
building-block theory 116, 131

Cartesian dualism 7, 142, 148, 244f.

Index of Subjects

Cartesian framework   128f., 138
Cartesianism   1f., 6, 113, 116f., 122f., 127, 130, 187, 189–194, 198–200, 205–208
causal explanation   59, 67, 159f., 163, 165–167, 169–177, 179f., 202f., 277–283, 287, 294, 298, 300
causal intermediaries   149
causality   141, 146, 149, 152f., 165, 179, 278f., 285–287, 293
causal law   165, 201f., 279f., 298
causal power   5, 181, 197, 199, 202, 280
causal relation   2, 12, 66, 152f., 168, 179, 202, 222, 277–279, 281–283, 286f., 291, 293, 298, 300
cause   4, 6f., 12, 54, 122, 125, 141, 146, 150–152, 154f., 165f., 168, 170–172, 179f., 197f., 201–204, 220–222, 264, 277–287, 292–294, 296–300, 302–305, 316
cement of the universe   152f.
certainty   35–41, 45, 47f., 51
charity   138, 207
clarification   4, 12, 309, 317
classical utilitarianism   265
closed sentence   131
coextensive predicates   25, 29f.
cognition   6, 37, 133, 145, 174
cognitive meaning   1, 75
coherence   14, 18, 35, 97, 118, 273
collective agent   212, 229
color   5f., 38f., 59, 110, 144f., 147, 182, 191, 286
common good   216, 249, 259, 266
commonsense psychology   196–200, 206f., 304, 309
commonsense realism   52f., 73f., 76, 83–85, 87
Commonsense view of the World   2
communication   117, 121f., 133, 146, 154, 206
communitarianism   241–243, 251, 258–263, 268f., 271–273, 275f.
community   18, 43, 57, 70, 73, 77, 80, 98, 182, 192, 241, 246–248, 251, 254f., 260, 262, 264, 268f., 275, 310, 322
complex expression   21, 116, 132
complex propositions   101

compositionality   22, 113–115, 125
computational state   199
concept   1f., 6, 8, 10f., 14–16, 20–24, 35f., 41, 43, 45, 52–54, 56, 58, 62, 68, 73, 76, 81–85, 89, 91, 93–99, 102f., 113f., 116f., 120–122, 124–128, 131, 133–136, 140–142, 144, 150–152, 158, 164f., 174, 185, 187, 190f., 193–196, 206–208, 219, 244–247, 250f., 254, 256, 258, 261, 270, 275, 279f., 282, 287, 290f., 297, 301, 306, 310, 316
concept of cause   152f., 168
conceptual content   142, 145, 149, 155
conceptual scheme   62, 70, 72
conceptual structure   140–146, 149, 152f.
conditional   18, 46, 88, 109, 113, 118
congruence   16, 18, 96, 177, 292, 301–303, 307, 309–312, 315–318, 321f.
consciousness   1f., 4–9, 11, 13, 100, 143, 189, 243f., 247, 255
constitutive feature   135
constitutive-non-constitutive distinction   135
content   6, 20, 41, 43, 67, 76, 81–83, 88–91, 93f., 96, 98, 100, 103, 114, 117, 119, 121–126, 128, 146, 150, 155, 169, 189, 197, 207f., 211, 216–222, 225, 259, 281–284, 294, 297f., 303
context   4–13, 15–18, 20–24, 27–30, 32–34, 41f., 44–49, 51, 53, 74–76, 78, 81–83, 88, 90, 95f., 98, 101, 104, 106, 110f., 116, 120f., 133, 139, 154, 159, 178f., 181, 191, 208, 227, 243, 245–248, 257, 261f., 267, 270, 276, 280, 292, 305
convention   82, 133
convention-T   131
co-reference   6-11, 24-28, 31-34
corporation   210f., 216, 223, 225–228, 275
correspondence   1–10, 12–20, 22–24, 27–29, 31–35, 52–58, 60f., 63f., 67, 69, 72f., 75–80, 82–84, 88, 90–98, 102f., 107–109
counterfactual   21, 104, 160, 167
covering law   201, 281
cultural institution   146, 154

Index of Subjects — 359

culture   5, 10f., 50, 145, 154, 156f., 183, 187, 242, 254–256, 269f., 272
culture of therapy   256

Declaration of Independence   241
de dicta   5
definite description   5f., 9–11, 16, 18f., 21–31, 33, 212
deflationism   76–78
demonstrative   5, 9–11
description   1, 3, 8–14, 17, 19, 23–27, 63f., 70, 74, 85, 105, 110, 126, 135–137, 140, 148, 152–157, 161f., 169, 172f., 178–181, 187f., 190, 198–204, 208, 213–215, 220–222, 225–228, 278–282, 285f., 293–297, 299f., 304, 308f., 311–313, 316, 318, 320f.
descriptive metaphysics   6
desire   2, 14, 31, 118, 126–128, 133, 146, 152, 154, 160, 162, 164, 167–170, 172, 180, 183, 185, 188, 194, 196–201, 203f., 206, 210, 216f., 221–223, 246f., 256, 259f., 262, 268, 277f., 280–284, 288, 292–294, 296–300, 302f., 307
deviant causal chains   296
dialectical construction   15
dialectical illusion   4
dignity   242–244, 249–252, 256–258, 266, 269f., 275f.
dilemma of reference   131
disagreement   40, 196, 207
disjunction   46, 101, 109
disposition   116, 132f., 145, 204, 280f.
disquotation   15, 108, 110
diversity   80, 242, 251, 253f., 256, 269–272
dogmas of empiricism   195
doubt   6, 13, 19, 36–39, 48–51, 77, 129, 142, 144, 174, 186, 190f., 205, 216, 277, 287, 293, 297, 321
dualism   1f., 6–8, 64, 153, 171, 200f., 245, 247, 290, 296
duty   250, 258f., 263, 265, 273, 275

effect   2, 28, 30, 63, 140, 146, 155, 165f., 168, 170f., 176, 183, 198, 202f., 246, 278f., 282, 285f., 293, 303, 316

egoism   241, 262–265, 267
elementary propositions   101
eliminativism   1, 196
emotion   133, 183, 220
emotivist self   260
empirical knowledge   133, 149
empirical verification   3
entities   2–4, 10, 13, 16, 18, 20, 30–33, 57, 63, 130, 170f., 185, 197–200, 202–205, 221f., 248, 278, 284, 290f., 293, 296
epiphenomenalism   169, 202, 286
epistemic conception of truth   67f., 76, 97f.
epistemic intermediaries   149
epistemological individualism   243, 248, 260
epistemology   5, 10, 52, 290
equality   7, 243, 249–251, 256–258, 266–268, 274
equivalence principle   54, 76, 83f., 103
error   18, 59, 79, 81f., 95f., 121f., 136, 149, 299f.
essence of the mental   1
ethical   18, 75, 243
ethical discourse   128
ethics   5, 10, 79
event   8, 61, 70, 106–108, 142–147, 151–157, 166–169, 172, 179, 197–204, 206, 208, 220–222, 277–287, 289–291, 293–300, 303, 307, 315
event causation   278, 287, 293f., 297
event statement   107
everyday experience   146, 148, 155f.
everyday life   24, 58, 195
evidence   8–10, 36f., 48, 58, 101, 106, 113f., 116, 119–121, 123–126, 131f., 135–137, 145, 167, 174, 176, 185, 205, 225, 247
existential quantification   26
explanation   8, 12–14, 19, 23, 54, 58f., 61, 68, 70, 75f., 93, 95, 116, 126f., 131f., 135, 140, 152f., 155–184, 187–193, 195–201, 203f., 211, 222f., 227, 229, 244, 248, 278–285, 287–289, 291–293, 298, 301–322
expression   1, 11, 13f., 18, 21, 32, 42, 46–49, 58, 65f., 69, 71, 75f., 88–92, 103,

105f., 116f., 119, 130, 132, 206, 212, 248, 256, 260, 276, 299, 301
expressive individualism   243, 252, 262
extension   6–12, 25, 27–30, 32, 68, 106, 151, 291, 293
extensionality   14
external good   261f., 264
externalism   113, 150
external requirement   8–11

fact   1–10, 12–22, 24, 27, 29–34, 37, 39, 41f., 50, 55f., 58–61, 63, 65–67, 70f., 73, 76, 80, 82–84, 92, 100–103, 105–110, 114–117, 119, 122, 124–126, 130, 132, 135, 141f., 145, 148, 158, 162, 167, 172, 174, 176, 180–182, 184–186, 188, 198–201, 207f., 219, 244f., 248, 252, 257, 265–267, 269, 271, 274, 278–280, 287, 299, 301, 303, 307f., 314, 318
fairness   271
falsity   21, 40, 47f., 79–81, 83, 95f., 260
family   7, 45, 212, 261, 263
fascism   254
feeling   4, 7, 50, 85, 105, 124, 129, 157, 181, 183f., 193, 197, 244, 252, 256, 260, 276, 301
feminism   241, 258
first-person   5, 127, 163, 289
first-person authority   127, 135
folk psychology   18, 158, 196f., 320
freedom   253f.
functionalism   74

gavagai   9f.
generality   11, 278f.
generalization   16f., 20, 41, 43, 47, 76, 81, 83, 90, 93, 98f., 163, 165–167, 175f., 197, 199, 203f., 278–281, 309
general law   177, 179, 197, 281, 283
geometry   62
God   5f., 217, 250
Gödelian equivalence   21
Good   1f., 4, 9, 15f., 24, 45, 59, 64, 68, 80, 83, 90, 97, 113, 128, 141, 147, 158f., 174, 180f., 197, 213, 216, 247, 249f., 252, 254f., 257–273, 276, 287f., 319

good life   253, 255, 259f., 262–264, 268–272, 276
groundlessness   36

Habits of the Heart   242f., 249, 252, 256, 258, 262, 265, 276
happiness   259, 263
Helsinki   6, 92, 186
historians   49, 186, 248
historicism   254
history   2, 18, 53, 72f., 84, 140, 170, 186, 195, 212, 250, 254, 287, 301, 319
holism   128
human experience   143, 145f., 148, 153f., 157
humanism   250
hylomorphism   5

idealism   9, 72, 156f.
ideal theory   65, 71
identity   2, 10, 16–19, 22, 24–27, 29, 204, 208, 250f., 254, 274, 291
ideology   226, 292, 296
illusion   8, 15, 49, 75, 86f., 192f., 319f.
independence   63
indeterminacy   8–10, 65f., 70, 84f., 116, 119, 132, 176, 307
indeterminacy of interpretation   9, 119, 132
indeterminacy of translation   66
indeterminateness   10
individual   5–9, 11, 16f., 19f., 23–26, 29, 63, 69f., 125, 145, 154, 157, 181, 186, 197, 204, 206, 210–220, 223f., 226–229, 241–257, 259–276, 281, 287
individual agency   220f.
individual agent   210–218, 220, 223–229
individual good   216, 259f., 264, 266
individualism   210, 223, 241–245, 249, 252–256, 258, 260f., 263f., 269, 273, 275f.
individuation   10, 228f., 252, 294
inductive science   6
inference   2, 16–19, 22–24, 26–30, 46, 105, 107, 109, 144f., 205
inner state   7, 153, 191–193

inquiry 10, 12, 14, 18f., 21, 35, 39, 53, 83, 140, 144f., 147f., 155, 188f., 193, 224, 288
inscrutability of reference 131
inseparability of intuitions and concepts 187
institution 145f., 154, 157, 182, 243, 246, 248, 258f., 261, 264f., 269f., 274–276
institutional role 250f.
institutional structure 212, 270, 272, 276
intellection 187, 193f.
intelligence 1, 4, 8, 86
intelligibility 72, 76, 86, 288, 305, 314
intension 14
intensional context 8, 18
intentional attitudes 136–138, 216, 220, 224, 229
intentionality 1, 5, 9, 150, 193, 311, 314f.
intentional realism 8
intention 2, 23, 114, 117f., 120, 126, 166–168, 183, 185, 197, 201, 207, 211, 215–225, 269, 277, 288, 292–294, 296, 299f., 302–304, 320f.
interest 6, 8–11, 14, 67, 90, 152f., 158f., 187, 208, 210, 216, 241f., 245, 247, 259f., 262f., 266–268, 272f.
intermediaries 149
internal good 261f., 264
internal realism 52f., 57, 64, 66, 68–74, 84f.
interpretation 9f., 23, 35, 37, 43, 57f., 60, 64f., 67, 69, 71, 76, 91f., 112f., 115–128, 131f., 135–140, 164, 169, 185, 189, 200, 204–208, 224, 258, 277, 285, 288f., 306f., 311, 314, 316
intersubjective 118, 207
intersubjectivity 206-207
intrinsic 3, 9f., 64, 94f., 124f., 148, 156, 200, 221f., 250
introspection 3, 8, 189f., 193f., 200, 225, 289
intuition 2, 6, 16, 20, 22, 133, 193, 195, 252
iota-conversion 21
iota-substitution 16

joint action 214, 219

Judaism 250
judging 37f., 42, 48, 50, 79
judgment 10, 16–22, 38–40, 42f., 48f., 78–82, 94, 112, 133, 144, 189, 198, 206, 225, 257, 260, 299, 305, 310f.
justice 180, 243, 257f., 265, 270f., 287
justification 17f., 21, 24, 71, 97f., 105
justified belief 98

kinds of events 156
knowing 2, 46, 56–58, 68f., 77f., 84, 137, 140, 143, 147, 162, 167, 191, 200, 222, 260, 279, 285, 299, 315
knowledge 6, 8, 10, 14, 35f., 39, 48, 56–58, 60, 63, 69, 74f., 83, 88, 101, 115, 118–120, 122f., 127f., 132, 134, 138, 140, 144, 148, 150, 156, 158, 163, 169f., 175, 189, 197, 218, 223, 225, 242f., 248, 260, 298–300, 306, 320

language 1–3, 7–17, 21, 23f., 31, 35, 37–39, 41, 44–48, 56–58, 60–70, 72, 74–76, 78, 81, 83–86, 91f., 94, 101, 104, 106–108, 112, 114–118, 120–128, 131–137, 140, 142, 145f., 150, 154f., 159, 182, 187, 190, 194, 196, 198, 205, 207f., 217, 241f., 245, 247–249, 291, 316
language game 11, 38f., 74, 85
law 78, 104, 110, 131, 153, 157, 163, 165f., 168–172, 176, 179–181, 185, 202, 204, 206, 210, 212–214, 246, 253, 265, 278–281, 285–287, 298, 304f., 319
laws of physics 141, 153, 156, 165, 169, 179, 285–287, 290
learning 59, 69-71
liberal 255, 269f., 272f.
liberalism 243, 254–259, 265f., 269f., 272, 276
libertarianism 265–268
liberty 243, 253–259, 265–276
life world 157
linguistic competence 116, 132f.
linguistic practice 208
living being 141, 143
living thing 142, 157
logical atomism 3

logical equivalence 17f., 21
logical form 107f., 133
logical syntax 1, 3, 7

making true 10, 67, 83, 100–102, 105
Marxism 272f.
materialism 1f., 5–8, 10, 290
material object 2
mathematics 6, 10
matter 2, 5, 7–9, 23, 28, 31, 33, 35, 38f., 41, 44, 47, 50f., 53, 60, 63, 65f., 70, 75, 77f., 82, 94, 100, 113, 115f., 119, 125f., 132–134, 139–141, 143, 148, 150f., 154f., 164, 168, 171, 176, 180–182, 184, 186, 188f., 199, 202, 206, 208, 212, 225, 227f., 242f., 249–253, 264–268, 271, 274, 277–279, 286–288, 292–294, 296f., 300, 303, 309, 312, 314f., 318, 320
meaning 1, 6f., 9f., 12, 14, 20, 34, 37–39, 43f., 47, 49, 51, 53, 57f., 68, 74f., 77–79, 83, 93f., 104, 112–120, 122, 124–126, 128, 130–139, 148, 150f., 188, 191f., 194–196, 201, 208, 244, 258, 265, 289, 291, 316
means 1–3, 5–12, 14, 17f., 21, 23–27, 29, 38f., 43–48, 53f., 56, 59f., 65, 68f., 71, 74, 83, 86, 92, 103f., 108–110, 112f., 116–118, 120, 125–127, 130–132, 136f., 140, 143, 146–148, 150, 153, 156, 161–163, 165f., 168, 171–174, 176, 179f., 185, 188, 196, 198f., 203–205, 208, 214, 218f., 224, 229, 242, 246f., 249f., 252f., 255, 257, 259–261, 263, 265–267, 270f., 280, 285, 289, 292, 300, 304f., 318, 320, 322
means-ends 161
mental act 215
mental causation 293
mental descriptions 140, 153, 156, 291
mental event 140, 156, 197, 202, 204, 206, 278, 286, 291–293
mental-physical distinction 193, 198, 207
mental state 2–4, 9, 33, 100f., 105f., 111, 123f., 126f., 164, 166, 170, 176, 190, 194, 197–200, 205–207, 289, 314
metalanguage 130

metaphysical realism 33, 52f., 55, 57–68, 70–74, 85
metaphysical spirit 3, 9
metaphysics 1–11, 14f., 17, 19, 22f., 31, 74, 77, 101, 142, 186, 189
metaphysics of idealism 1, 3
method 1, 6f., 10, 19, 21f., 51, 100, 109, 130, 141f., 188, 206
methodological individualism 223f., 243f., 248
mind 1f., 5, 9f., 12, 15, 47, 52f., 63f., 72f., 76, 88, 109, 112f., 116, 125, 137, 144, 146–148, 152, 156, 182, 184, 186, 192, 194–196, 199f., 203–205, 220–223, 225, 244f., 258, 277, 292f., 299
mindblindness 164
mind-body 148, 189, 200f.
mind-brain 6
mind-dependence 73, 84
mind-independence 84
modal logic 2, 12
modus ponens 46
modus tollens 46
monism 153, 287, 290–292, 296
moral 21f., 53, 208, 241–244, 249–253, 256–260, 264–266, 268–272, 275f.
moral individualism 242, 256, 258–260, 262–265, 268, 270f., 276
morality 243, 249f., 258
moral powers 257
myth of the given 140

name 1, 3, 5f., 8–11, 13f., 16–19, 21, 23–25, 28–31, 33f., 38, 52, 75, 92f., 107–110, 157, 210, 212, 246, 296
naturalism 3, 158
natural language 1, 44, 113, 120, 130
natural laws 165
natural science 126, 195, 202, 206, 224, 244f., 287
natural world 141f., 245, 279
Nazi 250
necessary condition 81, 99, 148f., 156, 203, 292
necessary truth 95, 121
necessity 16, 18, 22, 124, 168, 176, 220, 246

negation   46, 49, 95, 109
neural explanation   302, 315
neural process   293, 301–303, 307 f., 311
neural state   126, 301–303, 311
neurophysiological process   4 f.
neuroscience   158, 172 f., 301–304, 307–316, 318, 320–322
Newtonian   319
nomological   54, 168, 179, 278, 285 f., 304 f., 307–309, 312, 314–316, 321
nonrealism   59
nonsense   9, 15, 46, 48, 51, 53, 282
normative rationality   142
normativity   7, 78–81, 141, 199, 288, 305, 311
notation   7, 25 f.

object   3 f., 6–8, 10, 14, 17–19, 21, 25, 27–31, 41, 44, 54–59, 61–67, 69–72, 75, 84 f., 88, 91–93, 100, 105, 107, 109 f., 121 f., 124 f., 140 f., 143–156, 160, 172, 180, 182 f., 189, 191, 196, 198, 219 f., 262 f., 268, 286 f., 290, 318, 321
objective   2–7, 9, 36, 118, 122, 136, 141, 150 f., 206 f.
objective truth   121 f., 155
objectivity   122, 140 f., 150, 206, 289
observable behaviour   2
observation   3, 55, 57, 68, 137 f., 151, 168, 171, 176, 189, 194, 200, 207, 225, 299 f., 307, 315
observer-relative   3, 9 f.
ontological individualism   243, 245–248, 260
ontological relativity   65 f., 70
ontology   3, 18, 32, 108, 196, 210, 226, 229, 292 f., 295 f.
open sentence   6, 8, 25, 28
ordinary experience   144, 156
organism   4, 7, 10, 165, 196, 198, 246, 254
ostensive definition   193
other minds   122 f., 197

pain   1, 3–6, 9, 93, 100, 103, 105, 149, 190, 294
particular   1, 3–6, 8–11, 14 f., 20, 23–25, 29–33, 40, 42, 45–48, 53, 55, 61 f., 65, 69 f., 76, 78, 90, 96, 98 f., 102, 106–108, 111, 113, 134, 145–147, 152 f., 158, 165, 188–191, 195, 204, 206, 208, 211–213, 215, 221–223, 244 f., 247 f., 253, 255 f., 259–264, 271, 273–275, 278–281, 284, 306, 308, 312 f., 316, 322
particularity   256, 274
passing theory   208
Peircean realism   70
perception   61, 71, 85, 133, 137, 141, 143, 156, 247
perceptual belief   149–152
person   2 f., 9 f., 48, 50, 59, 74, 89, 106 f., 110, 117, 120, 122–125, 127–129, 134–136, 138, 150, 154, 164, 167, 172, 182, 189, 198, 200, 203, 205, 207 f., 210, 212, 214–217, 219, 223, 241, 243, 246 f., 249–259, 262 f., 266, 268, 275, 280, 289, 293, 302, 306, 313, 321
personal identity   2
perspicuous representation   6, 86 f., 187 f., 191 f., 208
philosophical individualism   242–245, 249, 251 f., 255, 260, 265, 276
philosophical investigation   8, 21, 86, 105, 187
Philosophical Investigations   7, 9, 11, 13 f., 35, 40, 47, 105, 187, 277, 320
philosophical reflection   22, 24, 41, 90, 191, 197
philosophical theory   13, 19, 193, 196
philosophy   1–4, 6–12, 14, 18 f., 22 f., 41, 52 f., 76, 78, 86 f., 100, 112, 114, 118, 124, 128, 138, 140, 186–188, 193–195, 198, 207 f., 244, 271, 300, 320
philosophy of action   201, 210, 221, 223, 228, 277, 302
philosophy of mind   10 f., 94, 186 f., 189, 193, 195, 197, 199–201, 205, 207, 241
physical event   202–204, 206, 286, 291
physicalism   9 f., 64, 100, 142, 171, 174 f., 186, 188, 195, 277, 286 f., 290–293, 296, 300, 302
physicalist description   153, 156
picture   3 f., 8 f., 19, 22, 38–40, 50, 60, 63, 77, 85, 102, 131, 147, 151 f., 194, 205, 224, 287

pleasure 259
plural agent 211f.
pluralism 228f.
point of view 2, 5, 7, 11, 13f., 19f., 23, 28, 31f., 35, 40, 52f., 60, 71, 73, 78, 84, 86, 95, 109, 117f., 122, 126–128, 138, 152, 163f., 167, 199f., 205, 207, 248, 258, 271f., 289, 306f., 309, 315
political liberalism 270–273, 275f.
positivism 57, 186
possible world 2
practical knowledge 57, 225, 299
practice 2, 4–6, 8, 33, 82, 142f., 182, 188, 191–194, 197f., 208, 212, 250, 256, 261f., 264, 272f., 276, 322
pragmatism 97, 140, 143, 241
pre-conceptual triangulation 151
predicate 1, 4–8, 10–13, 15f., 18, 20f., 24–28, 30–33, 45, 47, 54, 58, 65, 88f., 91–93, 95, 102, 107, 179, 190, 205, 208, 222, 286f., 290–292, 296
predicate logic 2, 16f., 27, 107f.
predication 27
preference 259–268, 272, 281
pre-modern 245, 251, 269
primary reason 31, 75, 79, 203f., 220, 278
primitive action 292, 294f.
primitive expression 116, 132
private interest 259
private language argument 193
privileged access 3
pronoun 5, 9–11, 89f.
property 4, 14, 21, 30–33, 41, 43, 53f., 65, 68, 77–79, 81, 83, 88f., 92, 94f., 101, 147, 196, 206, 222, 246, 262, 289f.
property dualism 5
proposition 1, 3f., 6–9, 12, 21, 32, 35–51, 75, 82, 91, 101, 141f., 164, 184, 196f., 278f., 282
propositional attitude 126, 133, 163, 287
propositional thought 149
pro-sentence 89f., 93
psychological process 133
psychological state 125, 162f., 302, 307, 314
psychology 1, 74, 137, 140, 158, 170, 176f., 180, 186, 196f., 199, 206, 292, 304

public availability 126, 136
public interest 259
puzzle 15, 165

quantification 13, 90
question 1f., 4f., 7, 9f., 13–19, 22–25, 27f., 30, 32f., 35, 37, 39, 41f., 46, 48–51, 58, 62, 70, 79, 83, 90, 92, 94f., 99–101, 111, 114, 116, 118, 120, 122–124, 133, 135, 142, 151, 156f., 159f., 165, 175–178, 180–182, 184, 186, 188, 197, 200f., 206, 214, 219, 270, 282, 289, 299, 301f., 304, 309, 311–314, 316f.

radical error 129
radical interpretation 113, 117–127, 129f., 133, 135–138, 206, 289
rational agent 160, 169, 204
rational explanation 161, 165–169, 171, 175–177, 179, 203–205, 278, 280–285, 287–290, 294, 301f., 305–322
rationality 126, 140, 149, 152, 163f., 206, 288f., 298
rational sense 160–162
realism 53, 55, 67f., 70–72, 97, 290
reality 1–5, 9–11, 14, 16, 19, 21, 31, 33, 41f., 46, 53, 61–63, 66, 72f., 76f., 100f., 109, 111f., 114, 126, 130, 132, 136f., 174, 184f., 196, 211, 241–246, 248, 251, 290
reason 1–3, 5f., 8–11, 13–15, 17–19, 21, 23f., 27–30, 32f., 36, 38, 42–44, 48, 53, 56, 59f., 67, 70–73, 76f., 79–84, 88, 90f., 93, 96f., 104, 107, 115, 118, 123, 125, 129, 133, 140–143, 145f., 149, 152, 155, 161–164, 166–169, 171, 173, 175f., 178, 182–185, 187, 189, 192, 194, 197, 199–204, 207, 210f., 213f., 217, 220, 223–228, 244, 248f., 257, 259, 264, 270–272, 274, 277–285, 288f., 293, 297f., 300–317, 319f., 322
reason-explanations 207
reasons for action 10, 162, 167, 169, 185, 280, 283, 288, 300, 306
reduction 5, 57, 170, 177, 290, 311
reductionism 120, 170, 174f., 211, 215, 217
redundancy theory 13

Index of Subjects — 365

reference 1f., 9f., 12, 14, 16–18, 25, 29f., 53, 55–58, 61–72, 75f., 80, 84f., 93f., 98, 110, 114, 116, 123–125, 131f., 138, 147, 198f., 210, 217f., 246, 286, 310
referential use 9f., 27, 29f., 32
reflex 317
Reformation 269
relativism 68, 254f., 270
religious discourse 5
representation 1, 15, 17, 53, 102, 113, 130, 311, 316
res extensa 2
respect 2, 5, 19, 47, 56, 58, 65, 141, 200, 205, 207, 214, 225, 245, 249–251, 256–258, 265, 268, 270f., 274, 277, 280, 290
right 1, 3, 6, 8, 18, 23, 35, 42, 47, 51, 60, 65, 71, 77, 79f., 82f., 86, 104, 106, 108, 115f., 122, 127, 137f., 149, 151, 177f., 192, 207, 224, 226–229, 241f., 245, 251f., 254, 258f., 265–268, 271, 273–276, 288, 292f., 297–299, 302, 304, 309, 321
robust physicalism 195, 201, 205
rugged individualism 267
rule 1, 3f., 6f., 9, 16f., 19, 24, 27f., 30, 33, 39f., 44, 46, 62, 70, 82, 104–107, 116, 119, 122, 132f., 160, 167f., 170, 181, 184, 191f., 194, 200, 206f., 210, 221, 227, 247, 249, 264, 270, 272, 291, 298, 304, 320
rule-following 191f., 320

satisfaction 9, 14f., 91–93, 107, 114, 116, 125, 131, 257, 263, 266f.
Satz 43f.
science 1f., 5f., 10–12, 19, 52f., 57f., 70, 76, 87, 116, 124, 140–142, 145, 147f., 155f., 158f., 163–165, 168–179, 181–184, 188, 194–196, 206, 229, 247, 261, 280, 287–289, 303–305, 307, 309, 315, 317, 322
scientific philosophy 3
scientific realism 9, 33, 52
scientific revolution 141, 244
scientific theory 63, 76, 120, 199
second nature 310

self 1f., 5, 7, 20, 36, 86, 97, 128, 134, 143, 147, 165, 193, 198, 215, 241–247, 251, 254f., 263, 268, 271f., 312
self-development 243, 252, 254, 256
self-expression 252f., 256
selfishness 262–264
semantical primitive 116, 132
semantics 11, 14, 31f., 57, 74, 106, 113, 131
sensation 5f., 124, 190f., 193, 197, 247
sense 1–7, 9–13, 15f., 25, 27, 29, 31f., 35f., 38, 42, 44–53, 55, 57, 59–65, 68–71, 74f., 77–79, 81–83, 87–90, 92, 94, 96–98, 100–102, 104, 107, 110, 115f., 122, 124f., 128f., 135–137, 140–145, 149, 152f., 158, 160, 162f., 165, 168–176, 178, 181, 184, 186, 189f., 192, 196, 199f., 205f., 208, 212, 217, 220, 224, 226–229, 243, 247–250, 252f., 255, 257, 259, 262, 266, 268, 270, 274, 280–282, 284, 286–290, 292, 299, 301–305, 307, 310–312, 315–317, 319, 321f.
sense awareness 144, 243, 260
sense-force distinction 82
sense impression 144, 149, 152
sense perception 149
sentence 1–22, 24–27, 30–34, 37, 41–48, 53, 55, 57f., 61, 67, 69, 79–81, 88–94, 96, 99f., 104, 106–109, 113–116, 120, 124f., 130–133, 137, 150f., 155, 202f., 206, 208, 226, 278f., 282, 291, 320
sign 1, 7, 11, 16, 18, 21, 25, 27, 29, 37, 44, 46, 52, 63, 70, 77, 144f., 149, 246, 280
signification 1, 21
singular individual 252
singular term 1, 4–6, 8–13, 16, 18f., 22, 24, 26–30, 32, 65, 88, 108
Sinn 1, 49
skepticism 51, 113, 115-117, 123-124, 149-150, 175, 192
slingshot argument 1, 8, 107, 130
social agency 210f., 217, 221, 225, 229
social attitude 216–218
social character of language 134
social contract 268
social contract individualism 265, 267f.
social environment 143

social good   259–262, 264
social group   210–212, 215–217, 220, 223 f., 227, 255, 265
socially constitutive concept   246
social realism   243, 247 f., 260
social world   245, 255
society   5, 146, 184, 211, 241–243, 245–276
sociologists   248
sociology   140, 195
solidity   4
space   1–4, 97, 133, 151, 171, 183, 199, 244, 295, 305
space of laws   288, 296, 305, 307, 309–312, 314 f., 317, 319 f., 322
space of reasons   141 f., 288, 294, 296, 305, 307–310, 312, 314–317, 319 f., 322
spatiality   3 f., 44, 279
speculation   2, 5 f., 9, 14, 132, 164, 294, 298 f.
standard story   168, 210, 221, 226–229, 277, 283 f., 287, 292–294, 296, 298, 300
state   1–10, 13, 17, 20, 33, 43, 74, 125 f., 130, 135, 142, 152, 154, 159 f., 163 f., 170, 173, 189 f., 193 f., 196–200, 203, 205, 207, 220–222, 224, 229, 245, 269, 275, 278–281, 283 f., 286, 293 f., 302, 307, 313 f.
statement   1 f., 4, 13, 15 f., 19 f., 22, 53–62, 64–69, 71–73, 75–79, 83–85, 94, 100–111, 115, 162, 174, 176, 180, 185, 195, 212, 286, 298, 302
state of affairs   1, 3, 14, 16 f., 53, 55–58, 60–62, 64, 67, 72, 75 f., 80, 91, 94, 100, 102, 104, 106 f., 159–163, 166, 169, 171, 219, 289, 303, 306
status   20, 23, 38, 57, 62, 69, 100, 113, 121, 129 f., 138, 144 f., 158, 178, 193 f., 196, 211 f., 223, 242, 251, 262, 273, 283, 319
stimulus   151, 166
strict law   153, 163, 179 f., 202–204, 278–280, 285–287
subject   1, 5–7, 12, 14, 36, 52, 80, 86, 102, 117 f., 120, 122, 134, 140, 143, 146 f., 149–151, 153–155, 157, 208, 216, 222, 265 f., 275, 288, 321
subjective   2–6, 8 f., 36, 39, 65, 118, 194, 224
subjectively understandable action   215, 224
subjectivity   2–4, 6, 8, 256
substantive property   54, 68, 73, 75 f., 78 f., 84
substantive relation   55 f., 84
substitution   3, 5–12, 16, 18–31, 33 f.
suffering   143, 145, 155, 183, 190, 198
sufficient condition   81, 110, 128, 156, 168, 316
supervenience   64, 156, 159, 179, 208, 287, 290–292, 311, 322
synonymy   5-8, 12, 32

teleological description   161 f.
teleological explanation   159–161, 166 f., 174, 244
(the) False   1
The Great Fact   14
theorem   114 f., 131 f., 208
theoretical concept   113 f., 136
Theory   1–5, 8, 12–27, 29–34, 53–56, 58–61, 64–67, 69–72, 75–80, 83 f., 87, 91 f., 94–97, 102–104, 107–109, 113–118, 121, 125, 128, 130–133, 135, 138, 155, 158, 175 f., 181, 184 f., 187, 189–199, 206–208, 242 f., 251 f., 256, 258 f., 264, 267–270, 273, 285, 294, 301–303, 307
theory construction   14, 18, 21 f., 24, 188 f., 195 f.
theory of meaning   13, 57, 67, 94, 107, 112–114, 116, 124, 155, 192, 207 f.
theory of reference   53, 55, 66 f.
(the) True   1
thing in itself   63
third-person   2, 121, 124, 127, 138, 289
third-person stance   137
thought   1 f., 4–7, 10–12, 14–16, 18, 20 f., 23, 25, 31, 35–37, 40, 45, 52, 60, 62–64, 66, 74, 83, 85 f., 91, 93, 98, 101 f., 115, 117 f., 122–127, 133–135, 140–144, 146, 148–150, 152–154, 156 f., 164, 179, 181, 186, 188–190, 197, 199, 205–207,

241 f., 244, 247–249, 252, 256 f., 267, 277 f., 281, 284, 286, 289 f., 294, 300, 315, 321
thought experiment 2, 11, 18, 119, 122
time 2, 5, 13 f., 26, 40, 45, 50, 52, 58, 60, 64, 68, 70, 79, 91, 110, 128 f., 133, 143 f., 152, 154, 157, 161, 167, 169 f., 175, 182, 186, 188 f., 191, 215, 222, 227, 242, 244 f., 250, 252 f., 256 f., 263, 269, 274 f., 280, 284, 293 f., 301, 319
token 202, 213–215, 222, 291
token identity 10, 169, 202, 204, 291
traditional societies 252, 255, 263
transcendent 9, 14, 70
translation 49, 75, 103–105, 107
triangulation 122, 134, 138, 150–152
true-false 48, 79, 81 f., 96
truth 1–5, 8, 10–22, 24, 27 f., 31 f., 34–36, 38–48, 51–56, 58–64, 67 f., 70–73, 75–84, 88–99, 101–105, 107–116, 118, 122, 124 f., 128, 130 f., 133 f., 140 f., 149 f., 155, 170, 184 f., 191 f., 195, 199, 201, 205–208, 241, 249, 260, 279, 282, 291, 319
truth condition 13, 43–49, 55–57, 60 f., 65, 67–69, 77 f., 83 f., 93 f., 101–110, 113 f., 155, 192
truth-error 79, 81 f., 96
truth functional 13
truth maker 19
truth value 1, 5, 8 f., 11 f., 15–18, 20, 25 f., 32, 45, 65, 88, 103
T-sentence 54, 103 f., 107 f., 114 f., 130–132

under a description 214, 220-221, 227, 278-279, 295-297, 299, 308, 313
underdetermination 119, 125, 135 f.
understanding 1, 3, 6, 10–12, 14, 35, 39 f., 52 f., 56 f., 61, 67–69, 73 f., 76–78, 83 f., 86, 93, 104, 108, 111, 115–118, 126, 133–137, 146, 152, 154 f., 158, 167, 187 f., 191–194, 197 f., 200, 206–208, 215, 223 f., 241, 244 f., 266, 273, 283, 289, 292, 296, 306 f., 312, 320

unfairness 276
United States 269 f.
unity of science 128, 195
universality 251, 273
universe 2, 152, 157, 196, 278
Uppsala 24, 49, 51
use 1, 4–11, 13–33, 38, 42–47, 51, 53, 56–58, 60 f., 63–70, 74 f., 78, 80–85, 87, 89 f., 93 f., 96–102, 105–108, 116–118, 120, 124 f., 130–134, 136, 138 f., 144, 146, 155, 163 f., 171 f., 178, 182, 187, 191 f., 194, 199, 206–208, 221, 245, 249, 259, 270, 281, 284, 288 f., 295, 301, 304–306, 309, 316
use-transcendence 68-69, 71, 84
utilitarian individualism 243, 258, 262, 265
utilitarianism 263, 266, 268
utterance 4, 10, 41 f., 44–49, 51, 53, 73, 75, 82, 88, 90, 96, 106, 114, 122, 125, 130, 137

verificationism 57, 73, 77
verstehen 224
Vienna Circle 1 f.
view from nowhere 164, 306
vision 59, 191, 242, 300
Volk 250

warranted assertibility 55, 59, 64, 70 f., 73
we-intend 218
world 1 f., 4–8, 10, 14, 16, 18, 20, 22, 34, 39 f., 42, 48, 50, 52, 55, 63–65, 70, 72, 74, 76 f., 85, 91, 97, 99–102, 112 f., 119, 123, 126–130, 134, 140–143, 145–150, 152–154, 156–158, 162–164, 171 f., 179, 181, 184 f., 187 f., 193–195, 197–199, 207 f., 210, 221, 224, 226, 229, 241, 244 f., 247, 250–252, 256, 269, 271, 277, 279, 288 f., 292, 299, 306, 309, 314 f., 322

zoon politikon 247

www.ingramcontent.com/pod-product-compliance
Lightning Source LLC
Chambersburg PA
CBHW031418230426
43668CB00007B/349